Debox_Degrid Architectures Publications

PUBLICATION DATE: January 2012
(ORIGINALLY PUBLISHED AS *WOW HOWS THE HOUSE NOW*)
TRIM1524_2286
Read & clarity adjustments June 2012

ISBN   978-0-646-57126-3

PURCHASE, DISTRIBUTE OR PUBLISH

HouseFandango

for
your Library,
Friend, Passion, Designer, Teacher,
Developer, Politician;
as a House Warmer or to Retail.

Go to
bookshops
bookstore.bookpod.com.au
amazon.com
deboxdebox@gmail.com

CONTACT

For very welcome feedback to author, enquiry, comment or purchase:

Manager
Debox_Degrid Architectures Publications
16 Sanfrancisco St, Sorell, Tasmania, Australia 7172
deboxdebox@gmail.com

facebook.com/HouseFandango

Search: debox degrid, Monte John Latham, HouseFandango

ACKNOWLEDGEMENTS

Thanks to those who have read and commented for me, Malvina Reynolds for the ticky tacky boxes on the hillside, Paul Kelly for the horses galloping herein, David Gulpilil for his inspiring public face, Mathew Fisher and Procol Harum for the shades of pale and the humming room, Jimmy Buffet for the sound of the weather, Robert Dessaix for bringing out the name Cheekybugga, all the writers I have read and forgotten but whose information I retain, all those acknowledged deeper in the pages, my local professional mentors and colleagues, Del for the Rosny house and location, Jean for the crumbs on the table, all the other oceans that lap at my private island, Jesus for his being as he is, his staggering Dad and our Holy Spirit.

Albert Gallopilong, Cheekybugga Talkabout and the Harmoninnies are fictional characters and in no way represent any real people, but I still love them. They are profiled as Australian Aborigines only through the limited understanding of the author and so the profiles may be flawed. Reference to Sitting Bull similarly arises through the limited understanding of the author. Global and Maggie Pale, Bobby and Little White Cloud Dazzler and Low Carl are all loveable fictional characters.

PRODUCT OF
TASMANIA
MATEI

YOUR HOUSE .. ANYPERSON'S:

Your own house actions and circumstance.

This nutshell, with humour and passion on serious rock, explains housing uniquely.

For owner, renter, designer, planner, builder, homemaker, sociologist, economist, environmental practitioner.

Introducing the industry and diverse, colourful people around camp, boulevard, cottage, rooms, breadcrumbs and modern dwelling: a surprisingly important cause for humans in a modern very troubled world still with its paradise.

Houses are **huge** *to world and homemaker. How do we manage it all? How does it manage us?*

With each of us is our activity that bonds us with domestic contraption; the activity of housing and the returning action of houses. "House" is more than architecture.

Dweller in the driver's seat; do your own special housing. Share in the perceptions of others, experts, curriculum drafters and authorities commonly blinkered by their own streams of focus making decisions and blocking the wholeness in wholistic housing.

This is offered at least to students as a guard against the blinkering educational stream silo effect. The students need to be on fire of their own generational movement! And knowing the indigenous and the nomad have held us in hand eons ago while today they are surveyed into a corner.

Read it all easy down-home as by an architect off an organised cuff. Anecdotes, technical and poetic allusions, recalled from a well-read and design experienced mind. Crack the mystiques of design, bureaucracy and the built. Find the lay person in the heart of the professional and professional in the lay.

HouseFandango

A Guide
for our
Domestic Romance

Your Dwelling Contraption is a Key

THE ROOTS

No author is an island. M. John Latham grew up in the outer suburbs of a small scenic capital city in Tasmania Australia amid abundant countryside burgeoning with new residences. Currently he runs a small architect practice in rural coastal Tasmania; deep in the island down under Downunder. His experience in architecture ranges through cottage construction, corporate interior design, and urban and building architecture. A home handyman, he is also a keen expressionist painter of what he calls *enviro-mental sharing*. Born mid 20th century, he has moved through thirty five residences; upper middle class houses, flats, dives, grand old farmhouses, share houses, in the city, in the country and with plenty of camping in between. He and his wife have five children and during the course of their romance have lived in a score of dwellings and half a score of different locales; some dwellings briefly and two for a decade. Intent on practicing Architecture since mid high school he began the course of work but left it indefinitely, dissatisfied with society's values, working as possible as farmhand, handyman, artist and draughtsman. He once swept the streets of the area in which he now lives.

Eventually circumstance had him impassioned and available to write. He found the draft would double as a thesis for his Bachelor of Environmental Design, the first leg of his passage to the practice of Architecture. Thus he returned to mainstream Architecture eight years after departing it. Though straining at the leash, being far too busy with all of the second leg study, jobs, moving locale and children he was then unable to publish. He worked across a broad range of architectural projects in Hobart, Perth and Wellington including house design, public buildings, corporate fit-out, remote area townships and housing, municipal architecture, community-based townscape, local government reports, urban development appraisal, urban art and settlement heritage. In these projects he has liaised with local dynamos, politicians, bureaucrats and built development trades/professionals of many specialties.

Since the original draft the author compulsively kept notes; for example, one on a discarded pie bag at a Wellington Bob Dylan concert. The manuscript, as renamed, is now preened and updated to his current worth.

In *HouseFandango* he discovers and melds life experience with professional intent. He has been passionate, compulsive. Unfolding as he explored and persevered, relying on logic and nous where early research showed nothing, his enunciated aspect on housing seems to be unique. He considers, that among all else in the book, there is something special about the idea of '*nomurbics*' (refer 'Glossary'); the light it may shed to aid the sad plight of the indigenous and the refreshment it may give to the house dweller, who may be in sad plight also or simply creatively housing.

No author is an island; this work draws on a broad education and the very very tolerant contribution of Sandy, a very very special piece of New Zealand and wife. He sincerely hopes you enjoy it.

Smaller follow-up books are planned –
The Lounge Room, Architecture of Fire and *The Nomurbic Urban Office*.

To

Every Dweller
toward means and mind to be optimally housed.

Sandy most especially and
Jabra, Adam, Jasiel, Saul &
Anaya.

Mum & Dad & the Molloys,

and to
Wattle Hill, Porirua & all other
Locales with Dinner Tables.

The

demanding
romantic science & doing of housing:

A marriage of;
builder, engineer, artist,
dweller, academic, layperson, politician;
the nomads, the
settlers
and
those between.

§

CONTENTS

42 ♪

Holdup
Houser ...
dwell a moment
...

HERE ON THE
FRONT PORCH

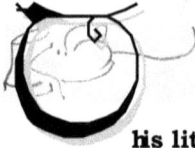

his little wad of words may assist the bow-

tied professional and the layperson dynamic in motion.
For enjoyment. And very serious business. A stranger on
foot, even a Building Inspector, is circumstanced to visit
whilst aptly subliminally reviewing his own and another's
dwelling-arrangements. Or maybe it's a beautifully toned
ballet dancer. Having clacked the cast iron knocker she
waits, intrigued by the mosaic floor, the cat and the
butterflies and the invitation of the wooden seat warmed
with the sunlight that is showing the filigree shade of the
veranda trim. The door is almost designed to allure, like
most. A fragrant country zephyr visits - they seldom
knock. It swings open a little. You look ... listen ... the
science and the romance of your own housing quietly
touch the heart of your life; your nostrils recalling your
own residential scents. This unfamiliar hall is as strongly
introductory as was that now numberless front gate, with
its easy swing perfectly set by a casual lean. Yet an
angelic shaft of sunlight, visible obliquely through the
prismatic glass of an inner door, is now the beckoning
welcome. This book beckons but begins not only here, nor
does it end where the toilet brush cleans, nor the inside of
your back door. *It begins only as it infuses with your own
dwelling future and those of others.* The infusion is
induced by aspects of its interior. Nobody home, but you
know it's proper to enter. The first room, surprise, is egg-
shaped in plan. A shallow dome in an otherwise flat
ceiling. It's a large lounge. Archways, doors, windows,
ancient tapestries; in a house in a native grotto and with
simple gray-weathered unpainted axe-split boards and
lichened stone. A modern cable from the gable, soon to be
again updated, runs overhead to the ravine passing over

some very very old circles chipped into some outcropped
stone. Comings and goings have worn a foot track, the
only significant peoplemark in declining nature's vegetated
surrounds. You understand this house like any other.
It's already built so in one's stride the founding stone has
less priority than the front door. To begin at the
foundation and look to its sequential development,
through the floor and *mother of pearl*, hoping to find, in a
pointed end, an understanding of 'house' is a square
approach. This may suit some, but not the dweller, nor
the visitor. The only approach for them is through the
wistful romance generated by the *room* spaces and
touches of home; *the first kiss from person to natural place
is an emotional happening* - not a freshly cut stone re-
contacting mother earth. Houses are more than square.
Machines, construction, space and economy do reign hard
with the quadrangles of orthogonal procedure. People,
though, will seek the *quicksilver* of personal abstraction
and the sensuality of organic surrounds with which to
intersperse these indispensable right-angles and the
varied stuff of which they are built.

In this context this rectangular page and the others,
hinged at the binding, like doors, produce arc zephyrs as
the hand of an organism turns them, seeking for the mind
some pertinence for application to your own housing
decisions and lifestyle. Houses, like books, are subtle and
solid. A book once could take no other form. The
bookshelf will always be. There's one against the wall
basking under the skylight, the sleek *shadow* of a
beautifully handcrafted iron-bark spear hatched across its
French-polished beautifully machined woods that stir
emotional under bound mellowed papers and the fine
plastics of a sleek digital reading device.

Thankyou for having removed your muddy boots and
entered with acknowledgement and meek demeanour.
Powerful courtesies, protocols, taste – people interfacing
domicile. Houses being so close to home, we must talk
about them in concert with their people. In here are walls,
encampments and cultures; and also some characters, to
relate us directly to the hearts that command house. And,
to be complete, the hearts that command the flip-side of
our sense of civilisation and mortgage – the hearts of the
nomadic. These people relate us to owners of different
ways – the owner being the measure of the house. Thus

4

are seen the logistics of design, masonry, curtain-lace and sheets of glass in the province of the ubiquitous layperson, as refined by his or her academic attributes and helpers. We're talking about getting you what you want and need, by way of domestic facility; 'house', if you like. *Not just building it.* You will learn as much about calling your own shots as having them called by others – and as calling them yourself for others.

Offside the lobby, a reading nook an arms-spread in diameter is carved intricately inside the stump of a huge English Oak. Slowly decomposing roots reaching for water spread below the polished end-grained floor. The tree trunk has been cut to fit under the roofing iron. In the spell of the deep rich now oil-buffed shining grain, showing the knots ringing the many moons suns and bird footprints, are the dweller's mellow leather hat ... and a well used yellow ochre butternut gourd with a leather body tie. The gourd contains a personally vital accumulation; once the **only possession** of a Yaqui Indian, now gone. Household warmth billows invisibly outward, through the iron and an acrylic skylight dome set concentric with the growth rings. The warmth is passing through the sun's oblique radiant heat and rays which below bend spectral through the prismatic door-glass into the hall.

The READING NOOK

HERE ON THE FRONT PORCH

The hat affectionately keeps another's thoughts, language and appreciation of this place and its house. In this nook is a panorama across many a literary countryside.

There is knowing and optimising your own dwelling place; some may say your dream house. It's about anything that relates you to our housing - people's housing; a phenomenon, as are its creatures. Practical explanation, advice and inspiration are shown through true-life romance, adventure and frustration, entwined with pragmatic facts. Design-fertiliser, colour, quantities, art, acts, whys and wherefores. Dweller balancing acts. Misconceptions, problems and paranoia hopefully will be resolved towards deep understanding. We're looking at technicality, psychology, budgets, evolution, lifestyle and brave moves. Call it the *Housefandango*; us on the move, keeping the looming ego of science under the intuitive wings of our rhythm. A multiperson romance as we dance, leaving only bio-tracks, on this earthy floor.

Seas of citizen dilemma and private garden spa. Those already in spa may merely wonder. *Why in universal evolution or for the love of God do we need facility and shelter such as to require a house?* Philosophers, scientists, Hindus, Zulus, Generations X, Y and wonderers everywhere have many answers but to this one we still wonder. A tonic out there may help nourish and heal unwittingly ailing industry, energy and feeling associated with housing. The public needs persuasion to seek understanding and to continue seeking. The conventions of structured architectural thought some from an ivory tower in barely visible mist perhaps rightly may hooha the fuzzy discipline of your guide here; regardless you will note the critical movement and inspiration to which you may put your shoulder.

Most certainly you may put your shoulder to the enhancement of the essence of your house - *and any house on which you will have influence.* **This phenomenon of house**; your own awareness and that of your guide differ. Yet each is one with the air, space, roads and walls that take *room* somewhere there at a ninety degree phase shift from the page in the direct line between you and author. Like your dwelling history, house science is complex, simple, practical and poetic. Often it's outside our understanding. The book is as a house and unfinished garden unto itself. Variably it reads crude cold bare boards, miss-hit bent nails and fragrant polished surface lit with colour. An open door – an admission of some ignorance and your freedom to come or go. No chapter is a finished room unto itself. By some quirk, a mattress may be written into the kitchen, the blankets in the back shed, but if it's bedtime I'll have them in the unfinished guest-room for you. Please make yourself at home and look to picking it again from under the sleek shadow on the shelf.

Let me drift as you read through your own nebulous dream house. I speak to the common culture of the crew and passengers here on spaceship Earth. My colloquial flavour relates to Australia & the Kiwis, my home being in the Hobart and Wellington locales only a few hundred years after peoplekind have cultivated life with notably reduced urgent survival labours. Nobody will understand it word-for-word; it doesn't matter, I play with this occasionally as I play with words. Wholistic housing is a less-than-embryonic science about which we must also wax artistically. Essence of house. Some new words and notions arise, and some new slants on existing words. Spot-reading may cause minor quandary; the explanation of invented words perhaps having been skipped over by the Reader, and the dictionary doesn't know them either – *ecopical, nomurbic, synthetic aesthetic, armpit protocol, debox, ergothetics,*

6

Housefandango etc. They're all out back in the **GLOSSARY** – a read in itself. Sometimes the facts serve to support a parable-like expression. Some facts are unverified - an impressionistic painting of a recognisable scene. The sublime scientific anthropoid is simply generations of Mums, Dads and Kiddies. The ordinary is very palatable. Crumbs on the table are the heart of great architecture. Mankind is people. A house is a domestic arrangement, a *dwelling-contraption.*

The professional houser and the lay dweller; the romance is the same for each. Each must have some clue as to the other's doings.

DREAM HOUSE

HERE ON THE FRONT PORCH

Before we address the floorboards, budget, angelic light shaft and colour schemes we should note the house location. The Building Inspector snaps out of his dreaming. "It's only a building," he thinks, falling back to the pleasing scent-memory of his own refurbished pine wall-boards and ... again into his unaccustomed dream. An orchestral backing; let's look around. Across the world. History. Future. Through our ancient genetics, psychologies, religion. The wham-bam creation - BANG!? Now, from all this around let's look at where you are. Holding these chapters for your reason. Having had various dwelling experiences and looking to more. Your domestic future? Dreamfully housed - we hope; '*ecopically*' I'd prefer. Well, you might die shortly; but even then, there may be the wooden overcoat, heavenly city, fiery inglenook or, yes who knows, a short bardot as a trapdoor spider or beaver. Oh for a window to the afterdeath. Maybe in fact there is a circumstance that one day will terminate your housing experience - hopefully not some disaster or oppression. Or an ancient padlock on a big pearly gate.

We wonder; the mind needs rest, but the head has no bedroom. We don't see dolphin houses. The traditional native Australians are very scant with housing. But the impact of housing on people and environment is vast. Now critically dangerous. Always delightfully potent. There is much to be said and conveyed, simply, to a *multi-minded* public. There is some in-depth significance in our need for the right house and there is plenty in our reactions to the need.

We do dream. Domestic perfection. Are you *doing* it now? What is absolute domestic perfection?

Are you happy with your lot? Do you properly know it? Are you changing it? Do you understand its romance? From her womb to the door of death, our very own housing trail; more like the snake's skins than the snail shell. Building or staying where you are? The coming outlook may change your mind.

Rolling stone, millionaire, woman's magazine addict, stick-in-the-mud or eccentric pauper living in a cardboard *box* on a freeway; there is something here to enhance your house doings. *Owner-builder or director of national housing policy;* there is something here to feed your dream and your job (we're here firmly eye to eye, director). Utopia versus reality, wants versus needs.

The power of our housing is of course part of your shaping and the shaping of society on Earth.

> This book is to encourage the true adventure and fulfilling creativity and doings of home - using the house. But why bother?! The dolphins don't.

DWELLING-ARRANGEMENT

HERE ON THE FRONT PORCH

"*It's an exciting* little *dwelling-arrangement*," you find yourself laterally thinking as you approach the prismatic glass in this cottage of unique character. That's it, in a nutshell. Every person and family has some physicality that serves toward their domestic requirement; their *dwelling-arrangement(s)*.

For some the *dwelling-arrangement* is mobile; for many millions of others, a campsite, a hut. For other millions it's as American Malvina Reynolds wrote in the 60's - "Little *boxes* on the hillside, little *boxes* (and, in the 2010s, big ones ♪) made of *ticky tacky*, little *boxes* on the hillside, little boxes all the same..." For some it is an immense building, or even more. Or merely the sparse welfare of city fabric. Less; the ether of hope.

Or the sparse welfare of a nomad's roam. 'Wander'. Is it a converse to 'dwell'? A wanderer too must dwell at least awhile - with family, colleagues, friends, traders, circumstance or simply place. A place that, like the easy logic of flowing water, optimises the balances of a limited organism ruled by the mind of a person of character. The mentality of home - part of the synergy of logical existence. And there is a coincident inclination for a place of *safe-keeping* for things and family, which if carried may inhibit daily excursion or continuous 'wander'. A place of *facility* to totally relax, sleep, cook. And more.

This manifests as physical *domestic-arrangement*; which is variously homogeneously entwined with work, social and public life. Facility and amenity. Commodity and delight. The *arrangement*, for *dwelling* and *domestics*, is not always as firm as a house fixed in locale.

The well worn oft mundane word 'domestic' relates to the ethereal kernel of home. 'Domestic'. In some places it is as stupidly over-ruled as plain water – a commodity many are learning to seriously value.

We're looking at all domestic manifestations. The things that people *do* – domestically. So, the thrust here is about the *act of housing* and its consequence. This will facilitate improved *action*, for our planet, neighbours and yourself. It is about your responsibility to vote with your house. Encourage improved *action*.

"*Houze* me beautifully please sweetie," requests Little White Cloud, her heart gentle and satisfied with food and a fresh breeze. "And do it *ecopically*," she throws in; one word not at all well known. Loosen up, windows wide and open. Wait for the design. Think of earth, stomachs, time – and domestic facility, *contraption*.

Contraption – contrivance, equipment.

Domestic-contraption - made for dwellers. A house. House in locale. Coloured for life and culture.

Home.

For a Settler.

A GLOBAL TALE

This 'home' is a global thing; Earth, locale and people in motion.

Don't be self-centred, at least for a moment. An ordinary Sydney chap, whom I call Bobby Dazzler, lived with his inherent inclination toward enhancing an already superb environment. Looking to facilitate and celebrate the magic of people in this world, he became aware of unrealised potentials and heart-felt frustrations among people across the four-corners. Bobby's house was pretty ordinary. But then, so was his breakfast. "There's something very special and global about these ordinary things," he thinks in his kitchen as he oils the pan. "Everyperson everywhere rises from bed and swallows breakfast. But only I have this particular frypan, these fingerprints and ...." Somebody had spoken; he'd gone into a dream. He grabbed his coat; grabbed his hat; found his way downstairs in seconds flat. Stepped outside. Quickly tracked through nature's depleted vegetated surrounds. From the bus he glanced back at his house. It nestled in the picturesque grotto with a backdrop of contemptible suburban heater haze. He loved his home though, including his immediate neighbours idyllically endowed in carefully photographed crisp modern houses on small property allotments flanking his two acre nature nook in the suburban sprawl. As he moved on, through the unecologic repetitive shambles he could see the world collapsing - and the rich intrinsic beauties of the monotonous urban character. Rare trees going to rafters, page paper and smoke – just part of the fact. Wide eyed he dreamed of people in India dying of tuberculosis caused simply by the cow dung smoke in their otherwise quaint huts. Under their feet across the Earth, Mexicans were clambering back to their slums in preference to alien modern buildings. All of the characters on the bus were off to work with the loving compassion of their mortgager as their first awareness. Bobby's thinking, broadening from the egg in the frypan, acknowledged the sullage drain and foundation trench, moved across his suburb and vehicular locale, across the coastal strip and the mountain spine, drifted up through the *stratosphere* where looking he saw. Good earthy resources are being converted into unsustainable things at an unsustainable rate. Beautiful life-support landscape being eaten by the orthogonal dwelling things - *houselocusts*. As well, the *houselocusts* were running out of this food and their bodies therefore chemically mutating – less organic, more plastic.

A fellow passenger unaware began relating ecstatically to the dazed dreaming Dazzler. About her partly finished new house. Rich, earthy brick, clear sheets of glass, corners, shapes and *room*. Amenity, utility, surfaces, constructional *handmarks* alive. Architectonic. It would transform her daily self into accomplished freedoms. Open new vistas of personal life. He faced her with a cooking oil stain on his shirt, knowing the house location; "It's horribly good ...that. A fantastic abode for you. I hope we can find replacement rich local cropland for our population boom. And is there *room* for the consequent increment of industrial growth and road extension? I'll be designing a whole new suburb this week. I know what you mean, absolutely fantastic, but .... I read the news today. Oh boy! It's a global tale - horribly good."

Bobby reeled as he sought options to throw his effort toward a "*supremely* good" scenario. Fantastic. "Horribly good" is not real. Certainly an ecological scenario was a bare minimum. His thoughts came together. A clearer than day bolt of truth. He would have to leave his job. But he couldn't; his job was horribly important. It was indeed perpetuating the melee but at least it was also paying his mortgage. He was hamstrung by his own house. *To hamstring, is no aim of the house builder.* His tasks and priorities at home with his companions had him snagged. Domestic politics must be done; the family must weigh it up. Is it better to contrive your family's lives around your house and locale, or to bring your house around your lives - or both? Is there time to build, or is it better spent in some dolphinian way; is the unenhanced wooden spear better than the microwave cooker? This was an issue also for sociological and ecological politics.

Bobby was most perplexed by the complexities, problems, mysteries, lures and misconceptions as the knowledge moths fluttered to his illuminating enquiry; the politics of housing weighing against his love for his sunlit loungeroom and what it offered. His mortgage was an integral part of his housing process.

Housing process. The getting of the house. *The process is frustrated.* Frustrated. He was happy though - if he cared to be complacent. Bobby was straining at the leash. He wanted it all. He wanted everybody to have it all – perfect dream houses all round please, my shout. "But I was sure I had it all at breakfast," mumbled Bobby from his haze. "I just can't wait to hang the Picasso print," retorted the fellow passenger, basking blissful and lost in her own *interior*. House bound, she looked forward. "*Housebound* – hypnotised, trapped," reflects Dazzler, on the ambiguity of 'bound'. "Utterly over-cooked." And with others they continued in the bus. The driver's name is Global *Pale*. His address was originally Eden.

There was some lemonade in his refrigerator. "How do the Blackfellas manage without a fridge?" he mused, imagining a familiar face tanned from birth cheekily asking, "Now ... what you mean you say fridge, Global?" Global makes his eloquent reply in a voice of sand and glue; "The answer my friend is here in the drinking. The answer ... is here in the drinking".

"EXCUSE ME
PALEFACE ...
WHAT MEAN
YOU SAY HOUSE?"

O**n the inside** of her cerebral temple, Bobby's fellow passenger, like

the Building Inspector, is crossing a *threshold* in search of a domestic future. Yet she is locked into her own preconception of what a house can be – glossy magazine, leading trendy architect. Her word is 'vogue'. It may well be correct for her purpose. But, like a soaking of *oil into a parched, sun-bleached door*, her concepts may become enriched with new awareness and that which she had forgotten or overlooked. For many a soul has been unaware of even the air between us, despite its weight on our bodies, the sparkle it gives to stars and the way it carries our voices. Until reminded, say, by some persanal wind in a bus or small perfect room. There will most certainly be foul air with the fragrant, *armpits* and off-key psychologies. Because; the house is our product. Our useful rooms and streets are our product. It will take more than this chapter to explain what a house really is. Much is subliminal. Man's doings are people's – brilliant but on average, not sublime. His architecture, in the generic sense, is little better than his politics. You may wish to ventilate. Your medicine is coming up.

Shelter. Object. *Dwelling-arrangement.* A house may be a lot to you. Both simply and profoundly, to what are we referring with our word, 'house'? A style, cultural amenity, contrivance, *contraption*, a unified *accumulation* of domestic items. Some built fabric the embodiment of molecular forces. Facility for dwellers. A *box* with a pointy roof. Something in earthly synergy. Of social energy. Address. A major aspect of home. Interior and alfresco. What is a house? Something we can dissect and analyse.

Never on the bus, *absolutely never,* is a certain fictional grandfather named Albert Gallopilong. He has been initially unnoticed from the *stratospheric stroll;* lost and forgotten behind the urban blinkers of pitched roofs and street signs. His character and energy are reminiscent of a hero of mine, the real world character, made city-

famous by his acting talent, David Gulpilil - spearing roo for the family in the country one day, a dinner suit in Sydney the next. In a contrast to David, Albert has absolutely no contact with anything Western ... nor anything Eastern. An anciently traditioned Aborigine, of a fictional Harmoninni mob, Albert resolves his domestic needs in his traditional *ancient* ephemeral way – a minute modicum of interior, some alfresco and a vast amount of exterior. Global *Pale*, the bus-driver-cum-proud-entrepreneur of Western *ticky tacky* mediocrity, needs to know Albert – to understand heart-in-house. I feel that another character here, sketched as a *modern* Harmoninni, holds a key – which certainly is not a machine-cut Lockwood. His name is Cheekyfella Talkabout. Really, it's Cheekybugga, but it switches in mixed company, such as our Readership or his aunt's friends in Sydney. It's he who coined 'Albert' as a nick-name for old Gallopilong. Cheekyfella works with our swag of people, whose hearts command their dwelling arrangements, as does yours, to spirit the waft of cultural intuitions, inexplicable by science, through the plaster slurry and rooms of our domestic tapestry.

Domestic-arrangements, including houses, are very substantial generators of civilisations and personalities; including indigenous civilisation and Harmoninni personalities. A house is a romancer, a civiliser. A generator. "And it's a fryer and I'm an egg," grins a fragmented thought. "Hmm," affirms Bobby Dazzler," it's true; they always say a house is merely *shelter*. There's more to it. Amazingly, houses are neither properly understood nor valued." It strengthened his desire. Somehow those house-seeker frustrations must be resolved! "Though some may be proper, the house by-and-large is not in tune with wholistically healthy societal development."

For caveman, now-man and the progeny, what is a house?

SHELTER

Shelter – obviously it's shelter. Shelter, built where needed, is house. Only a romantic notion! That could be a bus stop. The impulse to shelter, contrary to loosely popular acknowledgement, is only part of the house story. From our perspective today shelter is a necessary accessory - a technicality. Never-the-less it is romantic - a pocket of safe, warm, calm air regains us some of the personal potentials that were lost to the blizzard now buffeting a shelter. Shelter in this sense offers a kind of gateway, back from the passion quashing storm, to the growing personal future. And it is a lure to the *traps and delights of interior*.

The elements. Inclemency. Clemency. Keeping out the wind-force, beasts, rain and robbers. Builders will guard, *screen* and *shield* variously for hygiene, security, seclusion, serenity, tidiness and unhindered activity. Having blocked out, we now induce. Induce light, view, fragrance and sound – *nature's nurtures* – and tap water and warmth.

Block out inclemency. Induce clemency.

However, to annotate our lay awareness:
the impulses to *houze*, more than by shelter,
are prompted by the following five factors;

H O U S I N G   P R O M P T S

PERSONAL DOMESTICS - hygiene, tidiness, eating, furnishing, mood, crumbs and egg-shapes ...

SECURITY OF POSSESSION – ancient tapestries, food, spears, kindred, chattels, tools of trade, goods, video ...

INCLEMENCY – ultra violet, creaturely adversity, any adversity ... grayed weathered boards ...

COMMUNITY & NEIGHBOURS - gregariousness, courtesy, seclusion, privacy screening, juxtaposition, memorable parties ...

ERGONOMICS - *room* to move, access, a place to be found, to be and do, floor in particular ...

Shelter is integrated amongst these five prompts. The building fabric that provides *shelter* is much the same fabric that provides for each of the five prompts. This integration is because adaptation, compromise and inspiration cause things to be used for any number of purposes. For example, some support timbers for roofing may inspire a location for a wardrobe; the pantry framework can be a rest for a roof – *as the grotto is a place for a house.*

The enclosure of our walls causes us to adapt to an appropriate style of movement; one that endures adequately to open the way for interior living. In the shelter, we may coincidentally find seclusion, solitude and privacy. "These also can be found variously in the wide-open world," jibes Global *Pale*, as he rudely envisages Cheekyfella hunched in a burnt spidery tree-hollow reaching, shivering for a non-existent door knob.

A visual-acoustical *screen* for privacy and a sheltering *screen* for seclusion are each screens arising from different motives. One keeps personal things from going out, the other keeps disruption from coming in.

More than by tree hollows, forest nooks and building; the amenity from such screening facility may instead be somewhat achieved by *social protocols* – protocol in lieu of building. "And so't must," returns Cheeky with a twang of wiry confidence. "Where home's underpinned by *a seclusion which is selectively in close distance to the community* (meanin' the tribe), sensibly it must be achieved largely by *behaviour protocol.*" A spear in the leg may be more practical than a prison. "*Protocol* binds our tribe, built walls would loosen, weaken it; albeit that walls may serve as *built protocols!* We indigenous campers *use distance for privacy* a fair bit. Young fellas are kept separate from the girls. Seclusion is likely more real than privacy. Maybe privacy is cowardice." ... Global wonders "Smart native ... must have been to university to be so eloquent," as, whilst privately smarting, he pulls away from the stop, and, without noticing a Mexican asleep under the bus-shelter seat – and, still completely oblivious to the huge significance of **social protocol** in housing.

> *Tribal togetherness lowers priority for walls.* Seclusion is made variously by protocol, stealth and/or walls.

It is when tribes are replaced by looser society that walls increase and thereto *dwelling-contraptions,.* Or perhaps that's putting the chicken before the egg. The *tracker* in Talkabout is finding the motive in Pale.

Household *room* and order will develop regardless of **INCLEMENCY**. You might find yourself in need of support for meal plates amid rain, boogies, ants and beautifully plumed birds. That's house and camp from the inside. It is usual that shelter is part of this development, but there are the *other reasons for walls and roofs*. And there are *dwelling-arrangements* with neither. And either. There is a vernacular in China preferring some rooms unroofed - how do we keep out the household fowls?

INCLEMENCY, among the five housing prompts, is listed third only nominally. Historically one factor may have begat another. Whichever was first is probably incidental. Today they are mutual and are responded to, with construction or lifestyle conventions, pretty much as one. Among the five prompts, priorities vary with *climate, resources, culture and tradition.* As the long drenching wet approaches, unlike the *Pales*, the indigenous nomadic Harmoninnies move to the *familiar* shelter & hallows of a distant, deep, dramatic, fire-flickered cavernous meeting place.

For those domiciles where there are fewer if any neighbours; the priority and physical profile of fabrication, an aspect of house arising from obviously the **COMMUNITY & NEIGHBOURS** prompt, is *lower* than that prompted by **INCLEMENCY**. In this instance, house and life can be quite different from the urban counterpart.

Location and *distance* may give shelter. You may have reason not to settle in the Arctic, close to the town's public invasions, or the lava flow. Forgetting the dolphin question; shelter, in its first sense, is nature's enforcement on our tender physical and mental

16

predispositions. And on our chattels. And even on our house itself – keeping it back from the tidal surge.

In this way housing is; people ordering community in conjunction with individual domestics.
"And please note, Global:
The **COMMUNITY & NEIGHBOURS** factor is a lever in the physical creation of, 1, Cheekyfella's minimal *ephemeral* camp-hut as well as, 2, the largess of your own *settler* dwelling." "Yes, not just either but both," observes a fair witness.

The work of making shelter essentially is not a bugbear in life but a support. Certainly this is so in good community – it is well that some solo housemakers may need help. Wrestling, muscle with gravity and the elements, or using foraged materials to adjust to hourly circumstance, can put one in closer touch with the healthy planet's country and community. It can be a thoroughly preferred activity. At home. The porch on a balmy day. Awnings in place. Waiting to reward the neighbour's building assistance with a beer. Things just could have been totally different though.

By way of Darwinian allusion. Two ancient characters, Grunter and Gina Palaeolithic could have chosen to go the way of the horse or seagull – unsheltered, open air, non-manual. Perhaps at this stage divergence from any evolutionary direction was too late. We should have taken a left at Salamander City. Does any homo sapiens have regrets? The making of housing could be the making of a rod for the back. Do any progeny of Grandfather Adam regret? Maybe Adam and Eve's Eden had natural housings. Ideal places to play house, to utilise for liaisons, eating, making contact or whatever. We don't know about the daily consciousness of these two unique forebears. Think of it as the *Z* factor. Maybe there was no need for domestic facility. Food was easy; straight from the trees. The meaning of *ecopicality* will unfold – in *Z* surely *personality* epitomising *ecopicality* was rife. It was pleasant enough to sleep on the grass. Perhaps the opalescent glow of the night sun refracting through the firmament discouraged sleep. They were tending the garden in consciousness *Z*. Moving a boulder to make a clear area in a place of splendour. A modification of place to keep optional implements for cracking coconuts and spooning passionfruit. Domestic developments would be an option. Sewerage would be negated by perfect eating, or something. But we really don't know all about *Z*.

No, there are no firm regrets. Our conditioning has shaped us, shaped us, aped us and continues to do so, do so. We adapt. Happily comply. Happy, nonplussed, to *houze* as we do today. As population, we can enjoy it immensely as it is. Shelter, utility, homemaking; the three hand in hand. And it is worth a special note that when thinking of seclusion for *privacies* and *solitudes*, we may tend to think of the individual alone. *It is very significant though; that couples, families, tribes and friends flourish together in joint seclusion.*

And that a regular and facilitated meeting place, some type of address, if not a shared physical home, is paramount in achieving this; be it in camp, tribal territory, aside in the bush, or in *domestic-contraption* amid the crowding of city.

Spare empathy though for the poorly sheltered, drought stricken and downtrodden. Perhaps a native Australian, an Abophile, a Harmoninni, thrust into a depriving cell or an early 'welfare' *box* house. Away from, all three, the songs of the land, extended family and tribal camplife - some serious stress. Severely over-sheltered, shuttered, blinkered. *Housebound.* Deprived; by the stuffy interiors to which the Anglophile subjects even itself, as it acts preconditioned by crowded, medieval public-domestics and streets devoid even of the likes of effective subway escapes – today extruded through the *ticky tacky box.* Sensory and tribal deprivation. *Housebound.* Or spare a thought for a molly-coddled old lady finding herself ship-wrecked on a cold, hard, treeless island.

An extreme in this story; traditional Abophile shelters are generally very scant. These people barely know interior - certainly not as the landowner does. Openness is strongly present - generally no isolation from outside activities. The distance protocol they use between the numerous camp domiciles is ephemerally flexible; not a built straight jacket, rather - easily adjustable to social and natural exterior and location. Their shelters, merely a minor part of their *domestic-arrangements*, are a usually a small secondary adjunct to open-air encampment - perhaps at times with a special cultural acknowledgement imbued into a forked stick prop and ridge rod. The shelters variously have aspects of domicile, within their overall family camp domain. Essentially, they may be as a shaded, waterproof or windscreened bed *room* locked only by social lore. Rudimentary, like any minimal humpy. The *perception of its interior* is less than a whisper. Global *Pale*'s generic industrial *ticky tacky box* invents a new air of stillness, if not stuffiness. So conversely the *Pales'* *perception of exterior* is well short of complete. This is so, even considering a drug-free psychedelic exterior moment that Global experienced during a sojourn with Cheekyfella Talkabout at a Harmoninni Corroboree – or "… a sort of barbecue party," as Global called it, unaware of the rare and highly special privilege.

> The *Pales* have a **patio adjunct** to their sheltered *dwelling-arrangement*. The Gallopilongs have a **shelter adjunct** to their alfresco *dwelling-arrangement*.

Shelter is *shielding, insulating* and *screening*.

> Albert manages these three as he relocates a piece of drying, leafy, limb to balance his sun, smoke, privacy and warmth in accord with a new mood of the shifting day.

Shielding is protecting and making *room*. Maybe with sheet plaster about the bed or eave and paint to save the graying weatherboards. *Shielding*, or *filtering*, away the sun is making shade, maybe with corrugated zincalume - making *room* for activity or facility that requires shade. Perhaps we even shield ourselves from darkness - using light. From winds, dust, sun. From bacteria and dirt, from car headlights, neon signs, crassness, rudeness. From 'adversity', from external inclemency and intrusion. We screen ourselves from neighbours for the most obscure reasons at times; and often out of courtesy. By physically screening visitors we are making *room* for privacy, seclusion, protocol and inner sanctum. Gate, portico, buzzer, door, lobby, guest lounge. *Shelter* from the vision of community passers-by with lace filter curtains, tinted glass or gruff expression. Tiki repels. Knocker announces.

Insulation screen's the outgoing. Often for warmth it stops some heat going out of the house. *Shelter*, stops something coming in. So one could include that *insulation* also includes fabrications for visual and acoustic courtesy, shyness and solitude - stopping sounds and sights from going out. These often need to be kept in for psychological comfort - community screening. Bundle them into the meaning of shelter anyway – hmm; perhaps it's not heat going out but cold coming in.

Shelter provides an interior-creating amenity. This is *room*. So also do community screening and domestic order provide *room*. For each of community screening and domestic order; the created interior amenities differ. Notionally, they are the amenities of *enclosure* (fenced, requested or walled) and *domicile*, among the amenities of *utility* and *owned place*.

Shelter excludes more than inclemency!! By the nature of its materials, it also unintentionally excludes desirable amenities - *nurtures*. It excludes – some daylight, outlook, fragrance, social contact and, quite significantly, ventilating air flow. The excluded things, *clemencies*, now more than ever, include some fundamentals of what I term *nature's earthy nurtures* – that is, the nourishing sensualities of Earth's organic surrounds, at one with the 'songs of the land'. This results in *box* syndromes, ghettos, vitamin D deficiency, dastardly frustrations. A prime excluded fundamental is *'extensive open space'*. Shelter supports exclusion of extensive open space - enclosure, containment, limits. There may well be other things, beyond the average ken, *excluded* or *impacted* by shelter fabric - a metal roof may toy with magnetic fields.

Shelter promotes expansion and evolution of domestic interior; as does community, within its own enclosure limitation. Interior is a lively catalyst for imagination. With this - and art, security, facility, ownership, comfort, cosiness and, when spare time arises, the concept and rooms of home boom. Be conscious though; **exterior is a catalyst also - an immense catalyst!!** Bringing in *nature's* *nurtures* is in fact selective externalisation of interior – **timber panels**, potted plants, soaring ceilings thrusting through windows and a potter's wheel breathe lively clemency into a *pale* white *box.*

Whilst the interior-creating processes of fabricated shelter catalyse for most; the not so naive native nomad named Albert Gallopilong sits happily with his grandparents, cousins, children and wiry nephew in a newly found natural lee, sharing the open air energy of a lashing humid storm – never having more than simply heard of anything *ticky tacky*, not even so much as a match '*box*'. An opportunity to 'be', the likes of which Bobby has not really seen. Another day, another hand-built lee.

So with this broad understanding of shelter; we do wonder as to whether it in fact was shelter – shielding, screening, insulation - that did encouraged most of our forebears into houses and that it too is the promoter of our *accumulations*. Our domestic imaginations. Our fixed, *accumulating*, consolidating abode.

Did peoplekind's Harmoninnies simply not succumb to the enticements and procrastinations of interior originally established by camp and shelter? *Did they not recognise some extended potential of interior*, or enjoy the amenity? For them open sky, community, family, socially flexible encampment and 'nomadic' movement are supreme - and ceilings perhaps a star-blocking idle tarry. Fly them away the dolphins might say. It seems unlikely that being gentle on the earth is reason for the Harmoninnies' building-free lifestyle, as, they would burn huge areas of land to flush out goannas for food and to create green grass sprouts to lure their kangaroo prey. They were however recreating the circumstance of natural bush-fire, but never-the-less, in this process the slower animals would suffer. But further, the Abophiles in this state were exceptionally tough and more accepting of harsh death in their own lifestyle.

Some of the housed peoples have followed similarly in their living without chairs. They build but, they sit and squat on the floor. Why? Mood maybe, or perhaps some simple practical reason unique to the early development of each people – lack of materials or time, a liking for simplicity, a genetic tribal habit, no room for them, no clutter, more flexible space. Why do they not build houses? Why do they not make chairs?

Hermit crabs and shrimp have shelter for security and stealth. Dolphins don't need a house as a wind and rain shelter, nor for privacy it seems. Is privacy a result of innate coy, the serpent, or generations of built interior? Before houses, domestic life was often quite public and this was carried through to early and medieval house interiors. However, fig leafs, clothes and enclaves with whispers surely were around before *ticky tacky boxes* too.

Hunter-gatherers, of all walks, as a matter of course have a home base - where they divvy up food, store tools, make snares and baskets. They therefore need facility. A home-base, of some time frame, is a necessity. Shelter, at times, is simply an option, an occasion. It can be developed as environmental control; though it is not always the winner - burglary, virus, spiders, rats, earthquake, telephone marketing and peeping Toms. A hurricane may challenge a shelter - we rely on the builder for shelter, more so than the building. House me beautifully darling; we'll spread nacre together.

A symbol for house ...?
It's not an egg – a house doesn't hatch, it opens and shuts.
A symbol for shelter?
The front door perhaps is more appropriate than is the roof.
A symbol for domestic-arrangement?
Might be a pot or a food store.

The house is more dinner-table than shelter.
The ephemeral camp is more lightweight than table and chairs.

HOUSE EMBRYO

EXCUSE ME *PALEFACE* ...
WHAT YOU MEAN YOU SAY HOUSE?

The embryo develops into the fullness of an optimum house. The house over centuries has been affected by technical and cultural developments; but not in its fundamentals.

Some cultural aspects of houses are *non-fundamental.* These may become more pronounced and significant where ego and creativity have time to play and where leisure and wealth are abundant. With inherited skill and understanding, houses grow in accommodation - in commodity. One plain crowded multifunctional room nextdoor to others becomes a multistorey mansion in a leafy *boulevard* – the owner leaning yet to a humble but cute egg-shaped lounge in a tranquil grotto.

Thereby the wholesome residence may grow from its primitive and economic minima into something quite elaborate. Or even *deviant.* It may be that a debt-free house without excess, laziness or immoral facility is not deviant. In its full development a house is a different thing to different people and different locales. But the fundamentals are common to all. This is so, even with the most advanced industrial evolution. However a house does become less in the fundamentals for those who live in unnecessary deprivation in the *palest* of *boxes.* These fundamentals, before built *room,* are those first essences. Encampment. Domiciled land - an alternative use of the word 'house' is to describe a male person's family, as supported by place.

The common sense of house is much the same today as it was in the roots of our dictionaries. Dwelling also means 'diversionary waiting, procrastination'. It is also 'abiding'. Abode is 'an action of waiting, a stay before moving on'. It is a house too. The thing forms around the action. Abide is also 'toleration' - we compromise. Towns and villages were 'urbs' - urban. From the word 'hud' we have - hut, hovel, yurt, site, house. Place is 'stede' - homestead. Boundary is 'limits'. Cain built supposedly the first 'city', not a Big Apple, a smallish living place for some people - Jericho, the city where Joshua battled, was only 600 metres perimeter. It is interesting that Cain, as a doer of bad things, headed up this in his progeny. Was he wrong to have built the city? Residence, lodge, igloo, tipi, castle, camp, cabin, bungalow, flat, cottage, tent, quarters, interior, inside, exterior, outside, space, chateau, shanty, household, street, address, place. *Domestic-contraption*. All are words of abode grown on a vegetated earthly slate.

'Room' - a key word. It is based on the commodities of amenity.

Beyond mother's womb *room*, and the land, of early life, the physical manifestation of the home is surely the *dwelling-arrangement*. For a wife it begins at the physical provisions of her husband's arm. For the husband it begins at the physical place of his wife beyond which he cannot fruitfully go. For the baby it is mother. For the children it is the parents. Home in a house is underpinned by some family or communal aspect. The word 'husband' is from house – or perhaps vice versa.

The birth of the house in the noble savage romance is beautiful like a tree from a mustard seed. Caves and embracing trees as housing are fixed and limited but in they may provide of a genetic 'memory-notion of interior'. A notion that may spawn ideas for fixed roofs and huts to potential builders in open lands who must pursue sustenances or curiosities. And who therefore come to build where there are no trees or caves. Interior is but one property of *room*.

Interior is but one property of *room*.

Priority order. That which comes first in housing is surmised. *Room* for the settler to be and do, screening from the embarrassment of newly discovered nakedness and bad weather. Crowded almost public rooms; where private family home cannot grow. Whatever the historical truths are, they are there physically in our genome now - wow. We are the progeny from there. It is true though that our dwellings are both practical and psychological space – *room*. *Room* attached in the dwellers world by utility, fabric and access. *Room* enhanced with intended expression added to accidental expression. *Room* – if we can't find it, we make it; for cutting up vegetables or for ethereal explorations. We find it. We adapt it. We make it. *Room* in the cupboard, *room* for a loom, *room* on the spoon, some *room* in the room under the moon, making some more *room* soon one may assume .... Oh stop it; please ease up, for the fever may grow ... a choking room boom. "Room boom, ... room boom, ... room boom!?" contemplate the Palaeolithics and the Gallopilongs, raking their imaginations in the brief shelter of a foraged hut. Rumours abound, among the homo superiors, that it is the cause of rheumatism.

Within the whole, a human embryo begins with the three; sperm, ovum and womb, whose order we don't decree. Except for the effects of life span, the human embryo is totally definitive of the person on its threshold; and it is living. The house embryo is not living, even as a blueprint, which anyway is more like a placental umbilicus than an embryo.

A dwelling embryo begins with the *three*:

D W E L L I N G   E M B R Y O

1. CONCEPT - Maximally improved, local, at-hand, environmental function and aesthetic.

2. THE WORLD-CONTINUUM - The whole, the happening of world and life (people singing to enhance the sung creation, singing the right place to build, forgetting and wondering why).

3. PRAGMATICS - The time/wisdom structure within which is nurture and security and the *playdough of the Earth*.

It is the same for both the 'first encampment' and 'the last housing unit, perhaps in a distant future megastructure at the bottom of the Pacific', or a unit in a housing block in early Rome.

The beginnings of a fullness yet to be, the house embryo doesn't change much in time. Ahead of a place to bed, we find or establish a reasonably level and otherwise appropriate area. This area has been quickly developed into the fullness of a true and level floor. The floor! - a property of *room*. Some *room* may not require a floor; the room on a spoon. Once floor is in our life, it is inherent, assumed, relied upon, an ongoing nurture, a persuasion, cultural fixation, necessity, convention - a pragmatic or continuum. Our response to blind domestic foot traffic and practical placement of *accumulations* creates the flat floor – an ergonomic thing. The road is a kind of floor. Dusty earth, heavy with track marks between camp fires, swept oiled ground, bees waxed boards shine resisting tracks and looking fine, black and white checks, squares of dyed woollen mat, cool hard marble, grass green synthetic shag pile.

Once the fabrication ball was rolling other aspects were developed simultaneously. Anybody knowing people fully, such as a Lord of Eden, could predict the detail of development from the wide-open to the *pale* interior.

23

And of course it happened with the spread of culture and functions more than by a steady flow of singular a-priori. There was a time when the wealthy had durably surfaced floors while the poor had bare earth. That's why we say "dirt poor." Sometimes the floor surface was slate. It's slippery when wet, so straw, or *thresh*, was laid for better footing. As winter continues on, more thresh was added. Itself it tended to slip - through the doorway. A piece of wood was placed to retain it. That's a "threshold."

Anyway the 'floor', or, at least, the naturally level site, developed order - placements, security, shelter, screens and so on. These varied with cultural concept and geographic locale. The self-preservation urges and community courtesies mingled and interfaced as the dwelling contraption grew. We can bet which came first, ahead of social address – facilities for safety, nourishment and sleep.

A place to sleep, a lean-to and then, for those still wanting (most of us), the first sign of all-round enclosure - perhaps ahead of singularly conceived walls and the high-priority floor. From the (still contemporary) gorilla's circle to a reclusive, or maybe communal, humpy bed-sitter with external, maybe communal, living, cooking, washing and toiletry.

And with this enclosure; the *opening through*. The milestone. The *cute opening*. The beginnings of the mature machinecut door, doorway, latch key, threshold and front porch. Maybe parched, maybe oil soaked. Somewhere at this foetal stage; genetics will diversify. And so neighbour, society and the land mix in different ways. Different locales, people, understandings and mores strike out to various diverse breeds. Gallopilong's legs went walkabout - and this time it happened that he made a sleeping shelter on stilts above wet ground. Cain built a city, ingenious in Genesis, gorgeous says Gina Palaeolithic.

The foundation trench is not the first fabrication. Though a shallow post hole must be an early occurrence, it is low in the embryonic a-priorities. It comes only as firmness requires it - at the time of the toddler's first stumble or fall. That which goes to the dump or is lost by impact is the afterbirth.

Mother of pearl, some result of the ongoing *emotional kiss* from person to preferred place, is not the first fabrication – ah but, some understand it to include the exterior shell. Well, where does the exterior of the shell end and the interior begin??!! We have a sense of design and construction. The front door comes first but so does the founding stone. And a sense of inhabitants, like the oyster, making an intimate organismic comfort, fending out the sea aggressions, honing the raw basics, rough edges, finishing, changing, de-drabbing, decorating and colouring to personal delight and to coordinate with similar considerations in pre-construction design. The results of this we may call, for lack of an established architectural term, *mother of pearl*, the inner face of *nacre*. *Nacre* is the full thickness of shell. The outer face of *nacre*, a hand against the wind, is a foundation for *mother of pearl*. *Mother of pearl* is a key aspect of language as these pages go forward. We make it as we cover cushions, polish floors (flattening in the bent nails), round corners, smooth our wood, make our protocols, clear our air, place our talisman, plaster our ceiling, make our interior, hone aspects of our *room*. We give some *finesse*. Mind you; never overlook the finesse of perpetually modern nature.

We may give *finesse* to the outer face too. The oyster never goes out so to it this doesn't matter.

We may mentally grow a house by beginning from its completed *finesse*. Completed *internal finesse*, *mother of pearl* in form and place, and fully optioned. Mentally grown. This is **CONCEPT**. Probably *outer finesse* is an afterthought – self preservation coming before community courtesy. It may be that the noble savage in fact began with this refined ethereal fabrication imagery and that the mustard tree appeared before its seed. As we say, the idea that semi-obligatory rudimentary shelter, the outer face of *nacre*, began the house is perhaps quite naïve. It may have been optional rudimentary delicate interior subtlety envisaged over a feast of fish and dates on a clement shore that became, maybe, Turkey. This may be a best concept for embryo. Or some elsewhere where it's always fine but miscarries for lack of opportunity and resource.

Having found, or declared, ourselves vulnerable or naked and seeking, we in the end find we use the house to found a road to take us back to the Eden we recall we sullied and that an Iraqi despot has recently bullied; only to find in time that it is a long road to hoe and that Cheekyfella, our modern native Australian, beat everybody. Though he did need the help of both the settler and the lord of all logic; a very special person in housing is our young, broad-grinned, athletic Cheekyfella Talkabout. He has become highly *ecopical*, but he doesn't know this at all. Like you, he shall come to know of it later.

Ω

Apocalyptic times are upon us. This embryo of anyperson's house is now rhetorically only good for its stem cells in making our embryo today. In the fat West the individual house embryo is frequently afflicted with mutation. Once there was toleration of a bare wooden floor, no curtains nor cupboard doors until there is money for further development. Marketing, social psychoses and credit have appearances and luxury taking precedence over some of the *fundamentals* such as good *room* forms and ample play space. These embryos are those of the orthogonal *houselocust* breeds. It is good values that build an embryo into a proper healthy house - it's strong bones and a good liver ... rather than credit-card prenatal surgery and marketed pastiche implants.

ACCUMULATION, BUILT BITS & a UNIFYING MATRIX

EXCUSE ME *PALEFACE* ...
WHAT YOU MEAN YOU SAY HOUSE?

A singular object.
Is that what a house is?

'Domicile', 'place' and 'possession'. These metaphysical realities cast a *singularity* on the house.

It is a *singular* entity. Physical realities also, register the house as a singular entity – view it from a bus or the lounge chair.

But our house is almost a mere *accumulation*.

Our stuff. Chattels, vital possessions, camp bits, awnings, roofs, screens, block-outs, odds and ends. Ourselves. A yellow gourd. Look at your own. A house is almost this. To access, protect and use this stuff we also need *room*.
Room for nacre and screens.
Room to access the items of our *accumulation* (including parts of the house and its yards). *Room* to access, to move. *Room* for fingers to turn a door knob, arms to reach and swing, air to circulate, mind to soar, people to share – to access amenity, to use and enjoy.

Ergonomic room. "Ergonomic' pertains to work so 'domestonomic' might be better ... but no. *Ergonomic room* is what I call the detail and generality of that *room* necessary to access and live in a house and its place. *Ergonomic room* is a *unifying matrix* that brings a physical and metaphysical singularity to our domestic accumulations including rooms. In fact, it is a heart of the house.

This *ergonomic heart* is the fusion interface of dwellers and the *accumulation*. In the fusion is the spark of interior – which may be delightful.

> *As we know: room* is needed also for delivery of items to their place – grand piano to the studio. And for fat people, wheelies, tallies, blindies and parties. Oh well; for the goats and cow to keep you warm and a catflap for Sylvester and a stormy beach in a cupboard and a car trailer full of bricks on its road.

The act of extended abode itself creates further *accumulation* to fuse with the *ergonomic heart*. Take care this may trigger the *trap of interior* – the spark may be dampened.

There are *built bits*, which are anchored to site;
roof up there and some masonry elements. Expressive jigsawn filigree, to visually soften the edge there on the front porch.

There are *loose bits* that hover and patina between the built and the dwellers;

bowls, bedding, dunny tub, talismans, magazine rack, shelves, chair, basket, hoe, lawn mower, a cooker, refuse. Abacus, computer. Fig leaf, wardrobe. Footprints, scuff marks, hand oil dosing the door edge.

The house grows. The builder's client sees it grow in a different way; quickly - stage two, 'move in'.

Our *accumulation* relates to, and in large part is; the things, constructed accesses and screenings, the utilities that facilitate our various domestic activities. Always in some ordered chaos. Usually with options for us to 'do without', or to make-use-of facilities elsewhere in the community, city or the land - always there's some sort of domestic facility *elsewhere*, even in just the nature of land, a cup o' sugar next door or a table at the Greasy Spoon Café.

We tend to increase the utilities unless, having packed them back into a rucksack, we depart, leaving our site unfenced and unroofed, a warm brick chimney straining the flap. We tend to develop, expand, accrue, proprietise. The Harmoninnies limit their *accumulations*.
  "For us," explains Albert Gallopilong, "it is largely only containment by site, or conveyance, which casts a sense of material singularity." For Global the singularity is his ownership - receipts, land title and address.

That we accrue the items in a single place is an ergonomic matter. There may be value in the saltshaker being down the road and the attic-store being agisted in the neighbour's paddock; but we need most stuff at hand at home. And hopefully the single place, being the land-site itself, provides inherent in its nature security, practical comfort and whimsical delight. If it doesn't we do what we can to make these; or with Albert walk to them elsewhere.

There's something in both our assumption and right of use. The use of - and potential to use - the items *accumulated* on site give a perception of them as a physical singularity. Singular ownership.

Re this singularity, note the *demands* of the utility items; *demands* for containment, protection and *ergonomic access*. These *demands* lie inherent in the varying values of the *accumulated* items - contain the children, protect the money, *room* to access.

Note the **combination**, of these *demands*, with the dwelling *activities* that create the *accumulation*. Simple really;
  children running from the toys to Mum's cook-pot. Cooking,
  playing, sleeping, viewing television, reaching the remote.
The ergonomic heart pulses. This combination of demands and activities physically unifies the *accumulation*. The demands are satisfied firstly by *room* – she needs the *room* to reach the frypan.

Room is visible in that it is enhanced by landform, fabrication, amenity and *layout*. And obviously it is free of obstruction to the required *room* amenity. *Mother of pearl*, like interior and space, is an attribute of *room*.

Room to store, to enclose, to move, to access, to do, to put, to reach; custom-made *room* arising from paths, floors, halls, passage, scullery, stair, hoist, walls, doors, roofs, fly-wire. This visibility shows the unity of all the *ergonomic accesses*.

Singular *ergonomic access*. Unified in its direct physical connection to the dweller – from anywhere we can go via this access matrix to, reach and use anything. Stride to the washing machine, get our shoulders through, see, gather together, sit in order, party, manipulate, gain access for maintenance. "Get the frying pan from the cooker in the conservatory White Cloud ... please dear."

Accessible address. The singular house entity is reinforced in that this *accumulation* must, for both dwellers and visitors, relate *ergonomically* to the community – accessible address. Again, it must relate to the community as a conveniently single limited property and also as a point of coming and going, to nurture our singular and plural being; our personal, family and social identity. So house is an entity in social concept:

> Domicile. Ownership. Address. Highway, footpath, bus-stop, letterbox, visitors, search warrant.

Always on the settleable land – not really, there's 'always in the space-station' and 'on the ship'. And *in* the land. And so going with the wandering tribe.

Our *accumulated* stuff is extended by our creation of *room* for activity and such as egg-shaped aesthetic comfort. So *'room'* itself can be an item of the accumulation. The elements and components of the physical house accrue as we consolidate our property; shed, garage, barbecue, roof, hearth, bench, plumbing and curtain. Coats generate coat hooks and laundries. Bedding is enhanced by a bed base. Lawnmowers may need a shed. Shelves for books. An attic for suitcases. A barrel for wheat. A room for hobbies. A place to lean a spear. Chairs, if desired, demand a table, and eventually home theatre and their own remote controls, which in turn need a place – a place to be and a place to be manufactured and places to be resourced etc.

For Albert, seating is not an item - it can be accommodated by the nature of the site. A few rocks contain the fire. Some shelter offside or coordinated with the hearth if suitable and some other bits too. An Anglophile would have to have a chair, at least of sorts, maybe imported Rococo, and a porcelain jerry – on the red dusty ground. A jerry! - Cheekyfella bends over, grabbing his sides in laughter.

All of the various *accumulated* items fulfil functions in response to demands relating to city, society, family, personality and/or the dwelling-organisms.

Δ

So house is a conglomerate. *Accumulations* the rubble. *Ergonomic room* the matrix. And nacre from the *playdough of the Earth* is there - and the whole Earth itself.

Albert Gallopilong's is a loose conglomerate. And smaller. His *ergonomic matrix* about camp allows subtle social and land interface and flexibilities on site. His utilities are less permanent. He has no rucksack, but his family will help by dragging and carrying some of the stuff. Even the long-term home-base for the elderly is minimal – yet still the same Earth itself is there.

A ruck-sacked Mr Low Carl, an Amerophile of no fixed abode and few *accumulations*, hooks into the expanse of the city – a wallet his key, the stock exchange his meagre *hunting and gathering* ground. *Eco-social sustainability* his urgent devotion. A person who has known a cardboard *box* under a freeway bridge and, there, a home-cooked fresh salmon fillet imported from New Zealand for breakfast.

A DISSECTION
of this OBJECT

EXCUSE ME PALEFACE ..,
WHAT YOU MEAN YOU SAY HOUSE?

The accumulations, including the rooms and nacre, bring about this singular object – the house. It's on land or maybe on a raft. Having just put it together, and feeling a little pepped up with all this remarkable human progress, let's have another look ..... .

A simple object, the house. Intense too. Simple componentry; but complexly inter-mixed – made complex accidentally, incidentally or purposefully. Consider this: the house and its plurality is a **phenomenon** – like the glow worms.

Hmm, an observation; to be concise we must note that the material fabric (the nacre) is not the house. The material fabric is not the house. (In this scenario the ergonomic matrix is overlooked in its quiet presence like a spirit.)

We see that each material used is in the *action* of fulfilling its purpose - the threshold is holding back the straw.

These *actions*, combined, are the house.

These *actions* are the house:
>The physical *actions* of shielding, retaining, attenuating, securing, facilitating, nurturing, permitting, inducing, tapping, supporting. The *actions* of response to the dwelling-organisms – the floor may creak its support under foot. The *actions* of stopping the cold wind – the window strains against the gale. Of obscuring incoming vision. The simple magic of Albert Gallopilong's strategically placed bunch of perpetually modern molecules in a leafy eucalypt branch, daggy with some dead.

This acknowledges the vitality of both the fabric and the items of the house. Walls screen, as well as define space and culture. The staunch energy of the wood bears the load of the roof. It supports the jigsawn filigree that in turn fosters cosiness. The *action* of the wood, of the materials, is the house. Not the item, not the gray weathered board, but the *action*. When the wood is not *acting* to provide domestic bliss, it is not immediately needed. We simply need the reassurance that the wood will be there when required. We become *housebound* as we forget that we simply need the reassurance that the house will be there when required; and when the house is not *acting* to provide domestic bliss it is not immediately needed. Molecular energies in worldly order via materials are the house – dynamic house – shimmering with molecular activity, like Dr Who's Tardis at lift-off (albeit in a shimmering world anyway).

We see that a lot of things can exist only 'inside' - things that would be swamped by exterior, or require the support of the house fabric or the technology the house has brought. These are the difference between interior and exterior. An aspect of security is one. A David Attenborough or late Steve Irwin television documentary is another. One might expect the root of the word house to mean interior. They say though the root is probably 'hud', meaning hide. Hud - a simple place to secure vital possessions, spears, skins and kindred or to sleep safely, perhaps, or to hide, have personal sanctity, privacy, security for the hunted. An hygienic stainless steel pantry as part of a mudded, leafy humpy makes more of the hud.

Houses are more than humpy today - as was domestic activity then.

These material *actions*, that we utilise, generate the house. In this perspective there can be nominated six primary elements to a house:

P R I M A R Y   E L E M E N T S   T O   A N Y   H O U S E

DOMESTIC AMENITY – cleanliness, order, *nurture*, *ergonomic access, room to be*, cosiness ...

DOMESTIC FACILITY – cupboards, baskets, table, *room to do*, floor, yard ...

SOCIAL SCREEN – internal walls, external walls, locks, protocol, fences, lace ...

SHELTER – roofing, external doors, fences, walls, sound attenuants, vertical blinds ...

CULTURAL INTERFACE – orientations to neighbour, passer-by and visitor, style, 'welcome' shingle ...

CONSTRUCTION – trusses, footings, plumbing ....

These six inter-related elements rely, variously on;
material properties, dynamic molecules, cellular structure,
reflectance, visual contrast etc.
The elements generally exist in mutual fusion. There are indeed
complex overlaps. So having acknowledged them it is best not to
bind our story to them. We can analyse this fused whole from other
perspectives also.

Physical *actions* arranged for other purposes can be adapted for
housing. An unused barn is not a house until a person moves in to
dwell – utilising aspects of its fabric that the animals and the hay
never knew to acknowledge. That person may have a blanket and a
toothbrush. She must be in abode mode. That's all he needs. They
may even be a crowd.

One's minimum house may be this, but smaller. A small tent. It
hasn't much scope for permanent abode and so its house status
becomes questionable. A large reasonably permanent well-appointed
tent, though, will always be called a tent, rather than a house. And a
grass hut will usually be a hut. And a palace a palace. A flat a flat.
But it is clear; an eye is an eye, a father a father, a meal a meal, a car
a car, a residence a residence. A *dwelling-arrangement* a *dwelling-
arrangement*. Let us in this story talk about houses as being our
semi-permanent built *dwelling-arrangements*. *Dwelling-contraptions*
in fact. And camps as ephemeral *dwelling-arrangements*. Caravans
and other miscellanea we can get our minds around without tags.

A home may require a house. It may require only a people. A home
is not a house. "Any real estate agents reading?" wonders a reader.

A bed is a basic facility. As with both encampment and the hud, the
key fundamental of house is ordered facility, *domestic-arrangement*.
With it we may make an arrangement of *accumulated* facilities and
utilities. An Abophile encampment is a unique example. A small-
roomed suburban house is a very common example - we note here
this book's first direct allusion to multiple 'rooms'.

Fabrication components, amenity components, facility components
and space components. These all meld. Fabrication influences the
shape of space. Space is a basic property of *room*. Space may be
utilised to serve as amenity. Ether from a dome. Compact in a *box*.
Furniture components give rise to spatial components, give rise to
separating components – seat, *room*, wall. Components melded with
components. Within components. To accommodate components.
Making elements, *accumulations*, *ergonomic matrix*, corners, spaces,
shapes, bits, rock, lace, *nurtures* and whimsy.

To stretch a point, sentimental and spiritual ventilation, in the form
of artwork, picture, Attenborough/Irwin documentary and talisman,

31

are a component as well. Electrical, plumbing, and air and light
ventilation are components.

Facility and amenity - handy and cosy. A fireplace, sink, bath,
inglenook, curtain, pantry, cupboard, wardrobe, bench, studio, den,
galley, lounge, kitchen, loo, seclusive place, oriel, sill, window,
hearth. Interfacing these and people we have - furniture, blanket,
bed, seat, chair, table, chest, pot, bowl, cup, plate.

All these things need *room*. *Room* - space, scope to occur, space to
receive. *Room* does not necessarily mean enclosure with ceiling.

The facility of *room* as kitchen, bed-room, portico etceteras we see as
major components of the more recent evolution of house. **Toilets**,
perhaps porcelain, once were an item in a shared multi-purpose
room in England. In general it is probably only 400 years since
Anglophiles as a people came upon the idea of making separate
rooms for separable functions – something I think to do with
affluence of free time, fixed in place plumbing and expanding nooks.
One or two rooms, with furnishing flexibilities, for a large number of
residents were enough. I think though that multi-roomed houses
have been around since earlier times in other cultures.

The embryonic aspect of *room* might be bed space or clearing for
family circle. Each of the activities for which we require and make
room requires, or may be enhanced by, particular amenity; colour,
texture, quiet, privacy, blackout curtains, in-house and community
screens and so on. Each amenity gives us something that exists
nowhere in the landscape and is generally distinct from other houses.

Mother of pearl is an element of the house too. It varies somewhat
from *room* to *room*, activity space to activity space. A use and user
sensitive inner-skin. Limited by dweller economy, resources, mental
wile and inventiveness. Interior honed for soulful beingrowing maybe
in fact is ahead of shelter's preservation. In part womblike, but your
own creation. Its embryonic aspect might be bed-comfort or *smooth
serviceable* floor – those adjectives are valued functions.

But there is the cost to fundamental lifestyle.

> Albert <u>was not tempted to go in</u>. No interior. His legs his front
> door – for going out, not in. The horizon's lighted atmosphere his
> walls; or some handy landform. No such thing as a drain. A
> drain. A toilet brush. No such thing. For him, this *mother of
> pearl* is a thing of the psyche, of perception and a manner-of-
> *doing*. Not a mental wile, but an inherited reflex. Behind that
> particular *mother of pearl* may be the remainder of the
> Harmoninnies' house *nacre*, their living weatherboards, the body
> of the Earth to which they belong. Perpetually modern nature.
> Somewhere between there and their bush television-set is their
> house and it suits them just fine.

Space, *room* for interior, *room* for rooms, *room* for access, passage, doorway, hallway, porch, portico, lobby, entrance, veranda, balcony; or rather for the functions they serve. These make it possible for several people to do several things that may conflict if it was not for internal and external walls – social distance shortcuts. Copulate privately, move around, study, whisper, make smells and odours,

        quiet moment on the back step.

It may well be that activities are best done without devoted *room*; that is, in accord with some other social norm such as in the normal crowded multipurpose, multi-dwellered, one and two *room* houses of medieval London - toilet-bowl pongo right there near the communal bed and the stove.

Roof, walls and floor are certainly probably our first thoughts when we think of the components of a house.

Why not the *accumulation* of utilities? It is because we are relating to the synthesized entity rather than the ephemeral utilisations.

For a chicken in an egg, roof, walls and floor are three in one. For a family in a dome they are two in one plus floor.

Inherently the priorities of construction raise the awareness of components as being in an order different from the priorities of dwelling. The constructional embryo, the growing building, is different from the dwelling embryo, snug *room*. Our first thoughts of abode may be bed, cooker and toilet. Or are they for womb-security. They are not for foundation stone. Having said that we must note that the foundation stone - with, depending on technique, tooled level seating and concise ends to meet the next stones - is in fact the first support for the front door and the *mother of pearl*. And symbolically the first physical action of that *emotional kiss*. The kiss lingers through to the reflective and fragrant floor polish, lace curtains and the front door of tomorrow's dream. Of course there may in fact be no foundation stone, but the principal remains – a tipi for instance. The foundation is simply earth.

A door, front or otherwise, is merely the fusion of a wall component and an access component. The floor is the singular most distinctive component - a camper may agree, subject to some windbreak.

Some have formed or sculpted their floor to double as furniture. It may be ramped, stepped or adapted to stairs. On-ground or up high. Multiple storeys or split-level. But always it is substantially horizontal and desirably flat, flush and finished to enhance comfort, hygiene, cleaning, movement, balance and maintenance to say the least. It is prime for visual and tactile enhancement also as part of the *mother of pearl* - perhaps mosaic.

To a pilot or an eagle the roof may seem the singular distinctive element – a feather falls to Sitting Bull. This roof is there though only to enhance the *room* that is begun from the floor. The first dwellers went through the door in the floor and found the benches and walls. If a roof were not needed against the weather, a version of it would insulate sound from the neighbours and keep birds, fowls and burglars from the table, maybe whilst gathering rain to a tap. It is to keep dry. A blanket. It is shade from glare, heat and ultra-violet. Some wind shelter. It relates to ceiling designs, reflected electric light, support for hooks, stabilisation of walls, acoustic impact, air and fragrance control, insect-wildlife-assailant screen, radiation fallout, droppings, cinders, smoke, object in landscape etc. "Okay, let's push on. I'm bored," yawns Cheeky Talkabout. Is ceiling for our womb comfort? "Wake me later! ... and I'm not sleep'n in an air-conditioned white vinyl-painted cube with fluffy white carpet. This rock ledge is warm from the sun ... up there in the ceiling." Is there a need for ceiling that is separate to the need for roof? Ceiling, the upside of floor. A component in itself. Ceiling is certainly related to *mother of pearl*, smoothing the under-structure of roofing *nacre*, of an overhead room or a stack of apartments. A distant contact above the bed. A junction with the walls. We usually colour them light and airy, but we do not imitate sky. 'Ciel' is French for sky. And sometimes they are mirrors, just to play the marriage between the dwelling and its organisms. Like rooves, ceilings are not always flat with wings.

The structure as well as supporting the domestic amenity must support snow, wind, dweller body weight and its own weight and thermal movements. And resist termites and rot.

Building itself generates various items, trusses, boards, but these we will not refer to as components. They are the fabric that makes components. Adaptation may make some of them useful as components however; a constructional roof space becomes an attic; a column a rest for a red wall-phone. As we've seen, the fabrication requirements for each facility and amenity are often common with those of the others in the house. And if not identically common, they are generally mutually adaptable to a fabrication solution that is a fusion of the various requirements. An external wall, glass aside, serves all - keep out the weather, create privacy, insulate sound and heat, support shelving and roof, at times to suit outdoor activity, conceal wires, hang pictures etc.

In the dissection of the house we note the front, back and sides of the common *domestic-contraption, ticky tacky* or otherwise. These external aspects of the house in its setting relate to practical and cultural address, domestic yard, the pragmatics of shape and the requirements at cadastral boundaries. Like the attic, the flat of the land and the space between wall and fence, we use what we can about the incidental and accidental quirks of the house.

The garden and yard for some are merely an optional part of a house. Nomads and apartment dwellers don't have them – certainly no lawn-mowers nor a place to store one and its petrol. And its noise.

House is a component of town. Town is broad community-based fabrication; for trade, meeting, parliament, industry, gregarious dwelling. Urb. Where there is a house there is some ergonomic connection in a track, a subway or a road, and, for a minority, cables and pipe. If the house is an apartment - maybe an escalator, elevator and a long hallway. A sense of address, if not a formal street frontage, the letterbox, a number and jowl-to-jowl neighbours. Where a house is a camp the connections are vibes, smells, simple vision, sounds and ground.

It is no small matter ... "Ay, what was that?" It is no small matter ... in the industrial world that a portion of the public arena must be considered an aspect of house.

> Address, roads, services and support industry are part of the whole responsibility and quanta attached to your wittle bit of domestic domain; including adding to its total impact in land consumption probably the area of its site again. And this is with no allowance for food production processing and delivery lands.

MINIMAL HOUSE

What symbol might represent minimal house?

EXCUSE ME *PALEFACE* ...
WHAT YOU MEAN YOU SAY HOUSE ?

Not roof - a barn has a roof. A door, lock, wardrobe. Table. All of the space imbued with meaning from use ... or, simply, *room* prepared for sleeping. A room full of stuff linked to sustaining provision. *Room* and utility, appropriately in locale.

Minimal house, including physical frugalities, is achieved through maximising domestic time and utility outdoors – patio lounge, alfresco cook and dine, tree-hung shower. It reduces the psyche tendency to substitute healthy open space with expansive interior. In winter we may tolerate a tiny shower cubical indoors.

Cheekyfella Talkabout spends huge amounts of time in what some call 'the outdoors'. He is of a different People to Albert Gallopilong - whom he anyway loves to call 'Uncle'. Like Albert, Cheekyfella Talkabout is an everywhere nomad. Full of wisdom and humour, together *they value a strong pair of legs more than any front door through which they might walk.* They value and live the land more than can be seen through any 'view window'. With their kind they value home and society richly - *without the house.* Gallopilong's physical trappings are exceedingly scant - because of his cultural understandings. Talkabout also is scantly trapped, except on his rare, bare-foot 'beige suit'-clad, visits to the likes of Sydney, which he artfully enjoys as short sojourns ... in psychedelic interior - and jibes as to that which the Whitefella, *bound* and lost amid his immense *accumulations*, is missing.

A traditional Inuit, maybe Inuophile, is minimally housed in an igloo - mortgage is no issue. A contemporary Egyptian office worker needs substantially more - because of culture, regulation, *accumulation*, automobile and city life. The minima in settlement life vary hugely, reflecting the complexities of personal *beingrowing*. A large lavishly detailed house could be a minimum, in the locale of opulent natural resource. Complexity of lifestyle, and the nature and the activity of the inhabitants, may justify expansive minima. Ego, pretension and greed establish false minima - and often deviant housing values.

The number of dwellers considered, the size of *domestic-arrangement* and house is based on all of; the *room* to move, to do and to be, the fabrication *nacre*, built bits and the extent of *accumulation*. For some size is impotent. The bigger, the more work and resources. We may choose to utilise space that we can do without. Minimal is a little optional. It is the same with lavish amenity, utilities, and other *accumulation*, as it is with space. We can be frugal or enjoy a little abundance. Astronaut Major Tom's orbiting tincan is a minimum; no *room* for visitors, but you can squeeze in your wife and cleanly defecate and pee. As much as needed and as little as possible.

Social norms are indicative of mediocrity's pragmatic minima rather than optimum lifestyle minima. *Our social values warp our sense of minimum.* As a rule the West including New Zealand and Australia has far more floor space than it needs, yet standards for other house amenity may be too low. An illustration in point; tiny *boxed* yards for children to spend the core of their childhood. Less than optimal minima and therefore inadequacies, deprivations may arise from societal values, apathy or limited resource. Nominally eighty percent of the people have twenty percent of the wealth – in the West at least. Twenty percent of the floor space is owned similarly, surely.

For some, *sharing floor space with a group* is beyond frugal – it's inadequate. For others it's prime. A group household who are happy with the privacy and domicile arrangements can be an effective form of minimal housing – economy of scale. This can be expanded to cities.

Both building and town planning regulators have been inclined to specify house design and construction that does not allow achievement of satisfactory minima for many people. Minima are very important for pockets, working hours and ecology; also for *mother of pearl* psychological subtleties such as *synthetic aesthetics* and lifestyle. We cannot properly have less than our own personal minimum. We cannot properly be obliged to borrow or take welfare where land ought be available for a tent. In Africa are people who make home under a tree, planting a garden around it. Well now, that's a romantic minimum. It relates to the welfare *box* – but where do the tree people go jobbies?

The dwellings of both the pastoral nomad and the settled indigenous builder are limited by resource and often time. Food gathering is first priority. For these people, house scale is such that ecological sustainability is an accident - if not a fundamental religion. A Namibian or was it a Maasai cow-herding nomad, typically incredibly fit and good looking, said on the tv, *"God intended us to farm animals by seasonal movement and not by planted boundaried farming."* We see in this a very significant choice that says no to settled housing. These people as I write are threatened with flooding and its dire implications for them, which are supposedly justified by the need for a dam to provide water to the houses of others. They are balanced, fair minded, highly articulate people. I am certain they understand *ecopicality* – as you will. If it wasn't for the ways of the built cities Talkabout would know of them not via tv but as faint distant energy in his dreaming.

Around Earth we have millions of houses yearly adding to the billion existing. Many cannot be classed as *houselocusts*. Ecological and industrial sustainabilities weigh substantially into the concept of minimum. We assess this critical issue by weighing all motivation to fabricate *nacre* against all impact. We juggle, like some do with credit payments. Economy is key to beauty and balance in life. Picasso knew. I think it is this 'look' that sparks the Minimalist style of architecture – wholistic-'balanced for all values'-minimalism is a different thing. And who wrote 'waste not, want not'? And what do we know about excess?

Sometimes we setup some *domestic contraption* as a minimal basis for additions. This concept Cheekyfella has well resolved. A sunroom may be an optional extra in Chicago; Cheeky finds it in the wild open spaces. An essential sleeping slot, one of an accommodation provider's stack in Tokyo, is a tight minimum if you eat out, laundry out, defecate and pee out, meet out and store elsewhere. The urban nomads love them. Ceiling (roofed by floors above), walls, floor and bed - say three cubic metres - a slot. A house in a van without cooking or stand-up space - tight. This is a potential of big city life – bituminous in context. And there is similarity to Gallopilong's offside bed-*room* – dusty red in context. Yet its true the fragility of city life cannot compare with the indigenous intimate stabilities in Earth and family. In this sense the *room-amenity* of communal campsite and creek has far more support to humanity than theatres, online cafes and laundramats. And far more than simply *utilising outdoor space* on a purchased town-planned site in order to reduce fabrication; urban outdoor living. 'Outdoor living', 'alfresco dining' - Cheekyfella reels again with laughter - but then perplexes when he registers that this is how many like Global *Pale* exist. He notes however a tantalising 'potential' for a perfect blend, a *nomadic-urban* architecture-lifestyle.

Yes we may find our temple in a bush nook or our body, the bed in a commercial lodge, the dining table at the Greasy Spoon cafe. Many facilities, such as these, for which we require a house, can be found away from our domicile elsewhere in country or town, apparently minimising but in fact merely dispersing the dwelling facilities. But we will never find in this dispersion the privacy, appropriate solitude, simple stability, intimate familiarity and purity of the individual; the requirements of at least the modern Austrophile's minimal longer term domestics. The bed-slot in the city lacks. A gas heater is only a partial substitute for a stone hearth and log fire. The latter being closer to a minimum for a healthy heart, yet further from sustainable today, in light of current city eco-status.

Minimum is a practical thing, **an abstinence thing,** *an affordability thing, a fundamental necessities thing, a cultural and social thing, a thing of the mind and a very personal thing.* It is time away from home as much as time at home. Economy of housing activity – not merely house construction. Usually it's most beautiful to the dweller whose economy it is - usually giving some freedom from cleaning, maintenance, building and guilt. There should always be an option for a person to have a plot of land somewhere practical, where an encampment is allowed to be begun and slowly to grow into exactly what the dweller wants. An option for a Gallopilong to camp in town.

Minimum. It should be the maximum.

Oodles of money can confuse and change these values. And really the only stop on those capitalist sorts of minima is educated acknowledgement of ecology, town planning, hearty needs and environmental beauty - of *ecopicality*. Sustainability is a down-to-earth subset of *ecopicality*. The global *accumulation* has surpassed ecological minima. The bridge is cracking.

What is minimum for you? If you are part of a growing sprawl it is too much. When it comes to eco-minima it's hard to beat renovation as a limit to your *housing activity*.

A MAKER of FOOTPRINTS & RIPPLES

EXCUSE ME *PALEFACE* WHAT
YOU MEAN YOU SAY HOUSE ?

☼*An urban architect's perspective* follows:

Under the footprints of the world's housing are some exceedingly complex issues. I simplify these with custom-made language.

Nomadism and urbanism. We can surmise that behind both is a common ground. A *nub* of thoughts, a *crossroads* or an unaware reflex. A ground from which we either;

☐ **Settle** into place, building and farming or,

ʒ **Move** through places, with the mood, the hunt, the herd or the seasonal foods - which may lead to a place of abundance, with an option for non-urban indigenous settlement.

Thus, we venture into the mind ethers which underpin our basic domestic options; the vapours of the motivations underpinning both dusty campfire and plush penthouse. Whichever, from this common ground, we variously diverged, still taking our ancient circadian steps, making our *domestic-arrangements*, *doing our housing*. Dancing the *Housefandango*, *Campfandango* and *Localefandango*.

There's a flip side to this common ground, this *nub*. Another common ground, real but rarely visited. A ground of convergent mutual acknowledgement among the nomadic and the urban. A ground fertilised with the unification of the advantages of both lifestyles. A ground to minimise the adversities of both. On this fertile flip-side common ground, nomadic lifestyle breeds with urbanic lifestyle to produce a mutual overarching domestic ethos. Call it, *nomurbism* – an ethos producing a humane but strictly protocoled urbia alongside the *room* for the nomadic roam. *Nomurbic* understanding assists the *Campfandango* and indigenous settlement in their daunted interface with rampant cities. *Nomurbics* is also a facilitator for a full range of urban/country nomadisms.

A spectrum of *nomurbic* options lives between the two extremes.

Call this perfect urbia, *Ecopia*. '*Nomurbia*' might do as well for a name but a link with 'Utopia' is descriptive.

These 'cities', with their remote outposts, urbs, surveys and houses are mutually protocoled to sit happily organically and spiritually within the nomadic realms. And the nomadic realms within them. With this, *ecopicality* is uncovered; an urgent modern way of dancing the *Housefandango* and the first-principles mindset that includes environmental sustainability also for its ethic, beauty and lifestyle.

Campfandango is in not my focus here.

These, probably heretobeforeanywhere unmentioned by any name, rhythmic sciences of *ecopics* and *nomurbics* are not teased out in this discussion. The ogres of current pragmatics devour the flowering romance. These sciences can be observed faintly notional and intuitive in the creative activities of many people today and yesterday, non-descripts included. Perhaps some are Carlos Santana, Paolo Soleri, Arthur C. Clark, David Suzuki and John Smith. The covered wagons loaded with settler people and their embryonic residential *accumulations*, rattling through Sitting Bull's nomadic indigenous heaven, dangerously threatened his livelihood, as their noise and numbers scuttled away the buffalo. The railway brought it on heavier and the opportunity for mutual *nomurbic* togetherness, incorporating *ecopian* townships, in lieu of a fight for survival, was gone – a faint hope that it might come right one day. Give me a house; rather give me no more than a tipi-village with horses – and perhaps a gentle trading neighbour in an *ecopian* town.

Modern times and urban ways have grown a *megamonster*. It sounds like kid stuff, but look behind the name tag. It is the commonly acknowledged *untamed* unecologic giant multinational current pragmatic of industrial society which harms more than just the nomads. The deeply urban individuals are plagued with unfortunate mindsets, from the *dodo* that creeps into their unwitting thoughts. Undoubtedly, without a blast from the sun, the rampant city end of potentially *ecopian* lifestyle would swing around and swallow the nomad whole – as it does currently, still.

The *dodo* is urban deviance caused by ignorance, apathy, greed and desperation. The *dodo* feeds its decisions to the *megamonster*. In turn, the monster spawns the orthogonal *houselocusts* – the *machinemarked grid* of *boxed domestic-contraptions*. The *houselocusts*, with their *theodolite*-surveyed industry, consume the wonderful world of the nomad, the land, the country; and the resources too - the *playdough of the Earth*. The *dodo* is responsible for *pale* people, *boulevard* excess and deceptive opulence.

Ecopical attitudes and actions, having no scope for deviance beyond practical compromise, will convert the *playdough* into *tame* balanced urban solutions. Thus, providing variously an abundance of health-giving natural physicality; *nature's earthy nurtures*. And with it domestic *room* as a basis for settlement that is sensitive to environmental beauty, creature habitats, ecology and nomadic realm. *Ecopicality* will also renovate, *debox*, *degrid* and defang the *houselocusts*. But comfort zones for most must change. Comfort zones will change.

☼ A tracker's perspective:

The dweller is the trackee. Its bed may be housed comfortably under a tree. Or in a *room* of colourful vinyl-coated walls. It defies rain with roofing and mosquitoes with net or smoke, even though we love to see the stars from bed. It's an historic prehistoric compromise - house components may obscure natural wonders. We counter this compromise with design, décor and affable materials. We make the place nice and a romance grows – imbued with palaeolithic glow.

Various *ripples* roll out into our community and our world. Yours is yours, not just anybody's. The world is eventually everybody's - a piece of a broken door washes ashore at Tierra del Fuego concurrent with an ultra-violet inclemency through holes in the ozone shield. Ultra-violet footprints, sprawl and depleted natural amenity lie broken and discarded on the track. The *houselocust* shoots itself in the foot. The additional inclemency it brings upon even the nomad creates more purpose for the house, more mutation for the *houselocust*. A deviance from sane simple values – trading scenic delight and fresh air for crisp synthetic slums, effluent and smog. But with tv and the *soma*s of entertainment and irrelevant luxury.

It can be done well. Changing trees to rafters. Wide open space to interiors. Lifestyle. House has worldly impact. As it adds, converts and complements; it depletes, marks, modifies, opens. Woodgrain and quarry-face are revealed to the light of day. The foundation trench consorts with its pile of dirt and the manner of its extraction. *Housemarks* - the resultants of the construction and existence of house. A tree will not sprout through the porcelain bath. A worm cannot poke his head through your road. Eye can't see through your brickwork. Time spent, *playdough of the Earth* used, energy burned - to produce a house. Especially for you - or for a welfare number.

The egg is fried; the mind is civilised, tantalised, homogenised, tempted and romanced by the cultural concept and existence of house. Sometimes Globalised, never Gallopilongised. An amazing range of impact when multiplied by the number of houses and factored with the number of people who ever will have lived, multiplied again by our tendencies to crowd together and go for more. The innocent little house. Oink - the deviant *houselocust* pigs out. Global *Pale*, plagued by a long nurtured *dodo*, is driving. Everybody on the bus is skipping the *Housefandango*. Some, nourished by the skip, are mobilizing, unwittingly towards *ecopicality*, like Bobby Dazzler. *Ecopical* architectures must multiply.

The *ripples* continuously go out, washing over people and earth. Holocaust and *fandango*. Lifestyle, identity, health, doings, feelings, appearances, society, ecology - are all house affected. Substantiated by utopian purpose, house, or at least *domestic-arrangement* is the burning torch of unique personal *beingrowing* in gregarious settlement, planetary participation. Holy holy. But, plagued by our foibles and inadequacies - houseless people, incubated people, dirty people, stuffy people, tasteless, unfortunate environmental impacts and hopeless interiors. Walk on Blackfella. Apes born in cages from apes born in cages - **mere *shadows* of apes**. *Pale shadows*. Years moving back and forth. Cage removed. His movements remained the same - despite the freedom to go further. A frozen mind without scope to liquefy, he was never to cross the threshold from his limitation, his familiar life. The steam engine and the internal combustion engine once developed each began immense unstoppable cultural transformation. Both bane and joy; the evolution of house has had far greater impact. Carbon monoxide and tyre dumps; *shadows* of people and sewerage. Cheekyfella, like the Namibian nomads, intuitively *ecological*, has compassion for Global.

Some people push on without houses. Some with gentle impact or indigenous houses. Will they all be overcome by the house-burst phenomenon? The *houselocust* holocaust. The room boom. Bang bang. They need the oil oil (again as I type).

Skipping the *Housefandango, doing our housing*, opening a window, manufacturing a doorknocker, felling a tree to make particleboard, a dollar in a charity cup, so many hours of one's job, a photograph of the landscape, an optic-fibre cable to an acrylic-rendered gable; they all relate to our housing quanta. They are all new things on the clean slate of a houseless world. A house is a responsibility.

Without house a whole lot of physical stuff could not happen. Smaller *accumulations*. Fewer children. Once one is in a house its potentials expand. Given a base to work from we see the hierarchy of personalised developments unfold. Like the horse to White Cloud's forebears the house gives freedoms, doings, enjoyments and snags that would not otherwise occur. We can create, party, worship, civilise like never before. Also we greed for more and more. And strive for more. Grow with more. The house when created inspires paintings for walls, architecture, lifestyle developments.

Night-time darkness is the shadow of the grass, rock, magma and water that sits under our floors between the candle and the sun. It blows away our day. With electric light the house is lit to the extent where night-time dweller activity becomes quite different to that which it is in the pre-industrial candle flicker and the simple soft dancing architectural dome of open fire-lit night. The lighted house, a new small world of manmade lights and other components. A world for which we are prepared to pay a high asking price or spend much time creating and developing. Daily rhythms are modified. Albert, simply, is happy in the circadian solar cycle dance; totally unaware of his cultured domestic reflex being exercised at his unseen *nomurbic crossroads*. His nomadic society could never have manufactured even a kerosene lamp, without first settling down. Such a lamp may be quaint in the face of the Dreamtime.

The light of the camp fire creates two concentric 'rooms' within the broader world. One, nearest the fire, has the amenity of the vibrancy of light, allowing good song and hand-working. The other, outward before the dark, is the nearby amenity of calming half-light, handy psychological amenity for conflict resolution, quiet romance and stars. Stars without cars. Without street lights. The introspective night-lit house world, with its internally reflecting, star blocking windows, has grown from our basic domestic facility. We enjoy nonchalantly the 'civilised' comfort of an on-ground milky-way as we gaze out at the city lights across the river.

Are houses a *trap*? Do they create a temptation to live in limited space, interior, couch potato, insular, battery hen, lounge lizard, mollycoddled, comfort zone, sensually deprived mental fixation. Or is this just a danger of which to be wary in a magnificent evolution of houses? **Your call.** Call your architect – from deep within.

Housing is not necessarily as it might have been. The *housemarks* may have been different. Utopian. Imagine; the psychologies of the existing houses as compared with those of a utopian house; and the efficiency in work life and ecology. A lot less effort and a lot more environmental beauty. *Ecopian* is the same, but with a lot less *nomurbic* and ecological stress.

Onward from the simple perspective and artefacts of the hunter-gatherers we find that; new gadgetry, discovery, use and weather constantly impact the house – plaster, the tradesman's tools and ultra-violet included. Also impacting are the metaphysical graffiti of the tastes and impulses of the dweller, the architect, society and lawmakers. The house is both stimulator and receptor. There are, no doubt, many here unrecognised life impact and life potential factors in the principle and reality of the house.

> Mere *ripples* to Mother Earth may be tsunamis to people. Mere *ripples* to us may drown our great grandchildren; or us.

> Mere *ripples* sending out colourful cultural lifestyle and company.

A ROMANCE for the MIND

EXCUSE ME PALEFACE WHAT YOU MEAN YOU SAY HOUSE?

We note that the ripples *going out from the house impact mentality* – as well as environment. House ultimately is built for this mentality purpose. Some of this impact is unintended even unconceivable in the original intention to house. And we must acknowledge the impact of demanding daily work on our mentality also - and that this mental impact most certainly affects the development of our house. The tired man's house will grow in significantly different ways to the leisured man's house, especially if the growth is multiplied by generations of community.

Many things can exist only inside a house. This includes plenty of abstract, *armpit* psyche and domestic smog. There are physical, emotional and intellectual satisfactions in a good house – and let's not be stuffy, they're elsewhere on walkabout too. Interiors however can be the vital birthplace of much character and psychology through comforts, stimulation, identity and also frustrations. Mind matters – growing personae, security, cosy facility, rest, home, abide, reside, inhabit, cook, seclusion, neighbour sociology, local government sociology, courtesy, hospitality. Housed or unhoused we have many domestic mind matters. Hospitality, as one, is well known to the unhoused cultures, but the house catalyses it differently for the settler. The egg, a chicken and then an egg, hospitality and house, nomad and settler, housed and unhoused – all happened at once. Laziness is easier in a loungeroom than under open sky. The things of the mind relating to house are immense in number and complexity. They ricochet about the world and our psyche. There goes one now from your ceiling to the chair leg, through the wardrobe, round the cornice and off the ancient tapestry. Chain reactions. Mathematical expansions. From basic settler-versus-nomad mind impacts, to subtle interior matters. The room is humming hard.

From the joy of indigenous building to the potentials and stress of borrowed money. It is said that country Blackfellas don't like to hear Whitefellas' business talk. Is it that they anxiously opt out of crossing the threshold inward to the business of rampant settlement? Contracts, deals, industry, banks, legalities and – "Oh blimey mate! Those *theodolites* just don't suit!!" These things are dimensions away from the indigenous way. And also somewhat from the Japanese Kodo way; drumming is central to this culture and the town 'boundary' is set where the drums can barely be heard.

Mind both is applied to and responds to housing. Design and household organisation, brainwork and creative excellence. Ordering the establishing abode. The mind is at work and using our time of day while it is requiring, constructing and using this *domestic-contraption*. It is at work while it is merely associating with each of the individual parts of the house and their sum. What else could the mind be doing? Any dolphin might know, but unwittingly, we guess. The dolphin might be hunting - but not gathering.

We take refuge in the quiet of the bed-room. We do things in all the rooms that we may have. Territoriality, social constructs, etiquette, solitude, domestic protocol. Lifestyle and magic. Sharing. Aesthetical activity. Imbued meaning. Most of these concepts and actions of the housed mind have some nomadic counterpart – an ancient tapestry may be woven in the lichen on a gnarled limb broken by the wind many moons ago and reflected in the ceremony of a fork roof prop.

For the deepest sustenance that settlers find in their house, are there parallels in nomadism? Yes and no. Nobody seems to have looked at this very closely. Society, is an instance. Both Nomad and Settler have society. The societies are different probably because of the different lifestyles and because of our construction of interior. But maybe the societal differences come first – but after that *nub* of thought. Or was it the egg first for one and the chicken first for the frying pan. In parallel; both societies know seclusion and their own style of bedpost and washbasin. *And, of the deepest sustenance of nomadism - are there parallels in urbanism?* Consistency, familiarity; a new house frequently - imagine. Talk about walkabout with Talkabout; it will take us part way there.

A couple of gender opposites marry - Bobby and Little White Cloud. They romance ever on over the *beingrowing* of their housing - the copulation and coordination of two decors and habits, two genders and personalities. This, gently said, is the only fully synchronised marriage and best attitude for family house.

Some dream on about sea views, central heating, lotteries and hot and cold servants. More. More always comes, as patina, hallow and developing reality. The unfinished garden is the only state of garden. Always there's need and *room* for change and enrichment. Note the chunk of your life's aspiration and activity that even just the concept of 'more' commands. More is not banned from minimum.

There is so much in that pile of dirt from the founding trench. Its *ripples* variously pulse through our daily quizzical metaphysical. The house is an object in all four, our personality, gregarious nature, history and security. Less than this, it is an object in place, environment and world. Less to humanity, that is, for as humanity alone we do not really know if the Earth values the impact of house on our psychologies as less than its impact on herself.

In many ways the house that Bobby and White Cloud Dazzler have now, and those they have known, stimulate their romance of house *beingrowing.* Certainly psychologically, the house provides a flood of human and personal reaction. There is a huge wealth of undiscovered scientific data. Consider the relative house reactions of Queen Elizabeth and Shaka the Zulu. How much of their differing personae result from their domestic worlds and those of their forebears? Indeed how much of their commonality is simply psycho-reaction to bed, roof and walls - our own reaction to and affinity with our constructions? Interesting quanta indeed. And the one and two rooms of medieval London, crowded with family, servants, visitors, customers and large multi-person beds which are packed away for daytime activity; how do they compare with Zulu tribal life?

In the centre of the Dazzlers' holiday tipi is a circular electric heater in lieu of an open fire. Bobby doesn't care much about this psycho-house stuff. "If the larger order had not left us with two legs we'd be different too. There's no going back. Our response to our physicality is unalterable, so ... . Hang on! We do need to know these psycho-reactions to houses in order to reopen closed vistas; medicine for rampant domestic incubation, for pallid curtain-bound detached *shadows* and lounge lizards. To minimise. For the *Pale* children. And our own."

Akin to this is culture - the whole gamut of creative, accidental and cultural inferences, impacts and heritage. One can read a character by his face, clothes and body language. Read Cheeky's facial etchings, then Global's slick intent. One can read a lot from the expressions of a house - meanings, aesthetics, art, spirituality, the epoch of its origin, purpose and even some of the subconscious and disposition of the creators.

Yet more. Order. Without housing we would receive far less of the sustaining satisfaction and motivation that we get from the application of our own order to our world. Very significant to our psyche – *or is it?* Romancing the mind. We think so anyway. The fact and the exercising of household order; by nature there is order in our abiding and our hunting and gathering. Order is a clarity; the rubble and twigs moved away, for clear lubricated *room* for physical and mental activities.

Albert Gallopilong would react to the geometry of the Anglophile with intrigue, wonder ... and perhaps a growing inkling of mental resonance. *Box* house-forms, the interior, the consistent and light colours, the junction of two smooth walls meeting at a flat ceiling, rectangles, many straight and parallel lines - new and different in nature. Perhaps dolphins dance to the ether of this geometric wonder - antimatter, intangibles, sharpish geometric order. Interiors and exteriors, doors, inside, outside ... which 'side' of the wall ... of the fence. New concepts. Potent new colours. Nature *synthesized* by people. All in contrast to the character of land, sky and ocean.

House, like nomadic domestics, is heart, soul, earthly links, health, vigour, a temple. It depends on the culture, habit and bent of the dwellers. Permanent departure from their ancestral home has been known to cause death among some indigenous people - a thing of the spirit and mind.

Beingrowing. A house is not an end in itself. It facilitates. It is the physical support for home. "... *the* physical support for home!" from his dusty hearth at *home* Cheekyfella grins at my Freudian cultural slip. He says, "Whitefella wrapped in business and books. Blackfella homes are a little different – *and without a house as physical support.*"

Your *domestic-contraption* may be as crass as an obligatory stuffy flat near your place of work. Build on its beauty and put the rest away to dusty corners. "It's no worse th'n bein' obliged to sleep on gravel in an unfamiliar place in the desert!" comes the matter-of-fact words of another Harmoninni friend. A new room is strange; what's in the cupboards, how does the wood feel? The snug of a blanket, a cleave to a 'warm-and-soft', a contrast to a 'hard-and-cold'. The snug of a blanket, the inseparable interface of dweller and amenity, an essence of house. Inseparable by conditioning in mind and body. Inseparable by your cultured daily domestic demand; always there, even in the crass flat, we hope.

Reader; drop the book. Sit gazing at the floor. Ponder the myriad of mental complexity and simplicity associated with the physical reality of your abode. Imagine the same area with Roman mosaic. Without a floor ... blades of grass ... a fresh elephant pat.

A CIVILISER
of COMMUNITY

EXCUSE ME PALEFACE WHAT
YOU MEAN YOU SAY HOUSE?

*O*ur *billion houses are* romantically *rippling* their gradually civilizing community mind. The civilisation in turn cultures and evolves the houses. It is not a civilisation of nomads, nor low-technology indigenous settlers.

A rookery works well for penguins. People in a similar circumstance require *room*, space around them, social screening, commodious surrounds, protocols and maybe not fences, walls and addresses. The solutions to these requirements facilitate dwelling – dwelling, our being what we will and doing what we will, where we will. The interests of the individual are served whilst courteous consideration is given to the neighbours. People being people, a complex proprietary develops – call it *armpit* protocol.

It seems that people abide in place to know each other. To join for the benefit of numbers. 'Wandering' tribes abide with each other in simple knowing purposeful moving and in their encampments. People meeting Earth, and each other, has induced settlement and thus housing. Taking care of the fields first, then the house, which for Albert is a simple arrangement. Gregariousness. Identity meeting identity. Talent complementing talent. Strength in numbers – *this is more significant in housing than is interior.* Whilst inside in solitude we are not wholly alone, as we came together in nature also for vital security and built a dwelling place for a tribe. Our character, our persona, grows accordingly as we enhance our own domicile in this place. Character enhances gregariousness and the domicile becomes equipped with some *fabricated social interface*, that in turn enhances and unites both private and city living. Like Grunter, we can leave behind hallowed halls and address-focussed facades to accrue on our heritage. The romance of housing history sobers though as the settler notes that Albert Gallopilong, as a nomad, has some equal social mores and character formers. He has some additional social mores too, which nominally may balance those that others derive from firm expanded housing. Even so, a huge world apart, now that settlers' *domestic-arrangements* have become houses, the vast majority would not swap even deadly unecologically housed lifestyle simply for fine weather and a spear. *And more profoundly; for life together without walls and what they bring.* House is enjoyable and so is hunting. And so is inclemency - in its place, or when managed.

We may be held to a locale by the sustenance of agriculture, or some other rationale. To live in close proximity of each other we must make *dwelling-arrangements*, social distance and access routes. If it happened that Grunter Palaeolithic had resolved to go with the penguins and not worry about shelter, he may well have built for social reasons anyway. As noted, social distance, like screening, is a form of shelter. It is certainly a significant prompt to build. One simply cannot get on as a person in a rookery. The Building Inspector unwittingly reads the eons of *Houseballet* and orchestrated togetherness in the old walls. Even India's crowded villages show this. First up then; a couple of horizontal branches between tree trunks. Throw the spare quilt over them. A screen. But Gina could still hear the neighbours' televisory device at night, so Grunter extended his arrangement. Gina was satisfied – but, as usual, only temporarily as refinements and new options arose. In the world of creatures, people's houses are unique. Unlike animals, people have very refined personal faces to shelter and meet. *Our faces too are protected by our screenings and courtesy to allow ongoing personal abode.* No big oaf *armpitted* neighbour breathing garlic in your face.

Yards and fences may occur simultaneously in association with houses. Or firstly. These are also part of our *dwelling-arrangements* due to; need for open space, the nature of human defecation, domestic animals, carts, vegetables, trees, landform & social choice.

In Eden with its *Z* factor - things were undoubtedly quite different. Here, if population had occurred there possibly would have been no housing prompt from the adversities of social proximity nor for security – but perhaps from the making of meeting places, purely to facilitate the romantic plusses of social proximity. Seclusion in which to compose, contemplate and develop may have been a cause for some both distance and *nacre* fabrication. The Fall, however, prevented all social expansion in Eden. Whatever mistake caused it, it *rippled* serious consequences. Instead, reasonably honourable social expansion occurred outside ('elsewhere') barbed with the prompts of nakedness, murderous intents, bestial survivals and natural adversities – in part a similar housing road to Grunter but maybe the sun was quashed behind a firmament of water. Adam's crew, while they were not devolving, were off down the degeneration helter-skelter. A shelter-skelter gradually incrementally eased by medicine, luxury and cosmopolitan city *soma*; yet challenged somewhat by the indigenous options.

Successful nomadism makes settled civilisation a questionable activity. Is there too the halfway option? Nomad marries settler. People in motion through land and ocean, using people-made dwelling stations - or part-time settlers using the buildings of full time settled colleagues. Can we prophesy the nomadic urbia - *nomurbic* arcology. 'Arcology' is a term from Paola Soleri describing wholistic city design, integrated architecture and ecology. Yes I foresee a little balanced electronic city, Ecopiala. That's the tantalising blend Cheeky was seeing. And visionary Arthur C Clark saw isolated *ecopian* hamlets, by another name, linked variously by satellite, or indeed by the expanding *hypertech hypernet grid*, with a capital **G** - and a capital **R** and **I** and **D**.

In the helter skelter world, the progeny and houses of Adam and Grunter went on to develop the customary courtesies paid by millions in respect for the meanings of the front gate and the front door. The culture of hosting. The private party. **The *Housefandango* was all go.**

Yes, if you like, the house cradles civilisations, community and personae. A bit of romance. Yes. the dinner plate is pretty significant too; I say it needs a floor and a table, to be superb. *They are a cradle too.* The temple does not come first. Nor does the corner store. The central trading post though is a fair challenge for first place, or cradle, regardless as to whether or not there is archaeological evidence. Maybe trading post cradles the house.

Because of developing urban utility and production, the options for and the priorities of housing change. Meal catering. Call the laundromat. Install a spa. Along with urban utility the processes of social order enable one to gain a house whilst doing other work. As such the house is significant as merchandise and as a credit lure. This, with human natures the way they are, means trouble - the bus seat jolts over a small hole in the road. Ay! Bobby.

And still Cheekyfella and his noble Uncle Albert, on walkabout, do not bother even with shoes or hats. Minimum, but not absolute minimum, environmental impact. Scant and social. Uncrowded, happy, healthy and beautiful. Seemingly simple. Easily misunderstood for their more controversial learned ways.

And easily bulldozed.

They *'are owned by'* the land.

The *Pales* 'own' the land.

"WHY IS EARTH SUCH THAT WE MIGHT NEED A HOUSE ... MUMMY!?

Please **bear with me** Building Inspector, and the others of

more matter-of-fact mind in our multi-minded public. I like to involve our mammal cousins, the dolphins. I think it brings true grit to our *shadow*. Fly by these pages, if you please, to more technically furnished utility – your grit may already be okay.

We've seen what a house is - a singular stimulating comfortable collection of facility and amenity, internal and external, in locale. We see what a house causes - *ripples*. But looking deeper at the reasons. Why *houze!?* – when we might do without it. Why is Earth such that we might need this *domestic contraption!?* This provokes wondering about why we are what we are, where we were when so much of our inherited life was programmed. And how and what it has to do with tomorrow. We 'know'. But what we know is tempered by what people say. Cultural lore, religions, science. Moths and butterflies.

Our first limitation, in our designing in our life, is that we are what we are - *happening organisms* and beingrowing social individuals of earthly and spiritual roles. Maybe trying a stairway to a heaven. Our bodies. Organisms, housed initially in the bodies of others - but maybe we are a two hearted organism together with our mother until we first breathe. The organisms grow under the shelters and facilities of parents, fosters, community, providence and self-help. Unlike the dolphin organisms, we have hands and lie down to sleep, we are vertical and sit down to eat, we shelter from sun, wind and rain. Sometimes we 'go out' to gather en mass like penguins. The marriage of the matter-of-fact economic pragmatics of quadrangles with the *quicksilvered* matter-of-

The nomads know that it is not all about
'ROOM SWEET ROOM'.

fact romance of beautiful design may be like the compromise disciplines of husband and wife. Something's gotta give, so something happens. It seems kinda suitable to the *happening organism.*

"Why does God make us build houses Mummy?" Bobby's ears prick as he rolls the oil warming in the pan for Saturday's breakfast. The nurturing father's attention is drawn to his black and white checked credit-laden kitchen floor. The room was humming harder. The small child, drawn deeper into her shared daily domestic realm, had forgotten the question, possibly for life. But struck, Bobby Dazzler had snapped out of his own familiar daily ... *as the ceiling flew away* – flat, orthogonal and roller painted white. "... That's a relief," chuckles Cheeky, "Yer know, Uncle Albert wouldn't have a clue what a Saturday is! ... a moon cycle yes, but a month or a week-day, no." Dazzler, dazzled, was outside, having not left the flecked laminate bench. He had thought he already knew, but today his thought was new. His homely interior was already full of the nearby eucalypt fragrance and fragment spectrums of sunlight, by design, for their own and their daughter's delight. Some incidental beetles, also contributing delight, had dragged in their waft of *nature's earthy nurtures.* It spreads filling the house, as the ceiling settles, slightly skew, on newly lichen laden stone walls and long endemic grass with native orchids and caterpillars in the white squares of the checked floor. He wasn't sure if it was distant space nebulae he saw in the black. *"What is interior?"* he wonders. "A reaction to romance and adversities," ponders White Cloud. "White Cloud in a dank cave would give me boundless more *delightful home amenity* than 'the most beautiful house in the world' without her," Dazzler breathes, seeing his wealth as immense. He sees, joined with her mind, her languid organic forms united clearly poetic with the soft flexible comfort of an orthogonally woven square of red and black Maori patterned threads set at seat height above the worn oiled board floor. The profundity of the organic distraction left no concept of the square blanket. The mattress made a captivating frame.

Like she, he responded more to the romance than the routine, chill, dim adversity that put her there.

UNDER the skewed ROOF of UNKNOWING

WHY IS EARTH SUCH THAT WE MIGHT NEED ONE!?

*A*lternatives. One wonders why we hunger, tire, shelter, shy, reclude. Why most settle but some 'wander' – perhaps settlers have more children, ay. Why do you? Is evolution compromised? Is divine design mysterious?

We usually live oblivious to the essential, call it primeval, birthing of house! We do the same with the air between us. And with the base realities of our financial systems.

One may wonder under the skewed roof of unknowing. All the way. Why is Earth such that we might need one!? Life without even physical environment. Cosmic environment only. In this wondering is an inner something. No eyes to see. Clear darkness in the centre of a metaphysical cyclone. Total sensory deprivation. Can you imagine also; life without the ability to be selective as to place and movement? Like a tree. Why not just be awake all the time? No bed-room. Why not have flippers – no muddy boots to be stored in a porch? The world might have been one great clement indoors. To house all people. A sky high ceiling of mist, or water, to save wither from the sun. A vast indoors, pre-existent along with our dolphinian – I meant to say human - organism. If houses grew of nature like trees, it might not be a good thing. We might go looking for a tree with a community hall or a parliament house. And then try relocating it in the family forest. *Beingrowing.* Progressing a style of civilisation. Pre-existent houses mean pre-existent cities. A city already existent. What then, a stargate, or even pre-existent children? Stargate existent. Where to then, music, dolphin song? There'd be no genderhood. Freedom from, even departure from, physical environment. We ourselves might be an essence of the purpose of house, where that freedom is neither balanced nor anchored by environmental interaction. Where would we go ... woosh, silvering away dolphin into an astral sea – of joy, naturally. And ....; well couch potatoe having loosened our preconceptions, let's not imagine further how else we or the world might have been.

An educated and intuitive world can only wonder about this domestic nature. Preconditioned lay folk just 'know' or just 'do'. We flew in the face of social, climatic and environmental adversity in order to fulfil our hands, to farm, to make places of our own, to prevail, to confer our presence in place with our built graffiti, to give way to our simple reflexes and other reasons. As our domestic establishment grew, grows, we feel we owed, owe, it to ourselves to stay with the effort and wealth we had, have, put into it. We stick with it. The house is a habit. A ball and chain. Talkabout is nodding furiously. Henry Ford is not fazed - the ball and chain is simply a *limitation*, a *compromise*. It gives new freedoms and potentials at the cost of work and environmental impact, whilst limiting our potential to wander and enjoy the sun a bit. The gain easily appears appealing enough to override the cost. So people's evolution developed the house not only as protection but primarily as the means to gain these potentials and freedoms. Eggs first. Chickens first. All at once on the cooker.

A scenario begins. A three dimensional reality. Physical or ethereal. We need the body-world-house scenario to achieve what it is that we know we like. That which we like may be preconditioned by that which we are; humans and people with three dimensions. Our *dwelling-contraption* conforms to our relationship to our family and vice versa. Mind the step that steps behind the mind, but go in there - taking care not to trip out of life's acids. Spirit is more prime than primeval slime. Behind body and house, personality, ego. You will find your love for simple beautiful nature and your humble dwelling place as a part of it. You will find the tainting arrogance and shallow tastes of personkind layered over the ancient harmonies of a humble erection. Simple house. Personkind's ego culture is pertinent only to itself, and we do have fun with it.

We seem to thrive on pressures from gravity, air and wind; to savour what we have when we counter them. Calm interior, protected by the person-built structure buffeted by a dusty gale. A scenario different from a calm interior on a calm day. Erection of a building deepens our engagement with gravity - as does a successfully targeted spear.

A style of thought; "Why can't we fly?" "Because we don't need to," or "We need the limitation." We have two eyes because we need two. Why can't we live without a house? Because, though ultimately we can, we don't need to; or, *dwelling-contraption* is a joie de vive; anything you can do without a house you can do with one, given an attitude. Significantly, Albert Gallopilong unconsciously disagrees, though he may understand a strictly ethical settler - just let us walk this path through.

We need the whole world including *dwelling-arrangement*. We need house in response to the world as we fulfil our lives. We need the "firmness, commodity and delight" - the essences of building, as coined by a highly acclaimed architect. In particular, *domestic commodity*. If the world did not demand housing surely it must mean that satisfactory housing already existed in the world. Even in congenial weather we would still *houze*. Grapple with the butterflies and moths of knowledge. We still don't know; but yes we do. We increase our understanding. Bobby could see the Great White Spirit in Little White Cloud smiling, helping her arm around Albert Gallopilong, on the roof of the library to the culturally famous Bauhaus school of architecture.

We may mistakenly assume that the soul things that happen to us in our houses are all house-related or supported by our house. These soul things may happen regardless. The quiet meditative comfort at a flush powered porcelain bowl can be achieved just as well and even better in the shrubbery – if you time it right.

In a world such as where God provides all needed houses, if one wants environmental interaction, one is free to build one's individual house - or one for another. Why does Global *Pale* not exchange his fibreglass prefabricated, two bed-room, style-classified, plastic decorated house, squarely facing a baked-enamelled metal picket fence and sharp kerbed street for a loin-cloth and a gourd? Wonder!! Why, to him under the roof of plastic rain, it is obvious. He knows why! "Oh, come on now," comes a cheeky jibe from a lively shadow. Mr and Mrs *Pale* having given their faces to their own house interior grow ever *paler* for not having given their faces to the sky's molten looking glass. Talkabout sings about this looking glass; but has he gone behind it and so is growing dark? Bobby found it when his ceiling flew away. His wife unbeknown already grooms by it; her own house, an aspect of Bobby's, simple as a buffalo-hair shawl and sun-glasses – devoid of Maggie *Pale's* corset and foam shoulder pads.

Houses leave us with good and bad. Leaky roof, not enough *room*, no house, dirty windows, ball and chain, rates and taxes, failing ecology. Home sweet and sour. Romance and adversity. Rational limitations. That's life, even without houses. The sweet and sour quanta, and items, will vary from house lifestyle to unhoused lifestyle. But so long as it keeps happening, romance and adversity will meld - people binding together in inclemency. But there's more. Simple organic activities latch onto it – eating, kicking around for a spell. With further regard to the Dazzlers' daughter's question, we must acknowledge the prompts to *houze* from the romantic side of people's nature as well as from the adversities. A reaction of emotion with practicality builds houses. Knowing the first *emotional* ingredient of this chemistry would be of some value in understanding. The many belief systems and motivations cloud this knowledge. Although White Cloud may know, she cannot easily communicate it. Formal study may answer it one day.

Something about houses moves the heart and soul. Houses that is, not the humanity that dwells therein, nor the life they lead. Home is the glow, attached to the dwellers, which soaks into the camp and house, or is reflected off it. The hallowed molecular husk that is left when the homemakers depart for other lands is the house. The moving of heart and soul is from that potential of intimacy with good life and the power to foster good life. The moving of heart and soul is also from the part the house plays in that good life, through the exercise of our creativity and building skills. It can be found in a camp in a grotto too. It is a convenient and significant part of our togetherness with the natural and the communal worlds. Those psychologies are present. And they all fit into the conscious and subconscious motivation to dwell in place and to make it - the development and evolution of houses. Houses became necessary facility. Once initiated there was no stopping them; not even utopian ethics. Not even the naive automation that grew them. Not even the incremental *shadow* making - the apes in the cage were hooked on familiarity and tradition. Life must be a very big thing; there is so much meaning to be gleaned as we bus through suburbs acknowledging the values of one unique house after another - as the *settlers' television* wings us from one land to another. Never-the-less the *bush television,* the campfire, runs an appealing alternative documentary ... and the sound of the weather is the show's theme music.

One day when there's time Low Carl will elaborate the science of the architecture of the campfire – warm counterpoint to star, the search for site and material, the building and the spark, maker of a place, deflector of wild, cooker, comforter, cosy lighted dome, light of address, *cosmic symbol,* trodden ground, shared *domestic-contraption* of wondrous amenity owned and monitored by the makers and the cosmos. Under a megalopolitan bridge or by a billabong.

We know and read the romance and adversity that puts the suburban houses there. Beyond simple inclemency, the adversity may rest in the dweller's conformity to social mores and existing socio-economic locations and fabrications. Sometimes of course these present no adversity - we find a another way if we would rather not *houze* in a particular location or manner.

Ideally, having resolved the settlement, inclemency and modern ecological issues, our thoughts are largely with romance as we seek a house. Dream house. Get real.

Some of the adversity is the spike of the world but a problem lies in our own doings. Albert Gallopilong is 'unhoused'. He is unfettered, at the very least, barely fettered, by *domestic-arrangement* – not a lot of goods and chattels arranged about the camp. But who knows the full pan-out? Is nomadic food-gathering a toil equivalent to making *domestic-contraption.* **Domestic**-*contraption* - **that heavy fabrication that evolves the basic *domestic*-*arrangement* into a house.** Does Albert spend all day in his pantry hunting for the family, whilst others spend all day paying the mortgage? Is there a difference?

Domestic-arrangement need not be heavily cloaked in *domestic-contraption.*

There are puzzles about why we *houze*. There are many possible reasons. Some things we need to know. Some we do not. Mystery is a big plus. It supports our dream and sharpens our eyesight. "Mystery. Can you imagine a romance without one?" answers White Cloud, in the friendly fickle of sun and shade under her seductive silky-soft lighted brunette cloud of unknowing – the universe reclining therein. Stay away from my window. Stay away from my back door too. Partly the nomad's *shadow*. Facets of house, facets of you. Disconnect the telephone - oh. A perfect house, romancing true. Tonight's the night ... we'll sleep at the starlit skylight – but ... jolt! ... the seagull has dropped some baggage. Ah! who is the master of romance? Really it isn't you.

PEOPLE SAY
WHY IS EARTH SUCH THAT
WE MIGHT NEED ONE!?

"*It varies* with peoples and beliefs. It's no different if you're from Arizona," advises White Cloud. Why is it so? Who can say? Science, religion, philosophy, me, cultural lore, intuition. Plain as the nose on your face. The main miracle - cosmic bang, brilliant creator. Here we are. Homo sapiens of many different sorts. Many bound to make our own place. A will to wall. In many ways, we know why – in that we are happening as organisms and people.

Scientific understanding is very shallow; why didn't housers evolve cow-hide or slick molecule-shedding dolphin skin - rather than to eventually go with such delicate cladding as to require a hud. Architectural psychology and sociology do go at least a way to illustrate why, as homo sapiens, we make our houses. It's not all about shelter. These partial understandings must rest flexibly in intuition. And this applies to the hierarchy of needs that we address as we make our domestic facility; calm the stomach first, then let energy build, then chat up the spouse and on it goes. Once the prioritised organic preliminaries are achieved the hierarchy branches into non-linear options. Broadly the options are nomadic and urban. Architectural moods vary among; climates, nomadic preferences and those staunch monks worrying more about the other than the self. Even so, regardless of our organic inclinations, our predilection for social activity begins an architecture of at least *layout* and wind shelter.

Oh for a humpy. (Your own cosy chapter is only ten pages ahead.) Some say that the urge to make or acknowledge an *inner sanctum* in the house is related to our being conscious in the womb. We do dream in the womb, others say. We had some mind in there. We may not however know that we are in there, or that we are safe and secure. Someone is suspicious that until we breathe we are in that unphysical step behind the mind place. When born we notice the change. We eventually realise. We are now 'outside'. Do we, you, have deep memory of that state of inner sanctum; the little house with which we were one. The house from which we were separated by the umbilical cut as much as by the exit process. Tossed out of Eden maybe. Outside the womb. Yet still inside Dad's and Mum's dominion. This inner sanctum security and personal recluse may be what we seek as we curl up cleaving to a blanket in our bed-room. Some say it is so. This room may well have been conceived of our inherited memories. A little mud room in a jungle clearing. Some primitive Africans emerged from their huts through a cute opening which is positively mother-like. I think a few still do so today. As they go in, it may be positively wife-like, a symbol for the lady with which to identify and the man with which to relate.

Adam and Eve in *Z* mode had no umbilical cut maybe. So not a navel between them (but men do have nipples). And no womb memory. And I bet, no mud hut; and therefore probably would never have built houses in *Z*. They might have built something else; a temple, no, God was there at hand. Maybe a railway station and a hair salon. In this scenario we drastically de-elevated helter-skelter at this Fall.

Possibly we changed mode altogether. Cain was born into sin outside Eden. No direct contact with God, unlike his parents, Cain did experience umbilical life. His mother was his immediate sooth, not God. Did this genetic *inner sanctum* security begin here in Eve's womb? And does our sense of sublime destiny begin with the handmade Adam and Steve? Sorry, it's told as Eve. Always we are left to wonder, under our synthetic rotunda. Is the inner sanctum principle incidental in the origin of housing. I think so. However, like our cultural roots, genetic memory is reflected in our designs.

I see little about our subject in the Bible. Or the Koran. I feel a brightly coloured boldly upholstered lounge chair comfort in speculation that the various religious understandings lead to the conclusion that housing, palace, rotunda or humpy, like shoes, is not a significant matter in the greater scheme of things. "An inevitable poulticing programmed by God to heal us back to an Eden in New Jerusalem," says a voice. "A soul sorting process," says another. "A mundane matter," says another. A Christian or Islamic ethos may be that your house, like your dress, should reflect your integrity - maybe humble rudimentary exterior with an inner nacre glow of spiritual wealth. The Tao would have no scope for decorative trappings - just the fundamental without arrogant or frivolous addition. The Buddhists may be similar there. The ancient Feng Shui, known as Chinese geomancy, is perhaps some seriously valuable sensitivity and common-sense glorified with astrology, animism, good and bad spirits, mystique and silly superstition. Feng Shui, means 'wind and water'. It is said that it can improve health, wealth and good fortune. As with most esoteric activity, practitioners may vary in their application of some of the traditional fundamentals. Originally it aimed to align people correctly to the seasonal and spiritual elements. People of any ethic may adapt their housing activity to support their own religious beliefs. The Harmoninnis' blackfella Dreamtime activity supports their domestic beliefs. Call it religion, perhaps.

I am told, and I have many tellers near, that their Creator provided in Eden absolutely all requirements for Adam and Eve. This probably meant at least somewhere dry for them to pass the first nightly mists. Was there wind? Adam and Eve tended the garden, named the animals and talked to God there. Ants were part of the garden but they were ruled and so not a nuisance. Faecal hygiene was not an issue either – proper food for horses and people. There may have been no cause for the concept of a home base. Perhaps they cooked. Pots and a kitchen? Fruit and nuts would be enough. There is the Z factor. Yes! it was a physical world - space, gravity probably and air - God breathed breath into Adam. They slept we guess. There was night. I am also told, and Sitting Bull agreed, that animals do not have soul, the individual people sort of soul - some of them have houses of sorts. People have a soul. Does soul relate to house. Albert Gallopilong has a soul. And perhaps it is the lack of isolation, which results from built containment, that has allowed the survival-cum-development of his close tribal bonds. **Bonds unknown in the ritz boulevards.**

It is conceivable that a sheltered place, some community *room*, for ancient people to socialise or talk turkey could become a defacto group house; sparking a sense of residential interior. People eventually built individual domiciles around it. It therefore became solely a community hall again, but of a different spirit. As such the community hall may be significant in the development of house. If there had not been a Fall there may well have been in Eden just one big electric-like vital communal facility. No privacy, inclemency nor security issues for which to build. Harmonious personalities blending tribally in the fabric of human environmental participation.

As this author, I am lost to much of the Islamic lore. Considering the studious and wholistic interpretations by religion founders of the common and limited ancient documents, can it be so different in this regard? After the Eden Fall conditions changed. Maybe even the laws of physics changed. There are adversities, people's doings altered and their constructions impacted. Clothes some were made by God during the transition. Probably He did not create the house. Nor did He design us so as to *houze* by nature. But wait, possibly He did, in this round-about way. It certainly was an in-your-face practical option that we took up as we began the obligatory long haul in the tough land. And the plough. Not so much so for the men with the boomerang. The life sustaining kangaroo can jump fences. It must be pursued not farmed. Abophiles, generally, have managed notable but not total avoidance of cultivation and hence the built settlement that it strongly encourages. The first word in the Bible, after clothing, is of Cain's 'city'. This first child built a city. Presumably this was later on in his very many years as the genetic tree sprouted profusely. This 'city' would have been some ordered and fabricated arrangement to suit social mores as well as domestics and shelter, an ancient urb, maybe a couple of acres of habitation facility. The last word is of God's city, the New Jerusalem – a huge cube, on Earth, with pearly gates. Surely, it'll have no need for the light of day nor designer-integration of *nature's earthy nurtures*, as it will glow from within of the light of God.

In your own walls, right there around you, is the mysterious truth as to how they got there and why they, those particular walls of that particular finish, are around you now. The answer my friend ... is shimmering in the walls; the answer is shimmering in your walls.

The house needs to be in a world. The world shapes the house most. With no world there is no exterior. In this scenario a housed interior would have to have built links to neighbours. A totally internal 'world'. Climb into a star to see what it might be like - or recall your entry into your embryonic organism, if it is real. Or dive into the air up through the ocean surface to see what it looks like from outside. Without a world we would need a house more than ever. The world of Eden was the house of Eden surely - equipped as securely as a spaceship but far more abundantly. The world obviously is a domestic facility - in places, and sometimes in spread-out sparse places that require long distance foraging. Spaceship Earth.

"Life is a bridge. Don't build a house on it," some person says, seeing a crack down the track.

ORGANISMS HAPPENING

WHY IS EARTH SUCH THAT WE MIGHT NEED ONE!?

Like many animals, we might have found adequate comfort, safety and social congeniality in unmodified perpetually modern *happening nature.* How different is Global *Pale's* physiology from Gallopilong's? Surely Gallopilong would use bearskin and igloos in the snow. Just as surely *Pale* seeks an even softer, more private bed, and more electronic synthetic. More comfort. How different is Gallopilong's social congeniality from *Pale's*? One is more social.

Many have inherited and developed a soft comfort zone, attuned to fine modern interiors more than to the vigour and openness of the world. We accommodate with various degrees of incubation sparingly interspersed with recreational invigoration and sunburn on the lily-white. Creature comforts. That *happening organism*; the one with legs and a God heart, the special species with the salamander they say. They are us, and our cellular wisdom knows how *domestic-contraption,* housing, came about. We housers liked it this way, it was practical. People wanting and nature enforcing. Wanting art, security, facility, ownership, solitude. Ease and comfort. Enforcing cooking, shelter, planning, security precautions. Shelter, sleep, food, faeces, washing, bodily affection - this is your thinking organism happening. Our doings are prompted, demanded and harmonised-with by the environment. Well, we can't prove the harmonising aspect. Maybe it depends on how right we are.

But we are a very special organism in wholistic ecology.

In abode we are in action, *doing* - dwelling, making *domestic-arrangement, Housefandango.* Hands and mind go hammer on nail with a human movement to build. We do not know though that hands and mind do not come from building; when our great, many more greats, grandparents were building salamander city. Were they reaching out to make shelter; and so grew hands? Evolving to build as to walk and talk? A question, not an answer. Am I asking again, perhaps from a slightly different perspective? Did shelter cause house which caused domesticity, privacy, private life? Or did private life, *beingrowing,* cause house which also gave shelter which encouraged naked ape? So it may be that there are many possible species of house. Different people and peoples may have been inspired to *make* differently. Only camps for some. Houses may be no more in question than legs and taste buds.

A life with less inclemency can be created, by genetically selective processes. The dolphins may know this. Were we too dopey, or do we compromise to meet our noble goals?

We need house and inclemency both. There are times when we require shelter and times when we use inclemency for refreshment. Inclemency; mud, dust, breeze etc, and rain for life. Degrees of shelter - gumboots, umbrella, windbreak, privacy, isolation, bed. We need shelter for effective delicate doings and maybe these, like many activities that we consider to be part of civilisation, would not have developed without house. Stamp collecting.

Hygiene is big for organisms. More than licking, it is a domestic activity facilitated by dry washable conditions, refuse areas, basins and bowls to say the least. The city brews epidemical bacterial danger whilst Gallopilong's people refresh by relocating anywhere from a few paces or a day's walk aside. They leave it to sun, wind and rain, rather than mop, soap and drain.

A house results from some of our both natural and spiritual doings. Some say solitude is supportive of spiritual fulfilment. Solitude can be found on walkabout. But, where people abound or weather unsettles, it can't be found – or not easily.

The noble male, Grunter with his clan and magnificent body in the nature; in founding his life, seeks food and a degree of comfort. He ponders and wonders; particularly in the frail and idle of the evening and night where the organism and persona seem to blend - a key time for appreciation and invention of house. Tired of the jostle he stations himself, aside his tribal friends. Is he feasting on dates and fish at the shore, rather than warm raw meat? Here he abides, short sojourn, long stay. Gallopilong's station is a whole large locale. A tribal territory interfacing other tribes. Grunter gets to know the vicinity. A person must sit, talk, dwell. He faces his brethren. Faces his wife. Shares and passes. He arranges his station, maybe including clearing it of obstacles, to enable such activity. Makes it on level or makes it level. Floor. Sits around a circle at special times. Prepares food in a location. Keeps the area clean. Pees out of the way. Arranges meetings at this station. It's his place. He gives bent to his creativity there. If he stays, things of intimate value and implements accrue. His familiarity and memories with the place grow, hallow. He identifies with it. He feels at home - it is his home - he is safe, comfortable and happy. Others know where to find him. He expects that others should recognise his home. It is of great value to him, both in the nourishment of his life and in the time he has applied to develop it and in the feeling he has imbued in it. He will not abandon it in a hurry to walk with his friend, forebear of Albert

Gallopilong, in a huge territorial home. Grunter will always be like the boomerang, and come back to his home, which is not notioned as a potential empire. He will ask visitors not to break his creation, his order. He will ask most to request permission if they wish to enter. Today's homo superior may expect him to defend it by perhaps savage instinct rather than cultured diplomacy and primitive, then modern, law.

Territoriality and domicile. Are they instincts or learned traits, which perhaps do not exist in the mutual respect and trust of an ideal such as Heaven? Many creatures have a feeling for their own space, *room* - their lair, pit, rookery, home, stop-over. A place where they can rely on, discover and fight for safety, peace, rest, dream, identity, facility. And a place for family. Territoriality is primarily by domain, but comes from the seed of ultimate privacy, beyond the various ego spaces, into the very body of any creature. It relates to seclusion. And it exists with a nomad's intricacies too. Might territory be the separations that give us our selves and the ability to relate to each other?

Grunter the organism continues happening. *Doing his housing*, with mate Gina. Some of their friends stay with the old ways of communal domestics. But the single family house is practical too. Various ground areas are chosen for various domestic tasks and activities - *room* to be domestic, *room* to be social, *room* to be spiritual, to be comfortable. Belongings and furnishings *accumulate* and set physical definition. A way around, a way in, a way out – *ergonomic matrix*. Some shade. An awning. It rains, the awning had best be waterproof. New physical definitions and a hint of interior. And no sky, la ciel, when you look up. Or did a wind wall come first; the view was gone, but it did remain close-by – until the neighbour came and built. And the sunshade rested partly on that. And the presence of the neighbours and community integrate other constructional motives. The organism likes the sun to wake by. His motive is as yet unaffected by ingrained cultural inanity or gay perversity; creature comfort ahead of cultural comfort. Or spiritual truth. The man, organismic person, persists with his house activity as an impulse, a peace, a nutrient, a necessity, a pastime. It becomes a base for his art, society and our settled life. He went to more interior than did our idyllically endowed tropical islanders.

If enclosure facility was built first; for security of belongings or people, or to block out the smell of the neighbours - then the inherent shelter aspect would have been fairly incidental, though useful and therefore used and developed. Grunter's children would be a little more incubated. Softer and more isolated from the social and environmental informations of the surrounds. The house is inhabited by a clan of *happening organisms*; for warmth, affection, security. Or shared fire.

Some see that this is where 'man sets himself apart from nature and wherein he finds dominion over it'. Try telling that to a hurricane or a plague of soldier ants, a typhoid bacteria or Gallopilong. Or to those knowingly suffering from house impacted ecological depletion.

Other creatures in their shells and other places may find various dominions similarly – but not over nature. What are the various other creatures doing as they make house? Relative to our face, animal houses do not have both front and back door. That is to say they do not present to the street. Nor host *Housefandango*. Before the beaver-wise readers pull on the hand-brake; the beaver has a front & back door more for amenity and facility, as they simply access the dammed water on one side and the river flow on the other.

∞

Is the scenario that in fact we are evolving from organism to mind? No, more likely that the organism *connects* the current individual-yet-joined minds. The beingrowing house is the prime vehicle for this *happening organism* – doesn't sound like it should be hot air. A butterfly to be. The ball and chain the cacoon.

WE KNOW WHY

WHY IS EARTH SUCH THAT
WE MIGHT NEED ONE!?

Why a house?? "Asking that silly question again?" shorts Global. "The answer," as Henri Thoreau said of the deep mysteries, (But was it Henri who dropped the g?) "is blowin' in the wind; the answer is blowin' in the wind." Somewhat; but in practice the answer lies in the reason for the key parts of the household – the physiology of seclusion and security, beds, fire, sink, lounge, private places; our domestic needs in fact. We modern settlers know why we need these things - if we don't think too deeply. "It's in the drinkin' of the lemonade," smirks Global in his profound introspection. There is many a reason for a house - necessity, love of work, short sighted, furniture, things, facility, fulfilment by abode, making shelter to facilitate a task, playing with the *playdough of the Earth*; anything to be comfortable at home. We know because these things are now. What we don't know, or simply tend to forget, is the historical footings of our housing life.

We know we build for comfort. Comfort can be addictive. Indulgent. It can be mental. It can be a lemonade *soma*, keeping us in an illusory comfort zone. The loungeroom lizard sneers at the couch potato. A soft leather couch offers no comfort to a concreter; not until she is looking to rest. Her trowel handle is not comfortable to the couch potato; not until he is looking to smooth cement. Facility and amenity adequate to enable activity includes operational comfort. The supremely articulated and detailed person-cuddling ergonomic chair was *soma* to Gallopilong. But he was hardy to it. The language roots of the word, 'comfort', are there to be looked up, but we know what we mean anyway. Comfort is lack of obstruction. No pea under the mattress. We may be uncomfortable from the Fall. Comfort has degrees ranging from hardy to ecstasy. Is stimulation a comfort?

Bobby's house is a necessarily reliable and routine extension to his physiology. It enables him to power out into his work in a well organised fashion. It provides facility for his regenerative return. His well oiled front door is his seven league boots, but like Albert Gallopilong's front door, there is a fair bit involved in establishing and maintaining the critical nature of the lifestyle.

Who left the cake out in the rain? Nobody in their right mind. We need facility to store ingredients and implements. Domestic matters arise from our nature, family and community. We have beliefs. Why, Darwinian, did we elect to houze - and in the manner we have? We know! First a sleeping bag - the family under a buffalo hide. Then the bed-*room*. The camp fire, then the recliner chair, stainless steel and vinyl. Womb, unfold, grasp, become. Order and fabricate. Domesticate. House our children. Lions, gorillas, turtles, spiders, parakeets, beavers, bats and the others do their own things. Termites have mounds, wasp nests are all individualistic, and weaverbirds build intricate and beautiful nests. Their domestics are nowhere near as complex as yours Cheeky, or yours Reader. But dolphins do nothing to house, I'm sure. They don't cook, can't lie down any further – on the move horizontally. No settlement, no campsite. Why didn't we go that way Darwin? Looks easy! Some say dolphins are spiritual too!

The dwelling place is not the first thing in any person's life, though it is very high on the family agenda. It is there to support what you do with your day. You know very well why you make your *domestic-arrangement* the way you do. Your cultural mould though may limit or shape what you know. And your knowledge may not be academic.

Behind it you do not know why, but within your freedom to choose, you do know why you choose a place and extend your *accumulations*. We know! It is obvious that we select and operate our house as a meeting and social place. A selected, fixed location where we may reliably catch contact on chance, by arrangement or routine; dweller to dweller contact or dweller and visitor. We intuitively know ... . Wonder aside, we intuitively know ... including why we *do* it the way we *do*. And we are quite happy to do without or adapt where our *doing* falls short. Sometimes though we need to formally enunciate it, to help with design or social or environmental concerns. Both, the personal and social *beingrowing* reasons for housing are usually simply subconscious steps in that direction. We just know that our house is an esoteric craft to transport us through some of life's lengthy terrain, along with the day-to-day glide.

We know that essential *dwelling-arrangements* answer an a-priori, a continuing succession, of needs for our preferred development.

Freedom to entertain each successive need is reliant on the platform provided by the solution to the previous. Before these needs of course is the first thing, the initial substantiation of the spirit, soul and body. Without this even the first lee would never have been sought. It is our essential persona. This is with us regardless of floor, walls and paint. The colour of the kitchen walls does not matter until the floors are washed. However, I think I know; the answer is in the skin – the sensitive elegant veneer that gives purpose to the foundation stone. The pinnacle of our skin is eyes and face. Would you let your face wither ahead of your genitals if the choice was there? Our face is our uniqueness in animals. Our skin is our first embryonic. I'm suggesting. The *mother of pearl* is a primary. Once supported adequately by flesh and bone, our skin seeks the light of day and the nurtures of air – birthing through the vulva. It goes on seeking *mother-of-pearl*, a smooth home interface to the world or a holy communion, once found in the home of the land. Though it is honed in personal intercourse, our face, our persona, will wither, or simply change, without some house – even camp or molten looking glass. **Maybe this is a monkey.**

The house, from *organisation* and *construction activity* to *renovation* and *maintenance*, along with parallels in daily adventure, being *Housefandango* and chore, provides and fosters further chosen substantiation of spirit, soul and body. New development and renovation in their house property is a strong motivator for children too. They see the newness pointing to future - the spirit to which the settler builds. There'd be a nomadic equivalent of this.

We know house answers for us an *accumulation* of particular functions. An absolute myriad of them for most. We know the particular functions and we arrange facility, amenity and utility to suit.

There is no need to question house. Question the functions. We know enough about those to be practical. We can live happily in the faith that the answer is there - in the wind.

Some particular drop of enlightenment though may be very helpful as to the purpose of it all.

Primary facility may be for security of goods, woman and family. Or cleanliness and tidiness may have been the first house inspiration – they'd had enough of the flies, the muddy floor or dust blown into the food. Or the abstract family circle and identity and hospitality for welcoming visitors.

It is obvious to us as we act in our mode today, and it doesn't matter much as to what may have been first or second in history. We know may settlers seek a regular microcosm in which to search and unfold their persona, unobstructed by demanding fellow people or by an obtrusive environment. But maybe I would rather be that monkey.

Or is it *domestic-arrangement* and house that gives a new dimension that humanises my face?

꿋

Back in the city... . Knowing in
mind is not always enough. We
know we can do within what we
know and that we know more.
How often has the can-opener
been forgotten on the camping trip?
When it comes to family or
house planning we must rake
our minds for at least some
sort of a list. A list of items
and a list of prompts.
Because we are so unique, a
universal list will not be quite
sufficient. You and
yours is a closer
fit than just
anybody's. Similarly,
some authorities
providing welfare
houses and planning
and building
regulations do
appear to be missing
a matter or two.
Ahead is a
**CHECKLIST FOR
HOUSING**.

But first some more background to it; as we sit where we are – reading.
Maybe in our room. In a bus on the way to earn another mortgage
instalment. In a tent away camping miles from the
house-bound rat race.

Maybe a housing department waiting room or the chief executives
desk. At the hardware store or in the ute with clay on your hands.
Maybe this page is blotched with paint spilled from the
roller where you were painting the ceiling that certainly wasn't flying
away.
Your author is looking over your shoulder trying to
express what you
need to hear and would like to hear.

꿋

YOU & YOURS,

HERE & NOW

he **science of housing** must be learned by home and general community case-studies. University is not enough. You may be enlightened in a stranger's reading room or by the driver of a bus. People say that Man is the measure of all things. Certainly the informed builder is some measure of a house. Our measure, similar to a Building Inspector's, would vary diametrically from that of a dolphin; unlike to Cheekyfella's. But the ultimate measure of your own house is you; the dweller, feet up in lounge mode. It's okay by you, or it's not. ... aha! Just kidding.

This chapter is a tough one to write. Your situation and many of your needs and desires are a world apart from those of another reader or any author. You, yours, here ... and how. Your shoulders are outside these pages. Is your room egg shaped. Some of your needs are common to all. There are various ways to fulfil them ... to put those *accumulated* utilities into some *domestic arrangement* ... to enhance the *dwelling-contraption* that results therefrom. **However only you can specifically address your house. Not me obviously.** And *already there has been much read that you may interpret to you circumstance right now;* such as the impact of all those corners and the social block-out of all those walls. And the molecular actions of all the fabric in your house. And your broad geographic *houselocust* impact, as mirrored behind the *Ecosculpture* smokescreen. This

Ecosculpture is just ahead, at **PLAYDOUGH FOR CUBBYMAKERS**. Perhaps this chapter should be very small in that it binds into the entire floor of this book. And so as your situation binds into the entire floor of this book; it binds with any small part of your own floor, any seat, *room* or place on your floor, in your own housing, from which you may prefer to consider your next housing action. Gently hammer your head on your plaster wall. Count the strides to your boundary. Refresh the scent drawn into your flared nostrils. Your own housing experience is your measure of this story; of your *housemarks* on you. And the *housemarks* of others on you. And the measure of your true fit among the quadrangles on the land, the weathering of nature and of Cheekyfella's grin.

Where are you? Some sort of dastardly gray *box* barely supplied with *nature's earthy nurtures*; a gaol cell. You may make no alteration to it, barring some removable decoration. On another hand you're at some sort of *ecopical* island paradise. Different strokes for different folks. There's not always a lot you can do your housing - need or want to do to. Perhaps no bell, book or candle will get you out of a mess you're in. The *doing of housing, Housefandango,* for you in some extremely deprived circumstance may be mental **adaptation** enhanced by some ritual contact with *nature's earthy nurtures* and renewing, refurbishing your personalised *mother of pearl* – writing on the wall, finding *organic nurture* through future escape while valuing what is with you. If, worse, you are a victim of sadism or callous disregard, we're off the track – you need to somehow find home. Find your Mexican-hammock optimum elsewhere. Or for other reason, is it weight on your shoulders? What do you really know about your place? What is it doing to you and the world? Where are you going when heading home or out?

Do it as you do. Your *house doing*, house evolution, renovation or lifestyle. Fulfill your professional or social responsibilities that may coincide with housing. Look past the limitations in which you may sit. Expand your imagination or motivation for advice. *Ripples* from you and from your *contraption.*

The chirps of birds in your garden *ripple* outward, the gleam from your white enamel paint, the odour of your burned heating oil, the colour of your letterbox, the slaves that died to build it. The plans that you just okayed. Are you failing the world; no insulation, unsightly appearance, wasted land, using threatened tree species, cooping up the children, seeping sewerage ...? Is it right; in all the ways of the dream and the world? Are you happy with it? Do you see the significance?

Out go *ripples* – your voice in the locale, your renovation, your *doing of housing* as it affects you and as it affects others. Call a public forum, cut a circular doorway, put some money aside, plant a tree, vacuum the carpet, tear it up. Chat to a professional. Read a book. Read **OUR DOING OF HOUSING** a little way ahead.

DIFFERENT STROKES for DIFFERENT FOLKS
YOU YOURS HERE & NOW

*Y*our *trappings.* Your fellows. Your society. Your own time, geographic and cultural context. Your locale. And please note the *uniqueness* of any people, including family and yourself, for whom you may be designing, modifying, building, making town plans or drafting regulations.

Convention, orthodoxy, mediocrity, normality, universality and your individual genome; they're all are *ordinary.* Your individuality is ordinary in that we all have idiosyncrasies.

You're not necessarily designing – you're just you making your way. Depending on how docile you are, your way is set by automatic response to orthodoxy, marketing and knee-jerk.

I am knocking on your door to harmonise with your psyche, our id, dream, personality; as you read now that which I was writing then, or then that which I am writing now. For that moment, cast off familiar and cultural assumptions and all orthodoxy. Masks off that embryonic face. Armours, charades and frozen concepts all gone. Only a slight gnaw in your tummy, in your domicile. Where are you now, where do you live? In a recent timber frame house in a suburbia? Your house, then, now, to come - cave, cardboard *box*, mud hut, stone mansion on a hill, floating on a river, rude, sophisticated, symmetrical, random, cuboid, spherical, cheap, costly, home-made, or not, like it or not, ramshackle, or orderly, colourful, grey, artful, historic, stagnant or chameleon.

Maybe you are on the track already, growing with that vein of golden domestic, to refine or renew by *doing* it well. Maybe you are crippled in some way - no friends, no money, in a slot in a government building - or maybe you plan houses in one. Maybe you found this book in one of your hotel lobbies, you live variously around the world. The common needs and our unique personal requirements can be fulfilled in many ways in accord with our lifestyle and *beingrowing.* You are common because everybody is unique and with a similar body. You have private and personal aspects to your domestics. Here in the *room* you have for reading, your *armpits* are each located two hand-spans from this, your own unique chapter, and from your cut-off umbilical connection. When you sell or move on, your marks will remain. An architect may strive to produce a house as natural as the earth. Devoid of id. Universal, pure. Devoid of his own thumbprint or those of her client. This may not be possible. Because of *handmarks* and mind-marks. Rarely, no, never will you buy a house that is not imbued with the taste of others.

You enjoy your personal life best in a domestic circumstance that is properly, or coincidentally, tailored to suit the proper you - and to some extent is tailored by you. As if you didn't know. You *do your housing.* You *houze* – it's a verb. Innovation in convention. House. The verb makes the fact. When you've done it, you live in it, with it – more verbs. *Doing your housing* gets you a house. Money is often not always for the action.

Your foci. Your *attentions.* These set your domestic preferences and your aesthetic taste – your own character of housing.
If your *attentions* are turned your psychologies may modify.

ARMPIT PSYCHOLOGY

YOU YOURS HERE & NOW

Sweaty armpits, dirty nappies, the washing, inappropriate dress. Domestic arguments, mental atmosphere, vanities, untidiness. Mired pubic hair clogging the plug hole. Noisy, smelly ensuite detracting from the bedroom. Air from cavities and mattress. Innocent looking shoe soles from public urinal, footpath and 'brown daisy' dog turd, carrying horror to crawling baby. Defecation, nose picking. Nudity, beautiful sexual activity, secrecies, oddities, etiquettes, discretions, dignities. Imminent anal winds. These things may also emanate from your family, housemates, blow flies, animals and friends. And in many cases some, especially various noise, emanate from neighbouring flats, properties or camps. We now remind ourselves, yourself, of our, your, socio-eco-environmental impacts; and our, your, impacts on ourselves, yourself and your family. In fact *most of this chapter* could be in the **ANYPERSON'S HOUSE** chapter coming up. Of course the whole book is woven through this, your, chapter. Let the whole text in, to blend with all else you have in mind and imbue it into the items, form, fabric of where you are. Let your everyday familiar walls drip with their domesto-cosmic heritage.

So much is held within the partly sealed envelope of your own house.

Household smog is a usually dense reality. Not as apparent as cow dung smoke, it is largely flaked skin in the air from people and pets, supplemented with cooking odour, sneezes, air sprays, smoke, toxins from synthetics, the dust of defragmented plastics and the dust of locale. Some paints emit toxins for years after application. Household air may be as thick as a Chicago street, but it can't be seen because of the short depth of field in the house. It can though be felt, smelt and tasted a bit. It usually is most noticeable as one enters a stranger's house. Your nose knows.

Garbage and pipes go out. Houses grow into cities. Epidemics emanate from the brewings of the grime of settlement. An unanticipated cost of housing. You have your own personalised breed of bacteria unique to your house – yes existing nowhere else. It is adapted and acclimatised to your own brand of domestic grime; identifiable as being as unique as your residents. We grow familiar with our own grime but go to work immediately with scrubber and detergent when faced with living in that of others. Not much of an issue for Talkabout. "Except ... yours is spilling into the coastal sea. It's beginnin' to flavour my uncle's fishin' ... in many places!!"

Some domestic amenities very close to you are; ventilation, fragrance, privacy screening, ease of cleaning and crisp focus. We like to show discretion, cleanliness and order to visitors - in principle at least. Our traditional Sinophile uses a raised area of floor as a place of absolute cleanliness. No doggy-done shoe soles in this part of your house if you're a traditional Sinophile.

Privacy. Your nature, cultural conditioning and paranoias help generate those socio-domestic protocols, orders and fabrications based on *visual and acoustic privacy* - olfactorial protocols too. Social distance is a psychology that is in various ways common to most cultures. Yet it is special to each of us. It varies among people. It is associated with the variable desire to screen, from housemates, neighbours and the public, your intimacies, unsightliness, odours, sounds and arguments. You may relate to that. Only three centuries ago in London personal distance was hard to find, houses being small and crowded. This desire for privacy arises variously from courtesy, pretentiousness, social embarrassment, penchant for solitude, taste and to avoid distraction.

The *walls, screens, curtains etcetera* of such psychologies usually cost money in our housing fabrications and even location. For many, and maybe you, the *screenings*, that we may have there, associated with privacy, contribute very significantly to *sanctity, seclusion and the scope to be free and mentally comfortable* in our own house - highly significant housing values.

Samoans are traditionally relatively open about their interior. The household possessions, beds and furniture are open to view. The Japanese too are less concerned. Sydney neighbours are far less a witness to and control on our character than those of old Gallopilong in the bush. You may like to remove a hedge.

It is your household, you care what goes on here. There are often cultural and homemade protocols for activity in the house, even in ordinary 'cultureless' places. Ordinary in fact does have culture. Greeting strangers. Shoes off in the lounge. Hang loose in the back porch. It is tapu to wash your hands in the Maori kitchen. The children respect the location of a memento placed by Mum so the toys go elsewhere. Please ask if you want to wash the dishes. When in Rome. Mrs *Pale* insists on keeping a room for special guests – spotless white carpet, clear plastic over the furniture. "Stay out of the 'good room' kids," she calls. It all helps to generate the hallowed halls. "Maybe we can come around sometime?" ask the *Pales*. Her taste is atrocious. But then if she moved in, the wall-finish for which you paid dearly she would quickly demolish and replace– without knowing it wise to provisionally accustom oneself to a new house before renovating, as one may come to like it.   We note here also that to some people the surfaces & *mother of pearl* generally are of far more significance in domestic value than the *layout* or energy efficiency. Mrs *Pale* can make her mark with wallpaper but, wealthy as she is, she has no concept of installing a sunny widow for free warmth. She'll adapt to and tolerate the status quo in that instance. Surface is part of *finesse* & taste; contained by *mother of pearl*. Northern sunlight supports *nature's earthy nurtures* and ecology – or southern if you're Up-over. "She's all powderpuff 'n' clogged plumbing!" thinks a joker we know, "This's more her chapter-section th'n mine."

Your values and priorities in the arrangements of, and in, your own *domestic-contraption* are just that – yours. Order is not order – you are. It's not the Bauhaus it's your house. Do it your way of course, blue eyes or not. Take good advice too. To be practical you may accept the law and order placed by your culture, or a compatriot. Your house and the way you run it is your own unique order. Character, eccentricity, conformity, taste, disposition. I like the kitchen sink to face south – and conveniently the original house owner or designer did too. They saw past convention and I wanted it to be *different*. Many such psychological manifestations are shaping your circumstance. Of course *compromise is a necessity*, probably as much as food. The hope is that one's order matches that of the spirit and the world, for happiness, care and sustainability. Regardless, as yours grows out into the world it joins the world.

In the etchings of Albert Gallopilong's visage there is a vague hint of his domicile. Pursuing the lines and the light behind his eyes, for sure we see his family and his camp half a day away. But there's something deeper in; something he welcomes with the grasp of his feet. This broad distantly deep psycho-physical realm of ownership, at one with his visage, we see as we startle is headed by his tribe, tribal territory, his country. The light of his eyes and the sweat in his lines join in, by a moebius twist, with both the very daylight shared to our pupils and the close scent of the land, in which we stand talking to the person listening through his feet many miles from his camp and in a time before your floor was built. Global *Pale* of course is oblivious. The lines of his flaking epidermis culminate at a pin of electric light in the spy hole of his front door. Certainly he has country, but it's only politics and grab. His dream-time lies in the forgotten world that *gallops* behind the microns of disinfectant, sweat, mildew and acrylic paint at which he gazes blind and entranced from his industrial bath. Dazzler, in the middle, reveals, in his own little smirk, an unrealised dream-house in a natural community place of abundance of *playdough*, time and money – a water-wheel would be nice, and *room* for visitors.

In a house, as in a camp, there is some mutual control of *social distance*, shaping personal relationships and family order. The personal touches, from various dweller members, on the functions of the house and its aesthetic may make a somewhat collaged *mother of pearl* in a family or group house. Your own persona must flex a little – a colloquial accent develops in a house - as in a suburb, city nation and world. It's your household, you like it. Some people like their slums, with their familiarity and ingrained ownership, as some people like old shoes or complacency.

Part of the way you are feeling now has to do directly with your domestic environment. An artist may need to live in a slum. The psychology of a slum may improve the condition of a company-director-gone-broke. We move on. The artist may next need to dwell near a mountain stream, the businessman finding joy in a cajoling urban neighbour. An oil heater or cow dung fire may be causing a cough. The greasy hood over the stove may have made you feel a bit grimy. That distasteful wallpaper has been nagging you for years, but you are putting up with it. The beautifully turned, polished stair banister reminds you of your heritage. The fresh blue that you painted the kitchen cupboards has given you a new lease of life. The flapping of the tent is relaxing you and cooling the hot air; helping you to acknowledge how much you abhor your houseful of 'low flow' *boxed* corners. The new government-built flats are soulless. The developments planned for the hillside opposite will severely deplete your domestic bliss. Your participation may be imminent in conservations and developments in your locale. A nuclear reactor under construction over the rise is a worry. Or the hard slats of the park bench are tempting you to have yourself return to a softer bed in a jail. It is there with you. **Beating alongside your heart.** Your home, house, abode, pad, dive, slot, tabernacle, cabin. Your house may be debilitating, maybe filled with wealth and boredom, or inexplicable joie de vive; it's ancient vibration laid over with today's mindset.

More so than new building, housing is about *adapting* that which is already built or existent. There's a world of rich cultural built-heritage and cold harsh run-down poorly made truths. Compromise. Opportunity. Converted caves, barns and office blocks. A limb and

bracken lean-to leeward off some 'already built' very large boulders.
Houses too large or too small or too ugly. Too cheap. Old *armpitted*
building or camp may be a resource for fresh new amenity - maybe
you are in one now. Many people, but for lack of money, would build
a new house. Our economic views must be sensibly balanced.
Renovation is noble. Begin a new avant garde architectonic
renovation – lean it onto the old boulders. Don't use too much ... or
too little – as little as possible and as much as needed.

Economic values are very much the breeding ground for *houselocust*
deviance. House funders will often introduce visual and spatial
monotony because it's cheaper than nurturing the natural equilibria
that are vital to healthy dwelling. Cheap *box* houses for example
really must be renovated with complementary links to the lines of the
earth. A simple arch may help. Wood grain. An internal pond. An
interior-to-landscape interface. Half a wall out. A small extension to
the north. "Uncle Albert Gallopilong, if he was to live in one of your
cities I've told him about, said to me he could do with no less than
room enough in his pantry to fling a spear, plus at least a small room
containin' at least a small stormy beach," contributes Cheekyfella,
"Lest you find me mentally ill in it ...'f I couldn' get away', he said,
thinking of life with no 'song of the land', no grasp for the feet,
tangled with urban wires, grid, straight tree lines and tar - **stifling**
nature's earthy nurtures. The *box* needs 'flow'. Global *Pale*, you will
not understand. Your *armpits* are conditioned with the fake scent of
aerosol brand-psychologies. You, you dear Reader, not Global, have
your own preferences, cultural developments and tolerances. Some
aspects of your *house doing* may well be considered anything up to
hideous by a future purchaser. In these circumstances it is
fortunate that you will take some of this eccentricity with you when
you leave this house for somewhere else. Sometimes though, in fact
often for those readers who are fervent believers in wholistically
refined, *ecopian*, houses; even the whole house carries the stench of
warped culture or hideously unique, differently stroked, owner
developments – something developers and their designers have to
watch.

It is delightful when it is the other way round. This is more facial
psychology than *armpit*. Fragrant spatial comfort from your
finesseful resident vapour trails. It is a north facing sink that'd be
perfect - for you.

Your intellectual understanding of your house influences your vision
of its beauty. It is similar for another's vision of your own house.
And in addition the psychologies of each, the indigenous nomad, the
street dweller and the opulent urban resident, are very different one
from another. Driver *Pale* arrogantly notes this, whilst Cheeky
Talkabout alights from the bus at his mob's temporary smog-free
urban-edge encampment. As Global's naive despicable thoughts of
the houseless camp increase a lust for his new highly plasticated
floor, his face, usually just ghostly, turns a whiter shade of *pale*.

Face recluse in vertically veiled hat, waiting for him at an inner city stop near the drapery, *housebound* even when out in rouge laden cheeks, Maggie *Pale* couldn't venture past the inner side of her soft pink crisp vertical window blinds, where she often stood gormandising the light of her personal interior, which reflected back from the blinds, and discarding most exterior that filtered toward her. She is restrained from reading the light of day by a fear of wasting energy normally devoted to her social ego. And for a fear of *galloping horses*. She modified in subconscious some light, melding exterior with interior, to build the social ego in which she was shopping.

But sorry, this is not about you and yours. But what do you do with yours?

The best way to minimise any impact of house on your psychology is to maximally ventilate with time spent in the yard, the garden and if possible in what we call the wilderness. We find Albert Gallopilong in the 'wilderness' with the tiniest swag of domestic psychology. His *armpits* may hustle; he is but a person. He may *be* wilderness.

An OPTIMUM domestic CIRCUMSTANCE

YOU YOURS HERE & NOW

In relating to your optimum, your 'dream house' perhaps, the, err ..., worldly wisdoms gathered in this book are at least a large part of what you need to understand and follow.

Compromise and the concept of *doing your housing* are keys to well tuned housing consciousness and housing environment. **Attitude** and *doing* are as significant as having. Attitude and *doing* are as significant as having. " ... Ay mate!!" Attitude and *doing* are as significant as having. "Gotcha. I understand. It's a wee bit to do with my personal attentions." That which I love seems to grow around us.

(As the nomad herself is the 'way', the establishment process's is the house.)

A shimmering oasis. A desert camp thirsting in a palm copse needs a drink fridge in an art deco loungeroom. A *boulevard* mansion spread widely inward, away from its windows, ceiling shaded, stuffy but beautiful art deco lounge, needs potted palms and a spot of moving sunlight. One person's palace is another's albatross. The world can support only limited house quantities. Any locale is the same; limited in what it can carry. One person's big house must be counterbalanced by one person's small house. A house in harmony with the locale's eco-beauty balances can be said to be the *ecopian* optimum – if it suits the perfect better side your personality. We overshot the mark. Maybe it was electricity that took us too far – and you and yours are with me and them. The utopian optimum; why don't we have it? It's a house of a nomadic settler or a settled nomad – in a nomadic urbia. A *nomurbic* house. *Ecopian* balance. It is fundamental to your house *doings*; your *domestic-contraption is a key*, when it comes to the urgencies of ecology and sociology; and also when it comes to you. Reach into your architect.

Your house now may be an inherited mansion, but you live only between the kitchen, bathroom and lounge. The rest is excess and not actually your own *domestic-arrangement*, nor your *ergonomic room* nor taste. This is obvious by the seeming dusty neglect in some corners and polish in others. A critic of that seeming neglect is merely a critic of something outside your domestic world; though perhaps you should screen it away – and that may best be done with a broom. Albert Einstein I heard has lived in a rough but ready house; there is a lot in the eye of a beholder - including the aesthetic of a practical understanding of the unused corner.

How do you feel, personally? Does your abode work well with your daily movements, jobs, activities, recreations and rituals? Is it properly weatherproof, and generally practical? Sometimes it's all so domestically dreary, but like your health it's worth the right *attitude*. And that simple ephemeral *attitude* multiplied by a billion is as important as an election. Does it present tastefully or eccentrically to passers-by and neighbours? Is it ecologically and socially responsible? Do you find various small or major annoyances with your dwelling, or your style of dwelling, and your character? Have you affection for your abode? Does it draw too much on your time and effort, leaving less for other important activities like sport, socialising, work or a cause? Does it lock you in, not let you out? Anxious to do something? Can't afford it? Can't quite see your way through it? Are you stifling your personal development by being stubborn with your housing development? Or by regarding it as unnecessary work? Do you think you have it all? Do you need to swap with somebody?

Have you unlocked all locks possible using your (or 'the' - for urban planners) *domestic-contraption* as a key?

You may need to prompt inspiration by a commercial enhancement of your inner architect. There may be plenty that needs *doing*. Immediate improvements. Plumb an en-suite to your bunk under the bus-stop seat. If your house sings to the tune of your own happy spirits, and reflects daily refreshment, keep it up. Make your adventure in domestic facility pleasant, as it unifies with your spiritual adventure. Fully realise the romance in your current reality. Use this *guide to the housing romance*, your forever modern ancient nous and your genetic inclinations. Acknowledge the pragmatics of your ephemeral domestics against the ideal of your dreams.

Millions are stupidly unhappy for what they don't have but think they should. Millions more wrongly adapt totally and permanently to what they have been given. Those are two extremes. The long term, the social circumstance, the earthly facts and the dwellers dreams all interface in the ephemeral lightness of your house – 'horribly good' as Bobby saw it. *Doing* your ephemeral domestics with *attitude* is as important as doing government and industrial chores.

Gallopilong, experiencing the high drama of his first and only Western contact, sings with Talkabout and a tall, tanned, *ecopically* inclined, *dodo*-immune, urban nomad in basketball boots. This is Low Carl, a staunch advocate of urban sustainabilities. *Pale*, a cyst in his belly, has delivered them on Talkabout's charter, to talk with Little White Cloud, the purest of tummies. Bobby is at an urban planning conference, aboard a nuclear warship - big steel thing with *room* for 5,000 navo-domestic beds and its own communal intent; a kind of ant nest. Gallopilong, in his way, notes that the warship floats there, in the balanced brine, symptomatic of a broader epidemic rash from the settlement mire, rolling oily in mix with the well sung water of cities. They want some action out of Bobby. His consciousness block, the cause of some marital ill-ease, has caused him to grasp a false optimum. He had settled for less; for complacency. Domestic politics, through White Cloud, they feel is a way to move Bobby in his conference presentation. The conference circumstance presents as a crucial nexus, an international and topical fusion point in the body industro-politic, which will do well from an inspired acupuncturing with the needles of *ecopicality*. Bobby was refreshed and empowered to deliver the therapy. Simultaneously he resolved a key ephemeral domestic issue at home, for his out-speak had conveniently cost him his job. His house had to be sold. It made them debt free with a four wheel drive and a tipi. *No longer hamstrung.*

You have broader and narrower contexts. And complacencies. How far does your imagination, and understanding, of housing possibilities and subtleties go and how honest to you, and yours, and practical to Earth, is your optimum hope in housing?

This query should rest easy with you if you feel you are optimised in your current abode, or if you are anywhere between there and being able to slightly modify or build what and where you want. You have responsibility to yourself, your children, visitors, fellows, those who may come after you and the ecology. Optimum may be slum or luxury. Certainly it is practical. You have some power to enhance the settled environment. Perhaps you have the resource, position or expertise to enhance the social and industrial aspects of housing. One vote at every opportunity. *Wow! How's the house now!? Your*

dwelling-contraption is a key. Here is a *guide to the housing romance.*
To be real, especially in the urban explosion, we must have a
physical attitude to every molecule of our house property. Every
vibrating molecule.

Your situation now. Within the practicalities of your housing life,
which we see is of substantial proportion in your whole life, it may be
made up of many different factors. The factors have varied through
your life and will vary further. She has become pregnant. You've
moved out of the parents' home, out of the nest. A realisation has
occurred that you are lacking some vital housing need. You think of
horrible problems when it comes to your house; tasks and
complications too much for you. A 'for sale' sign has been pasted
over with a 'sold' next door – you know it's ominous. Making do with
or just shutting off your surroundings is not always the best answer;
even though moving can be tricky. You don't want to move. Maybe
you should. You have newly moved into a house. You don't like
something. Give it time to get to know you - provisional
accustomisation. Adapt within comfort. Your house is to provide for
you and yours; so you know what it gives. But do you know all it can
give, or do you not recognise some of what it gives? The *wallpaper of
locale* elsewhere and the associated house may be calling. Your
abode now is part of the district, of course. The beach may be near,
the crèche, your work; all that can be reasonably reached, they are
all part of the facilities of your house and should be considered in
your house *doings* along with the intimacies within your private
boundary - something which is today extended for some by the car,
public transport and the local services. Some cultures have it, that a
house to the neighbourhood is as the lounge is to the kitchen. Some
aspect of the locale may save some *mother of pearl* work on your
interior. In fact the locale is so good that you settle for an old shack
in which to live, just to be there.

Another person's house also provides for you. It keeps their dirty
linen from sight. Provides a place to visit. And a lot more. The
comfort of a suburban street. The benefits of your help to build it.
The visual experience. In these ways, your house may be there for
others; a cultural contribution, a building block of a town, of a locale.

Looking at housing power, at you and your house now; as possibly
you sit feet up in front of the television, around a card table, or at
your hobby bench. Ah! Caught you, little lounge lizard. Clarify your
understanding of exactly what it is in which you live.
    Using your imagination picture the locale, walls, floor, ceiling, and
    furniture around you as that of an Indian tipi, a Mexican adobe,
    an Egyptian pharaoh's palace, a Georgian mansion, a plastic foam
    building, a small flat in a huge block in Taiwan, a house boat, the
    house next door, an igloo, a geodesic dome, some nomad's
    walkabout camp. The materials and textures around you would
    change through a broad spectrum - translucent animal skins,
    reinforced concrete, polished wood, wool carpet, reeds, mud

bricks, animal sinew, painted cardboard, plaster, ice, canvas, rough-cut boards, fibre glass. The colours, lighting, and general atmospheres would vary in a myriad of different ways, affecting you with the sensations. Shapes and sizes, indoor-outdoor relationships, maintenance aspects, warmth, homeliness, cost, tastefulness, delight, permanence. All flicker in thousands of different combinations before your mind's eyes, nose, ears, armpits and toes. Desert sites, tropical islands, suburbias and hilltops flitter outside this spin.

By nature you conjure a dream of sorts. By nature the dream is in the same world and your pragmatics guarantees you will be able to access the location.

Further, your optimum living conditions will be far gentler than the ailing conventions, buoyed by complacent dwellers and *dodos*, that result in the settlement mire. That is not to say that a future dweller will not destroy it as quickly as laying bitumen on the path of a llama.

Your dream! It may be impractical, fragmented; an adoption of something you have seen or had done. It is limited to your experience. It may enforce a house marriage and eventually falling in love. We must consider your just deserts and the firm realities. The best domestic arrangement for you may be an unhoused one – with a deeply embered bush television, without a power-point. There is a lot of wholistic pragmatics involved in the achievement of a dream. Dreams do not appear as simply as roasted marshmallow. Optima are artful wisdoms.

WHAT'S IT DOING TO YOU & THE WORLD

YOU YOURS HERE & NOW

What's it doing to you and your world? *Armpit* psychologies, health, snares and function affect you. And a lot more. House-based work has its influence on you. Time spent in and about housing, and in travelling to and from, is closely related to psychology, in its influence. The time we spend in any relationship with housing is variable in the extremes with individuals. You can assess the time you spend.

Don't panic, but do listen. The *ripples* of social and environmental impact, going out from your house, are your responsibility. We shall note the depth of this responsibility. Circumstances vary as degree of ownership or custodianship varies. Practically speaking, there may be relatively little you can do about the impacts of house. What you can do, and what you do do, can be measured and assessed – can be terrific or unfortunate. Where have you and your society got to and where are you both going? Are you a *dodo* or a Low Carl? That which appears as optimum for you and yours may not be so for environment and society. We are working on this one through this chatter. Watch the *ripples*, *mindmarks*, freedoms and coercions. Do not let a bad house bring you down or corrupt you - as they certainly sometimes do.

Do not strive for that which you cannot afford - that which does not fit into your peace pipe. Acknowledge the worldly wars of mortgage and residential corralling. Orientate yourself in the urban landscape. You don't want to foster the grimy oil against the good water of the gatherer-wanderer's landscape; that which lies flattened underneath the pavements lawns and floors. Foster only the valiant landscape remnant shaking the joyful fist of organics at the immense oily settlement fabrication.

Accepting the fait-accomplis of a purchased item, your abode should reflect all the worthy human attributes. Dignity, tidiness, courtesy, citizenship, celebration, earth values. Much of what you can do though is dominated by your society and industry.

We may all develop our homes in a variety of ephemeral ways but the reality of the fabric and the town plan must be formed by profoundly considered action; and more so, as each individual addition adds to the staggering immensity of the housing impact on this planet. Affluent excess in housing is foolish. Abundance though is a joy and can be achieved through understanding of ecology, planning, purpose and doing more with less.

Global's minima are more than Cheeky's maxima. What are your quanta? And their *ripples* going out into the world and into your heart.

TENURE
SECURITY
AUTONOMY

YOU YOURS HERE & NOW

*C*laim. Lair. Critical need. Our hunting ground. ... our own. You are where you are, for a time; a spell, a job or even a life. What does ownership mean to you? A dream! A maintenance problem! A mobility snag! Freedom to renovate! Investment! Ownership is a fundamental in house psychology and pragmatics. Fighting for ownership and autonomy; desperately clinging to it or simply enjoying it. Even a little shrimp will fight fervently to fend off intrusion on its little undersea cavern. The sense of ownership, though, flexes with realities.

The house drifts from the indigenous principle into the formats of industry, market commodity, mortgage, rates and land taxes. It drifts further from the lifestyle guarantee of the dweller's own *handmarks*. Ownership is a means of retrieving some of this guarantee. The process of achieving ownership can be drawn out. It can take a very significant quantum of the inhabitant's time, effort,

80

money and perseverance to gain full ownership of a house. Sometimes we are our own enemy in this regard; but in the city-economy housing should be streamlined in its ease of ownership. *Frustration* is the name of the game for most. So much of your life paying a mortgage; conned by some Cheops to build the pyramid in return for what? Still, there are cons and pros. Whilst Bobby can enjoy working as a town-planner as he buys his house, he can moan first about the interest he pays – and then about social egalitarianism and values. It is this, payment for land and our own high domestic ideal that frustrates our aim of ownership.

In order to maintain a credible asset for the bank, or indeed our own retirement fund, the house under purchase loan must ideally be limited. Limited to popular market-commodity, the grey suit and shiny black shoes of its social mediocrity, the easy to govern majority, the cholesterol problem of fluid society, the pain-in-the-neck that stifles the id, the socio-economic *box*, for which many urbanites learn some adaptations.

As the nomad herself is the 'way', the establishment process'is the house.
(Attitude and *doing* are as significant as having.)

That's a punchy statement. The *doing of housing*. Whatever it is that we go through, to achieve our domestic profile. It is our domestic profile. That which we go through is dependant on our wants, resources and skills. And opportunity. Owner-building offers a profile that is significantly different from outright purchase. There are many ways.

Some sort of legal ownership is necessary, in most societies, to protect us in our domain, our domicile, against discourteous intrusion. Just how deeply rooted is your domicile; are you founded on the rock of, either, morally honoured or legal ownership or are you teetering on the edge of a flimsy lease? Or in the path of some discourteous disaster? You may think you are well set up, owning your own house. What is it costing? Are you free to move easily? Does it inhibit? What right have you to ownership when so many do not? This question *pales* a little, in that; many people prefer not to own, to be able to move more freely, to avoid borrowing.

There is a concept that ownership is theft. We can own the process, the effort, elbow grease, money; but all the material is taken from the Earth originally. Nature's bounty. How do people come to own parts or pieces of the Earth? God grant. The *playdough* of the builder. Take some, it's mine now; but wait – the *Pale* family owns the quarry.

In essence we do not own our houses but are the custodians of them for the course of our temporal sojourn, or more precisely the course of our habitation.

If you do not own the walls you own what you have put into it - tenancy, décor, vibe, spirit. There is no *mother of pearl* on a bare cave wall but there is on a mud wall. The dwelling oysters have smoothed, cherished and coloured – owned, honed and created.

Are you secure in your *beingrowing*? House ownership is one consideration. Securing your ownership by paying continuous rates and taxes, and maintaining your abode with continuous services bills and coats of paint are snag – a pea under the mattress maybe.

Your autonomy must be maximised. Ownership is a community thing that affects anyperson's world. Subject as much to community vagaries as to its immense values. If we look at a worst case scenario, we must ask; where is the honest society that will allow the poor to begin ownership on a shared piece of sewered urban land with a free permit for however many dwellers to lodge there in snow-zone bags under foraged shelters and Abophile styled camping arrangements? Ooooh, better not allow such allotments in the wealthy zone. And they'd be bound to cause trouble in the poverty zone. They'd be better off in the welfare housing zone; it's for their own good. This dishonesty, snobbery and bigotry is one key to the *dodo*'s passage into the mind.

Your autonomy must be maximised. Ownership is a community thing that affects anyperson's world. What you do with what you own or how you manage with what you don't own is dependant on the way you lay your uniqueness over the anyperson templates. These templates, though not tagged as templates, lie throughout this document.

Attitude and Do

ing are as valuabl e as Having.

ANYPERSON'S
HOUSE

Ohe **unique master** of these reading eyes possibly by now
has one eyebrow sitting slightly skew. You in some regards
are just an anyperson on a bus recalling a midnight gone star-
dusted in bed or pacing the hall and banging the wall for lack
of funds to pay for it all. Some aspects of your *domestic-
arrangement* are common to all. They match anyperson's
house. Some aspects of your *domestic-arrangement* are
common to your locale only. Some to your country only. And
some to your culture. Some to your planet – no wooden doors
on Mars, no trees. Those *domestic-arrangements* in your
locale are very likely to be far more similar to your very own
than are those a jet flight away. To the eyes of that distant
culture, the differences between yours and your neighbours'
are relatively unnoticeable.

The house is universal, suiting anyperson, only in the
fundamentals of minimum facility; the fundamentals of camp.
Camp may be comprised of depot, *hud, ergonomic room,*
cooker, some storage and a place to sleep. This is *domestic-
arrangement* without substantial *domestic-contraption* –
without house. Throughout the many cultured lifestyles, any
person's house in most of its fundamentals assimilates with
its neighbours. Also, each neighbour's own unique
requirements exist in detail - and sometimes in larger
respects. Idiosyncrasy abides with commonality, with
universality. This abiding relates more to soldiers on parade
than to hippies at Woodstock. *Commonality supports
uniqueness. Uniqueness agrees with and modifies
commonality.*

The universal fundamentals of house are not universal in
appearance. Local resource, construction, taste and
orientations all cause varying visual outcomes. Outcomes as
solutions to the same fundamental needs.

A healthy HEART in COMMON

ANYPERSON'S HOUSE

We turn frying pans in our own localities, distant but over the same Earth centre. A house-mate at the table spills crumbs from the bread knife. We all *must* meet cosmos and culture. With domestic provision. We all, nomad too, need domestic order. We all need our human, national, tribal and individual spiritual evolution. Our spiritual adventure. Social ego in territory and expression. For most, this means house. Nomads are few, they don't procreate profusely, are kerbed by hi-tech bullies and perhaps the lifestyle is less popular. Consider what might be *the practical, wholistically-based, average housing desire.* What might be a *heart* for urban utopia, a basis to fit ongoing housing desire? Not a house based on ailing mediocrity, like the welfare *box*, but an individual ideal and whim. Meek, humble, affordable. *And not just the physical aspect but also the processes and culture. Place, lifestyle, materials.*

Tahitians don't rely on the house for warmth as much as do Alaskans. What is it that all of us do share in housing? A first thing that often comes to mind is the 'nice place', a good spot, which suits the daily excursion. Then roof against sun and seagull droppings – or it may be the lockup depot for vital goods. A commonality grows from the embryonic simplicities.

Little White Cloud Dazzler washed the dishes in a plastic bucket for five years – her husband had given priority to a television ahead of a plumbed sink. Likewise, fabrication to screen neighbours, visitors or passers-by is a lower priority for an Australian country recluse than a Mumbai ratepayer. The wanting of anything occurs only following the satisfaction of apriority wants - except for the first want. As the wants extend beyond the primary, they become more eccentric to the individual. The common *heart* drives the extended priorities; to suit the id of the inhabitant(s).
Once we have security we want identity, stimulation and so on. We don't desire to compose music, collect stamps, or adorn our houses when we seriously want food for an empty tummy, or safety from an advancing bushfire. Likewise there are things we cannot do on an empty house - nor with no house.

Likewise there are things most cannot know without going walkabout - a consequence of generations of settlement.

The rooms, *'bricks and mortar'* that some may consider common are but the variable froth on the hearty reality.

A little like Grunter Palaeolithic, the settling settler, a nomad settling temporarily one day can see clement weather ahead. She may establish a bed first. But the days are long so she prepares temporary seating - a bark pad over the pebbles. Meanwhile he takes the children collecting shellfish. A table to prepare them - a handy flat rock or a clean shell of bark. The *accumulating* utilities and artefacts are ordered, placed around the mobile source of the *dwelling-arrangement*, its people. Its 'people', the dwelling organisms, are the mobile pulse of the *arrangement*. No fabricated part is the *heart*, not the hearth, kitchen nor bed. Pulse and ventricles. The *ergonomic room* available to the dwellers is the left ventricle. The right ventricle; the utility and implements - including the vital necessities for which we must return when on extended excursion or moving on. The ventricles do not work without the pumping inhabitants, the *pulse*; the interface between dweller and house.

The actions of permanent habitation convert *dwelling-arrangement* to *dwelling-contraption* or house. Any house has this *heart* in common with any campsite, any *dwelling-arrangement*.

This *heart*, to suit both dwelling *arrangement* and dwelling *contraption*, is comprised of;

♥	.. Inhabitant(s) inhabiting,
৲	.... *E*rgonomic *room, room* to move, and
+	.. Utility and implements – facility.

Can we be more specific as to the *heart*? Cheekyfella Talkabout out on walkabout finds the campsite used and vacated, with the nominal extra of a handy constructed sun-shade. Perhaps with modification, demolition and/or addition, he revitalises the vacated facility with his own habitation and thereby incorporates it or part of it to make his own personal *dwelling-arrangement* – it was cloudy, the shade was useless. It may be that, having been through this process, the campsite is not changed in any way. What actually was it that Cheekyfella found? Well, yes, it was a campsite or 'dwelling arrangement', but in the hollow sense of the words. When discarded it became a part of nature's cycling. A husk – incoherent *nacre* components. Cheeky used it as he would a handy eucalypt branch to adapt it as his *facility* – and of course there was plenty of *room*.

This *heart* is *inhabited room* and *facility*. But the *heart of hearts* .... No, this isn't smart philosophical fluff. It points out that the *doing of housing* is inseparable from the inhabitant's house. Inseparable.

Climatic, geographic, ablutionary and circumstantial variants command that no domestic *facility*, and therewith *room*, is the same for all across the globe.

As we zoom in closer to locale, tribe and hermit this becomes a lesser truth. But never is one inhabitant's, unadapted, facility the identical fit for another. The inhabitant itself being *adaptable*, we can however rough it, compromised, in a standard unit, especially if we match the culture of its makers; and in the *heart of hearts* our culture is essentially common – people active, being people.

All houses have roofing in common to enhance facility, but surely:-

The common house *heart of hearts* is;

⌗   The facility/amenity of its sitting comfort after the evening meal.

And it is so also at the campsite.

A city tenth floor flat inhabited by a café diner has one too. *The heart of hearts extends out* **through the halls and paths of ergonomic room in** its *connection with the full* **heart**. This extension grows, driven by the heart. It is at its best when it pulses out to and also receives the energies and specialities of the most suitable locale.

Nub butterflies flitter and sleep freely at this *heart* **of hearts** in camp, lounge and singularly intimate butternut gourd - where *dodos* cannot go. Some house *hearts, we know*, repeat ailing shades of *pale*, rather than beat uncluttered like the shell of a snail. Where *nature's nurture* is inadequate for them, the *nub* butterflies disappear until conditions are right; emerging sometimes in subtled minds that may still survive in ailing organisms stifled away from *nurture* in *pale* hermetically sealed urban *box*.

Our extended priorities will deviate from health, if our developing house embryo has *placebos* that confuse its needs. *Artificiality*, a quality lacking in organic integrity, is a form of *placebo*. Television sets with magnificent nature films may be adopted as *placebos*. *Placebos* may leave us wondering like naive babies as to why a belly full of factory chicken leaves us queasy. And *placebos* may in some way be beneficial.

Technology, philosophy, art and indeed the house are not the end wants. These creations of society and individuals are merely the pots for the plants to grow from. It is the *blueberry pie* we are after not the plate; the rest, not the seat. Housing is for people, families, groups or individuals to bloom from - flowering into their doings in the open world. Not mutating isolated from the days passing largely unlived outside the curtained windows. Days like wild horses, *galloping* to a Gallopilong distance, across a sea of dolphins, all embodied in the organism of an innocent beetle, with lungs beating too fast to breath; dying by insect spray, crashing, from the spotless beautifully manufactured light-fitting, to the dusty toxic steam of nylon pile below, inside the curtained windows of all the tired houses in the sun. How's she s'posed t'get any riding done? Blooming, healthy dwellers moving dynamically with the horses, inside in the harmonic texture of wholesome rooms joined bravely to the long distance. This is the ultimate gauge of supreme housing - dynamic life. A facility, showpiece or an end in itself your housing should not be. Nor a shackle, a hassle, an idol, an error, an obstacle. Nor a little inadequate. The dynamic *blueberry pie*. This *heart* in our houses provides it – provided the inhabitant sits truly intended.

Another *common heart* consideration is the popular need for *privacy*. The fabric and facility required for privacy concurs a little with that for *womb sanctum* and for inclemency shelter. Privacy for nudity, for decorum, self-consciousness, discretion, secrecy and security. Fabrication for privacy is merely to shield against neighbour, paparazzi and pedestrian attitude and aggression; with a measure to shield against other house occupants. Heavy gates, bars, shutters and no children on the front lawns in South Africa as I write, and paper walls here and there in Japan. We do also fabricate for *seclusion* and *solitude*. It is handy that this also serves privacy. In solitude we escape from the disturbance, coercions and aggressions of those around. The freedom provided by that particular *room-amenity*, which we construct purely in order to support *solitude*, is a reasonably common requirement of housing. Our continuous spiritual evolution, *blueberry nay the consumed joy of raspberry pie*, is supported by this freedom. Albert Gallopilong's solutions rely little on people's architecture and more on social protocol. Never-the-less solitude is another facility in our common heart. And another; where there is solitude, there is the architecture, or optionally only the social *protocol*, of the doorknocker.
A buzzer, banger, knuckle knocking, voice hoying or subtle coughing. A visual wave or courteously sheathed eyes and ears coming into personal distance. The knocker's presence is also a demand. 'The remains of any trespassers will be prosecuted', states the tiki's fearsome face or the nun's simple request.

On the other side of solitude we have in common the big wide world. The *outer sanctum*. Mum's and Dad's big world. Ancestry and societies with the huge horses *galloping* hurricane on the horizon. The rich land and sea. Wild wide open space. The outside of house *room*. The big, big mutual portico to all *domestic-contraptions*.

We bind all of these needs as we create the *heart* of our house. We create urban utopia when, in the right locale, we bind together with facility and *room*-to-move creating this *heart* maximally with local resource and local culture in the foundation of air and ground.

Privacy and *womb sanctum* are not necessarily part of the *heart*; they are not apriority needs and, for some, are not needs at all.

Where does womb sanctum fit? Any house is a substitute for the womb! It has been said and held as sacred. Profound. Inner sanctum. Our foundational psychologies, security, seclusion and whatever else are shored up by our own fabrication. So says the womb statement. Is this retrogression in life? Probably not. Perhaps you may recall being curled up there. We had it inside our mother and we need it now inside our world. The architecture of inner sanctum does not carry weight with all peoples. It may perhaps be assumed as a fundamental, a building block, a heart, but only due to the conditioning of generations of walls and ceilings, or sheltering trees. It is incidentally real once an interior is established, but there is doubt that it was an original motivator for housing. *Womb sanctum* is though a popular value of housing. It does not necessarily have space dedicated to it either. It is an organic consciousness that is relative to the coordination of the inhabitants. Womb sanctum can, anyway, be found in the *heart of hearts* as described. Some may find this sanctum in the sphere of extended family and tribe. They do not need to build it.

Can this common healthy heart fit a *ticky tacky box*? Adapt the *box*.

COMPROMISE
ANYPERSON'S HOUSE

*C*ompromise. It's a pretty big issue in getting anyperson's house together. On one hand compromise is second best. On the other it is achieving through dweller *adaptation* something that otherwise would not be. One does not, though, expect compromise in a dream house. Allow me to clarify to you the gains and surprises of your compromise ... suddenly the mystic sees the universal unfolding, the surprises and nourishments of providence ... the unfolding dream. If you do not comprehend providence you must comprehend compromise.

Location is subject to compromise dealings. And so is each *accumulated* domestic utility and room. So are the extent of ownership and the values of each new resident.

Everyperson is compromised. What does this mean? Suppressed *beingrowing*? Reality? I want to be, but I cannot be, an artist; I do not have studio *room*. Money, expertise, resources; the dream is compromised by pragmatics. The owner with minimum compromise has the most realistic dream. Compromise merely adjusts the dream and makes it appropriately real. The occurrence of husband and wife working together creates adjustments to individual ideals. Similarly nest builders and society in nature strike a balance – the tallest reed bends best with the swallow. It may be a political sort of balance, sometimes anarchic. Yay, that is the truth; in some ways our hands are tied by forced compromise so that we cannot attain that which perhaps we should. It is in the nature of people and their nests.

Home is where the heart is. A happy heart humble. With a little heartfelt resourcefulness and simple reflexive adaptability a compromised situation can become a perfect one. Our compromise though should not be lax. Ignorant acceptance, negligence and inactivity are different from compromise. These are reasons for dream shortfalls; dissatisfaction and inadequate housing. The first problem of housing lies with the nature of people. As part of this nature we generally settle for less without question; *if the 'less' equals the status quo.* We settle for *excess* in this way too; so the ecology meekly cries for relief. We do not compromise adequately. We compromise our ethics instead. It is reality – harsh truths. We fowl our own nest for lack of compromise with economy and ecology. Compromise is not a dirty word. Make do. Economics, practicality, availability and understanding; seasoned with hope, if in the face of anarchy. An ill-affordable carpet to impress; lose it to compromise, this may in fact be gain. Subtraction of the trappings of social pretentiousness so common in housing is a subtraction of zero; and a significant addition to your housing dream. In the presumptuously built decadence, many limited options are bemoaned, fanciful expectations and wishes are expounded. Yet already those people live in mansions relative to their ancestors. A minimal domestic provision may be a sobering compromise for these people - aside from vital contemporary utilities.

Even more sobering is a thought on our residential evolutions. As resources become sparse, an application to government for right to build may be treated like an application for welfare. One may be compromised into wearing the errors of our fathers. "Sorry sir there is a dwelling unit available for you and your family in the northern sector of uptown Smogton. And so, regretfully we cannot acquiesce to your request for new construction in the rare and diminishing land areas of Fern Hollow." The lady, mournful, hugs her two children and waves bye bye to the family dog.

HOUSE
at HOME
ANYPERSON'S HOUSE

*H*ouse is one foundation and symbol of a home-life; as a table can be a foundation of joy - and a plate of pie. There are those who have a table but are not aware of its depth of value. There are those with plates on their laps in a lounge who don't notice that the table is not there, but that the dining company is. A nomad campsite is the same; with a home-life that is perhaps more intimately gregarious, being less affected by interior and physical constraint. A small crowded house that mixes family with an aspect of public, in daily and nightly life, allows only a dim glow of home. This is so because the genetic liaisons and intimate identities, associated with central home, require the nurture of *appropriate seclusion*. Generically speaking, this sense of seclusion may be implicit within the broader meaning of the word privacy. The outer layers of home of course do include public liaisons and public places.

Home is from 'homoe', related to 'dom', meaning 'the-same-as' and 'like' – also 'village', 'place of dwelling', 'nurture'. Homini and homo pertain to man, people. Like dom, dome, hominus too - domestic. Domain and domicile are village and 'place-of-dwelling-or-nurture'; territory. We know the word is more in its most developed use.

Bathe a moment in the mystic myriad mirror-like magic of home. Is home any larger to the owner of a mansion than it is to the mud-hutter behind in the rent? Probably the extent of your satisfaction with the extent of your interior freedoms is a kind of partial measure of home. Does Albert Gallopilong come home? Well yes. He does so, to his family and friends in *social mores*, the exterior being their interior so to speak. "You're jus' lookin' at a diff'rent style o' home," Cheekyfella Talkabout grins still. Our Maggie looks sideways; silent by the blinds of all she can conceive as credible home. She is too staggered to scoff - more likely not virile enough.

Does the fact of home support the motivation for housing? Or does home develop as an emotional land-place concept as a result of the house? The egg is in the cart. The road doesn't go anywhere; it's right there where it is. The road hatches. Omega the chicken knows but can't say. The horse is free. Evolution will not answer. Knock and let it open. House may enhance a home. That's all a house is. If your house vanished, would your home go with it? Well yes if you like; but home is what you make it. It is community, only optionally, with particular locale as much as gate and hearth. Home will unfold in a new setting. It happens free of house but, being based in the time continuum and the hallowed patinas of residents and loved ones, it can be heavily bruised by abrupt change of people, place or routine. In nomadic lifestyle, also, hallowed halls happen equally - in land, paths and places. Memories, rituals, ceremonies and appointments. Personal, facial and social spoken addresses. And embrace; a *nomurbic* commonality we all share.

Ownership has little to do with it. Personal, family, tribal and social **beingrowing** build home. Yet, too, home is from whence one starts. Familiarity, sameness, fertility, id. Home sweet home. Where the heart is. It is a place, locale and country. It is with the heart of why we build. The heart of the inhabiting organism is the heart of the living house. It is the house of our spiritual evolution. If your *domestic-arrangement* in any way barbs the lifestyle and magic of your home, adapt, renovate, coat the irritation with *mother of pearl* or vacate.

TRANSIENCE
& OWNERSHIP
ANYPERSON'S HOUSE

London is owned by only a few; mostly by inheritance - ask a prince or a duke. Transience and ownership strongly relates to both chapters **YOU, YOURS, HERE & NOW** and **ANYPERSON'S HOUSE** - hence it is complementarily itemised in each.

Individual ownership is my point here - racial and other ownerships are left in abeyance.

A house may be well weathered before paid for. Houses cost. Why? Materials, labour, regulation. Land. Many an indigenous people had no concept of land ownership - before, a certain type of conqueror dropped by. Tribal territory paints its own sense of belonging. Perhaps the financial and/or inherited ownership systems are incorrect.

In the West maybe two percent of people own their house outright - caravans and bedrolls aside. Every house though is owned by somebody or body corporate. There are degrees of ownership. There is stewardship, custodianship. Joint ownership, partial ownership. Rental and lease rights. Landlordship. De facto ownership. Territory is more a matter of living rights than ownership.

Dominion alone isn't quite ownership.

Work has something to do with it, and inheritance. It is written Biblically that God gave lands to some progeny of Adam, as reward for effort; to own. Were there title deeds? There were fewer people in the world then than today. The people were on the same amount of land as our current global population - the very same land. Is this gift perhaps some sort of slight return of Eden. Is this the dawn, even merely in principle, of genuine ownership – and in fact righteous boundaries. By right rather than fight. That very same specific land was, and remains today, saleable commodity.

The Abophiles traditionally feel themselves *owned by the land* – or so I have heard from some. They have dominical *protocols*. Perhaps firm private ownership is something of which they are barely aware. Their proprietary connections are relinquished as the encampment, possibly with hut, is abandoned. The hunting ground remains tribal territory.

Custodianship, in some circumstance, may be more convenient than outright ownership. And in fact it may be a greater personal commodity. Of course a property's custodian may also be its owner. As other than commercial-commodity, a house is often sacred to its custodian. In that regard the custodian logically has priority and all first rights in all three - its use, its development and its hospitality potential. Yet as a facility, not as a home, the house may well serve others approved of by the custodian.

With no sense of ownership there are no boundaries. But there are indefinite limits made by the operational *room* of the strong. And mutual limits by neighbourly agreement. With no sense of ownership we are penguins wandering in a land with no land based corporate structure. And why not?

Ownership is never strictly outright. Council rates, like the weather, demand maintenance. If the infirm cannot keep up to the demands, then others must go in to bat for them. Ownership is big these days. How does one do that? Own. I'm doing it now. Now, own, won. I own. Now I've won? Wow! Or is it more to the point to say that owning is sharing that which is established as mine by communal *protocol*. Whatever, having achieved ownership, insofar as it means nobody short of an army or a rate collector can ask us to move on, **a major new scope in our life occurs.**

Ownership creates limits, quantities; theodolitical boundaries - with their implications. And it creates the form of the public common land suited to the character of the politics of its creators - roadways, parks, squares. This *common* is the community's *ergonomic room* - plus its possessions. But! Owned by the creator of mother nature - whether abstract or real.

There are limitations today. Limitations on achievement of ownership. There is a mortgage culture. Blend this with avarice and other social ills and we have problems that severely stress happy compromise. In early times feudal ownership was vaguely similar. But earlier still the personal domain was pretty much the rule. I made it. I was here first. I need it. It's mine. Society though was still often an all-pervading influence - leader dominance, group *protocol*. But, at least, there was always another empty valley to be taken.

Whether you own it or not, a house can be there for longer than your earthly bardot. You could well be on your way through your house from your previous to your next. Your talismans and artefacts may travel with you. We may take our house only as we can carry or within the bounds of our practical imagination.

Ownership may limit your movement, for psychological or practical reasons - procrastination, slow resale. That can be a very significant thing in lifestyle and *beingrowing*. It can be a cumbersome thing, moving house. In addition though acceptance of a long abode may add a new dimension or answer a need that opens a door.

There ought to be places where we can lodge freely. There ought to be places we can own, where we can dwell freely. Be an occasional nomad, or a perpetual nomad, as the fancy takes us. Settle in your Way. Settler and nomad. As settled rocks and flowing waters. A fine sieving event; all in the way we settle down to a chat with the nomads flowing through town. All in the way the nomad settles down. Transience and ownership. Urban nomad. Nomadic urbanite. People in motion. *Doing housing* and roaming – *nomurbic.* Creating houses, lodgings and happy tracks. There are caravaners, at least one community of them, this very day finding a hard edge to this romance as settled people in England find them contrary to their own scheme of things - the nomad, the woodpecker (once classified extinct) and the dinosaur.

Financial ownership, from mortgage, correct or not, is a significant compromise factor. Render to Caesar and support the long long movement to win him over. Seek to 'inherit the Earth'.

The SPIRIT
of CULTURE
ANYPERSON'S HOUSE

*T*he culture and nurture of spirit. *Lifestyle,* locale, people in motion doing their domestic things. Together they grow more than mere convenient facility and shelters. **If we choose to house, rather than lodge,** we will always embody cultural developments and spirited design. *In some, this will be compensation for that which we lose the minute we go with permanent abode.* The cultivation of our spirit. Things of the soul. Anyperson's house will do something of this. Anyperson's house has some expression or design pertinent to the spirits of its conception and construction.

Not everyperson knows it but their *domestic-arrangements* really must suit the whims of the soul. Different things for each of us. But in our locales and communities we grow alike, spiritually and culturally; in many ways mutually attentioned. Birds of a feather and people together grow together. Culture, we know, is more than 'the look'. But the appearance of the house to the community and to the dweller, externally and internally, strikes a loud note in our thoughts and activities of house and home. The visual aspects arise from the nature of the world, the design, broad culture and construction. The pastiche of intentional visual expression, enjoyable or otherwise, is not a mandatory requirement for a beautiful house. But people often prefer cultural expression ahead of the look of natural pragmatics. *Homemaker; if looking to construct a new or an established architectural style for the delight of your culture, and for the aesthetic it gives, ensure that you see the style in its full urban context and measure its true and total impacts.* Make the style *kosher*, if not way beyond – even if necessarily radical. A big ask, to secure a big lifestyle on a big planet. But it's only for us people. There is guidance herein.

Community culture and community spirit are manifest in the house. In this regard, community may be local, national or ancestral - and usually it is all three. It can be interpreted right there in any house; cultural markings - succinct sometimes, unconscious others. You can celebrate anything that you want in the cultural attachés of your house. The rising sun of Australian Federation is filigreed into the slowly aging gables of early twentieth century Australian houses. The social more of frugality pervades traditional Japanese dwellings. And if we have the wisdom to read it, the minimal intervention of Albert Gallopilong's accommodation is also culture attaché – celebration occurs with Albert's accommodation; perhaps as simply as others celebrate the bus as they step onto it.

Cheekyfella Talkabout once used a worn out family car, which he had turned onto its roof, so that he could lie under the engine hood out of the sun, his spears protruding from the windows. He has rejected, aside from a sideways smirk, the cultural connotation of the *'Classic'* model of car and its fading *husk*-like circumstance and imbued the arrangement with his ancestral ethic of rudiment. Anyperson's *domestic-arrangement*, anywhere, embodies patterns techniques, curios and reflexes emanating from their culture. We can modify this by the act of creating some cultural heritage for our children, or some new invading race - and thus advancing the culture. Culture is a valuable broad social asset, which includes colouring our abodes; and to which we contribute with our abodes.

Cultural spirit imbues in the Mediterranean. Some, in *doing their housing*, customarily frequently touch up their whitewashed house fronts and footpaths. After meals the window frames may recieve a fresh coat to keep away flies. The urbane vernacular handmade nature of the houses and the purity of white cleanliness is itself cultural spirit. Lesser in cultural comfort, and begging of spirit, is the daunting, wrong way taint of monotonous mediocrity, shown through Australian semi-industrial lowest cost universal necessity suburban housing. Perhaps visiting foreigners see the beautiful spirit of these dwellings which is lost in the banal acceptance and tired familiarities of the locals – heroes are never recognised at home. So those at home constantly furbish. The cultural spirit here sometimes emerges by way of expressive overlay on the mediocrity, like an art canvas being covered or adorned with domestic passions to sprout at times great diversity. Those people active in their housing *adapt* to, colour, and develop this suburban environment. You may find gladiolas and concrete Aborigine figurines in some renegade Australian *Pale*'s faded rose front garden. Beer bottle walls to a back shed to contrast the street-common machined monotony of the old brick veneer or the older gloss painted weatherboard house.

Seashells set in cement-render on the brick base. Plaster garden gnomes, old tyres cut bent and painted to look like swans, dressed up dolls adorning on hooks to the weatherboards. And sometimes house names produce colloquial patinas over the base housing reality. A shine from the dwellers leaves the once universal weatherboarded or brick monotony as incidental white space on the canvas highlighted with honest passion. Ethic and integrity; the right way and the wrong. **The spirit of the action**; a key to *doing* it well. Simple brave integrity exercised in fabricating your house, or just in daily decor, shows up as awesome beauty. The beholding eye of the house buyer, however, may not see the beauty; being unenlightened of the romance as to how the appearance came about. In your nature is a free spirit of creativity toward household. It may be weak or strong. If you snare this spirit with dishonesty, timidity, or other foible, you make it difficult. It is common, and only sometimes wise, for excessively capitalist people to limit their creativity to the measure of money. When renovating or building, to always consider the resale value, and therefore to likely remain in what is conservative mediocrity in their effort. Better play it safe and stick with a *pale* kosher – some lesser vogue. For what price would these people sell their souls? Same as most of us.

Planting and landscape can have a huge depth of immensely sustaining cultural impact – from gladiolas to jungles with treasures therein. The same variety of expressions may apply.

Integrity sometimes means acting with courage and certainly without negligence. By being in touch with the culture, times and taste of your community by making, or only modifying, house with integrity, as a fellow culture creator - a step beyond the basic you - you will make something beautiful, and something more valuable to yourself, and thereby your community. A top class kosher or something in the *ecopical* beyond; which may even be a lonely abused hero. Ask for help if you need to, even if you are the Minister for Domestic Culture. This is all part of *doing* your own housing – or that of others.

The way we live and think shows through. The traditional Japanese ideal of poverty; the house being merely a temporary home in the realty reality and materialism and grandiosity being superficial. This ideal shows through with usually a better quality of standard materials and workmanship being all that elevates the house of the well-to-do. For some the ideal leads to a trait in house appearance that leaves wealth and prestige discretely concealed behind a humble front. Build this ideal *next door* among houses of some raucously bold Hollywood *boulevard* ideal - among opulent pitstops in social whirl. Both of these cultural ideals reflect reality and sustaining arguments. Perhaps a greater sanity of culture may produce something in between. *It does seem that East and West are meeting.*

The profundity of the Feng Shui meets pitstop opulence. Synthetic materials are set in place by elemental truths. Polypropylene, earth, water and fire. **Fluorescent purple acrylic, earth** ochre, pigment and opal. **All cultural ideal is amalgamated by some fission.** A most innocent architect, the swallow, arcs its *room* in a winged roam through the surrealistic forms and space of artist Dali's residence. Cheekyfella's country-with-*Classic* dwelling place melts away the sheik's imported-marble-and-gold. The house of the individual is forged by one's community culture and sharpened by one's very own spirited contribution – one's citizenship of physical expression in the city of the simple tolerating street.

So very integral with our life; our *dwelling-contraptions* carry indelible *handmarks* from both our culture and the personalities involved in design and construction – builders' thumbs smear in the formed-up *playdough of the Earth* but this is often obvious only to an architectural tracker. Yet once seen, these *handmarks* are as obvious as the very brick and wood. And therefore usually today we find it easy to identify the economy and resource persuasions of industry in the appearances and limitations of our dwellings. Existing industry; blunt ogre, hard geometry, toxins, deceptive economy. These *industry-marks* are given life by the owners' physical expressions.

Culture is art, technology, values, vernacular, different strokes, ordinary or special for the day. It is cherished as heritage and celebrated as expendable. In housing, it is more excitement over visuals than over functions. Though it certainly pervades the theatre of *room*. How long before the truly great tradition of country kitchen vanishes to meals-on-wheels, restaurants pre-packaging and take-aways. Low Carl tells, "it's been, for a long time, popular to have no kitchen in New York; always eat out or bring home the cooked finale. The same thing has occurred with the outdoor clothesline, for drying. And the art of the brick chimney seems to give way to the city's version of a didgeridoo party, the home theatre - in-lieu - of - barbecue – for less than one percent of the world anyway."

The cultural expression from our houses is both intended and unintended - part intuitively spontaneous, part cognitively intentional. Pragmatic and sometimes unfortunate visual impacts sit in posterity. *The physical expressions communicate to our psyche and senses.* Sometimes it's a psycho-physical harmony, if not a punk thing that is expressed. Other times industrial pastiche, low integrity or careless workmanship. Expression comes through the visual things - arrangement of materials, colours, shapes, lines, and masses. It comes through aesthetic and legible things. And audible and smellable. Expression conveys ideas, concepts, emotions, images or customs via the intellect, imagination, passions or emotions. In a different way to the nomadic landscape, house-based expression significantly impacts our destiny through our reaction-based *beingrowings*. Colloquial tastes. Period fashions. The unavoidable cultural truths of trades and industry. Some *dwelling-contraptions* can be compared to a fascinating organic miracle and a most exotic masterpiece of art - that swallow, that Dali. They are beautiful **and so is the ordinary sprout of integrity** – a happy shack.

Things cultural are usually not well achieved as a worthy balance against prefabricated components and synthetic materials - at our current phase of development that is. The cosmic things cultural faint against murderous orthogonal town planning - the drab bitumen streets, once the territory of a that *Classic* family sedan – now upturned by a strong organic hand. Dali is a swallow, Cheeky a Dali. The story is poetry. The dunny an icon. *A labelled fluoro-purple plastic detergent bottle shackled to a sublimely simple wooden spear.* A detergent bottle. A wooden spear. *The interior can be out there.* The tales abound, variously sacred, of generations of Harmoninnies reflected and anchored in Gallopilong's country. A big gnarled tree where an old grandfather sang a song of a wealth-of-meaning, some rocks flung there by some rainbow serpent, some pigment painting by some indigenous Dali, carved circles on an overhanging ledge. In which culture does the Reader grow? Is his or her house imbued with it?

The philosophy and poetry behind the intended architectural expression, as we say, is of the epoch; the society of that epoch. That's not all that should be said; it is also of the personal principles of life of all those involved in fabrication of the buildings. It is of the social and time-of-life circumstances of some small number of individuals, even one, who built - designer, builder, renovator, adaptor, decorator, gardener. Like a good book or didgeridoo, the philosophy is linked to a spiritual aspect which is beyond the physical-psychological facility of the construction. The Australian dream of ownership of a small plot with a good house is materialistic in part, but ultimately it is communal, cultural and naively spiritual.

The reality of this publication is some witness to the socially all-pervading influence of *domestic-contraption*.

There is some designer control of the cultural persuasions of our houses. Houses can be made to express specific whims or disciplines. Cultural cringe, culturally inept, uneducated, punk, eccentric, ego, the good bad ugly, Art Deco, the architects frustrations with all of these in his clients, and vice versa the clients wonder too. Houses, *boxes*, suburban *layout*, community *layout*, urbane design. We aren't looking good – over all. We are beginning to look uglier and we seem to be taking the gentle and the meek away from their inheritance. Not all. Only most. *Sustainability is coming into the spirit of culture.* **Building only that which at least seems to be sustainable within balanced ecology.** Sustainability - the beauty of nature, an *ecopical* aesthetic to be expressed. Very quickly, urgently, please. "Lissen 'ere, a bit, to my Uncle Albert!" suggests an unheard voice.

Culture. There is nothing all that special about it. Culture is simply what we like as people. We do things the way we like to do them and we like what we do. Traditions build. We pepper them with our own idiosyncrasy. Our *culture nurtures* our spirit as we *do* our very own little bit of housing.

ORDINARY IDIOSYNCRASIES

ANYPERSON'S HOUSE

It seems always in these times that the big urgencies are with the big scales. Environmental and industrial ecologies, water pollution, hurricanes and earthquakes. The gnarly catastrophe ahead of the riders of the *galloping* horses. Global and national economies. The media and politics don't talk much about towns, neighbourhoods, houses and ordinary individuals. The new environmental needs of the crowded consumer age become, through wisdom, the needs of any individual. Each individual brick needs to be good. Do not crumble. Play your common role. I wonder though; Little White Cloud's grandfather, or rather some real person like him, did prophesy, decades before our ozone layer knowledge, to be proven fairly correct, that if we had not balanced ecologically before the holes came in the sky, then the only hope was spiritual; the world will be lost. Our common role at times must be modified in the light of our arising unique individual initiatives – idiosyncrasies.

Our own thought and reflexes inform us pretty much as to what we need by way of a house. But education, social persuasion and discussion enhance the situation, sometimes profoundly. Sometimes profoundly. Instances of housing that are impacted by substandard status quo, commercial pressures and globalisation of culture and industry can be fought - only with that education and persuasion.

We relate to uniqueness and different strokes. Our own and others'. Idiosyncrasy. Equally, probably, we relate to commonality - the joiner and divider of individual worlds. *Commonality, the stage for id.* Architecture by its nature, and our tendencies, enhances this relationship between id and common. The normal forms, materials and expressions are a working basis through which uniqueness is integrated, intentionally or otherwise; like the canvas of weatherboards.

Anyperson's house has idiosyncrasy. Even those who try hard to be normal Joneses make their own id. Your house is not just anyperson's house – "Except when it's on the market," Global comments with a greedy grin. We all have thumbprints. In common all houses carry uniqueness. It's a very ordinary thing. We like privacy. It's very ordinary. Simple self. Ordinary old me. We are all one of those. With thumbprints marvellously complex and unique like snowflakes. Like 'old blue eyes' we do it our way. Albeit, very often, our way of handling the over-riding adversities. The mundane ordinariness of repetitive technique and appearance. Familiarity, ordinarily breeding contempt. Ordinary *little boxes* on the hillside. Innocent little cultural extrusions. Don't you just love 'em.

> Mix together the ordinary and the id. The rooster shows his own *unique* colours planted in his *ordinary* poultry meat. Let the ordinary be your canvas. A setting for the jewel of id. Id the basis of human society. Little *boxes* with garden gnomes, unique colour schemes and the odours of Irish stew. Where one's id is joined by others the ordinary will change – just a little. Then a little more. Trends, fashions, avant-garde, vernacular.

It is not only the individual dweller who requires the amenity of house. Humanity, the nation and society make the common demands. The ecology is making common demands too. Over-riding demands. Your own special demands, arising from your taste, family, hobbies, eccentricities etc, in part concur with those social demands and one would hope, *the ecological ones too.* All in all, one would hope, the *ecopical* ones.

Sensibly we utilise convention but add our own *persona.* If necessary, modify or remove convention to make way for our persona. This is easiest in new construction on 'unadulterated' land. Redevelopment of a Mumbai flat, or a dwelling unit in uptown Smogton, plagued with the personae of past tenants and designers is not so easy. In addition, in our gregarine way, we are able to enjoy the persona imprints of others as part of the fabric of our house – so long as the *armpits* don't exude garlic odour.

> As it happens most people are in houses not specifically built for them. A disabled person may be the first to declare this, and an architect the second. Adapt the ordinary. Universality in houses is a basis for adaptation and conformity.

There are QUANTA in the CONTRAPTION

ANYPERSON'S HOUSE

Flip the coin from this psycho banter to the muscular facts. Consider the weight of your own house. Tent, mansion. A few kilos, hundreds of tonnes. There are maybe a 100,000 square kilometres of house floor in the world - concrete and carpet, woodchip and glue, tamped earth and oil. Albert Gallopilong has walked none of it. Footings, walls, ceilings, roof. How many nails and power-driven screws? How much steel? Rich earthy brick, clear sheets of glass. How much fuel to bake brick? Mining, processing, manufacturing, trucking and selling. The gathering, processing and using of the *playdough of the Earth*; and the *room* used on the Earth.

Those in a house have added to as much roof as is necessary to house the floor; plus, they have added to gardens, roads, sewers, factories etc. You individually share responsibility, even if the house is not new, to be pedantic. Rather than build new in Fern Hollow you may see that logically you must go to reinhabit an old house in Smogton. The lust for the new house is sobered by the realisation that a sixth generation house is only one sixth your responsibility - simply speaking. That's quite a potent observation. All new-house enthusiasts should think about it. Reuse of a cast off *husk* can be quite smart even if the sunshade is useless.

Quantities. Materials, time, effort, space and land. They relate to economy, limitations, sustainabilities, human potential, effort and money. When balanced against the potentials of the builder, quantities limit the sizes in house fabrication. Against our ecological ineptitude, they destroy, somewhat, whilst they create. As consumption for our avarice, they bloat and impoverish. They tire the muscles and provide scope for dwelling.

Five buckets of mud, a bag of coin, cubit by cubit sums a house, and its land. Traditionally for folk, primitively or indigenously houses are quite small and in scale with the hands-on build potential of the dweller and some friends in trades. Compact, shared and close. No need for a crane.

To give the perspective of quanta in the whole housing thing we note;

F I V E   A S P E C T S   O F   H O U S I N G ;

---

1. **PHYSICAL** ASPECTS   -   *playdough*, land, *nacre*, shape, location ..
2. **PSYCHOLOGICAL** ASPECTS   -   *handmarks*, persona, *synthetic aesthetic, nature's earthy nurtures*, contentment, security ...
3. **CULTURAL** ASPECTS   - cost of address, *synthetic aesthetics*, style, market, contribution to locale ...
4. **PERSONAL LIFESTYLE** ASPECTS   -   party *room*, taste, eccentricities, effort in *doing* it, *synthetic aesthetic, mother of pearl* ...
5. **ECOSYSTEM** ASPECTS   -   seeping sewerage, excess, native locale, energy efficiency, resource balance ...

The **PHYSICAL** includes the quanta relating to the site, the extraction of materials and the energy and the processes involved in building. Similarly, the other four aspects have quanta breakdowns. These, however, are too extensive to convey right here. Imagine for example the quantities of one's **PSYCHOLOGICAL** that are affected and formed by just a shiny floor. Or the change of **PERSONAL LIFESTYLE** impacts when moving from one house to another. And imagine the **ECOSYSTEM** impacts of industry. These are vast and complex notional equations which I can but encourage to seep from their realities in your life through the tapestries of this book. The **PSYCHOLOGICAL** value of a free option for long deep hot bath outweighs the stress put on it by society's arising low-energy-use regulations. The regulations mean well, but the makers and the culture behind them, sometimes are locked into calculations that isolate the subject from the complex equations of the socio-cosmos. The *armpit* arts of common-sense and intuition are necessary in the leadership of regulation. *There is no doubt that we need regulation to tame our ravenous abuse of the limited quanta available to housing. Regulation is a kind of detention. An insult that we have to have.*

The more glorious your house the greater the quantity of time you put into it. Wealth may dispute this but truth demands a basic person-to-environment balance, where the load is always carried by some number of someone's. So don't forget, when deciding to devote effort to housing; compute the glory minus the time that could be spent elsewhere, maybe on walkabout or scientific research. Like the worth of a hot bath, the capacity to compute this is limited. Time can become a lesser factor, subject to money, providence, inheritance, giving and inventiveness. A woman of a specific culture can make a grass hut with that which is around her in a short while. A builder with industrial resource can do a lot more in the same time. This is a development in quantity equations that enables us to have mansions relative to the houses of years gone by. Cheeky and White Cloud though are not particularly phased by that. They enjoy the hut scenario; the concept of achievable floor area per indigenous debt-free builder - with time remaining for the other things in living. The economy of action availed by that upturned *Classic* sedan gives provision with a grin - who needs to shelter or secure a magazine rack, a birthday cake or a plasma televisory contraption?

In balance there is only so much one can do. However, attitudes modify the outcomes. *Attitudes* weigh into the quanta. Innocent excess. Practical abundance. Minimum standards. Cultural orthodox. *Nomad minima, boulevard bold.* Buckingham palace, though it pales meeker in the face of other palaces, can take care of itself - is it real? The barest essentials, humble economy. The most wicked excess. Many of us look with restraint - toward minimum housing. An optimum dream may well be lavish. Nomad maximum is scant. Or is it as vast as that outdoor interior.

How much fabric and money does it take to facilitate just the privacy amenity that we seek? Each *accumulating* domestic facility and *room* amenity contributes to the quanta bill. How much time can we afford for finesse of finishes - Indonesian woodcarvings, finest quality paint? Can we do with less bedroom floor - bunks, roll-up beds? What proportion of cost and worth is the roof? The cost of being orthodox, conventional, in your particular domestic circumstance - it might be cheaper to build a dome. A proportion of effort per luxury. Per necessity. Running costs, time spent on maintenance, warmth, the view, image, aesthetics. All are cost, time, materials, effort, land. Cost priorities and balance. Payback periods on floor slab insulation and double-glazing. A second storey may save time in moving around the house. The area of sun receptive windows is balanced with cost, insulation, privacy, wall space and desired sunlight. What balances the length of fences and garden paths? Area of lawn, verandas?

A huge amount of money is circulated because of housing. Not all effort is money orientated. Sometimes there is no economic exchange in house making. This can be by indigenous exchange and mates rates. For most Terrans, especially the Suburbophile, this is not normal. Generosity and barter are responsible for say half of Australian exchange and all its giving. The social place of housing encourages this non-economic exchange; unlike the construction of retail facilities or stock exchange offices. Similarly there is a *vast* unknown cash/housing exchange – until fascism squeezes it all out.

In our national economy. The fundamental of housing is about three percent of the complete market. This does not account for personal refinement, landscape or furnishing. Nor any of local government rates, public works, mining, forestry and factory facilities that are directly associated with housing. Around one percent of all Australian government outlay goes to constructing housing. A similar order of money, twice as much in England, is spent on all the other forms of construction that make up the nations overall fabric, towns and cities; offices, bridges, roads and so on; but these in turn are partly joined to the housing effort. Social welfare rental assistance, and defence services housing are extra considerations. Australian domiciles. The house is about 3/4 of total family wealth, usually a consolidating asset, sometimes a hedge against inflation. And usually 3/4 of their debt! It is this portion of personal wealth that is of main significance to the individuals' operational buoyancies. It is about five years of average earnings (comparable to about a year and half in the 1930s, for a smaller house of different quality). That money takes a lot longer than five years to accrue or repay.

People borrow most of the cost of building. People borrow to build houses! **Build debt!** Small to huge interest amounts are paid! Home sweet loan. The rich get richer, the poor get the picture. Frustration or simply wanting more? Both – even the land costs too much, if you'd be happy in a hut. And, subject to location, the regulations may not allow you to build anything less than an orthodox *box* – 'less' having a variable meaning. The process of getting housed is very often frustrated ... *"and frustration is not an aim of the builder."*

If somebody developed a housing construction system that allowed a house to be built with one month's earnings, would the market ultimately swing the economy so that it would take five years to earn that one month's money? Would it be rebalanced by gold taps? The ball and chain principle. People and money. The more prime the necessity the more we will pay for it. More likely; people very often will spend as much as they can to increase their house.

Money goes in all directions when a house is organised, is built, maintained or is developed. The costs support a lot more than the work *quanta* in baking bricks, producing plastics, enforcing regulations and milling timber. Site aside, more than half of the direct cost of a suburban house is for the effort of on-site construction - as a rule of literary thumb. The rest of the cost is in design, materials, components, connections, advertisings and administration. This applies to all, *ticky tacky* to *boulevard*, and would reduce with the application of *ecopicality*. Indirect and inestimable costs arise with the societal and ecological *ripples*.

Enormous *Housefandango* effort has been expended as the very cause of that grave ecological concern, and to drive every residential nail, place every single brick, weave every grass hut, manufacture every porcelain toilet bowl, make regulations rather than spears and sell every sold house. One could go on page after page. What percentage of all human effort is this? **What percentage of your personal effort has it been so far?** Why do we do all this?

Effort in science, sport, art, theatre, travel, agriculture, education, food supply etc comes before, with, and following effort in housing. Some effort is prerogative, other is clearly mandated.

Like Bobby you may have been in a job, repaying a loan on the house in which you now live. The proportion of your pay going to your mortgager is plainly a partial measure of your housing effort. The actual work you do in that job may be effort to some other cause, say, space travel, solar system walkabout effort. Money converts some of your specialist work-a-day job effort to housing. The interest picked up by your creditor may fund his house also. For some, housing comes in conglomeration with all they do and achieve, for others, it is a sole goal. For some it is a motorcycle and bed-roll effort, for others it is life's goal. Wisdom prevailing, the effort and return can be congenial, depending on the temperament and *attitude* of the dweller. One ought to be shrewd at times, lest the market-place enslave one, with housing as the shackle. Some ways of housing take less effort than others, and sometimes there is more return for less effort. That depends on how honest you are with yourself, and on good design and masterplanning.

National economy is often assessed in accord with the number of houses being built. This is odd, in that when the farmer finishes building his house he is relieved to be able to get on with farming – but when the nation finishes building it panics. At the times when the nation's people are all but fully housed, this is foolish. And when we are combating serious eco-problems, this is small minded – unwholistic. We do note though, that when housing stops, its industrial and services support stops also – huge in the *Ecosculpture* – & hence the worry. When the farmer's sheep are sheared the shearers stop. Certainly populations grow and need to be housed, but the increase is minor in regard to total consumptions. Perhaps it's not that there is decreased demand for houses but that more people than usual can't afford them. Surely there is a serious issue here to be addressed by the nation. It costs people lots of money to foul the ecology – and more to fix it.

Is the line we need to draw drawing itself?

In Australia about 1/3 of all full and part time workers are employed directly on housing construction. Around say half of the of the remaining 2/3 worker energy goes ultimately to housing; that is through forestry, logging, mining, electricity, gas, water, transport, communications, finance services, business services, property services, public administration, retail and wholesale trade, manufacturing and even agriculture. In this scenario, of about twenty million people, there are about a 1/4 of a million houses completed in a year, and about eight million existing. About 1/6 of that spent on house building is spent on alterations and additions. In the volatile global world this may change, as we move on in the early years of the twenty first.

These limits, along with the physical forces of nature and cosmos, and people movement, and common sense limit what we can do in building. How high can we go with a house? How far underground? How much floor to sweep?

The cubic capacity, weight and ground cover of house for each inhabitant? Think of a **set of scales**. You are on one tray of the balance. The other tray holds your own housing quanta against you. A pile of iron ore, gallons of fuel, telephone bills, rich earthy brick, clear sheets of glass. Trees to rafters and smoke. Ecology and economy. How important are the quanta equations? The figures for the equations are clouded in emotion, pragmatics and culture. We shall talk more on this.

The conventional Australian house is the most 'economical' Australian house, the *box* on a block of land. But it's not the most complete. **Well alright, for those who love their orthogonal *box*, there is nothing wrong with it, but is it lacking?** Are the quantities optimally juggled to produce the best entity? Budgets have limits while, for some, imaginations do not. The work of those of us who contribute to the orthodox, regulations and commercial promotion

106

could do with a quantity of imagination. Why are we not utopian today, or better still *ecopian*?

HOUSEMARKS AFTER HANDMARKS

ANYPERSON'S HOUSE

Now: the influence of housing on a person. What proportion of all influence on this earth is the influence of housing? The indispensable *right-angles*, the stuff of which they are built and that so many love to intersperse; to whence do their *ripples* pulse? This is difficult to trace, because other substantial worldly interventions and reactions are woven inseparably with housing - social ego, art, cultural life, natural environment and events, energy use, income, education and roads, to name a few. Some broad categories in which we might measure the **influence of housing** are economics, *psychology*, ecology, work effort, time, progressing civilisation and gregariousness.

Looking at *only one* of the abovementioned; does housing influence *psychology?* Architecturally, among psychologists there has been some disagreement. This is odd! Functional impact aside, *architecture does influence our feeling.* And our *behaviour, psychology and in fact our lifestyle.* We know this from experience. Dissenters must surely be mere *shadows* of psychologists. Those not acknowledging house impact on psychology simply do not understand that circadian rhythm & aesthetics are as much a part of time, motion & space design as ergonomics and mechanical efficiency. Did you get that?! A light hearted feeling, can be encouraged largely, slightly or completely by a beautiful house or place of encampment. Or even by cleaning a dirty house. Perhaps it cannot buy eternal happiness or even a continuous joy, but it can form a sustaining base (that at times may fade). Or shine. Or simply somehow subliminally assist. Or sometimes detract. A good dose of delight from a beautiful *room* assists anybody's internal power. Imagine *the world's most beautiful room.* Cheeky with Uncle Albert in heart weighs the beautiful *room* against that which it obscures, infects, deprives, depletes; and the fullness of the time it took to build. Well okay, in *defence* of the house ... there are no locked doors in nature to raise a happy sense of physical security.

Interiors may be created as extremely synthetic environments. We can put ourselves away from the sustaining scents and fragrances of earth, plants and animals for example. Deprivation can be near total, 'provided' by a *float tank*; not a house, a senseproof *contraption*, incorporating body-temperature water; one floats oblivious, allowing the mind to journey almost 'unfettered' by *nature's earthy nurtures* – an ultimate *seclusion*. Houses don't go this far, but **they can get you part way there** – the *paling trap of interior* may transform the *housebound*, whilst the wiser enjoy tropical balance. Unlike the *galloping* exterior the interior, powered by its grip on our time, wings us to seats, screens, lights, gyms and many things civilised; so much to our joy that, tv bound Anglophiles, Aussies, Kiwis and Yanks, average maybe 20 hours of their day in various interiors – cars, sheds, shops, subways …. "Ah!! The land of sun, surf and great outdoors?! …" articulates many a cross-cultural Blackfella, " … Th'old days mighta been tough, but bring 'em back please!".

While it is definitely not all-powerful, architecture does influence feeling. However, psyche activity being what it is, people can at will encourage, consciously accept or counter that influence - a little.

Little White Cloud was overcome. She actually shed tears over and totally rejected but then she rather loved the dazzling 'Thai Red' that Bobby had quietly and courageously painted the kitchen wall whilst she slept. Illustration of the power of colour relates the intricacies of architectural *psychology* generally. Colour in our buildings influences mood and feeling. It contributes to the immeasurable motivational beauty in the world; the land, cosmos, buildings and interiors. It has bountiful practical use in housing. By subduing glare it improves amenity. Warm and cheerful colour can make us alert to our surroundings. Cool and muted colour won't challenge our concentration. In our emotion, colour can stimulate us, defeat monotony, cause a change of pace. We can note, as others have, that red excites, green tranquillises and blue subdues. The contrasts and interplays of multiple colour benefit the spice of life. And in housing we see colours, colour quantities and colour combinations that we do not see in nature. Some of what I refer to as our peoplekind's *synthetic aesthetic*, our *quicksilver* of personal abstraction is less available in the ochres of our mud hut. It is partly brought by our colour-extracting intervention in nature. Colour is part of the *playdough* for our *dwelling-contraptions* and, therewith, our *synthetic aesthetics, mother of pearl surface and finesse*. There is no doubt that housing lifestyle has cradled incredible developments in our *playdough* colours.

Colour like this is not a feature of nomadic life, but nomads see more sunsets. And have a more subtle appreciation of the ochres.

Wonderful residentially adventurous character that she is, Maggie *Pale* once had everything in her house a shade of pink –
walls, blinds, laminates, pressed-plastic lace, doilies, carpet, washing machine, everything. It left Global sapped of strength on the pink couch, wondering if it was a figment, made of pink powder puff, aggressively speaking eloquently to him, or was it his cherished beloved. Maggie was espousing her disappointment

at the unavailability of pink lighting. Barely breathing and finding courage from his desperate recall of Cheeky's healthy face, and a huge appetite for the chocolate in his bus, Global dragged himself across the floor and trickled eternally through the crack under the door. He spilled off the slippery china-tiled landing onto the resuscitation of the green freshly vacuumed lawn. The ghastly taste of some misplaced blood-and-bone fertiliser was a relative pleasure of revitalisation in the cold light of the mercury-vapour lamp, which he'd recently installed to enhance the welcoming of the always bland filigree-free front porch.

Coloured illumination, pink or otherwise, has a different effect to *surface pigment* of the same colour. There are influences even on *physiology* - note that that doesn't read *psychology*. Chromotherapists have mooted that red light cures rheumatism, arthritis, poor circulation, stiff joints and chills and soothes inflammation and the effects of high blood pressure. Green light apparently is a remedy for infection. It has been shown that in red light time seems longer and objects seem bigger and heavier; while in green or blue, it is opposite. Black *boxes* when painted green felt lighter. *Note that we're not talking* light *here but* surface colour. Blue appears to recede, so blue cars have more dents, blue walls have more scrape marks - being closer than they seem. Red and blue. A lecture in a blue room may bore you. In a red room it may interest you. "So with red we make *room* for interest!" It seems that red physically stimulates the nervous system, blood pressure, respiration and heart. You may find yourself setting a thermostat lower in a red room than in a blue. Warm colours maximise social contact; and cool colours minimise it - such as the *surface* effect encouraged from the mercury-vapour lamps on Global's front porch. Blue-painted walls may have a calming effect. In a dining room blue feels cold. Orange is one that's better there. The ever delightful rats, in blue environment breed more females and in red more males. Maggie *Pale*'s pink has been used in prisons to reduce strength and angst - it brought on Global's appetite for chocolate too. They say noise in a white room sounds louder than noise in a violet room. Lime green relates to nausea – it reduces loitering in toilets. Some yellows can induce nausea. Others have been used to improve children's classroom performance. There's a wide belief that yellow stimulates the intellect. But your child may be more prone to damage his toys in a yellow room. Research also suggests that pink, lavender, pale yellow and green hold pleasant association with odours. Coral, peach, soft yellow, light green, vermilion, flamingo, pumpkin and turquoise have pleasant association with taste. These in food preparation areas make *room* for appetite.

In addition to the example of colour as influence by housing on psychology, we have the influence of space, egg shapes, squares, cultural kosher. Synthetic materials. Organic. Sunlight on the pillow. A clear full-view mirror screwed with a grin to the inside of the toilet door. Amenity, *surface*. Boundaries. Nomad hatters hall no house at all. Formal studies would show rooms-full of tapestried *marks* and response on our psyche. *Our environment significantly influences and creates our behaviour.* This occurs throughout species *beingrowing*, or forefather genetics, and the behaviour of anyperson today. It is scientifically held, that in early life, environment can be made to enhance development of our cerebral cortex. Some say the environment is more likely the creator of behaviour than we ourselves - is Jaweh in here? Cultural environment is heavily supported by housing.

We shape our buildings and they shape us. We've all heard: our hands *mark* our house, then our house *marks* us. We abide in houses that are good, bad and ugly. Just like the people who form the cultures that make them. By the time you finish with this book you will be feeling somewhat touched, if not positively tattooed, by your *dwelling-contraption* and also the others you experience around the place - and the rest of the building about us.
We become *accustomed* in many ways. *Acclimatised*, to our environment. Don't change the newly purchased house too quickly; give its quirks a chance to speak to you. We become accustomed to our compromises too. Accustomisation; a kind of *mother of pearl* renovation of the mind – **sometimes there's no need to physically renovate**. This *marking* of ourselves follows fairly enough from the nature of building, as well as from the *hand-markings* of our house. Minds, emotions, hands and tools in design and building; all are *marks* on the house. It follows that *marks* occur also from the thumbprints of definitive natural law, in that the ceiling is over, the floor under and the walls will sit perpendicular.

Our emotions, behaviour, persona, edification, and family relationships are impacted by the whole environment. And notably, house. Psychology from brick, lace and space. Health too. The world also is significantly impacted. What better point of reference than the place you call home at the moment, and perhaps those places called home by your neighbours. *Housemarks* may set our social measure and self-perception, set our sense of failure, success or adequacy. Am I kosher? Neighbourhoods and class segregation weigh in here too. People, in part, feel socially higher and are healthier and with fewer social maladjustments in *better finished* housing. Bad stables shorten the life span of animals and may cause even sterility & disease. We seek proper stimulation, we adapt and harmonise our housing as far as we can to meet our racially and personally inherited tastes, quirks, and vital housing needs. By far the largest fraction of people on this tender blue-green planet, flecked with roofing tiles and paraphernalia, would be seriously hampered in their personal *beingrowing* if deprived of even these lesser aspects of their housing, let alone, say, a roof, as millions are.

As well as the impact and influence of house on the dwellers themselves; the house places not only freedom, but ha ha restraint and limitation on lifestyle factors such as social life and eating. ***Freedom together with restraint and limitation*** *– yes, a real modification of environment.* In its perspective within environment, society - and alongside nomadism - house fosters a substantiation of

110

spirit, soul, body, lifestyle and magical experience. The extent to which this fostering effects what we are is variable and unknown. It is related to the *quanta* of time spent in relation to housing. It involves personal initiative, standard of design, gregarian security and delusion, creation worship, broad mindedness, ego, the a-priori of freedoms, dweller relations, health, contentment and so on. To actually *measure* this extent is beyond our comprehension. We would be weighing taste, philosophy, delight, dream-house wants, colour, kitsch, problem, expression, heritage, culture, genetics, keeping up with the Joneses – or, heaven forbid, the *Pales* and more.

So one thinks one has made it with one's mod coloured luxury pad - one may be better off in a caravan park if we look at the whole picture.

As plain as the nose on your face. If some of its *ripples* did not make us feel better we would not associate house with romance – but then settlers are a bit *pale*. This is highlighted in the modern world where the options and extended creativity of houses have a few people exuberantly changing them like hats, for fun. Fun is profoundly psychological. Very deep and very meaningful. Very plain. Like house.

PLUGGED IN
ANY PERSON'S HOUSE

S*et in its civilisation,* its socio-industro-cultural order; the house optionally may be *supported* by services and physical infrastructure from industry.

Toilet brush tied to a spear

GRID PIZZ

Supported in its conception, construction and operation. Plugged in, that is. Plugged in at design time. Into industrial fabrications, cadastral boundaries and public accessways. And in particular plugged in by way of its operation.

You may be in a house; plugged in. Maybe with Maggie *Pale* nearby; a short distance away; across the kitchen, through the plaster, the brick, across the gap between the house and the fence running along a cadastral boundary, through the fence, another gap, another wall and across part of another *room* – in her bedroom she powders up. Happily plugged in together in suburban bliss, anxious for the catalogue deliveries and the Tupperware. Or it may be a rural bliss – beautifully buffeted with cows and corn. *Many houses are not plugged in.* Albert Gallopilong's camp is thoroughly plugged in - to the land and his community.

Electricity relates to candle wax, wood stoves, boiling water. It comes by cable from communal power stations as part of what is sometimes called the *services grid*. One may plug into power from one's private waterwheel, wind generator, solar collector, carbide generator or other invention. Most commonly power is from this *grid* or the likes of home fire and elbow grease. The *grid* may also provide incoming tap water, and gas, pipes for outgoing gray water and sewerage, radio, settlers' television, telephone and internet transmissions. Public transport, pizza delivery, laundry services, social services, post and garbage collection variously enhance *grid* lifestyle - the whole town/city/region/'global' provision. It influences the visual geometry of residential property too; a corporate community stamp as well as the languid lines of natural landscape for the house geometry to meet. No *room* for Albert's spear here.

The further from the *grid*, the less opportunity for industrial construction and components; and the more indigenous and self-sufficient the house. The more *grid* plug-ins you have, the more neighbours - an urban styled house - no country orthodox. Switches and ceilings. Spears and stars. Globals and Gallopilongs.

We do however look to the further potentials of satellite transmission – one can be off-*grid* with no neighbours but still access wireless internet, radio, television, telephone. Can we get away from the road?

The car is reaching further and wider in its impact. More cars per house and more houses with cars. Mobility reduces some demand on domestic facility. It modifies lifestyle and therefore house use, location and development. Cheekyfella will make use of a car at times for a variation on the walkabout, a 'lounge-roam' as he calls it, and when it will no longer roam he may leave it, upturned, to natural resource – "Correction Monte," Cheekyfella languidly comments as he turns his head from the dust covered windscreen to the 'Roam Sweet Home' shingle on his dashboard, "I think '*living*-roam' conveys the message better." The impact of the car on the house isn't quaint, not really. Look at it;

a carport or multi-purpose garage or more, parking spaces, the jewel in the driveway, driveway crossovers, oil stains, groceries in, night light, more roof and walls, a strong integration with the street, big bland dominant doors, gaping gates and concrete paving. Where there once was some garden, stable or house – now the mobile interior, the key *grid* connection, the romance of the big bright streamlined freedom, the car. The garbo. The delivery truck. The bus. The railway station. No butterflies. Peaking oil resource.

All of these plug-in services are significant. In-house componentry. Power, tap water and sewerage are valued ahead of carpets, furniture, floor area and so on. A power outlet in a tipi would significantly impact lifestyle. Instead of a fire, centre-floor of the tipi, is an electric radiator. The flap-bell rings and the postman delivers the bill. Certainly a redesign of today's conventions could cope with all-round heat radiation and the power cord could be concealed under the ground. In reality have we found greater value for indigenous life in the *services grid* than in the simple earthly traditions? For most, regardless of coercion, we have; there are plenty of televisions in simple mud houses. Traditions are remodelled around the *grid*. The draw of the modern world, which supports the *grid*, itself sees the tipi in its magical context replaced by a *grid* environment. As we see our failing ecology though we wonder if those staying with original indigenous tradition are the more honourable. And that their housing is of greater integrity. There are many options in this world. Communal power supply by small local *grid* appears a reasonable option.

The in and out links that we make, between modern urban houses and public or community services, can make our houses easier to manage but also subject to hard to manage perpetual bills. One cannot always do away with services in favour of various degrees of autonomy. We can't easily be off *grid* in order to be independent and maybe away from roads. It may for instance be deemed mandatory, by state authority, to use the power *grid* if it runs by your house - this can be challenged. It is however possible to build an autonomous house. Self-sufficient. Off *grid*. You do not have to plug in. This provides both intricate and fundamental variations to house and lifestyle. On a community scale in the West, its potential remains largely unexplored. The location of an autonomous house is not constrained by the pre-planned *services grid* – the *grid* traditionally is based on *urban centralisation principles*. Urban decentralisation possibilities exist, in balance with centralisation, on domestic, suburban and city scales. Today any community planning based on *decentral* principles is pretty much by accident; or left-over from the old days, or only a radical future plan. There are significant eco plusses for this autonomous style. Waste, can be treated and

used or recycled. Your own body waste can produce methane gas for home use. There are various ways to make optimum use of water. Perhaps drain your bath into your toilet cistern and so on. Ingenious systems have been devised. Power can be generated privately using tidal movement, ocean currents, geothermal energy, wind and sun. Old bike wheels may make a wind generator. There's a pedal powered washing machine and you have mini-hydro turbines on your rainwater downpipes. We invent. Solar energy equipment can be made by a handyman or purchased as sophisticated equipment. If necessary a twelve volt battery or sadly a petrol powered generator can backup. We *accumulate*, but we maintain some freedom from giant corporatism & the stifle it brings to *nature's nurtures* & lifestyle.

An 'autonomous' house may also be self-sufficient food-wise. Some exist under the name of Bioshelter – *biohouse* or bio-*dwelling-contraption* are names more to my point. A *biohouse* is a hi-tech maintenance regimed, maximally modern, fully autonomous *dwelling-contraption.* It is also a grass hut and garden with a waterwheel in a stream. Looking to go all the way, *biohouses* may also generate excess power and so feed electricity to the *grid* supply. If there's no stream there are fish tanks for food, everything. You might not need to go outside for a year, hence the 'bio'. The 'shelter' as a descriptor is a hangover from the 1970s. There may be no reason to paint them pink throughout. Biohouse potentials are minor in the econo-ecological circumstance. *Biocities* - might be our only hope. Correction, surely; it *is* our only hope – improved by the cultural sensitivities of simple *ecopicality* and supporting *ecopical* ecological principles.

There is a psyche thing with this. You are very likely to have a plastic switch in a wall near you at the moment; to make an electricity flow. The flick of a switch is a reminder of industry, invention - capacities generally beyond the individual or small community. It is also a bread and butter thing - a regular invoice to meet. Meter and its reader. Furnace, tower or dam and street wires, cable to gable. All for the switch on the wall. Gallopilong will switch his attention to light, cooking or warmth but he will look to the moon, the morning and fire. His pizza will scurry by on the ground, should he care to fork it with his spear. But facing a less romantic reality, the quanta of time and effort he spends out hunting and gathering may be something similar to the time *Pale* spends earning to pay for the *grid*.

Somewhere over the rainbow beyond the conference on the nuclear warship there is a
domestic lifestyle eco-sustainable *grid*-autonomous-house balance:

E c o p i c a l i t y ...

♫Walk with *ecopicality*, talk with *ecopicality*.
Swing with switches, spears and p e r s o n a l i t y.
　　'*Ecopicality*',
　　　　　　　... sing it as 'Personality' (the old '60s
Lloyd Price song, google it now) — THIS IS HOW WE
SHOULD FEEL ABOUT OUR FIGHT FOR
OPTIMUM ABODE; sing it in the kitchen with the
crumbs on the table....

♫ We've got *ecopicality* ♪. ...

It's a new name for a common nameless body of understanding that
claims psychoecology critically in tandem with enviroecology. I may have to
pen another little book about this:
check Dazzlers Dictionary in the back porch.

ecopicality:DD; a wholistic quality of any environmental interventions (incl. housemaking); aspects
of this quality are harmonies in: ecologies, economy, community, dweller compatibilities, *nature's*
nurtures, dweller personality, urban design, *synthetic aesthetic*(DD);
an urgent modern way of dancing the *Housefandango*(DD), of *doing our housing*. *ecopical*(DD),
ecopology(DD); if a house has *ecopicality* it's a winner, so we sing to the tune of the old L Price song
"she's got personality ...
"she's got *ecopicality*, walks with *ecopicality*, talks with *ecopicality*...";
term developed during the writing of this book.

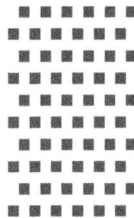

■ ■ ■ ■ ■ ■
■ ■ ■ ■ ■ ■
■ ■ ■ ■ ■ ■
■ ■ ■ ■ ■ ■
■ ■ ■ ■ ■ ■
■ ■ ■ ■ ■ ■
■ ■ ■ ■ ■ ■
■ ■ ■ ■ ■ ■
■ ■ ■ ■ ■ ■
■ ■ ■ ■ ■ ■

Houses come together in a world we share.

We may seek to 'inherit the Earth'; fascinating concept. Why would
somebody say such?

EVERYPERSON'S WORLD

Slipping sideways on a rubbled embankment, landing among butterfly fertilised bushflowers and scampering thylacines, banging her head not so gently on a very earthy sunbaked brick; "It's *everyperson's valley*," declares woolly-headed activist Leone Neolithic. Back here now Paolo Soleri, Bobby Dazzler and Mr Low Carl feel the *ripples* from her jolt in their true grit aminos. Mrs *Pale* at home in support of Global feels only a mild percolation in her pressurepacked aerosol-stunned cortex reminding her of her ownership of a fine *ticky tacky* lawn - she is moved to run the vacuum cleaner over it before dosing it with blood and bone fertiliser. You may sit somewhere in the middle. "*Everyperson's planet* ... changing with everyperson's house," declare the homo superiors along with Greenpeace and Silicon Valley. And I think to myself, "What a wonderful world." The remnant wildlife declare in unison; "Imagine our world devoid of houses, rooms and corner shops". Albert Gallopilong's people to all intents lived this but in an overcoming parallel comes an imposing new manmade expanding environment. Almost a different world. Suburban tar and letterboxes displace treed valleys and bushflowers from our daily life where we need them most. The *houselocusts* consume. The many years of protest songs *pale*. Revolution among planning bureaucrats and commercial industry is too slow; maimed, by some *dodo* that creeps into the mind and discretely economically rationalises (or powerly rationalises). It creeps into most minds affecting all sorts of consequences including the creation and sustainment of red-necked commercial industry that has become nothing less than a *megamonster* . Apologies to the innocent.

Reader, please don't feel engulfed by the depth of the *land* discussions here, seeing them discursive from the subject of house – and particularly your own up-to-the-minute domestic developments. Rather feel *nurtured* by the land and connected with it through your house. Feel your house or apartment

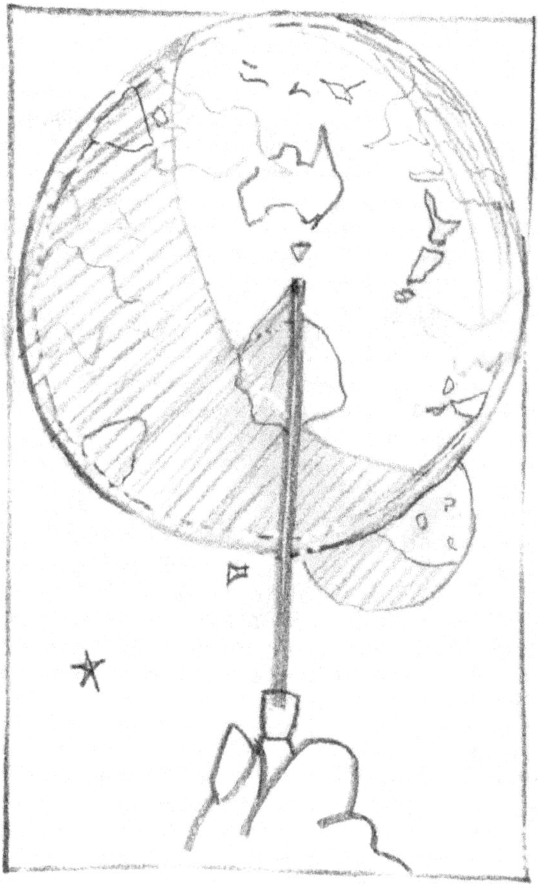

block floating like a hollow cork on the land. Feel the health of its links with the land - *nature's earthy nurtures*. Feel the realities of its links. Don't feel engulfed either, by the *megathing*, but rather wisened to *do your Housefandango*. Selling, maintaining and furnishing. Manufacturing tools and vehicles towards housing. A whopping great part of all building is house related. **The quantum impact of the house relates to the world as it does to the dweller.** The developing world, generated by housing, extends the house. An extended asset. More possessions. Greater domestic *accumulation*. Cities. Towns. Regions. The land, which we note is within the sphere of air about us, is places and substance. A balanced living aesthetical resource, subjected to imaginations and plunders. Sunbaking clay, grandfathers' thumbprints and adzes. People and building materials. All people love to grip and play with the physicality of mother planet. Plenty of clay for a little womb-shelter and concrete for a little bomb-shelter. A satisfying sufficiency? The doors of ecology may close on the *crowds of domestic-contraptions*. No doubt there is a noble *ecopian* balance - unless recovery from the Fall involves unknown transformation. The heavenly city, compact like the Tardis, immense and endless **room** taking only a modicum of space, a twist of ether its *playdough*, a macrobiotic diet for its builders. Hope.

Step out for a minute; from the grotto, up the street onto the town common. Lie with your face to the stars; that which you can feel behind in touch with your head, shoulders, hip, legs, feet is the core of our global sustenance and our global delight ... together with the air, water, the exciting hum of people energy, architectural bliss and stars. It is our world of course.

HOUSE NEGATIVE
EVERYPERSON'S WORLD

As *we note,* there is always some sort of *domestic-arrangement*; always pots, pans, chests or family circles. But somewhat optional are the permanent, heavy, immobile **domestic-contraptions** - houses. A house can't be carried, nor can it be built during a camping transience. The open space it takes, the *room* the whole housing thing takes; this is the raw space that would still exist if there were no rooms. Animal habitats would

118

not be interrupted. Understand what a house is from a geological-cum-biological viewpoint; just a material object on the land. Not to forget the attachments to the object; the lawns, roads, industry and dumps. The world would be different without them - a very different environmental happening, society, civilisation and industry. How different we would be is an interesting speculation; having all housing removed instantly, leaving us rolling on the ground for sudden lack of chairs. No Vegemite, no cupboard. This thought provocation is a little unreal. It needs to be enhanced with a narration of the inevitable physiological and cultural changes that would arise through a history without houses. It may be that Talkabout or Little White Cloud's ancestors are good role models. It may be utter folly; permanent settlement for some peoples in conducive circumstance was always inevitable - though originally nobody imagined a crowded damaged world. Now today, there's a theodolitically lit *room* around the nomad, and a lounge lizard even in his desert. In these thoughts we may sharpen our perception of what a house truly is to us – regardless of its architectural vogue.

Gallopilong knows a depth of *egalitarianism* in his communities that Global *Pale* does not. A house becomes some person's possession made possible by settlement. And as it happens many houses increase, as market-commodity. Some more than others. Eventually we have ghettos, welfare housing and Hollywood *boulevards* or those of Queensland; very significantly *inegalitarian* we feel as we look at the extremes through the eyes of moral compassion, a corner of *ecopicality*. This is cultural adaptation, unknown to Gallopilong's people, that comes from housers' subconscious priorities.

Something else that the Harmoninnies did not know, until the Anglophiles arrived; the common cold. As well as the *inegalitarianism* come bacterial dumps and epidemics. Only a limited number of people can house themselves in country retreats, because of economics, space and social dynamics. Also, people like to crowd. Thus epidemics. No houses, people on the move - no epidemics. *Nomad minima, boulevard bold.*

Always on the move, or soon to be, a nomad has a healthy sense of orientation that is lost to established settlers. *Cultural, psychological and physical adaptations occur in accord with the domestic circumstance.* Putting up and taking down tents are prayer for some who are nomadic. Real prayer – not quaint ritual. Some people never ever go out of the house. A few have never been in. Once your culture is what it is, it is very difficult or impossible to change. For most there is no alternative to the house; we may go part way by doing more outdoor living. The more we are outdoors the less we need of a house; so our house will change in atmosphere. House or no house we all will become - but differently. No house, different chores, no garden, different civilizing. From the *nomurbic nub*, our predilectional priorities extend.

We have an option manifest in this *contraption* for cups, chairs, stereo and love nest; set in motion by some human nature. What might have existed about me had human nature not existed? Or rather than human nature, is it just an aspect of id that many of us share? I love to make a settled home, another likes a settled roam? We all, settler, nomad and urban-based nomad, move across the firmness, commodity and delight of the ground. Natural landscape and dense cities have lots in common - sky, gravity, the earth, locale, time, and people in motion. From Manhattan, Low Carl's bitumen-scorched voice exasperates, "That clever chap, lauded by the universities and their progeny, who coined *firmness, commodity & delight* as keys in architecture was simply hi-jacking nature!!" " ... Or maybe harmonising with it," the ghostly bus driver shyly muses. And I'm surprised he has a copy of 'HouseFandango' at hand, in his glove *box*. "I have a Bible too, but I do not pray," he elucidates.

The 'clever chap' can only be excused if, rather than being blinkered in a professional *silo*, he was rightly assuming no separation of the natural and the architectural. The 'architectural' aspect of *firmness, commodity & delight* exists in combo with nature and the act of architecture; and so the act of housing. For example we simply 'find' the commodity of warmth in nature but we usually must induce it in our housing. And ideally; enhance it by temperature control if we want it in our house.

ENVIRONMENTAL BEAUTY
EVERYPERSON'S WORLD

The magic of a home locale.
There is more to the awesome beauty of the world than merely visual beauty.
The kinetic wonder of a glaciated valley.
The spatial vastness of a plain.
The path of some llamas.

Our vision and sense of the original environment is obscured by the erected buildings, albeit they're made of the *playdough of the Earth* anyway. Obscured simultaneously are the neighbouring encamped tribesmen living in unison with the land. Change is one thing. Loss is another. This lost awesome original magnificence should be replaced, compensated, the loss minimised; compensated by replacement aesthetics and environmental engineering – to some reasonable degree. People and animals gain immense motivation and satisfaction from this magnificence. is power. Ask my wife. So is aura. Ask the flora.

Thus the appearance and scale of our housing complexes and each house is important. Some natural sites are enhanced by houses and their trappings. Some sites should never be built upon. Some manner of houses and property enhance the landscape. Others reflect too much of people-kind's vanities and carnal sludge;

not a sight to behold. Subdivision cadastre, roads and power poles; driveways, fences, water tanks & car headlights may be attached to the house, frequently leaning heavily.

Trees to wood, to wall; ore to waste. Ecology, sustainability. Natural rhythms, patterns, cycles, wonders. Rich auras of fields of grass. Beauty. In our ability to modify nature lies the responsibility of a caretaker-cum-cosmetic-surgeon – mayor-cum-architect. Cottage in a valley, house in a street, suburb in a valley, a town full of streets. This all *ecopically* made, carefully with a balanced regard for the environment itself and its components *and its benefit to us*. We are also components of the environment, like the tribesmen. We do this. This is beautiful. A swallow's nest is beautiful. But swallows do not plague. People now are medically resilient against natural selection. The *houselocusts* relentlessly consume. Mainly through manufacture, the *houselocusts* ooze about a growing third of the industrial pollution. There's not a lot of environmental beauty in huge houses on small lots and there's no *room* for trees – so we grow inward to fantastic interiors. We grapple to acknowledge the other implications.

A SATISFYING SUFFICIENCY
EVERYPERSON'S WORLD

The global scale and a simple local perspective: an organic house by Mali's indigenous Dogon people is a pleasure to celebrate. It's no *houselocust*; but this is only in that it's in tandem with its industrially uninclined little society. The house is laid out metaphorically to unify with their religious culture – a little more on it later. The ever-globalising West has lost such pleasure. For example, **Pale still cannot grasp** Gallopilong's sense of exterior. He feels a little drowned, more than engulfed in the bush. The pleasure can be regained only by a familiar application of studied and learned priorities in *beingrowing*, *doing*, culture, materials and methods. This probably will never happen. Except in the event of some cosmic or divine revelation, the easily grasped simplicities of Western orthodox house-making will come only through the *megamonster* thing, feeding on our *dodo* mistakes. Homemakers will not know to be able to have trust in any ultimate safety of the orthodox. We may exercise discipline, wisdom and sensitivity by feeling and by design. However, for the keen homemaker to know a truly satisfying sufficiency of balanced *quanta* and footprints in newly built domestic amenity is more to hope. *The system cannot provide such* pleasure.

Never-the-less, in terms of long-range survival and ecology; rather than being guided by style, custom, direct-owner-cost economics or commercial advice alone, it is vital that we use systematic analysis in our environmental interventions. Don't be frightened; that's a job more for social and government attention. But a builder - in his real contract context - should be attuned to that understanding and also be wary of the now obvious mistakes of modern civilisation.

We hug the tree we relish a polished dinner table. We hug the ecology we save our nature. We pass the oil peak, we rediscover surviving local feudalisms; the scum of sufferings between them and the future neo-indigenous – or is it some timely technological release, some lunar H3, a blast from the sun or something triggered by the likes of Low Carl.

Ecology is akin to environmental beauty. A sacred harmony. Easily crushed by a *pale* naked ape with a bulldozer and a drum of chemo-waste. What potential harm can a polyester carpet do to the world? It covers a lot of square kilometres. It may cause ailment in production, use and house fire. And when worn-out, it is dumped. Multiply this by its global popularity and the passing years. Lungs and flamingo begin to flag. "From trees to portico chair and toilet seat. Here in this book's dunny. Protein processed in our tummy. The bricks of life building our body. We eat too much, we flush our money. **Building waste.** We flush too much - that aint funny. Visual and ecological pollution." Yours faithfully Talkabout, but do not laugh. "I couldn't have written it on your mirrored toilet door. I go in the bushes. But I see houses are a bit like that, ay." An item from a local supermarket conceptually miles from any bush; **a translucent mauve polyester toilet brush** sits in its little tub down in the disinfected *three-planed-corner* beside the porcelain, some dry soiled tissue over its inward *non-biodegradable permanently settled l i p* , no glistening thought for the *ripples* of its production, just waiting to be flushed clean by a sponge in water bound for today's S y d n e y H a r b o u r .

Clearly the exterior effect to which we nearly 'all' add when we build, buy or rent housing, is what Bobby Dazzler - as indicated so well by Paolo Soleri - sees from the stratosphere whilst on the bus. (I note I am guilty of assuming that the Western-styled, or similar, residential occurrences are lived in by all. Did you notice? In fact, though collectively speaking it is we few who make this ghastly mess, there are 96% of peoplekind who don't - so very very many who aren't messy at all. The vast majority.) This is the effect since the factories started to hum several score years back of the *housing* (cum-civilisation) *locust*. A growing smog of dust and fumes developing. And a shrinkage of the green around the planet. A very serious change to the Earth's complexion as it scabs the countryside with an urban web of *houselocusts*. Discoloured water moving to sea from most estuaries. A huge swirl of plastic flotsam now a feature of the Pacific.

The sun gives out cosmic radiation, heat and light; the Earth gives terrestrial radiation, magnetism, heat, electro-magnetic fields, noise, gravity; houses give out too. Houses are part of the planetary ecosystem – or bust. Cheeky is stunned - oh no, oh no he isn't. "Not fra'minute!" The delicate biological balances are part of other more subtle and invisible balances about which the dopey *megamonster* begins to learn. We all depend on the vegetation system that the *houselocusts* consume and fowl. **"More so than 'stop it', we must reverse the problem,"** Paolo bravely expounded quite some time ago. It may be that the luxury of a *satisfying sufficiency* on our housing plate is no longer available - unless our satisfaction is derived from wisdom.

Energy conservation is a key urgency related to the environmental depletions. Our capacity to forge metals, transport house components and warm our houses may wane for lack of alternative energy supply. A broad-scale return to energising by people power, oxen and water-wheels is not feasible in light of the current motions of life, and indeed the globally dispersed availability of materials. The indigenous nomads may yet become the teachers.

Consider a small 1970s *box* house; uninsulated, timber floor, brick veneer. It uses sixty percent of its energy in space heating, twenty percent in water heating, ten percent in cooking, and 10% in lighting and appliances. These spheres are close to you. When the fire goes out, the chill quickly wraps the dweller. When the oil runs out and the coal darkens the sky... A quarter of the heat loss is through the roof, an eighth through single-pane glass, a third through walls, a fifth through floors and a tenth by infiltration. This is merely the body of a fine *houselocust*. **Fortunately such brazen insects are being discouraged.** But there is further scope; a slowly closing, gaping chasm of unrefinement in global housing industry to conserve energy. The simple goal being to protect wilderness habitat, our environmental aesthetics - **and** ourselves. As well as through refinement of design efficacy and manufacture and construction energy, conservation can be achieved at the dwellers' doors, and in part it is, by taking action in existing houses; insulation, draught proofing, cooling, rational use of *playdough*, suburban renovation and so on. Money is saved where energy is saved, eventually if not immediately. But of course there is the minimum bracket of costs; a blanket, walls and roof - but the better the blanket the less heat energy will pass through it.

There are many matters to consider. *Some decisions regarding energy conservation are very complex and even unclear* because of industrial pragmatics, design time pragmatics, real world on-the-job pragmatics and limited accessible information – such as the value of a cowgirl's hot bath. One concrete building block uses the same manufacturing and transport energy as about three hundred mud bricks made of on-site soil – so to speak. It would seem that the other matters associated with energy conservation in brick/block construction; manufacture of mortar, insulation etc would make the mud a clear winner without detail calculation. However design matters arising with structure, regulation, taste, wall thickness and available skills will vary the optimum energy outcome from project to project. Variables like construction longevity, aesthetics and recyclability may make it impractical to calculate comparative energy uses and environmental impacts. *Gradual refinement of building conventions* is the only substantial avenue for detail refinement for energy conservation in traditional dwellings - that is refinement of the *little boxes* made of *ticky tacky*. They can be easily measured and refined; ultimately they are slick, flying-saucer-like, tuned to hyper-industry. Mediocrity is frustrating if we do not consciously make allowance for it. Let's make it awesomely, beautifully functional. Yes, let's renovate the dreaded mediocrity; make it a hyper 1970 Volkswagen Beetle instead of a throwaway pack of unserviceable electronics.

Design for insulation, cooling and heating is always financially and ecologically valuable. This design is not only in materials and detail but also in location, form, size, site details and lifestyle – all these value variables are the bones of *ecopicality*. Regarding the *nacre*, the shell, the walls, floor and ceiling of the house; heat transference from inside to outside is limited by both bulk and reflective materials – *the materials are in the actions of performing their allotted tasks*. Reflection requires air at the face to work and, as a rule, it is air in bulk materials that holds heat; a bird ruffles its feathers to keep warm, the reflector at the back of the heater throws the heat out. Reduction in surface area also reduces heat loss - snuggle up. Orientation in accord with the elements, adjusts heating and cooling - maybe bury the cold side of the house with an earth berm. Garden planting, colour, windows and massive materials come into the heat play. Material mass will store heat and give it off when the air is cooler - feel the warmth coming from a brick wall after sunset. Approximately; water stores 4000 kilojoules per cubic metre, granite and concrete half as much, brick, wood and plasterboard half as much again. Heat pumps will surely evolve; refined transference of heat from the hot spots we want cooled to the cool spots we want hot – from summer to winter (let's digitise heat and wirelessly transmit it from the Sahara to the Patagonian lounge).

Cooling can be achieved by refrigeration; or by evaporation using a sod roof, a wet towel or some Middle-East vernacular. A cool air space is sometimes made, in the hot parts of Australia, by building a second roof to shade the first. Double glazing reduces heat loss. It has been used extensively for many years by nearly all in Norway and the United States and many other countries. Triple glazing too in extreme cases.

Wherever there is sunlight its energy is available. Solar energy use can involve techniques that allow gain through adjustments as the sun moves and weather changes during the day – adjustable awnings, tracking collectors, open the window. Sail your house, tune it each day, read conditions and adjust as necessary all controls. Daily *doing* in a *biohouse* may include gardening, feeding the fish, cleaning, adjusting shades, closing vents and so on. Electronics can take care of some of this too - sun and temperature sensitive switching for shutters or anything.

Outgoing air carries warmth or cool, depending. Ventilation is important. By sealing the house and ventilating mechanically or manually we can reduce the rate of air change. One total change of house air per hour, by draughts, is fairly common in *boxes*. Air locks and plant shelters at external doors and weather stripping are effective here, and garden wind breaks also help. It is nice to have abundant free air flow through windows and doors but times are **tough**. It is nice to have a fire too, and a bath, but times are tough.

Our cheap *playdough* of course includes industrial cast-offs. Houses are being produced of tyres, cans, bottles, packed earth and straw. They are powered by sun, wind and/or rain, with biological sewerage and mass-balanced heat control, okay for both freezing winters and searing summers. A use-all water system. Water – another global urgency. Eventually dilapidation and obsolescence passes it all back to nature or re-recycling. These are exampled in New Mexico:a *satisfying sufficiency* more so than a new mansion in a Hollywood *boulevard*.

These houses in essence have been around for years; the Harmoninnies adjusting their bracken shade by a billabong and Cheeky nearby skinning a wallaby in his camp, supported by the shelter of an old car, using a hub-cap to collect berries or the idyllic streamside mill residence in Fern Hollow. **It's the plague factor, the vast growing number of houses, which is a huge issue.**

With the use of industrial cast offs; with the adaptation, to houses, of standard products produced for public works and industry, eg very large concrete pipes, prefab silo hoods ....; with the hyperindustry potentials, *biohouses* and *biocities* ...; with careful individual design ...: we shall make a difference. Shall we overcome? **Looking to a *satisfying sufficiency* we make our way from *boulevard bold* back along the road toward *nomad minima.*** Will the hi-tech shoes justifiably give way to a new generation of moccasin – eventually? From microwave to spear. Likely something betwixt.

The INDUSTRY

EVERYPERSON'S WORLD

*I*ndustry *suitable to igloo* and to penthouse in orbit. Romancing the options. It's Robinson Crusoe or a range of paid experts who get the job done. Some of Earth's *playdough* is converted to tooling; ranging through drill bits, sandpaper, timber mills and total prefabrication factories. Management and pay-packets operating precision square machinery - the joys of handmark excluded. **Local vernacular is replaced by everchanging**

industrial neo-orthodoxy - which is, and most say sadly, foreign to locale. Will the future—shocked architects ever compensate? Will the naked-ape *shadow* psyches, deprived of *handmark*, cope? Will the money economy of the *machinemark* compromise the house? Some say no, some yes. A dignitry's quote from a generation ago reminds us; "... building has become too easy, architecture too difficult." **There are ways of compensating nevertheless.** *Dance your housing* properly, using all your own values spectrum; commercial producer, government official or dweller. A potter's wheel under the *handmarked* dob of clay in the precisely built industrial corner. Keep industrial form subordinate to natural form and local manifestations. Subordinate but proportionate, *ecopiate*. The sense of organic local construction provided by the likes of thumbprints, adze cuts and *handmarks* is a vital nexus point for *nature's earthy nurtures* and our diverse *synthetic aesthetic*s. Like the mass-produced caravan once towed by the old '*Classic*', a small hyper-industry spaceship-style house is pretty much satisfactory, if there can be nature at the door and the dwellers' dusty footprints on the threshold.

If we are to stay housed peoples, aside the nomad's way; **this machinemarked industry is, in essence, the way we will go.** The fallback option, all in home-made villages, would require laws against mechanical aids, unless the aids run out of oil first (and don't hold your head in the convenient sand of day to day folly). The fallback option; imagined only by the Luddites!

The industry though, like politics, is big, heavy, cumbersome and ssslloww; but with the occasional volatile flare or catastrophe. Technology lags well behind design invention – except where it inspires design. The old *megamonster* is a bit slow – **let's get him**. Economic rationalism promotes persistent persuasion to buy the redundant. But the likes of a breakthrough in autonomy-creating solar power uncurbable by vested interests would modify the soul of the industry, and the house, in a flash.

Industry has become so much a part of our planet that it is well beyond being simply a tool or a clever process. It has swallowed many people - engulfed them. *For them it has become bigger than the real original terrestrial world.* Industry comes close to us through the house. Very close. Bobby still reels. The established patterns of action, skills and machinery, together with avarice and economic survival sway the manufacturer to sway the designer toward maintaining use of the established. Good invention may go undeveloped depending on the value options of its potential industrial developers. It is also a tendency of the designer to be over-influenced by these established patterns. We cap our invaluable convention by stifling our vital innovation.

Leonardo da Vinci was probably the first to toy with modular wall panels. In 1850 'tin' shed kits came to Australia as goldrush houses. The luxury model had glass windows, canvas scrim and up to three rooms. In 1945 the first hyperindustry (the then hyper)
'dwelling machine', the Dymaxion house, was prototyped; a prefabricated house looking a little like a T Model saucer-style spaceship. Made of sheet aluminium and plastics, it is a flattened bubble shape with a rotatable weather vane roof, deliverable to site in a tube by helicopter. The tube was also used as the central support. It was however deemed to be socially untenable, ahead of its time. It has not gone into commercial production.

We cap our orthodoxy by preferring familiarity.

Industrial production, by its nature, produces repetition; identical mass productions and precise reproductions. And with plastics comes non-biodegradable permanence, Pacific flotsam and windblown litter - and a taint of petro-chemical poison. Everybody's aesthetic and healthy world is hurt. We react to these things. But we are an odd bunch of biological marvels, for though we complain about suburban monotony we do not mind so much the repetition of house design from hand-held tools, off identical plans. We make them *little boxes* of different colours. But we do not as a rule like a machined reproduction as a house. Only as a car, caravan or a boat!! Or a washing machine, sink or letterbox. Our typical housewife is her own interior designer. "I note that she is so, in the face of any expert," adds Global, as he counts the cost of resolving the pink problem. Our own ingrained Western worldly culture is as sluggish to sensible change as is the damned industrial wonder. "Come on Honey! I could retire early if we ordered a Dymaxion." As any marketer knows ecology, economy, resource, aesthetic, timeliness and corporate profit must bow first to the magic of whim; be the whim informed or otherwise. Houses need some sort of customising; like the individual graphic work on the repetitive tipi. In itself repetition is why people are so much alike. It is a sane way to go. Peoples' hearts though don't repeat. They beat – unless they repeat shades of *pale*.

CROWDS of DOMESTIC-CONTRAPTIONS
EVERYPERSON'S WORLD

Where **is our control of the neighbourhood aspect of our house**: the regulated free market fait-accomplis; where in this reality is the flock of tipis, Camelot, Holy City, Arcosanti, *Ecopia*?

This is where the house strikes us most profoundly as being a little bit adverse. In the 'burbs. Where the house often has clipped wings. Where it is blinkered by fences, footpath strips. Rectangles for 'parks', for community halls and fire stations. Where the undeveloped allotments become a shaggy eyesore. Where the beach is too much petrol & time away and there are no roo to hunt. In the 'burbs where the local dance gives way to four wheeled buzz boxes and the barbecue complements the fresh scent of cut grass and reeking *armpits*.

Suburbia, like big industry, is not a daily part of everyperson's world. Suburbia. It is however very big in the world. And very big as an embracing part, or should it be 'a receptive' part, of very many *domestic-contraptions*. Suburbia, **the thing**. The thing **that you or your friends may personally support and construct.** Villages, towns, cities, huge blocks of flats: people crowd their domiciles in a number of ways. Jowl to jowl in suburbs, conjoined houses and flats. This is all okay, but we need a healthy serving of *nature's earthy nurtures* in there. Wholistically (read *ecopically*) planned urbanisation is one thing – our realities are another. We have come a long way in some regards. 250 years ago Anglophiles tipped faeces from their night-time jerries outside their front doors from whence it went, as in some third world settlements today, unlidded down London's open street gutters. However, the bulk of people, then, still lived on the healthy land. We have come a long way; now, like this, we abuse rivers with industrial waste. The health depletes. *Nature's nurture* is built out and poorly facilitated crowded life is built in.

Symptomatic of a social dilemma that some of us cause; some shantytown residents, after a short obliged time in 'nice new' apartments, objected, resisted the socially inadequate expedient modern solution and returned to their familiar surroundings. Same psychology as the Dymaxion saga.

Multistorey accommodation blocks, suburbia and urbia, modern or not so modern. They may be a vast big mistake. Can this be, Bobby? "No! It's a vast *accumulation* of little mistakes." A vast *accumulation* of little mistakes. The *megamonster*, planner and subdivider cannot win if we do not make a little purchase. Nor if we do not wain from joining voice against obligatory possession of a fait-accomplis - the no-option-but-to-buy-it scenario. Let's heal suburbia for lifestyle and magic. *Renovate suburbia, renovate mediocrity.* Of course, not all domestic locales are suburbias. There are beautiful little hamlets and there are central city flats and not all suburbias are devoid of beautiful domestic locales – lush sun-facing residential hillsides with magnificent long and short distance panoramas a short walk to bustling centre. Wellington City we love you. We go where we must.

What is it that we are trying to achieve with our suburbs? What do they mean in our lives and societies? How do they fit with our world? Are there alternatives?

Imagine. A house you do not like. And one in which you would love to live. Imagine the most banal modern suburb. Flat land, no vista to distant hills. A scantly treed flat monotony. Now imagine a suburban paradise. Stimulating treed, steeply variable New Zealand style topography and a water-course with roads following the contour quickly to a city and houses flooded with *nature's earthy nurtures*, vistas and *room* to pee in the yard. There are not many. And there will never be many. There are other ways though. Those cultures, a very small fraction of peoplekind, with motorcars and the hyper-tech web have elements that give wider scope for utopian addresses. Even this though may well be unsustainable. The essence of suburbia is access; access to each in the crowd of houses. Roads and house faces. The aesthetic relationship of roadways to the land, not just the bitumen but the whole road requirement and services adjuncts should follow *ecopian* design considerations similar to those mentioned for house properties and subdivision. Shape the allotment *layout*s to access the sun and the roads to modify the winds and ground waters; all with consideration of the many other domestic design issues. Empathy is best, but instead; too few heroes amid too many one eyed developers and weak or restrained bureaucrats corralled by office partitions, mortgages and time of their own. The suburb is shaped through the best means of making access; in accord with all three;

‡	Social planning,
~	The land and
¬	The pragmatics.

Suburb location is another delicate matter. In practise it is more an econo-politic matter, often gripped tightly by sometimes fascist, sometimes fair, private rights issues – and convenient owner-developer ignorance.

We group houses together in many ways variously with community facility. Very often it is house after house each side of a road. Or we stack them, and our people – a few storeys and sometimes tightly, sometimes delightfully into large buildings. As the street, and old fashioned corner store, are a neighbour interface to suburbia; so, the stairwell, corridor and any shared kitchen or bathroom are a neighbour interface in apartment buildings. The old techniques of Cyut still today have front doors in the roofs and the roofs used like streets, a kind of reverse to vertical stacking. A differing neighbour interface. Of course you will have your own feelings. The traditional Sinophiles divine what they termed as natural forces about their houses. They see the realm and its *layout* around the house as being as important as the house. Western *ticky tacky* suburbia is a road, nature strip, front yard, narrow side strips and the back yard, all toward perfect rectilinear relationship to the road. Usually little thought for relationship to even the sun. The Sinophile used walls and landscape to make a succession of room places, each a preparation for the next, which were used to give an order to their immediate surroundings. They make an entrance courtyard between a wall to the street and the house eaves. An artful gateway is used as a transition from the street - an entrance experience. There may be no other courtyards. More humble and more subtle and soulful than the capitalist subdivision, yet of course in some ways similar.

The various house forms in the old Sinophile village each fit cosmic principles and lines; who knows what the new will ultimately do. The playful Abophile throws his eyes toward our driver. "We could say Global *Pale* understands cosmic lines to be roads! Lines that are governed by the four 'cosmic' points of money, expedience, ignorance and saleability. Lines that usually form quadrangles into the land." *But with this we have the significant impact of the staggering potentials of automotive access* – to neighbourhood, city subway, seashore, airport, workplace. Contrary to its poor design, the shady patch of road at the house gate sometimes does in fact catch the sun. From that patch, we may be at the beach, away from the quadrangles in minutes, and pleased to be back home later bringing some *quicksilver* energy and a piece of driftwood to our little *box* – " … which is certainly not 'tacky', nor 'ticky'," points out Maggie's nephew as he browses for real estate located closer to the rising sun at the surf beach; taking the temples and community halls as passé; but a bit of fun at the main street café and bar is great. Of course the agents will try to sell him their well packaged dirty dishwater short-changed facsimile because he has no money for perfume; nor the wherewithal to realise what he's bought until it's too late to back out. Like everybody coaxed into any excitingly drab new 'burb.

They don't have to be drab though. Like the Chinese, the traditional Indian town plan is based on the cosmic cross, the points of the universe. The town, with its temple, to represent the city of Heaven. The Hottentots, of the Near East, apparently made a circle of round huts about a circular cattle ground. This form, they believed, was favoured by heaven - certainly not the capitalist developer. The chieftain's hut is at the rising sun. The other huts are sited hierarchically in the direction of the sun's, seeming curved movement. Some ancient Baltic villages feature a north-south main street with houses in order on both sides. The houses are numbered following the sun, from south to north on the west and then from north to south on the east. It sure beats naming streets after the developer's old girlfriend. Cosmic cues once set the basis for many architectures and town plans. Certainly colloquial understanding and culture formed the crucible for planning the community order of *domestic-contraptions*; or in the case of the Abophile, the order of seasonal relocation, game, *domestic-arrangement* and walkabout.

The housing requirements of people living alone or tribally in nature are different from those of people living housed closely together. The style of the traditional Abophile, not even any tables chairs driveway or letterbox, looks well against the truths of that average slot in suburbia, be it properly leafy, or treed with power poles and satellite dishes. *Visual and acoustic screenings* are resultants of the need for social distance and *room* to do and to be, arising from perennial penguin crowding; walls, fences, ceilings, hedges, ravines.

Places in suburbias do vary, especially with newness, but the main theme is minimum property allotment sizes. These are supported by authorities as the ecologically sustainable option (looking to *ecopicality*), by commerce as the dollar option and by local governments as the 'less infrastructure for more rates option'. Okay as an option maybe, but as a *houselocust* plague?! Economy at the cost of soul. Less gardening for less value. Lifestyle, road domination and vote seeker kudos in public works. Food for driver *Pale*.

Honey for slow developers; bees on the move make their cells of a shape that holds the largest volume of honey - no Global, you didn't hear 'money' - with least consumption of precious wax, and probably of time and energy. Wax is *playdough*; more precious with more people. Even the greediest of our range of developers only crudely apply this principle to maximise profits. We could save land and sustain ecology. Can it work? Some try. He may have been a Bobby, but he is our determined and not imagined but real Paolo Soleri, a long time frontier guru among the *stratospheric walkers*, and his colleagues who began building 'Arcosanti' in Arizona.

> Arcosanti was begun in the mid late 20th century as a way to conserve the countryside and house five thousand people. In its *layout* Arcosanti was designed to eliminate that which is most of urbia; long service runs, roads and yards. It is the first built step endeavoured under his arcology principles, which to me are *ecopian*. It's a battle moving forward in a world enslaved by the cost of war – and *pale* residential visionaries who are no more than *lounge lizards*. Soleri has sketched huge city complexes, peoplehives rather than beehives; some straddling valleys as dams and maybe powered by the water flow; some freestanding a kilometre high, and broadly ducted to bring in weather and sunlight. People would live at the face of the structures. They would work and socialise unfettered by traffic realm or by detachment from wilderness in these organic cities bountiful in *nature's nurtures*. A very short trip from organic urbia down into saved countryside and large pristine stormy beaches; perhaps to meet the great grand children of Low Carl wandering in hand with those of Gallopilong. At last check there had been no government support for Arcosanti nor other *ecopian* cities, hamlets, nor even the *ecopian* houses and encampments of its future. These are evident as only tiny fragments dispersed through all settlement. Today Arcosanti remains alive as an urban laboratory.

The savage draw of Orwell's 1984 well past, do we have faits-accomplis? Short of a global blast of pure consciousness, surely enough persons will not come aware to make a worthwhile change. Even the research necessary for housing and suburban improvement has been a low priority. The vote-giving people know not enough of the issue to complain. Incremental gain. Incremental pain. Lacking is adventure, courage, forethought and responsibility - that *dodo* that enters the mind. To be, or not. Sharp and adventurous. Stark and tortuous. Built change is effected very slowly. Very slowly. *The established old residential fabric sits heavily unchanged, belittling the relative microcosm of our radical advances.*

The suburbs suffice temporarily. Can they be eco-renovated? Urgent housing shortage throughout the world. This time it is Cheekyfella who, despite his cross-cultural discomforts, laughs. While looking at our beautiful solutions we are desperately providing only unecologic bare essentials. The beautiful being too costly. Bare essentials, though, as we have noted, are different to different people, obviously. The three quarters of the world's population who live in, what the West including the *Pales* terms as substandard housing, are not looking for the Western idea of housing – but monkey see, monkey do, they come to like the idea. Bare essentials; paradise. It seems the more we have the more we want. Even still, the regulations in part demand standards not properly suited to current socio-economic situations. *The bodies politic don't want even a temporary camp on a vacant suburban allotment, regardless as to whether it enables the owner to gradually build a house within his means and his no-mortgage ethic.* There are no suburbs specifically zoned for such domestic activity either. Whatever courses of action are to be taken they must **begin with rationalising the current circumstance by modified regulation of building and planning**, not just for economy but also for dwellers, and then to breaking the sprawl by improved urban decentralisation and possibly implementation of imaginative residential city complexes like Arcosanti. 'A Timeless Way of Building', the book by Christopher Alexander tells an outlook too.

Beyond greed, as our population grows, *there are places where suburban sprawl can no longer occur*, simply for lack of land; where huge ugly poorly located blocks of flats are growing, right now. Beautiful well designed and located apartment towers which are currently trending into existence thankfully relate to an aspect of Soleri's arcology. The cramming together of housing, so that precious seclusion and humane *ergonomic room* are minimal, is a fact of life today – as it was in Medieval London. "Is seclusion truly precious?" we may wonder. And yes we need our healthy *ergonomic room* and *nature's earthy nurtures*.

How can Global *Pale* conceive his case in favour of the suburban status quo? **These *Pale* people are real people, who are happy with and build the suburbs.** What are they saying? The suburban houses in all their similarity and conformity, like the human bodies, still show individuality and freedom – more so over time by the hand of the dweller. Do *ticky tacky* suburbs really have something going, for themselves, *which detractors cannot understand.* Some suburbs alluringly are quite beautiful. Hills and vegetation forgive dubious priorities and stimulating house and garden design ease the planning dilemma. Is it some sort of optimum assistance to their life and lives; the orthogonal order and the Australian old weatherboard, fibreboard, rendered foam or brick veneer house with its yards and concrete kerb out front? Wakey, wakey. It's okay on Saturday afternoon, but look. First, acknowledge that the suburban *box* dweller is, by generational incubation, generally more prone to be a mere *shadow* of a Neanderthal and therefore may not know. Despite the partial truth in the *box* house *grid* subdivision principle, much land is screaming. *Debox, degrid.* Ninety percent of Western houses are in suburbia. Often the *megamonster* has bulldozed, flattened and cleared the land of trees, everything nearly. Global *Pale*'s bus turns left, back onto the country road. Take me home! Do you feel your heart sigh in nourishing tranquillity. A soulful drive to that which is left of the bush. The car is an escape from bleak suburbs, a crutch. The bus will ultimately tie you to a street *grid* – and the power grid.

Even over a century ago nineteen out of twenty Austrophiles lived in suburban neighbourhoods. It still happens. Move on up from welfare suburb to *boulevard* suburb. And these get better; the Amerophiles have a few *boulevard* suburbs with highway checkpoints to control who comes and goes – a security for the dweller and a setting of 'tone'. Never-the-less *box contraptions* crowded on a bitumen togetherness - something they like.

Deboxing, now in the Dazzlers' dictionary, is action that avoids or resolves over-*boxed* housing. In general, *deboxing* aims to optimise the practical applications of orthogonal construction, whilst making *room* for the *synthetic aesthetic*s of human nature and the variations of landscape, wind and sun angles. Its focus is on the means of snaring *nature's earthy nurtures* for the dweller. The practical application of orthogonal construction has much ado with the potentials and the will of the builder. We can massage the angles and curves to suit your circumstance – even if we end up with a fully *boxed* design at your request.

Some town planners have tried their hardest. They have broken the orthogonal roads *services grid* with ring roads. Broken taboos by facing houses unparallel to the road and aligned to land and cosmos. Hidden the cars behind new landscape. Set character-of-place regulations. *And in fact they have created some truly beautiful domestic environments. But have we considered the ecologic and other dilemmas?* **And the supplanting of** pre-existent local culture **with disconnected planning and construction?** Okay, imaginative designers have better visions. Familiarity and duplication breed contempt. Inadequate neighbourhood planning is not good enough. Do not over-ride the adaptabilities and social overlays of suburban people. Suburbs of course are not overly sensitive to their people and their broader landscape. But they can be very liveable, particularly on an ephemeral sightline, given trees, gardens, local social congress and individual housing activity. And often they are best with the fading imperfect, adventurous unregulated owner renovation. The key issues against the medium density suburbs are ecology, local disharmony and natural landscape heritage. The old ones we can renovate. The new ones must be *ecopical*. *Ecopicality* involves *deboxing* and serious ecological and social coordinations – ideally properly wholistic, artistic and whilst socio-economically feasible *also uncomfortably frugal and politically courageous where necessary – ecopical.*

It is fact for some reason. Designers have a hard time improving housing subdivisions because **people love them as they are** . We have humanitarian battles over slum clearances because people prefer them to the new alternatives; again, the same force that struck the Dymaxion and I dare say Arcosanti. Familiarity may at times breed contempt. But it is a very substantial issue here – addiction, inflexibility, inappropriate accustomisation, old shoe, nostalgia, time and motion efficiency. The cage lifted from the *shadow* of the ape.

Ever expanding population. Apathy to change. The needs of *handmark*, belonging, land and solitude. These are things which entice many dwellers to leafy suburban optima. A seemingly good direction. The banal low-cost house in *box-grid* allotment is simply the bare bones of this optimum. Global *Pale* is a happy victim of this earthless consumer target. The bones though may be fleshed by owners as they individualise the faces of their domestic properties, but **the direction is to any Hollywood *boulevard* – agreed, a better version of the enjoyable faulty basis**. That can be a dream lifestyle, carried by somebody's money at the ultimate expense of our progeny. And quickly it happens that we are becoming that progeny. Our ecological sustenance wains. We drive miles to get to work or just to get out of the house. But by some quirk we can properly enjoy the leafy domestic dream if we work toward a balance. And we are only people - we grasp the floating things whatever they are to make a raft on the sea. To float in hollow corks. We rationalise, adapt and enjoy, even to colour any starvation.

PLAYDOUGH for CUBBY MAKERS

*A*nimal, *vegetable, mineral,* air, energy, light, industrial cast-offs - our *playdough.* Earthy brick, clear sheets of modified sand. Our house is not a part of us - unlike the turtle. We do not project it and solidify it with our genome. We do not glaze on our *mother of pearl* by some sort of bodily secretion. Our house is part of us as it follows in concert with the land. We build. We *box* up. We *grid* down. Some of us simply make a little arrangement with our hands - from foliage to humpy. A child makes a cubby – what is she thinking Bobby? "Why did God make us build houses Daddy?" – not likely, she's just in there making it.

Bigger impacts arise from the conversion of land to permanent site and substructure. From giant tree to finely milled wood and waste and natural faecal fertiliser drained 'away' – away to where. An old word for tree is 'beam'. For some a building is romantically rearranged earth. For others, it is an objective construction. To these others, building materials are passionless incidentals. Their *playdough* fun is forgotten after the childhood sand-castles moulded from plastic buckets. We all abide with facility made from the fabric we adopt from the Earth. Like we do with the air, we may overlook the vital support for the fabric; the time, space and cosmos needed to support it and also to make *room* for home and lounge. Building materials are from the Earth, whether or not they are theoretically incidental and lost under a poly-something hermetic seal, subservient to the dwelling facilities and the lordship of cultural imagery. Mud, wood, energy. Nuclear, hydro or fire generated electricity. Wood fire, coal, oil or gas fire. Sun and fire for direct warmth. Energy for cleaning, extracting, processing, transporting, building and cooking. "It's very sad that all this about the natural world has to be said," Cheekyfella acknowledges with Low Carl, "but I can see plain as day that most of you Westerners, who make all of the mess, just don't see it for yourselves. My country back home out back is incredibly beautiful. More than eat it, I want to be it. Don't want to lose sight of it, like you Whitefellas!!! Take a tellin' you dummies. Wake up. Australians wake. Cityfellas wake."

We use a cost-per-square-metre principle in evaluating house designs. Consider cost also as ecological-impact-per-square-metre. Let's see it culturally, sculpturally. Call it *Ecosculpture*. It looks like this;

E   C   O   S   C   U   L   P   T   U   R   E

- Please visualise :-

A 'developed' nation's houses (including its lifecycle matters, such as heating) weighed <u>against its resources</u>

PLUS the house *services grid*, (roads, sewers, neighbourhood house, cable from the gable ...) <u>against its resources</u>

PLUS extraction and manufacturing, (trucks, mills, factories ...) <u>against its resources</u>

135

PLUS commercial, real estate packages <u>against its resources</u>

MINUS alternative activity. (Cheekyfella can explain that.)

- Continue visualising:-

House (*dwelling-contraption*) = trees + ore + silicon + fuel + elbow grease etc. Cuddle a tree and then a wooden *dwelling-contraption*. A road and then a barrel of tar. Water, lots and lots of precious water.

Think of the quanta, the aesthetic and the *ripples*.

When a tree is taken, air flows. The air takes the tree's place and moves away from the space whence it goes. The roots turn back to earth. The taker uses food energy, perhaps transport and a chainsaw. The ground will be marked with the fall. The world is already marked from the Fall. Moisture will slowly go from cut tree to air. An eagle may lose its eggs. A sapling may subsequently find free space, but maybe not enough time to grow. Other things happen too; that we do not comprehend. All these multiply with the taking of a forest, influencing climate, beauty, fuel industry, roads, animal life, ground water etcetera. One medium large tree will suffice to build a wooden house. About half of the tree is burnt, turned to saw-dust or low-grade use. More of it is lost to builders' off- cuts. More of it is left in the forest, on and in the ground. So there is more to it than what we see stacked on site. The side effects of mining, of the use of animal products, and of the processes of industry, conveyance and trade may all be extrapolated so.

- Continue visualising:-

Add into the *Ecosculpture*; the processes toward the ultimate use of material, its disposal and replacement. Rock, clay, mud, tin, iron, copper, specific woods, grasses, reeds, hides, sinews, rubber, derived and synthesized plastics etc go to housing. How much? There is no clear global inventory. Housing, including the ancillary industrial *contraptions*, noted above, is responsible for about three quarters of all timber used - and probably clay too. A lot of energy is used to fire and transport clay products and metal. And a lot of precious water, especially in concrete and mortar. Well above half of the total use of glass and paints is in houses.

136

There's a lot won from the ground; roofing, plumbing nails, screws, hardware, concrete reinforcing, window frames, kitchen sink, stove, refrigerator, washing machine, electrical wiring and insulation. Envisage:-
Melting it, using some sort of solar kiln, into an amalgam - copper, steel, aluminium, zinc, brass. For one house we may have three cubic metres of amalgam – a lot more than a dentist needs.

Use the amalgam in making the *Ecosculpture*.
A solid metal interpretation of Cheekyfella Talkabout shaking hands with Global *Pale*, over a hot chain saw, by a cut tree. Place it on the vacant site that was under your current *dwelling-contraption*. It's impossible to place it here, ay – but it's there anyway among the form of your current *dwelling-contraption*.

In this amalgam scenario locate something like some barrels of oil and coal and assorted other items used up in extraction and processing of the metals alone. Where does the water go and in what condition? Global has photographs gripped under his *armpit*, of his family quarry, the very hollow from whence came the concrete aggregate. With the barrels too are piles of clay and sand, accounting for the very bricks, tiles, old fashion earth pipes, glass, concrete, and mortar that may be around you now. A pile of gypsum for plaster. Cotton, wool, and hemp soften the condition on behalf of soft furnishings. A modicum of rubber, from its tree, used in floor surfacing, doorstops, washing machine belts, carpet underlay.

As we use this *playdough* in the *Ecosculpture*, it grows in complexity; cotton shirts and rubber boots for the amalgam figures and mounds of miscellaneous query, some dead birds and a lung, half rotten from toxic emissions and waste. To be fair we represent Global as smiling. He's happy, a bit; the increasing use of plastics is somewhat justifiable by their economy as substitute for natural resources. And, because they are lightweight, they are an eco-friendly cargo. Plastics are made using cellulose, oil and various other natural materials.

It is hard to say but maybe, never-the-less, the *Ecosculpture* should show a plastic albatross around Global's neck. It died of toxins like the flamingos. Flatten his smile a bit. It will foolishly rise again as he sees a still living distant horse *galloping* a Gallopilong distance and a bug falling, beaten, to his nylon carpet. As a ritual, later when you've finished the expressive artwork, fling the plastic thing into the sea so that it too can wash up in Tierra del Fuego. Then send money to a Foundation to help the real birds.

To see the innocent reality make two sets of scales in the *Ecosculpture*. One of plastic. Balance the whole house material impact against Global's wallet. Make the other set of wood. Balance the whole against Cheekyfella's grin. It smiles for the land and smirks at built cultural ego. Just photograph his grin, enlarge it, glue it onto his boomerang and sit it on the scales with his most minimal and hard-worked spear.

And the grin against the wallet is measured in the art of the *Ecosculpture*.

- Next in the *Ecosculpture*:-

Consider, further, the forming of the ancillary developments that cradle modern housing production - factories, warehouses, retail buildings, extra transport, roads, waste, and yes, advertising materials and so on. More than half of this primary product goes to housing, less to other building. This can be represented in the *Ecosculpture* by a well used mobile phone, a calculator, cheque butts and receipts spilling from Mr *Pale*'s pockets and lockable cast metal satchel. And also a Greenpeace card in Mr Talkabout's torn jeans. It's actually Mr Carl's card. Mr Talkabout carries it for inspiration.

Waste is not so great in the sphere of direct owner cost; ie where the money is out of the pocket to match the assessable purchase; as distinct from the involvement of third parties and credit. Affluence however does ensure that one man may be appalled at what another discards. This is implied in the whole mood of the *Ecosculpture*.

Land, like energy, is a resource taken for granted. In a modern Western suburbia one house uses, all considered, about twice as much land as the allotment that it's on - roads, factories etc, but as we've noted, not including lands given to food. The materials stacked on site for building are what we are using in the sculpture. So, finally, we make a second identical *Ecosculpture*, behind a screen of smoke, symbolising the ignorance of education, to acknowledge the materials, extra land, construction water, ground water redirected by factory roof and huge amount of energy that are used off-site to support the house. It's all there for your *dwelling-contraption* too.

The influence of residential facility as an extended process is cause for grave ecological concern - in some localities. It is no concern in other locations, but of great concern generally. From trees to beams and smoke. Henry Ford's first car exhaust was a hint of future smog *accumulation*. But we didn't hear that anybody saw this. Nobody imagined the eventualities. From simple *playdough* for peoplekind's cubby to vast petro-chemical waste from the expanding housing effort of the peopled human organisms. Should we stop?

If we use the resources wisely, we can make fantastic house things, with great enjoyment and enthusiasm. But as the population grows, our creative autonomy must wane over to learned corporate wisdom and pragmatic agreement to mysterious regulation. This is because; we cannot get our minds all the way around the global scale. It helps to remember the simple joys of cubby making, building blocks and *playdough* being sobered by those realities of modern adulthood apparent in this *Ecosculpture* that we have just built, ... where your house is now.

More to the point; would we stop?

How close are we? Well a kilned clay brick, as in brick-veneer, uses probably more energy than our ecopical carbon footprint can spare.

POPULATION
ACKNOWLEDGMENT
HOPE

EVERYPERSON'S WORLD

We thrive on establishing an order in the seeming random land - a romantic notion. We are bonding with the land, if we are not raping it. We order our domestics and the associated civics. They say we all need this profound human order, but this order is simply the way we do it. If we do not do it this way we turn aside to another evolution. We all need our human, national, tribal, and individual spiritual evolution. These commonalities are scant in the cultural expressions of the *ticky tacky Pale* residence. If one is a settler, one's housing is a key part in spiritual adventure. One's housing is greater than the sum of its parts. It is more than mere *accumulated* facility. More than an orderly living machine, *dwelling-contraption* or real-estate commodity.

Order is the pattern of our minds - some say, the human mind. Some think of order as that which is not us. We see that our *domestic-arrangements* are idiosyncrasies fused with a common heart upon which they vary. Likewise order varies among dweller, designers and town planners. A collage of orders prevails - variant with earth, locale and the happening people. From countryside with no houses, through the gentle *nomurbic* crossroad town, to a missed pocket of the *box-gridded* sprawl, an air molecule, freed from under a paint bubble in Bobby's house, has ventilated a flower somewhere and is now in your blood, on its way to foster a piece of wood, which some child may use in her cubby-*contraption*. Acknowledge the magic of the place and fabric of your house. And of the myriad of magical mentalities working to its betterment, from many perspectives, and notching together, like individual dwellings in an *ecopian* suburb.

Regardless of our choice of rampant industrial endeavour, it seems quite appropriate for peoplekind to establish mass settlements. "Cities, not well exampled by the contemporary ones, are a way to go! Even Uncle Albert Gallopilong would intuitively agree, I reckon so anyway," Cheeky suggests. The inimitable Low Carl clarifies "But, all creatures are neighbours. Love thy neighbour. Honour *ecopian* limits and have the courage to say no to medical life-support industry that will overstep ecological fairness. For this is all *doing housing*."

Biohouses are comparable to organisms in that they have a miniaturised ecology;

solar energy, fresh fish from indoor tanks and horticulture. The acts of operating them contribute to the energising homes that they are. Though not yet easy commodity, at least one version is proven in ecological and domestic efficiency. They support hope. Yet aside from, and even in addition to government mandate, they will have to be effectively marketed if they hope to make adequate impact. They will have to become kosher, as proven by the Dymaxion saga and there would have to be some radical politics to shape a true *ecopical* economy to meet the common pocket – *biohouses* in today's values are not cheap.

When it comes to the nitty gritty we could survive for a good while yet, only by sharing world resources, by just using up what is left and then tightening our belts. We would be living in a sea of suburban and urban scenery in desert, the weather conditions would be changed, and we just could not remain as fully people of Earth as we are today. Abundance of time, timber and space. But that was yesterday. Abundance of indifference, shame and waste. And yesterday's gone. Without a yesterday tomorrow has no basis. Will there be enough yesterday in today to base a vibrant tomorrow, to base a new house and its world? The doors of technology open fantastic housing frontiers. The using up of the oil may save us too. Pollution will be more difficult.

Already we are very heavily overstepping the limits. There are better solutions and attitudes. It is not as bad to build in the Grand Canyon, Tasmania's magnificent South West or to encroach on the environment of other housing areas, if what is being built is beautiful, rather than wasteful, polluting and stifling of nature. Yet it is still very stupid. *Dodo*. We can build huge energy efficient houses. But it is still very stupid if we build too many. As many know, who see past their own Neanderthal *shadow* status, we need across-the-board rationality – *ecopicality* as we are calling it here.

Authoritarian acknowledgement to date is not proper. Short corrective programs. No corrective programs. A lot of little over indulgences do hurt. A termite takes the last fatal bite out of a timber house pile. We learn the hard way. We cannot recreate heritage or the full hearty environment. We can slowly, very slowly do a tiny bit. We can survive living tortuously on barely enough. And how's the house? Just think about the dream house.

YOUR PORTION

There are those who have drawn a *courteous boundary* between our neighbouring wilderness habitats and our corporate self. Respect for a ravine in a 'burb, an old oak, a swathe of hills. The nomads, the frogs. The tall and the small. Much will surely fall ... to the settlers' careless maul.

Except we hope.

We, who are not nomads, are all creators in housing by rental demand, renovation, purchase demand or building. Responsibility.

Specialists meeting jobs in a professional manner, existing alongside the base beauty of the one-man-band, forms a logic and interesting combine of people in the whole housing process. Beyond these common denominators and by contact with those in touch, or specialising in the various aspects, we exist as individuals seeking continuing abode, be it a changed or unchanged abode.

In the global scheme of things there is only so much you can do and only so much you own. Keep your campsite or string of factories courteous to nature like the vast majority of the world's people in meek villages or even sprawling Indian simplicities which may need only better sewerage and water – architectural *delight* proceeds *ecopically* from there.

Low Carl chooses not anonymity. Anonymity of intervention is a problem. It was not I who stole the cookie from the earthen jar. It was my Mummy. It was the giant multi-minded corporation *megamonster* that levelled the forest and spoiled the valley with water-wash mining or a whole new Chinese megacity. I'm trapped in this system. I'm the Jew who aided the Nazi. The Sinophile who evicted. What else could I do? We can empathise, but we refuse to know. Those *ripples* in our world are of good, bad and ugly. To think that some prefer only that which they are able to carry, whilst a glutton builds a fourth palace. And a million egotists build more each than they should. And the ancient valley lives & forest habitats fall to trans-national stupidity and even to native decision; lured by the potential *pale* trap of glamorous city interiors. One house, your vote. One purchase, something green goes to smoke. One house, one set of bourgeoning inhabitants; another tile in the cultural mosaic. The manner in which we go about *doing* it is absolutely crucial lest pollution, starvation, and low energy defeat our hopes. Politicians and lobbyists drawing from the social resource ought to have this in hand as far as is allowed by public consciousness and assistance. For the individual dweller, residential building and ecology come down to three;

- × The decision to use any, or a particular piece of, land;
- × The resource efficiency of construction and;
- × Natural intervention on site.

Talk to your designer. Insulate. Even dirty light fittings encourage people to buy stronger globes, which use more power; clean them. The key is to be sensitive and responsibly aware. Don't forget. Any product purchased is of raw material taken from Earth and in reaching you the product has involved the use of other resource also. And this is because you say you want it, even as it comes that way. It is as if you yourself took directly the resources needed to produce that product. The product may be say fibre-cement cladding or a garden tap. It is on your demand that the ecology is intervened with. You are either naive or responsible. It is also possible to upset water tables, animal habits and to be the straw that broke the camels back, causing various minor and semi-minor ecological effects. All this whilst building a house; perhaps with the avant garde architectural profile or the eventual unveiling of the new Picasso as the first priority significant in their own little mind.

If you have two houses, a long-term hotel *room*, a camper van, two holiday shacks and a tent, you may cash them in and possibly have enough money for a *contraption* in a Hollywood *boulevard*, ever conscious of the *Ecosculpture*.

The houses that are causing most of the housing industry share of the problem seen from the *stratospheric stroll* probably number 2,000 in one 100,000 in the world. Probably most of the people holding this book are from that group. Probably something like 1 in that 100,000 of the worlds' houses are 'Architect' designed. Your portion is significant to the world. To your locale and the people. No house is an island – not even the first ones (well look at what they started).

EARTH, LOCALE,
PEOPLE IN MOTION

Our **domicile**, home, domestic locale. Its air, clock, vibe, fragrance. People, heritage and lifestyle. Smell it. Move in it. Meet in it. Find a builder in it. Find a bus stop. Evolution, *cosmic symbol*, land, site, continuum, neighbours and the intimacies of everyperson's world. Various attributes of our chosen locale are domestically valuable, in conjunction with the personally *accumulated* and constructed items that enhance our dwelling place. Within the broad scale environmental beauty already discussed, we look at these more intimate qualities of the geography of domestic locale; but only those qualities that take on additional dimension when **felt as amenity in house**. We compromise on some of these intimacies; we can't have it all. They increase our home with context and in-house amenity for *room* and yard. We develop and *accumulate* domestic amenities and facility. We also move toward them as attributes of locale & site.

LOCALE

EARTH, LOCALE,
PEOPLE IN MOTION

*H*ouses will last longer than people; becoming local heritage. But in the *doing of domestic activity* nothing lasts longer than the first element, the Earth. The tribal stories of the nomads roll on for centuries. The technical and cultural evolution of the house rolls on too.

Your locale may provide the intimacies of a city, a farm valley or a suburb. Or of anywhere else. Your house is a organic centre of your locale. 'Locale' - a notable entity in place, a bend in a river, a village; you, your old school - there is many a part of a life-story explaining how we arrive and move on from our locales. When it comes to people's settlement, in what originally was countryside, there comes a great wealth of natural and social value. The continuum of *people in motion*. Most die within ten miles of their birth place. The bus ride to work of course is but a fragment of the story. Bobby has come to realise that he's a flea on a feral culture while people do

tardis

GRID

Cable to gable

three

planed corner

nacre

motherofpearl

Natures nurtures

however care.

Another sense of locale is the one, there ... radially, about your house or settlement. It's the natural environment about you – if it's not so far away behind urbia that you can't see or smell it. A zephyr in your face carries a bug on a leaf from yonder tree, the roots of which are cracking your neighbour's footings. The sheds on the forested hills behind, unlike the hills themselves, are not part of this locale. This locale belongs only to the wildlife, the river and the noble savage. It is not on Global *Pale*'s map. Its millennia will ultimately digest everything we have built, puked or gently placed, including our neurons. Influenced by *dodos*, we most certainly tend to spit onto it our arrogant street *grid*s. The Feng Shui weeps. The underground water may be unpotable - faecal particles from bowels within names. **The feral sludge is as real as the wholesome culture;** somehow its odour takes the front seat.

Leaning *ecopically* on his bedroll under a bridge near Harlem and not long back from urban China, our totally *nomurbic* urban nomad, and new friend of Cheekyfella, Low Carl sees the folly of the race and the dangerous *soma* of plastic laminate and the '*box* with a screen' within the *box* without real windows in the bitumen and lawn squares laid over God's mighty thumbprint. Low Carl carries the city in his pack. His feet feel the nearby underground stream deep below the tar and cement; deep below the floor vinyl and particleboard. The star is as close as its light, but the air may be soiled. If this little book begins at its heart it begins here, centre chest, in Low Carl's locale. He is a man of talent turning away from extreme locale-squashing urbanics – sacrificing luxury for a hard principled life. This is his housing vote.

It's not difficult to **love your locale ahead of your house** – letting in *nature's earthy nurtures* and letting-in secondly the desirable of any local urb (*people's synthetic nurtures)* while *screening* and filtering out the disagreeable odours with walls, *protocol* or mentality. This is first nature, rather than second, to Cheeky.

The place that suits for your housed abode is that which you seek as an outer aspect and a *nurture* to your house – more than *galloping* holographic wallpaper for your windows. The place we seek will also tend to imbue its culture and materials on the interior of our house. There are locales to avoid for reasons pertinent to the individual or for reasons of natural heritage or other use. Land care, health and safety underpin a variety of checks to be undertaken before we move into a locale. The type of house we want may not fit there or the local backdrop may not blend intimately with your domestic requirements and preferences.

The LAND
EARTH, LOCALE,
PEOPLE IN MOTION

The land, with its atmosphere and sky: don't get swallowed up in it; rather help it *nurture* your life by adding good housing. The land is *far* more important than your synthetic architectonic visual profile. The

Building Inspector had been thinking, "With some exceptions, it should all be under buildings, road and plantation", and he's talking *boxes*. He's talking habitable land and waters – land being merely a convenience for all-important constructed interior: the more beautiful in his eyes the better. The small house (hut, igloo, houseboat, yacht): in itself it's a **cosmic symbol**. In the context of the land and cosmos, the places made by people for home in the universe we can reflect with a *cosmic symbol*. Larger houses and huge residential buildings in cities become amorphous unless there is *cosmic symbol* design provision to mitigate that which is lost to size or sprawl, screened out by roof and walls, fences, lawns, snappy designs and pavements. We cannot see the forest for the trees, the apartment for the building - cosmic context is vague. The *cosmic symbol* binds a relationship between dweller and land. A tree or a sundial may suffice or a familiar landmark, a filigree motif, a fountain or a telescope mounted on a rock found under the floor boards. Or the house itself may say it clearly. *Cosmic symbol* and the *nurtures of nature.* We need them both. Deep in crowded cities both are difficult to establish. For this reason many will easily understand this talk about the land interwoven with our architectural cultural frontiers and the heritage that runs before them.

Today my writing station is moved to the unfinished pantry of a house under construction. Friends are upstairs, building. I could be helping, but it's okay, I drew up their plans anyway. The concrete floor has puddles from recent rain. The breeze blows through the openings between the ceiling joists at the top of the double brick walls. There is little to block out the whistling of birds. It is as if nature is streaming Feng-Shui-like through the house from the hill behind to the inlet below. When the lounge walls just above are plastered, carpet laid and the plasma screen is in, and especially if too many synthetics are used, there is potential to deplete or lose that stream. The inhabitants in their interior would be deprived.

On the nearby peninsula is a house where this could not happen. Among trees and bushes are their earth walls. The floor was the same ground. Continuous as you walk in. It was kept dry with drains but the people were seeking a way to stop dust forming and to avoid mud, from spillage. The fireplace was a development of the original campfire, by which they first slept under the stars. This place should not be called a site, for as they camped in the wild they *did their housing,* as it happens, about them. There was canvas and tapestry for doors, and lean-to awnings. I asked them about the draughts. They just dressed to suit and enjoyed the breezes. Their fireplace was simply stacked stone, effectively pointed with clay. We laughed about the probable reaction of the Building Inspector, who in this instance is a symbol of bureaucracy. He had shrugged it off to date. He would, however, be stymied when the nature builders eventually fitted their plumbing - thus making it a more obvious affair of the local Council. Vegetables abundant in a hanging basket, lounge chairs with the legs cut off, glass skylight, natural wood poles, no corners and an external appearance that was as natural as nature - beautiful little manifestations of home. **An interior of maximum natural nurture.** "Maximum!?" cheeks Cheekyfella, comparing it to Albert's camp. But you know what I mean, no shortage of *nature's earthy nurtures*.

Land is nature. **An interior can be tuned from maximum nature to minimal nature.** Minimal is sometimes a problem, and so is maximum if you are not bred like Cheekyfella. Warm grass hut or cold white *box*. Poor design can switch down the value of the land in your lounge – filtering it out. Some people need more *natural nurture* than their house provides. Some nature is always there, of course; the air is there, even if modified, and so is the nature of the dwellers hearts and toenails. Some say that housing should spring from the soil - organic, Feng Shui, earth, air, fire, water. <u>Bonded, integral with the ground it should be</u>, by materials, locale interface, weight, ground structure, kitchen water from the spring, sewerage pipe connection. Others say that this presumption is only a throwback from our use of the handiest materials; stone and earth. Gina's palaeolithic heart bleeds. Plastics and hyper-industry are now handy. So there are other ways to do things - the Daleks are happy. <u>A house can be relatively divorced from the land</u> - renovated buses, space capsules, factory-made dwelling machines, inner-tardis flats; all are much freer of site organics than covered wagon, yacht and stonemason. They're freer too than the organic dwellings, but that freedom is not all that is to be considered. Simple natural orgone, earth, wind, fire, *rich earthy brick* and water are nourishment. Balanced microwaves. Zesty auras. *Nature's earthy nurtures*. We can get them as we work and enjoy the land, but if we are housebound or synthetic citybound we need them inhouse. It's easy though to step out of a *roomy* hermetically sealed caravan onto healthful earth. Variety. There are so many options, but our renovations and designs must be wholistic. We must use our life-saving industry in concert with *nature's organics* on which to tactfully hang our *synthetic aesthetic* – our architectonic delight or our simple down-home personalised vibe.

The houser may choose to block out the land, but when it is greatly abundant he can't fail to leave plenty of it indoors. Two centuries ago in some North American plains, people were happy with an abrupt land-house relationship. After a hard hot working day out of touch with each other in the often dry windy air between the pungent sky and flat dusty earth: **they went inside**. The door, heavy timber, if timber was handy, shut away the hard hot day. The sod roof and thick earth walls, a few small windows and cramped rooms welcomed with suitable cool protection and family closeness; alfresco dining on a patio was not at all popular here. This puzzles Albert Gallopilong - he simply **didn't go in** like that. Never-the-less the physical *nurtures* of the plains, the land, was there inside that sod house. Things are radically different right there right now under the highways of today's techno-social interiors - the valiant plains remnant shaking the joyful

fist of organics through the cracks in the footpath and the distant
skyline at the immense oily settlement fabrication.

Our consciousness of land in association with house changes. In the
past people knew their houses as 'on the land', springing from the
soil. Today, consequent to the depth of cities, cars and industry,
increasingly the land tends to be 'conveniently under the houses and
lawns'. The priority, once the land, is now the house -
the global *pale*. The house, like tap water and electricity, is part
of the three dimensions of the Earth. "Never forget children that milk is not
from the fridge from whence you took it – and the cow may not be from your
continent and the cow's body may be genetically modified." The abode in which
you are, even with its failings in planning or aesthetics, and social
inanities, holds together like the land as a result of living principles,
physics, organics, delight as the seat under you is keeping you where
you are now. For many today the land as a backdrop is substituted
by a city of steel and glass. A very different amenity; the land; the
view. Imagine there's no housing, it's easy if you
try, around us only land, no homeless here to
cry; nomadic walking man, instead of concrete
blocks and urban shapes against the sky.

If all today's billions were nomadic would there still be as many?
Regardless nomadism is not an answer to the progeny of these times,
the house-burst generations – breeding like cane toads and locusts.

In many ways, the qualities of the land and locale are not always
sensibly incorporated in our designs. The lifestyle traditions of
people linked to foreign places and times will often dominate over
land sensitivity - cultural comfort ahead of creature comfort.

Cultural first. Natural second. Bum on a daisy. Burger wrapper
left behind. Somewhere an acid rain falls.

Eccentric fashion too; we sometimes allow it to fly in the face of good
taste in the name of our own uniqueness and conservatism. And
also there is no doubt that people can be very very silly. Very silly.
We note incidentally, in this silliness, profound scholastic
architectural psychology. The qualities of the land do not strike
romantic thoughts of earthly intimacy into everyperson's
Housefandango libido. The Abophiles, sure. The Samoaphiles too.
Those whose houses float on rafts of reeds on Lake Titicaca too. The
staid establishment conservative, and the 'great pale western
incubated suburban televisory machine support organism', no ...
... ♫♪There are red ones and there are green ones,
yellow ones and blue ones and they're all made
out of *ticky tacky* and they all look just the
same♪♫.

Building may be as rearranged earth – *playdough* - or as objective
construction. Planet Earth is soil, rock, vegetation ... and air. To be

intimate with the Earth is not to cling to the ground only. The jet has shown us the potentials of air not only in manageable force, but in magnitude. Peoplekind have in some cases over-developed their awareness of the air in proportion with the ground. The Age of Aquarius is about air. Many of us have our houses set in air, with a seal of plastic membrane, concrete and carpet sitting on the soil underneath. Lawns sometimes are all but synthetic in spirit. Living in the air, the ground is the dirt untouchable under the floor - maybe forty stories down. Come out you Hobbits among us? Our response to incorporation of the land. This is probably the first key to balanced design. Response in shelter. In sensual enjoyment. Sharing. Utilisation. And that mysterious supportive soul. Our response is coloured by our *attitude.* Our attitude may be foreign, locally ignorant cultural bias. Perhaps our attitude is philosophical, based in aesthetics or in respect; or our attitude is intuitive – or at times very silly. Attitudes, all, have social and ecological consequences. Our philosophies and perspectives vary. The West traditionally tends to order nature to suit. Dominate it - fit the site to the house. The 'old' East tended to suit nature. Respect it - fit the house to the site. One knows more about inclemency than the other perhaps. One builds a bastion, the other an integration. Each approach may suit their home land but not that of the other. And indeed respect, or lack of, for the land is in the measure. Some build stark, white and rectangular in opposition to nature. Others are organic, nuts and berries and others a blend of the two. And others lie over it, or with it, their contemporary architectural delight.

The genetics of the Dazzlers' 1970s Austrophile house spilled into the Great Southern Land two hundred years ago, about the time of the sod houses in North America. Fertilised by locale the first house sprang from foreign cultures, makeshift wattle and daub, mud brick and stone with shingle roofs and no glass. House builders were mostly displaced Anglophiles and Irophiles in those days and so, even as designs emerged from basic options to sophisticated, the houses in an oft balmy Australia were like drab-weather retreats. English houses were built in Australia and as it happened in New Zealand, America and elsewhere too. Different climate, landscape, resources and spirit should generate different architecture. Cultural roots and established industry are slow to change. Even today Australian houses in themselves are not strong in land character. They do though, in some number, honour the land – including of course its coast. As do the architects in growing strength. Even in Australia's tropical Queensland we built these drab-weather bastions. "The twits ... sweat soaked *armpits* and trying to get warmer," smirked some of the easy-going Talkabout mob whilst their cousins a little earlier were at what was to become today's Sydney Harbour, unhoused, refrigerator free, dwelling the idyllic clean smooth golden sandstone, sun-soaked beside sparkling aqua waters, abundant with crustacean, fish and fish oil rubs in this impromptu domestic place and fresh swimming glistening naked, free of marine petrol slick, cleansing that snot crusted in the hot dry hinterland, biodegradable above their healthful swarthy *walking indigenous ephemeral-settler l i p* , now glistening above snowy teeth. Determined but snagged in not so refined *box*, up north, the antipodean style rooms were too hot. Following the sweaty lessons, a deep shady balcony was added all round; still inadequate for the climate. They eventually lived on the balconies and also eventually raised the floors. The rooms were abandoned to incidentals. Like the weather, local materials and landform were hardly acknowledged. Southward in Tasmania the beautiful appearance of native Huon Pine and Blackwood, handy and easily workable for doors and household trim, was painted over with imitation grain as an 'elegant veneer' to look like English timbers. The principle of this somewhat *pale* cultural inclination remains today in various manifestations, whether between adjacent locales or faraway countries – in individual designers, their clients, house purchasers and renovators. A dose of it as part of our *synthetic aesthetic* is desirable, perhaps a visual placebo of sorts. But to swamp away the local land and culture; no. Talk about ignore the indigenous wisdoms. They went ahead *palely* on pattern with the 'old country', creating England inside and in the garden, and in the town. Admittedly they did this to accommodate the value of their traditional interior facilities, *synthetic aesthetic*, and an anticipated lifestyle – largely for psychological security. In tropic they remained dressed *dodo*-like in cold place clothes, ate big hot meals in hours that suit work in English weather – a Mexican siesta would be better. It was pretty much the same in cool temperate Tasmania here, but more tolerable. The Talkabouts lived in close physical and spiritual association, a totalish harmony, with the same land, but to say the very least, they called it by names different to those appearing on the new maps of the cultural conquerors. In Samoa we built lightweight houses, without walls, raised from the ground to catch the cooling breezes – I wonder what toilet arrangements their community had. This eventually came to happen in Queensland. **The land had won**, in the limited way it can, considering the momentum demands of the Anglophiles' customary interior character comforts, amenities and facilities – the Governor's Sunday dinner suit hot iron pressed on a rack in a shellacked English ash wardrobe against a lathe-plastered wall and on a broad-boarded floor, an ink-welled writing desk with leather inset and *room* at the side for gushing velvet drapes currently on the ship from London, all framed in axe-split eucalypt to the delight of the white ant. Wind shelter, seclusion and privacy needs are resolved in Samoa by their culture and broader environment - though it would be nice to know how they found no value in walls and if they used a form of fencing. Perhaps Minimalism was their way (like one modern kosher).

It's not just a house. Properly done, it is an individual solution to suit first the locale, ahead of the cultural character of the inhabitants. As we noted; people will tend to *suit their character first*, but the sometimes gentle yet always relentless disciplines of site and land will make themselves known. The colonist folk woke up and somewhat submitted to the new tropical land. Their houses adapt as quirky *contraptions* at least attempting compromise with the land. **Wherever; respect and appreciate the land first.** Especially before dozing it; as there may well be financial benefit in its functional and aesthetic values in integration with the flora and lie of the land; and value in conservation, for the world as well as the dweller. There are many potentials. Bushes and trees can be used to insulate or catch some snow. Deciduous trees lose their leaves allowing the sun through in the winter and sheltering in summer.

The way of Tolkien's Hobbit is a rare way of integrating with the land. It is by in-ground or earth-covered building. This technique is not orthodox kosher; it's too invisible, no architectural or suburban statement showing to the street, vague as to address and a bit more costly - but can be nicer to the countryside. Sheep may be able to graze on the roof. However, the commodities of in-ground housing are not widely appreciated. Building in, not on, the ground, is not as dark and musty as one might expect and it can be sharper and more avant garde, even than that which delights a Hobbit. Dream houses are not always of cloud and ether. A small number of happy cowgirls have emerged from the hot bath in a pool of solar gain while four metres below the grass roots. These houses can be made as fallout shelters, are safer in earthquakes, steady in temperature and more sheltered from neighbourhood sounds. In contrast again is the notion of the Swiss Family Robinson tropical tree house; a huge limb treaded with sturdy textured bark as a ramped front path. Earth is more than the *playdough* to build with. It is also the land with which to live indigenously. Not just for people, for itself perhaps and at least the other creatures. You might find more body weight in the millions of worms under the pasture than in the cows on it. Caution is part of the land marriage too. Rare radon gas may creep from rock and ground and cause cancer in the dwelling-organism. Beasts, crawlies, flood, all manner of inclemency, bushfires and polluted ground water demand our design vigilance. Earthquake fault-lines, pressures and chemistries in the ground by creating geopathic stress may make life a little uncomfortable. The mental and aural power of a mass of water in contrast to that of a mauve field full of fragrant flowering lavender - *the land has many empathies with our organism and spirit.* No architect can give you a field of lavender, but the architect/planner may deliver the lavender to your lounge by artful design - if you have a field nearby, your house will not be requiring so much fabricated *delight* and so may be cheaper to build. Oneperson's gold may be another's charity. Industry's electromagnetic fields add something new in the land - everybody's garbage we suspect. Your architect will be prone to block it out – maybe we should adopt lead lining as a new convention.

Natural conservation gains importance as the local lands fall under the *theodolite*. It's not just distant 'wilderness' that must be conserved but also local natural lands – local 'wilderness', natural heritage. **It's for our health too.** The *Ecosculpture* rings in. Bush, plains, desert, swamp and other terrain has gone under housing, domestic land, associated public works, roads, sewerage plants, power generation, water plants, crèches, and local halls. What proportion of buildable land is built on already? How much land is needed and used for housing related forest, mining, and quarrying? Amazing quanta these days. Even the major jungles are being stripped – taking the leafy skin from the indigenous Borneo inhabitants only this morning living *boxless* pampered by branch and leaves away from pungent sky and howling air. It is said that we are running out of land to build on, yet we see open spaces and vast wilderness tracts. We can find, and grow, billions of tons of trees for house building. Tons of *room*! Tons left for use! Yes and no. It is a complex world. Peoplekind's values are of vital consideration here. If we give up eating meat we regain vast areas of pastureland for other development. If we care little for the realities of natural inheritance, we can over-rule the wilderness areas. In Japan, where trees are now rare, we see how people live with relatively little *room*. Western cities and suburbs may be luxurious with land in comparison. All over the world people are fighting for natural environment to have final priority over our poor development effort. It means we are beginning to encroach on areas that our vote does not want developed with housing. Each house, as we've seen, effectively takes up more *room* than just the land under it and its yards, baggaged with roads, quarries, factories and more. Why not honour the Kyoto protocol? Hallelujah, they will say, because the heavenly city is on its way. Ten, nine, eight … . Bring it faster with our master blaster. As to the land so to the weaker. *Dodos* worth billions. (They're invading again as I write.) Wilderness heritage, environmental ecology, beauty and recreation are the reasons for land conservation. Simple domestic righteousness. Very often we want these in close accessible and enjoyable proximity to our crowded residential areas. We need to limit and coordinate built growth in locales to enhance the land, not to consume it; for our own pleasure and wellbeing and that of ecology and creatures. The deep and meaningful *delights* and motivations of the land are invaluable. The house introduces a new aesthetic element. It must be sympathetic, if it is to be. *Nature's earthy nurtures* is married by our *synthetic aesthetic*. We would never build in Grand Canyon, on Uluru, One Tree Hill or put a house boat on the local swimming hole but *we have over-ridden some very beautiful places with our houses, gardens, roads and residential industry.*

You may get on better with the neighbours if you acknowledge their cultural lingo and familiar visual preferences through your house expression – your dynamic ego and leading edge expression should still be there.

Your site is your vote in the land – in the country, in a city or at sea.

An AGREED PLOT
EARTH, LOCALE, PEOPLE IN MOTION

A tribe following the *seasons*. Yams and song. Others have little or no time for this, being busy with crops and concrete footings. And they don't miss it. Elsewhere in the time-place continuum a nomad king may settle, in order to continue growing himself. There is water. He has food brought in. So a centre is established. Grains begin to grow at home as if by accident.

As is for any travellers; for the nomads, as persons and as tribes, a new domestic *locale* applies with each ephemeral encampment - a familiarity prevails if the encampment is a revisit. If all people were once nomadic, what number of causes led to permanent settlements? One cause may have been the magnetism of some beautiful place abundant in fish and yams. Who would leave such a place? Pretty likely such a place is a 'place' for settlement.

Differentiating between 'place' and 'site'; a 'site' is a planned subdivision, an agreed plot, associated with a 'place' of settlement. The planning may be cursory or broadly public.

A national colonising party selecting the same virgin place for a township settlement might call that place a site; a portion of proclaimed lands. But once settled it is a town. The proclamation of colonising rights over broad-scale lands is an act from dubious values. The proclamation of a town-plan to organise community development is surely righteous. If people were righteous all the way, there would be no argument as to who has which site. Give me the West bank. People will argue. We could draw lots; but no, an inheriting or conquering somebody, or body-corporate, claims ownership, so we may be allowed to buy a site as a supply-and-demand commodity. Having drawn lots, sites may become commodities anyway, but this is within the measure of daily work gains. Ownership of vast continents may be achievable, on a daily work-gains basis, by the uniting of towns and regions. It then becomes politics as to how the land is made available. Ownership in truth. God grant. Albert Gallopilong values differently to the *megamonster*. It is the legal/bureaucratic/self-interested principle that we all know today, the *megamonster* that can feast only on the *dodos* that creep into people's minds. It is any individual's careless regard for utopian truths that create the *dodos*. And so - buy what you can. This is the rule of thumb. The dream-house bubble bursts. Buy what you can - of the paradise 'place' that was.

Those are societies' acts of siting. Our individual acts of siting are limited to assessment of options, choice and arrangement of tenure; aside from gift or inheritance. If we site ourself on a vacant allotment rather than a developed one, we propose a deflowering establishment of domestic facility.

And so here the principles of site selection are homogeneous with the principles of house design; what is a house, what is a site?

Our house design checklist overlaps our site checklist. Simple selves relate to places for home. We know that some of the amenities they would build into their houses may best be found in the undeveloped site; the tree shade, the mauve of the field, the 'mud' for the bricks, the water supply, aspects of landform, the quiet. Citizens and customers relate to sites as links between place and society. Unlike ancient times sites now more often tend to come already encumbered with *dwelling-contraption* and/or community urban development requirements.

Our site is limited to boundaries, easements, codes and common courtesy. Its shape is based on straight lines except where some natural element such as a stream may wiggle it. The land may wiggle the underfoot which is yours to a depth – but somebody other than you might rightfully claim the minerals that may be therein.

Probably all have either some legal right to sunlight or no chance of losing it, various rights to the river water that may flow through; and reasonable access. Usually no legal right to views, desirable outlook, subject to planning regulation regarding the extent of neighbouring houses and our own. There may be some provisional right to privacy. We have law as defence against intrusion by person as we have for ownership responsibility. Natural and cultural heritage conservation may limit or inspire your development potential. No mining rights without a stake, and perhaps your site may be forcibly acquired for public works or military use. In some places, such as the Philippines, bureaucracies are morally flexible; the titles office may tell you that there has been a mistake – somebody else owns the land on which you have built.

Site aesthetics: people will vary on this - beauty and expression are in the beholders' eyes. There's often a strong case, sometimes a lawful one, sometimes also awful, to say the site should, in construction thereon, show a certain neighbourhood flavour of natural or cultural aesthetic or expression, because a planning code says so – some locals fought hard for the code. Consult your experts thoroughly. And more by way of purchases, we must cover the cost of our regular share of the *services grid* and community services. A site has both land and social context. And neighbourhood.

This is subdivision for *crowds of domestic-contraptions*; but more pointedly for people. Some will grow *pale* therein. Others will be born of *pale* parents. Yet others will burgeon in well provisioned *nurture*. It has been happening for thousands of years in a very similar fashion, simply because we have feet, hands, *domestic-contraptions* and like to crowd into where the action is. There is no other way to do this. A communal gathering of Gallopilong's Harmoninnies has similar indigenously styled arrangements; more social than *theodolite*. The Harmoninni boundaries within encampments are fluid yet clearly articulated. Typically Abophilic, the arrangement is not for distance between walls and from street

Mid stream in the mystic

but firstly for togetherness of kin and as drawn by social ties. There is always flexibility for visitors. Despite varied and occasional use of orthogonal huts among other options, their scale of things allows self siting which is quite distinct from the cumbersome Western *box* planned siting. The hut, merely a lightweight offside aspect of the physicality of their domicile, is designed for occasional limited seclusions. Seclusion is generally from other people, but can also be from the distractions, discomforts and disturbances of the land and locale. The seclusions within the settler's house, quiet private niches away from it all, you may find bear no relationship to the locale, the heat of day nor the rustle of the wind. These sometimes tenuous aspects being forgotten until stepping out from the shaded depth of their interior into the glisten of the sun. The portico and veranda, even whilst they may be partially secluded, bear a direct relationship to locale - the kitchen too. Relieved to be back out in the stable comfort of the road-linked orientations of the unchanged portico, the Building Inspector has a slight concurrence with Bobby's *reeling* as he recalls the vapour of the passing Gallopilong cracking the repose of the lounge lizard in a dim corner of the egg room – Gallopilong, a living example of *nature's earthies*, inhabiting momentarily in a house which values the *nurture*.

Driving the message home: good development of the site protects against and values that which the land and locale offers - while contributing to it. There may be sad loss caused by development,

156

Many build with our plastic

however.

Today with population, global economy, town planning conventions and the free Earth being expensive, handy vacant sites are increasingly harder to obtain; except in re-subdivision and at the frontiers of the sprawl. In order to cast an optimum vote for Bobby, maybe we shall go to a developed site and demolish or renovate in order to improve things. Compromise appears to suck, but the ultimate temporality of realty reality eases the strain. The greater cause gives worth to compromise.

Building on rock is a way. The land under your house is a structural component usually, helping to hold your house together and supporting your floor. It is always there holding the house away from the centre of the Earth or wherever it is that the draw of gravity would take it; or is it the inertia of the house's mass. Sometimes it's buoyancy keeping the houseboat above the riverbed. People site themselves in all sorts of places. Good, bad and ugly. Large river-rafts, ocean yachts, underground, on the land or devoid of *cosmic symbol* deep in a recycled city building. Whole towns and eventually cities have been badly located, very unfortunately both for residents, animal habitat and environment - Pompeii, San Francisco. Banda Aceh. Look twice before you follow suit and add to the unfortunate *accumulation* - no matter how cheap or convenient. Your beckoning house foundation may also displace some valuable ecological link, impinge on an important neighbourhood natural recreation spot, or cover some prime growing soil. This may be a difficulty for you, as today there will always be somebody trying to sell it to you, and as sure as you give the spot away to nature, a llama's lounge, or social commonsense:- somebody else will coldly jump on it. Pragmatics sometimes help us to avoid unpreferred compromise. That is to say that you might as well buy. Or should you?

Sit yourself mentally in a favourite nature spot. A real place. Not imaginary. Smell the grasses. Feel the breeze, step out of the car of knowledge and walk barefoot on the land unrestricted by any track. *Nature's earthy nurtures;* imagine what you would build there and the impact it has. Now include favourite settlement cultural surroundings ... and review your ideas. Now still mentally entertain the same notions on your site allowing the realities to temper them. Now formally assess your site and locale, take advice and either design or move on - the neighbourhood may be rank.

SITE QUALITIES
EARTH, LOCALE, PEOPLE IN MOTION

In selecting a site we must check thoroughly its locale and its position in the locale. Or should we go to the antipodes. Narrow the options to a manageable number, checking them all for the domestic qualities which are there, remembering the sorts of things that people need, and like, consciously and subliminally, and that you need specifically.

"Ah, diss is th'place, jus here,see!" says Cheeky's nephew. As we have noted a site may coincidentally answer some of one's domestic building needs or in addition offer unimagined enhancements. A *delightful* outlook may save you the work of fabricating to make *delight,* or there may be spring water to hook straight into the kitchen tap. The nature, *nature's earthy nurtures*, which you can have inside, may be your site's best asset. Open access to the sun's rays gives some opportunity to avoid construction of a fireplace. The domestic checklist overlaps the site checklist. "That was worth repeating," agrees Low, "The Gallopilong's don't take care of hygiene with disinfectants. They use the sunlight and mobility." "Security and seclusion may be answered by location alone. No need to build for them, if you can dwell in an appropriate place." Seclusion within your tribe, suburb or family may require built screens or protocols however.

On the other hand the *adversities* are there. Like. Future developments - a highway or sewerage plant coming next door. Existing conditions - thorns, fire, snakes, midnight noise, nuclear radiation, factories, flight paths, electromagnetic fields, pollution drift, gas, mass murderer next door, cholera in the neighbourhood, no fresh local vegetables available. Will there be an earthquake, tsunami, bushfire, flood or eruption one day?

In some locations and seasons, bushfire may be a very serious issue. If you must take a site here speak with authorities, neighbours and professionals. There are many practices, design considerations and evaluations. Location of the house on the site may offer a wide variety of domestic options. Site features and landform affect fire movement, wind channelling (for shelter and for ventilation) and yard forms. They also affect the design, detail and shape of the house as we build for fire resistance and general liveability. Some plants are fire retardant. Water mains pressures will drop during a fire – the *grid* is frail in some regards.

A Feng Shui plan for the site may be appropriate – involving analysis of so called male and female land points, orientations, when to build, materials, colours, windows and doors placements, appropriate flowers, furniture and patterns with respect to arrangement in Taoist yin yang harmony, for good 'chi'. Feng Shui may, weird or not, involve throwing earth into the air and reading the resultant effect on the ground, like tea leaves – a form of dowsing or divining. The willow-wood manner of dowsing, for energy points or water, may turn up some interest. Running an eye over with your own idea of beauty and conservation may be all you need. All are land assessments. Make a character value analysis - delightful granite outcrop, grasshoppers, particular trees and grasses, microclimatic peculiarities. The lie of the land or other surroundings will form airflows, secondary to prevailing winds. Sunlight is good for you. Humidity, dampness and mould will bug you. Sub-surface rocks, clay or tree roots may make footing work more costly. Seasonal or permanent water flows or seepage are serious concerns. Use what you will. Remove, lose & screen what you will. Avoid what you must.

Under all that suburbia was once native life; you may wrongfully continue its destruction. The bulldozer may cost the loss of some irreplaceable advantage in vegetation or other heritage. It may well be best to remove some *adversities* such as weed plants, contaminated soil; but we cannot obliterate all such things. If there are potentially lethal red-back spiders in the house they or the dwellers must go, but if they are away in a wild bit of garden take care and live with them.

The varieties of flora and fauna on a site may offer value to the dweller, or others. Grasses stabilise soil, retain rainfall, and harbour insects, birds and small animals. Shrubs stabilise soil, make good ground cover, screens and creature homes. Deciduous trees provide summer shade and mulch for the ground, house birds and channel breezes. Evergreens make good wind and snow breaks, screens and pleasant music when the wind blows. Domestic amenity like this is relatively free of cost.

Soil types vary; silt, loam, clay, sand, gravel, rock. There may be several types at various locations and depths. The type and circumstance of surface and of subsurface soil and rock impacts drainage, percolation, structural potentials, stability, heat storage and insulation value, planting, ease of construction, adobe potential etc. Even its colour and odour. Does it stick to your boots and carry inside? Does it soak your garden water away? The scent of earth supports optimum health – part of *nature's nurtures*. Let it into your house. This scent in its many forms is often flattened by tar, cement, exotic (foreign) plants, lawn, dozers and building. Give thought to your soil type and general terrain as you might for your brick choice.

Confirm availability of *grid* services and community facilities. Find out what you can from the locals - demands, rates, local development plans, availability of builders, materials. The nearest sawmill may be hundreds of miles away, making timber expensive or changing your options. A wooden house may not be allowed in a particular suburban area. That gravel road you like may be turned to bitumen next year. You bought on a hilltop, forgetting that you ride a bicycle. Some locations may pose health problems from natural, societal or industrial conditions.

The whole site is domestic realm, but often the house is designed as though detached from the site and then placed upon it. Landform or feature may be adapted to suit *room* amenity – a solid stone outcrop may be cut to form in-situ internal stair. S*ensible use of the domestic commodity available from the site is seen through integrated house/site design.* It will baulk much of suburbia and the town planning world if your house is located other than centre front of your site. But it may be wisest, subject to circumstance.

And so we also note, it is a lot more than simple *domestic-contraption* that contributes to the amenity and evolution of housing. The changes to the land around the house cause changes to the house. The key contrast here is the city apartment compared with the grass hut. Can you imagine arranging to build a grass hut or mud house in the city. Could be quite expensive. Illegal. No skill in the industry. You'd have to do something about traffic grime settling on the grass and fumes coming through.

The CONTRAPTION EVOLVES

EARTH, LOCALE, PEOPLE IN MOTION

Here we go ... doing our housing. Evolving this contraption – steeped in our orthodoxies. Orthodoxy, to be healthy, is backboned by convention and fingertipped by innovation. Innovation is achieved through renovation, invention, necessity, addition, conversation, discovery, accident, meekness, ego, passion ... . Innovation contributes to evolution. So; a healthy orthodoxy may evolve.

*Staidness, innovationlessness, is the stigma that taints our common
interpretation of the otherwise honourable institution of orthodoxy.
The convenience of convention reclines like a couch in the jungle of
innovation. There to be honoured, utilised, modified or discarded at
will; discarded for a lack of need, or by inspiration to make new
innovation. New innovation must precariously face the many traps
that the jungle conceals. If successful, the new innovation will join the
old to become evolved convention – racy updated couch reclining in the
same jungle.*

The evolution of the *housing-contraption* does not necessarily have a
parallel in any evolution of species. Certainly the charisma and
spirit of settled people in some ways brightens as their housesdevelop
and evolve. And in some ways the charisma may be dulled in
shadow. Neurological wealth of a certain kind accrues from housing.
Settled society evolves only in a settled way; regeneration after a post
Fall degeneration perhaps, rather than new development through
evolution. The evolution of peoplekind is conjectured. House embryo
already begun, Gina Palaeolithic, maybe out of Eden, finds some *red
and yellow lycra sail cloth.* "It was just lying there. Draped over that
wheel thing that Uncle Ugg has been whittling! Maybe it dropped out
of that Dr. Who's Tardis thing!! It doesn't smell or feel like hide. I'm
sure it's going to come in very handy," she marvels, movingly
sensual, as she feels her familiar feminine domestic innovation
coming on. The evolution of resources, ownership, society and
design is a phenomenon witnessed by simple dwellers today as it was
yesterday. And this relates to housing itself and to its construction.
Our characters are probably more complex today, but Cheekyfella
and Low Carl wonder about that, as they share thoughts about a
current figment that is *Ecopia* – a domestic quality that has been
bypassed by urban evolution. They note the dangerous evolution of
house-based debt and environmental harm.

Indigenous vernacular houses exist still today, their dwellers
subsisting with basic facility. In addition we have very rudimentary
urban vernaculars, such as in outback Asia, by far the most common
housing form across the globe. The other end of a spectrum is in a
Hollywood *boulevard*; with new amenity in additional interior and
exterior *room* and the new aesthetic of its locale. The designers may
well have deprived the *boulevard* house of nourishing indigenous
amenity in earthy materials and simplicity. Today in the West we see
good bad and ugly diversities happening in housing. The house has
sprouted many varieties. It continues to sprout; providing different
amenities and with different processes of design and construction, in
suburbs, everywhere.

The ease of changing abode is a significant aspect of today's
evolutions. Another aspect is the introduction of a modern public
interface within the domicile, inside the front door - work remotely
from home, telephone canvassing. Nobody knows what will be

common place – *for this 0.1% of all peoplekind.* An electronic inglenook - a new *room-entity* - for the computer, remote control of windows and blinds, plasma wallpaper - all things electronic and chemical. Turn on the surround sound and vision *room* - electronic sky on the ceiling. The existing old built fabric though will remain in use as long as it can be economically maintained and renovated; and cherished for its cultural epoch - Art Deco, always a popular one and always will be.

Contemporary housing motives include creation for facilities which are additional to those that motivated Gina and Cain - the future will include motives additional to ours now. Piped water and sewerage have been used for thousands of years. Our facilities have not become, so much more refined as more in number. More items in our *accumulations* - tv, pools, piped gas, more rooms, more cars, boats, more complexity. Clever refinement has been exercised in secure and artful construction of even contemporary primitive dwellings - using very basic materials. We exercise the same clever refinement - with our own modern resources. In the future, when we of now are the dumb homo superior of the past, people will exercise the same clever refinement with their own heritage and modern resources. The items and facilities themselves become more refined because we have the benefit of previous invention and status quo as an additional resource; the benefit of heritage - and population; thanks to medicine.

Our household amenity becomes lesser in some ways too. The chimney and hearth give way to electricity, gas, oil, insulation and solar arrangements. Kitchens reduce and vanish under the influence of city provisions. The *cute little opening* becomes all manner of doors, lobbies, porticos and paraphernalia. Values change with industries and extinctions. Glass becomes cheaper, a great plus, and wood, sadly, dearer. *Rarefied raw materials become more expensive.* It's the same with skills. How easy is it to find somebody to build a fireplace that doesn't smoke, as fireplaces become fewer ? It was around the 1500's in Norway, it has been said, that the first chimney appeared - I suspect earlier they were about outside Europe. The chimney was made abundant in London by Henry V111. Do fireplaces bear some house amenity parallel to the 'home theatre'? Home theatre is *synthetic aesthetic,* rather than the *nature's nurtures* of fire and brick. However home theatre does bring imagery of nature. Additional facility used in contemporary modernity is in ultra-violet protection, water purification, finance, *room* for cars and dishwasher, and the rest. We are not cleverer, we're more broadly stimulated, having more at our finger-tips.

Here

we

go

evolving

Today on one hand we depend on the *services grid* and on the other we have potential to return to some domiciliary autonomy in the likes of *biohouses.* Construction and modern domestic *accumulation* is heavily industry-reliant, rather than owner autonomous. We are slow like the mighty *Mega*. **Owner building is surely a natural right and of very healthy value.** It is seriously frustrated and in fact is threatened by industry specialisations, mediocrity's law-suit psychologies and government standards based on, to be extreme, *pale* expectations of the kosher *ticky tacky box.* "Keep those grubby slum people out of our neighbourhood. Put them in a welfare *box.* Same for those nomads. I can't imagine how they can be happy living in those home-made shacks," demeans a *pale* voice in *boulevard* incubated politics, sweeping more dirt under the rug. Originally houses perhaps were not as much fun as they are now – shacks, no glass, leaky roof, no hinges, a single *room*, limited colour. But there were no building regulations and we could own them faster. They were simply houses - in use in daily life - *and easier to owner-build.* Regardless the daily domestics of Albert Gallopilong didn't leave him envious after his spirit visit to the house with the egg room in the Austrophile's grotto, and this is not because it didn't have an in-built vacuum cleaning system.

Thousands of years ago some Egyptians would head upstairs to a 'cosy' toilet and bathroom. The developments in plumbing and particularly sewerage are the milestones that substantiate and intensify permanent settlement. These developments go hand in hand with disinfectants, scrubbing brushes, river pollution, severe water shortage and crowding - the settler brings disinfectants into his house but all Albert needs are herbs, if his body ails.

Innovations, developments and discoveries are hand in hand with the feeling of growth and direction. People, though, being usually comfortable with a staid, self-owned, orthodoxy are very slow to grasp innovation when they are accustomed and attached to that which is already serving them - slums included. The time involved in the evolution of any development in housing is extended therefore by industrial and political factors. Industry, process and investment - the momentum of its status-quo has always sobered manifestation of invention. (I trust reading remains easy – I'll be in the back room making a cup of tea.) The industry man says, "Man will never fly ... and anyway we are flat-out building today's order." On the other hand the discovery of electricity has had a staggering impact on construction potential, household amenity, household devices and manufacture; easy hot bath, water pumps, heaters, refrigeration, windowless rooms without candles. If you are worried about the industry *megamonster* and its interruption to the rhythm of the *happening organism*, blame a lot of it on electricity. Or, rather, our use of it. It is very significant in the evolutionary phasings of the house and its locale. Motorised transport has a huge impact too, on house evolution and house location.

The house is the most conservative of all our developments - unlike war planes. Perhaps after all Gina was a little slow to make use of the lycra fabric. That is to imply that our neurons in fact have expanded; or to that effect. The Dymaxion house was ignored in favour of some asbestos-cement clad cottage. Nevertheless sooner than we think the new direction in our built establishment may be in 'Classic' bio-Dymaxions in under-sea cities, satellite space-stations or *ecopian* arcological people-hives endowed with super materials from nano-technologies. Little *ticky tacky* octagons in the beehive – people won't change much except the moral polarities will be an issue, the *Pale* progeny will be paler. It will just take some decent 'new world order' – somewhere up front of Israel, people at the mercy of the only food corporation (somebody suggested it'll be Woolworths).

After millennia of building we have a **huge stock of existing building**. Therefore renovation, adaptation, extension and conservation are huge aspects of house development. Renovating the old will still incorporate advanced skills, technique and style. *In a sense, we in fact never have built newly. We are always adapting the existing environment – existing landform or house-form.* Even the, once nomadic, Neolithic revolutionaries, who found themselves planted next to their innovative crop fields, adapted to existing environment, all-be-it natural environment, as they established possibly the first permanent settlements. In many ways the activity is truly as it was. Furniture and shoes may have been the beginning of nomadic domestic facility; a rock dragged over as a seat and skins for the feet. Today facility for walkers is simply hi-tech. Long into the future we will be renovating, adapting, upgrading except that much of what we build today will only be fit for demolition – can you imagine the horror at the tip face.

Farming and fishing perhaps encouraged settlement and land ownership, which in turn demanded and encouraged permanent dwellings. People got busy and loaded down with doings, even despondent; *trained to stay home, not trained to travel.* We built and enhanced what we built to occupy ourselves and to generate the newness that we no longer see in changing nature or that solves our contempt for the familiarity – the same old house, let's 'makeover', as the Amerophiles once liked to say.

The beginnings of housing have occurred in a number of separate places. Different locales, culture, sociology, attitude, climate, resource. Different house development. Social initiative using the *playdough* at hand developing one vernacular here, another there. Our day of globalisation brings a cross-pollinated hi-tech transition still anchored with vernacular soul to the land-cum-cultural context of site. Lightweight, energy-efficient materials, plantation timbers and machined and glued bamboo. Recycled toolmarked stone and brick infuse the clinical industrial with *nature's earthy nurtures.* As the years roll on the costs reduce to the houser of the

Couched in convenient convention

...

evolving

industrial construction fundamentals in his house and the costs of natural materials increases. What charge for a sheath of thatch grass? .... for a tamped earth floor and fireplace?

The evolution is exciting but there are contradictory costs if we are not shrewd in maintaining our earth and body contacts. In the evolutionary amalgam - and in the *Ecosculpture* – are skills, materials, hand tools, pre-made components and industrial tooling. The advent of saw milling (early 1900's) revolutionised building, making possible the lightly framed and expedient structures familiar to many lands; in so much contrast to the rough, heavy timbers of old. Timber stud framing where it is available has sped and cheapened construction and assisted owner-building. It has also changed the 'look' potential of houses and enabled the *box* sprawl. Metal studs followed clawing for a share of the industry. Thin timber veneering too has been fantastic. Industrial precision now enables also practical double glazing. This is a key new gene in the evolution toward houses devoid of fireplaces, chimneys, warm earthy hearths, heavy drapes, heavy power bills, energy production pollutions - and shivering as we disrobe for bed. Some enjoy a bracing shiver but some assume that in the long term it's cheaper to live in a sealed envelope without it. They say it's cheaper to heat the whole house in order to keep a cosy lounge. Alternatively we may use as much heat as is popular for the living *room*; if you then choose to shiver, close the bedroom's door and open its window to welcome cool air.

Constant industrial research improves housing potentials. Conversely and harmoniously traditional vernacular handiness continues to improve it also. *And so certainly the dwelling contraption is refined with the mighty silicon chip and vast mass produced deliveries. And certainly it is also refined by the initiatives of* **handymen and tradesmen**, *honed techniques, contagious ingenious innovations and* **new domestic necessities arising from evolving lifestyles**. The industrial research fails to link well with social politics in any organised manner. We do not have wholistic intelligence. The housing doer must be shrewd – streetwise. *Few of our buildings are anywhere near state-of-the-art in culture and technology; let alone wholistic with geopolitical strategy.* Why so much unemployment; rammed earth footings hundreds of years old have been found, still serviceable. I hazard they are sufficiently eco-effective to balance their labour intensiveness. Without wholistic government, modern industrial research can't assume the revival of past skills lost to redundancy. Earth floor can be truly beautiful, like polished marble, and near as hard; but simple as it is, where is the know-how today? Can you make a decent spear? I know you can't make a modern Olympic javelin. Can you build a proper brick chimney? I know you can't make the plastic switch on a modern heat pump.

Amid the industry, the handy tradesmen and the 'expanding' dweller; *playdough* and techniques are other ingredients of the evolutions of house. House - our practical and cultural domestic facility - with a pot of tea in the back room when you're ready.

Natural materials themselves are generally a constant but affect our housing roots variously. Some locales used stone, some bamboo and so on. Houses sprouted along varying lines of induction. The techniques in using and processing materials are what have created the most notable evolutions. We see developments in structure and fixings resulting in new form, shape and expedience. It is where we see industrialised materials providing new commodity. The chemistry of these techniques, social agendas, the 'expanding (and contracting) dweller' and construction efficiencies caused the expansion household *accumulation* and functions. A growth lifestyle develops.

From the original resources of wood, stone, mud, grass and 'all that' our techniques have given us concrete, glass, baked clay, aluminium, plastic-laminate, plaster and all that. Yes certainly, 'and all that'- so very very much. Concrete, something we don't imagine in the slick future house - brings its unique qualities, including diverse uses including as blocks, ferro-cement and slabs. The diverse potentials of all materials are modified by the pragmatics that give rise to cultural and industrial orthodoxy. So the evolution of mainstream techniques is *accompanied* by the incorporation of opportune individualistic design and/or minor trends and fads.

That is to say; some builder-specific innovation of material potentials may be incorporated with the orthodox basis of a single dwelling and perhaps never be repeated or carried further. And so, we have **creative individualism** and trends utilised in association with the orthodox in individual one-off houses. This heightens cultural options, taste and fashion. (This book seems to relate to other housing books in such a fashion.) Housing evolution is cultural, people in motion in past and long future whilst also pragmatic. We noted Reader that because of shapes, industrial repetition and newness the Dymaxion fell flat – to make *room* for nostalgia, individuality and owner building. People will have their *handmark* ahead of the *machinemark* – except where circumstance, economy or greed and the *dodo* eventually come to win regardless, like the hard queue to the only, obviously mercenary, supermarket.

Here we go evolving – *doing our housing*. Mud and branches; kilns and blades. Needs and whims: preferences and urgencies. Glazed tiles and shingles; trucks and saw mills. Porcelain and fine joinery; chemistry and lathes. Huge glass panes; and fibreboard. And with it we go through the accompanying design developments. Evolution motivated through people more so than Man. The evolution of the tooling and specialised factories gives us highly

Innovating to make convention ... evolving

processed natural materials. It takes us from raw material through chemistry's sound barrier into synthetics, and through the transformations of incredible machinery and glues – many new manufactured building 'products'.

I haven't done it but to track these developments using dates would be interesting; the first milestone development of glass, of electricity, of larger panes, gas-filled double glazing, metal window frames; of concrete, wallpaper, bakelite, plastic membrane, electric hot water, steel, copper, lime, flush toilets, paint colours, wall to wall, the car, bus service, the truck, the cordless drill. Early developments were made with the house as the focus. Today inventions are focused to other industry and adopted by houses - glues, acrylics, processes, production line.

A rambling sketch of materials-and-methods evolution, cut-up trees, rich earthy brick and walls of glass, follows in this text. It is in the context of this unfinished tome and relative to Mr and Mrs Dazzler and their diverse friends:

Glass sheets, now cheaper, have become acknowledged for solar energy collection and glass fibre insulation in energy conservation.
Albert Gallopilong, on Dreamtime walkabout in a clear blue day with a chill wind goosing his skin, felt the wind easing as he walked. "Strange," he thought "the bushes on each side are moving, but my hair isn't." Bonk!! He'd unknowingly bumped into a large sheet of glass - put there simply by way of yarn; nice tea! The radiant heat of the sun was now hotter on his skin as he touched and pondered in absolute awe at the transparent force-field. There he was on this day, all but naked, gnarled by 50 years of the elements, a specimen to behold, standing in the red desert, almost like Leonardo's man-in-a-circle, feeling the edges of this strangely sensibly sharply square glass phenomenon, whilst observing a wind-break effect, but oddly without the shade that should be there!!!
What a magic material. All thin and strong; square and flat too. Would he consider it worth the industrial work and associated environmental intervention to achieve this sheet of glass?

Glass. Where translucent animal skins, or small breezy openings, once sufficed, there came melted sand from the Egyptians; glass. It was motley and unclear in the beginning. As recently as the first part of the twentieth century it became available in sizes larger than one and a quarter metres. The English once had a window tax; if you could afford glass you could pay extra tax. The wide selection today would amaze any pharaoh. We have inch thick or very thin perfect flat clear glass; with heating wires in it if we like. Many types, tints, colours, curves and patterns. Mirror. Laminated with plastic for strength and anti-shatter or heat-tempered for strength. Acrylics and polycarbonates are available for glazing.

Wood. Twigs and branches packed with mud or grass. Driftwood and green branches in natural form tied or bowed into basketry. Bamboo. Bark. A Bedouin animal-skin tent is similar in principle to that which can be made from lycra, of any colour. Heavy logs as posts and beams formed various types of walls, which sometimes are integral with the roof - probably used earliest by the Japophile and Sinophile. Wood posts and diagonal bracing with brick infill - the Georgian Anglophiles' houses could take on the *finesse* of exceptionally fine joinery even externally. Before the mill, timbers were roughly sized and shaped by splitting and adzing. Hand-split studs, shingles and wall slabs were common. Laminated beams, plywood-boxed trusses, wall panels, curved pieces, compressed glued woodchips - particleboards. Specially machined sections as floorboards, weatherboards, window frames. All since the mill.

Stone, mud, clay, plaster for walls and floors. The early Egyptians made mud brick floors. Plaster floors have been unearthed. Mats were in use early - of course. Waterproofing of masonry or earth walls was originally by thickness; up to a metre. But in very recent history in modernish brick, we began, slow as we were, to use a thin outer wall supported by a cavity and a thin inner wall; moisture will seep only so far as it is diverted down the cavity and drained out. Walls have been of limestone, bluestone, sandstone, other stone, mud brick, rammed earth and often plastered. The old lime mortar, replaced by stickier modern cement, could be readily cleaned off for second-hand use; unlike the new. The burning of limestone to make plaster is significant in the evolution of the *housing-contraption*. It was very handy in building refinement but very costly in terms of fuel to make it, trees and labour. Paper-veneer plasterboard, a 1960's substitute for the old fibre plaster sheets, which in turn were a 1940's substitute for solid set and lathed plaster reinforced with horse hair; caused a huge impact on the construction quanta factors, through economy, buildability and speed. Huge impact; no timber lathe strips on every wall, no working off the floor joists to allow the slops to fall on the ground, no one layer and another, just walk across the floor, bang it on and trim it up. The paint roller and acrylic paints had a lesser similar effect on painting.

But were the Grunters pale also?

Still their houses were evolving...

Roofs in old times and now may sometimes be fabricated like their walls. Clay reinforced with reeds, thatched with grasses, domes of brick or stone, flat mud roofs in very dry places, tiles in China and wood and slate shingles. Thatching is still used; though expertise and the right grass are rare. Corrugated iron grew to a vernacular character of its own in Australia's settlement days, whole buildings were made of it. The once revolutionary short-length corrugated iron has inspired steel deck roofing, a boon in its spanning strength. Extra length and special profiles resulting from industry make possible large leakless areas of flat roof. Flat wooden roofs sealed with bituminous sheet were thus outmoded. Colour finished alloy now holds an improved roofing cultural currency.

Metals far more than before can be efficiently cast, moulded, rolled, carved, joined and treated; for use in latches, hinges, and nails, screws, wires, plumbing, roofing, wall framing, window and door frames, beams, concrete formwork, concrete reinforcing, decorative sheeting, light fittings, stoves, *Ecosculptures* and so on. In times of old metals were limited to forging and casting, but there is artistry and magic, like it was with wood.

Colour and finish. We have developed a huge variety of colours and surface textures, not imagined by the Palaeolithics; nor even the Victorian Anglophiles, despite their mastery of fantastic wallpaper designs. We have waterproof, bacteria resistance, mildew resistant, seamless, scrubbable, mirrored, textured ... all sorts psycology

ẽ

Evolution rolls on, *Fandango* full go. All the domestic *accumulations* and form, facility, responsiveness, construction, including suburbs, flats etc and changing needs and crazy whimsical creative or greedy endlessness ...full go. And it's all in the context of the floor-rashed land, the dirty rivermouths that can't see fish, the need for domestic screening, for facility and *nature's earthy nurtures* in the human penguin colonies; and the answer to our established huge need for vehicular access to a half a billion addresses.

Industry and technology advances. Old skills are lost. Houses come together with a new expedience. Existing components are industrially updated and new ones sometimes arise. Dubious qualities arise from synthetic components, fabrics, glues, paints, furnishings and electronic equipment. An eco movement begins; to design safe 'organic' amenity – ecological sustainability, a subset of *ecopicality*. We are now lumbered with our convention of plastic plumbing and electricity cable; the organic plumbing-pipe industry is extinct. An item not buildable with organic materials; an electronic heat-cum-photo-sensitive roof surfacing material and optic sheet skylights concieved – heat absorbing black in winter changing to reflective white in summer. And in parallel, the magic of hearing a custom-made electronic sound at the opening, even by a country zephyr, of your front door, though, allures the evolution. Alluring evolution alongside alluring, non-organic manufactures, alluring marketing and alluring front doors.

Looking at orthogonality and free-shape logistics - *corners, space and shapes*: the shape, on the land, of housing has developed from the humpy of leafy branches, stone, mud, skins; through the rough soft rectangularity of post, lintel and mud brick with assorted soft geometry roofs like gables of tiles. And on to the precise rectangles, cantilevers and curves of today. Interiors are similar. THE FIRST EVIDENCE OF **RECTANGULARITY OF PLAN** WAS TRACED TO AN ASSUMED RELATIONSHIP WITH THE EARLIEST MUD BRICK (7000 BC MANY THINK) IN THE NEAR EAST, NOAH'S KIDS, IN *CONSCIOUSNESS X*. SIMPLE UNSKILLED DOMESTIC SURVEYING LOGIC, HOWEVER, CAN ALSO PRODUCE RECTANGULAR OUTCOMES. IN CHINA THE RECTANGULAR HOUSE FORM, IT IS SAID, EVOLVED AS A DIRECT RESULT OF ITS RELATIONSHIP TO THE FOUR POINTS OF THE COMPASS OR MORE PRECISELY THE SUN. PERHAPS THOUGH IN FACT A PRE-EXISTING IDEA OF THE RECTANGLE WAS LATENTLY LOGICALLY COORDINATED WITH THE COMPASS POINTS. POST AND LINTEL CONSTRUCTION, LIKE THE BRICK, IN CONJUNCTION WITH EASE OF BUILDING ALSO SUPPORTS GENERATION OF THE RECTANGULAR PLAN. THE LOGIC OF ADZING BEAMS AS RECTANGULAR SECTIONS LENDS ITSELF TO THEIR RECTANGULAR PLACEMENT AS STRUCTURAL MEMBERS. A GABLE ROOF BASED ON A RECTANGLE IS FAR SIMPLER TO BUILD THAN ONE ON A TRIANGLE OR ANY OTHER POLYGON. IT IS EASIER WITH RESPECT, TO ALL OF, JOINING, ROOF WATER-PROOFING, NUMBER OF DIFFERENT LENGTHS, PLAN *LAYOUT*, FURNISHING *LAYOUT* AND GLASS AND CLADDING SHEET MANUFACTURE AND USE.

Designers, culture, contracts, regulation and civilised order; they all modify evolution. *People in motion* - Harmoninnies, *Pales*, urban nomads.

Housing evolves in line with popular whim and need. It is usually decades behind the available technological optima. Here in Australia, before our current passing phase; double-brick and brick-veneer became the way to go. By the late twentieth century the brick house was a cultural icon. "Nothing else would do!" pointed out architect Robin Boyd, paraphrased here. This is culture not economy – nor *ecopicality*. This design icon later found some competition with rendered surface, whether it be on fibre-cement sheet, concrete block or aerated concrete blocks. But the ultimate *paling* of designed integrity comes with the styling of prefabricated houses designed as facsimiles of the popular style. This assisted marketing - call one the 'Classic'. Gradual industrialisation of conventional construction is the only path broadly palatable to the consumer psyches and builder pragmatics. Style doesn't adapt quickly to innovation. Style. *The evolution of style in housing is a many-feathered thing.* To some, if it's double brick, it's style – "I insist, real style," the adventurous Global recalls his father's emphatic words. Today *boulevard* 'size' is the growing 'style' trend. In Queensland we're spawning four car garages, five bedrooms with en-suites and insane debt with small families. Real style is to do with all the pragmatics of architecture, as well as the dialects of fashionable culture, *synthetic*

...
using the very same molecules in the very same space ... evolving

170

aesthetic and the simple integrities of vernacular building. This includes cross-pollination among locales and continents. All to do with people *doing*. There is a very good record of style in buildings still with us on the ground and in books.

People's resourcefulness and expressions reflect and modify locality. There is local character in both personality and building. Ideas borrowed. Looking at something, we may find it suitable or perhaps an improvement on our own idea. We adopt it. She also likes it because it has a familiar aesthetic, which he has from experience come to like. He does not duplicate exactly; but exaggerates what he likes and adapts it for her purposes. This is a spread and evolution of colloquialism and dialect. Isolated culture is invariably unique. Pollination may assert itself through the migration of people with their entire cultural pattern, or through the importation of individual foreign ideas, industrial product and cultural achievements. Whilst in the past we sought and depended on closeness, modern transport has made closeness abundant.

Observe the igloo against the bark lean-to and the 'non-pink' skinned South African's slum shanty. Locale and culture are involved here in the evolution of housing – as in fashion. The Tsar's palace against Queen Victoria's and an Austrian townhouse. The accrued and developing cultural qualities are evident. Different locale and people happenings. *Available skills, materials, industry and craft in association with the people's aptitude for creativity, innovation, adaptation and development turns the wheels of house evolution.* For the Japanese a simple, direct structure of post, lintel and gable forms a basis, for evolving, asymmetrical forms. Their building proceeded with a genuine love of nature, and consequently the buildings became more polished than changed through history. This is attitude in building. They would adapt to nature rather than subjugate it. Today though, reinforced concrete is used in the same harmonious manner as wood - trees are now scarce in crowded Japan.

In Australia the huts of early settlement had no constructed floor, sported only small panes of glass and were not privileged with the potentials of lead flashings or hardware. Importing what they could from the mother country to a colony, people developed houses through many variations in style; basically, cosmetic variations on the practical development of the original huts. For a few lucky dwellers there were bay windows, stained glass and elegance of design. The inglenook, a fireplace with seats walls and ceiling, was also brought in as an addition to the *accumulation* of amenities. The towns were like English towns, as we have seen. With the twentieth century, development increased. The rising sun of Federation was stated in woodwork filigree on the house front. Then, starkly different, Modernism was adopted from Europe. For many years after the initial insurgence of the then current industrial machinery, domestic architecture, in the pertinent countries, drifted away from healthy natural design. Some acknowledged this drifting orthodox as being pretentious trendiness; ornate shut-off, deprived, big *boxes* made of *ticky tacky*. Stiff gardens. In parallel with the avant garde Modernism came the avant-garde Organic architecture from the Amerophile; with open plan, greatly reduced separation of inside and outside, shallow pitched roofs, double doors, sleek lines. There was much more of the health and benefit of the outdoors so loved by the indigenous people, *nature's earthy nurtures*, flows indoors via materials, vision, sound, fragrance, sun and air; not shut-off or deprived, just what the builders of the Queensland tropical houses needed to wake up to. This completely new approach to structure and planning fought its way through that current orthodoxy. It was also a Modernism, one with an urbane texture and a firmer grasp on locale. In Australia it was accepted as a back to nature movement, *nature's earthy nurtures*. Ceiling heights coming down from twelve feet to ten and later to eight - cheaper too. Flat roofs, lean steel window frames and the disappearance of ornament became the trend. The styles merged with the people and their resources. From around 1945 many of the Austrophiles' new houses were again owner-built after a lull of such activity since colonial times; so they had to be easy to build. Thus evolved the Austrophiles' suburban orthodox with its branch forks; one off into *paleness* while the other a wholesome honest shack or cottage – both still snagged with their own degree of *box*.

The future? Except perhaps from ecological discipline, it is doubtful that housing directions will take a particular singular development; other than that by industrial product and nature's decline. We are at a stage now where they can vary almost as much as abstract paintings. The differences are as those between automobiles – all manner of cars, buses, utility trucks, light planes, small jets, beach buggies. Many new ideas are and will continue to arise and develop in parallel. Prefabrication is very gradually finding its feet as the generations turn; Beatniks become Hippies, and then Punk Rockers, then surprise, tourists become the trend. Date. ... they're all clients and designers.

People in spacesuits beckoned by technologies & perpetually modern angels ... evolving.

Industrialisation will persistently develop in oft raucous concert with the conservative; in both parallel and blending. One day you may yet be able to phone a mobile facilities provider to request a *dwelling-contraption* on some mountain in a few hours. The provider would have the environment-controlled unit, tuned to your specifications, waiting for you at low cost, delivered by dirigible maybe. When you're finished with it; phone for its removal. This profiles the Dymaxion – envisaged by Buckminster

Fuller in a Glen Miller Big Band future of 1945. No architect is an island; we all happen with context, but maybe Bucky wasn't into Glen Miller – Lancastr bomber design maybe. The purveyors would provide;

> domestic air controllable in all detail – appropriate volume of air per minute per person, free of toxics, smells and dust, at a specific temperature, relative humidity, vapour pressure and dew point, a noise level below audibility and every essential refreshing and resting and sensing device necessary for happy well being ready to hand. This would, according to Fuller, be but incidental apparatus of a worldwide dwelling service; incidental like your computer is in regard to your internet service. One subscribes to the service as user only; no mortgage, no maintenance. The total *contraption* will provide ever-advancing standard-of-living conditions; whether you be speeding, poised, lingering, or dwelling on (or deep under) land, the high seas, in steaming tropic, on floating ice, high in the sky or a mountain top. The containers with all apparatus might average about 400 cubic metres per dweller, and weigh 200 kg in full use with all machinery. The mechanised dwelling containers will compact for pick-up and delivery into about 10 cubic feet per occupant. Pneumatic structure is the technique for this. Air filled fabric, tight as a car tyre. Houses per floor could be 1/4 the weight of today's suburban orthodox.

Don't you just love it. Infuse them with orgone and nano-tech bio-electronics. We can imagine living *dwelling-contraptions*! They will compete like motor cars and, who knows, race horses. Is this the simple truth of flying saucers? Unfortunately this will not happen in your future; even with longer life - maybe. But remember your optimum immediate future relies on your *doing your housing* fully.

A truth surely is that the ultimately fundamental joy of the grass hut becomes impossible to achieve, having given way to the modern conveniences, *crowds of domestic-contraptions*, regulation and grass rarity. More and more we must *debox*. In the likes of Mumbai we must make not only persona comfort but also we must divine *nature's earthy nurtures* to reinstate, in some way, an aspect of the grass hut amid the myriad of contempory sophistications of residential amenity in any single house.

And subject to population being restrained to match ecology and our need for environmental beauty, the separate individual house may become as difficult to achieve as the grass hut; as we all move along with *ecopian* arcologies into magnificent megastructures. It is surely true that as islands and continents have a limited population support capacity so do the other planets; and therefore it may be seen that the population balanced socio-settlement closer to Cheekyfella Talkabout's style is the raw truth.

Does the *dodo-that-creeps* digest this?

The CONTINUUM in the EPHEMERAL HOUSING-CONTRAPTION

EARTH, LOCALE, PEOPLE IN MOTION

*K*nowledge *may be valuable* of the history of your current *residential-contraption* regarding its fit in the cultural continuum. It is not a frozen moment – being in some way modified daily from its inception. Who once lived in it and what have they done to it? Who began it? The continuum of its use. Your own term of residency. Is it a mere fledgling – *but for the eons of the place that cradles it?*

We may value built heritage for the information and emotion it expresses; for the established facility, sentimentality and racial and cultural genetic links; for its adaptability and potential use. We may demolish heritage as being incidental or gross - perhaps by mistake. Others we absorb in passing with a mental ear and eye for the life the house has lead; the wealth of the past merged by our present. The continuum of cultural development and heritage should always be fostered as an aspect of our current house doings. Hallowed halls, ghosts and events, interpretive enjoyment, sharing, adaptations, renovations, scope to expand. Fresh new *room* gently joining the old. "Take care," says Dazzler, tongue firmed into his cheek, "not to scrape the original colonial 'imitation British Myrtle grain paint' off the native Blackwood doors to expose the beautiful genuine grain. That would be heritage sacrilege!" Some attitudes to heritage are a bit sick.

The fabric of any house shows the nature and resource of its builders. Thereby we gain clues as to its conditioning society, environment and the philosophic background. The fabric identifies its cultural epoch entwined with literature, painting or music. It locates the house in the continuum of cultural and industrial development.

A plain house may become an intricate one by the dweller's creative leisure. With this and additions and the weathering and patina of materials a house matures naturally, culturally and personally. The constant touch of your hand brings patina to a bare wooden stair rail. The wet-dry persistence of rain may rot your wooden window frame. Time in carving a door will warm the heart of some visitor. The development of a house by additions and alterations from one generation to the next develops family heritage and wealth. The Italians build a single storey concrete house and when the children grow they build and move up to a second floor and then a third for the grandchildren. They may go a fourth too.

The house is often a work in progress for the dweller - and a work being maintained. The continuum of servitude, by the house, in weather, demands maintenance . This is a plus insofar as it keeps one in some touch with time and earthly activity. Daily jobs have value for us; like cleaning, unblocking drains, replacing breakages, repainting, stacking wood or hanging a Picasso. Ultimately major components such as electrical wiring and roofing may be replaced and a time may eventually come for demolition. Houses may last hundreds of years or fade away. An ephemeral encampment pulsing with earthly activity will fade away very quickly except for the rearranged rocks, the carbon and the broken-away limbs. A common twenty first century suburban house today may last sixty years before significant maintenance renovations. It is reasonably possible to make them far more durable to time, but the initial investment may find competition with funds for more ephemeral expenditures.

As time goes by non-house building is added to our town *accumulations*. Other buildings eventually become houses. Houses may become offices, wine bars or shops. Disused offices are handier than caves for domestic settlement - Low Carl is the first to agree.

The forever ancient land about an encampment is far from devoid of heritage and continuum, but a *Pale* style suburb can damage it immensely. We should minimise our time in *pale* suburbs; except as we roll with the challenge to *ecopically* renovate. Of course the day may come when the author has a turn of psyche and a happy acceptance of that which he once deemed *pale*.

LIFESTYLE & MAGIC
EARTH, LOCALE, PEOPLE IN MOTION

Firstly, when considering lifestyle and magic, though I'm tempted to say debt and freedom, let's look at the two axioms - settlement and nomadism. A tribal land walk as home or a community locale as home. A gate, path, lounge and an increasing host of *accumulations*. Or a routine walk or wagon ride with what you can carry. Various blends of both is a third option. There is variety. The hunter-gatherer may roam to eat about the broad open-air *rooms* of his home, or he may settle and hunt what comes near and gather what grows in his garden. Low Carl occasions the hotel rooms and Cheekyfella visits his aunt in her suburban realm. Global will never leave his house but Bobby and family will roam awhile, truck and tipi, about Arizona.

In any city we find people of some 'nomadic' character living urban lives that relate to unenhanced space, pine to be mobile and are often up and away from the 'home' locale. Others though they look similar are as entrenched as the *Pales*, relating to fixed interiors.

Their personal and social psychologies vary in these 'extremes' and their mutual blending. Close tribal bonds we note are barely understood in the fixations of affluent urban settlement. They are stifled by the deprivation from walls and hard boundaries. Arguably, all aspects of people are house affected. The mind, the life, the world are thoroughly *romanced* and *rippled* - legpits are a concern if they are unclothed on your couch but not in the bush with the hygienes of indigenuity. Attitude and effort are points of reference. The *effort* given to housing and the *attitude* to housing are complex in society. They have highly significant impacts on our lifestyles and enjoyments

- ownership, debt, permanence, transience, civilisation, relationship with land and monetary exchange.

The perfect house. Of course there isn't one except in one's own aspiration and *compromise*. Pragmatics and magical Merlin the house - a place that in every detail is prepared for its unique dwellers. The towel rail is ready for your towel and your bed *room* will accommodate your preferred east-west sleeping alignment. We grasp this welcoming amenity, sustenance and security. It is not the most modern house either; a modicum of the agreeable of contemporality is all that is needed. The most modern in fact very often lacks *room* for complete refuge from television – a significant concern; especially for children. It also usually lacks adequate contact with *nature's earthy nurtures* with which the grass hut or merely the fireplace on the ground is integral.

Magic moments, sentiment, hallowed halls, sunlight through rain speckled glass, mottled on the comfortable cushioning of Persian weave in the back *room* where the tea courteously cools, an inspiration to open a new arch through an existing wall, the discovery of forgotten memento at the bottom of a well drawn drawer – some magic about houses. A slum dwelling too imbued with home and love holds these emotions often glowing gently behind deprivation ... perhaps this is the end point of this book - "Let the dog out. Goodnight!!" ... the ultimate value of houses is enhanced daily joy. It is important to make them and keep them this way. They are responsive to attitude, *Housefandango*, development and maintenance. Just like, but different to, the *Campfandango*; succour included. It's the art of making dwelling arrangement to maximally harmonise with home. Making house harmonise with home. For those in an outpost house, away from your people, the 'home' is a circumstantially modified understanding – for example there may not be a boundary near; allowing freedom of growth, privacy, sunlight and outlook all round.

In our world it all happens at once. Albert's young son receives in tradition his first gift passed from far away through many hands across an unbuilt land – a valued trickle of very real boundless country culture. Little White Cloud, as Bobby has always noticed and loved, ascends the stairs as she would a landrise on the nomads' prairie; the walls mere earthly molecules, as her focus is domestic bliss; the plaster ceiling a thin buffalo skin between the lodge and the stars. "The stairs!" says Cheekyfella, " You mean 'the wooden hill' author." Well okay Cheeky. Bobby always romps into the bedroom cube as a room in his house at his street address. The woman of ancestral nomads admires and loves this trait of her settler husband. "I see," advocates Low Carl, "one has to work at it mentally but one can be settler and nomad simultaneously." "Yer don't know," says Cheeky. "Dream-house and dream-time is two lives." But the daughter of Bobby and White Cloud innocently has it cinched; as the tailor develops national dress from the available resource so the designer with the dwelling. As the stage performer, sportsman and mechanic are dressed for their specific needs so might it be with the house. As the artist paints or the engineer builds so might it be with their houses. As the Taoist lives so might it be. As the female bird is the one that builds, White Cloud glazes *mother of pearl* over her husband's perplexity, using a lace curtain and some wisdom. So much of the magic is the fullness of land & cultural locale she shows. The orgone flows where it can. We may surmise as a puzzle of earthly energy fields, that the hard black and white checks of the suburban kitchen have set afield the warming ways of the soft blue orgone energy. We skip the '*Localefandango*' too. About my home it drowns in television *soma* and foreign rock as the fruitful neighbourhood-walk fades away, after the same fate as the indigenous and the orgone. We soak up our familiar air. It's different to elsewhere. Leave here and go there. But we need some buffalo hide and streetlife too to bring in the invisible warm blue orgone glow; or just remove the checked vinyl and polish the wooden floor beneath. Relocate the vinyl into the hall where the balance won't cause a stall.

In similar subtlety, the fully cultural Sinophiles will divine to enhance the delicate qualities of interior – that is to create interior in accord with their own unique perception ... neither inside nor out. This is the Feng Shui. Forces embodied with the environment, are detected by divining. I suspect today, still, this is ensured by health regulation. Up to the 1930s diviners planned houses using a blend of domestic and natural rules based on a set of twenty-four points. A toilet, entrance or kitchen must not be placed on a northeast-southwest axis. Therefore in compromise a a superb view may be faced from a toilet. The toilet, along with the whole house and particularly the northwest corner, was/is sacred. Many an Aussie's bush loo would concur with this exotic philosophy. To trap or control the forces, trees may be planted. Building may wait until trees are grown for this purpose. The Sinophiles' entrance courtyards might reflect five elements. The world was represented as a five sided *box* open to the sky. The central *room* of the house, the 'ming' (bright), connects the porch and the inner 'an' (dark) rooms an intermediate zone before the rooms of total privacy at left or right. Etiquette and worldly orientation rule the domestic *layout*. Respect is made clearly distinct from intimacy, the guest from the owner, the east from west, front from rear. The owner persuades the guest to enter. The two separate. The host takes the eastern steps whilst the guest the parallel western steps. Ascending, the guest follows the host's moves. The guest lifts his left foot while the host lifts his right. "I do not know what Albert Gallopilong does for lack of these wooden hills!" Bobby's neighbours roll in laughter but finish struck with awe at the cultural variations. Domestic movement in worldly space was planned to this precise degree. Raised terraces may dictate the path, as detail design, furniture placement and planning plainly show invitation and limitation of passage. No facade faces the approach, unlike the presentation of western suburban houses; instead there is gradual, eventful outdoor-indoor transition.

The intent is to net good luck and avoid bad by meeting the forces with design. *I prefer to think of it as making spatial comfort and beautiful connection.* The small humped bridges, asymmetrically placed winding paths, barriers and screens in their gardens are used in this process. Similar tricks prevail indoors. They say evil spirit travels only in straight lines and some directions are unlucky. Long straight thoroughfares do not make comfortable secluded places, nor do they promote intimate contact with good nature. Oh how many of us wish that suburban roads, kerbs, fences, gates, driveways and lounge *room* interfaces were as subtle. White Cloud's forebears adorn their tipi lodges with spiritual symbols and pictographic histories of the owner. Cross-sticks at the door say the place is locked. The flap open is welcome; closed, knock. No street numbers, ice-cream vans or stormwater grates. They loved to camp. In their own evolution the Japophile drew strongly on Sinophile principles. The Feng Shui defines a settlers' environmental 'interface' with a closeness somewhat akin to that of a nomadder.

Nomadder weather we settle; a toilet brush leaned on a bowl. Spears slung over a shoulder; *a toilet brush bound to a spear.* Settle down to a focused wander; a set of legs are the front door. The wide open interior; the microchip and genome. They will never outstrip a healthy river; nor a bed-*room* ceiling full of meaning.

We may be snagged by agriculture but we may be snagged more by following food. "It's good" Cheekyfella remembers in concert with Low Carl's thought "to collect things but just maybe it is gooder to go on walks,". Less stuff, more sustainability. Nomadic life, balanced population, no house-burst progeny, no extended health-care insurance; by natural selection.

A house is magic ... horribly good. There is adversity there. It is there in the story of a typical house and the story of your own, just like in marriage. Through this we find adventure and specific achievement; and doldrums and failure. The adversity in the romance though is a small fraction of the picture. The cleaning drudgery, maintenance, hard work or maybe a building collapse; all are heavily counter-weighted by the romance, as an average across the globe. People for sure have found disaster in a house. The planet is finding disaster and so is our mortgage-ridden economy. The country may appear magnificent at Kakadu National Park, as it quivers under the cane-toad, and in the national economic assessment but ecology is a worsening issue. And people do not need the lifestyle of mortgage. The adversity becomes a larger fraction. They do aggravate our own situation. Like politics our settlements are what we deserve. We must act.

Whilst many of my settled people walk through a city park internally dazed, neither a thought nor a clue as to where they might be in geography and in fact in ecology; nomads are on the ball in this way - some more than others. Those who house a little are perhaps not as sharp as those who do not. The Besseri nomads east of the Mediterranean are in a state of prayer when pitching and packing their tents. The Mongols once would indispensably pitch tents on twenty-oxen trailers and haul them cross-country. Houses on wheels were used by the 'Equestrians of the Steppes', who went perpetually back and forth between the Danube and the Don Rivers. The women built wattled huts up to nine metres across; huge wooden axles mobilised them. With them felt tents of goat hair and hides - a well organised village on the move. In the Balkans small sleigh houses for snow, mud and meadows were once common. Gallopilong's people, probably the most economic mobile housers, simply make do with what they can carry on foot combined with the provision of the land at hand.

Nomadic movement allows development of non-urban thought – something very significant that the arrogant foreign conquerors and their *pale* progeny could never perceive.

Any dolphin would suspect this to be true, equally as would any settler. Extroversion - no interiors. Interiors - detachment from nature. *No building noise, no interior clatter to leaden the wings of minds in the flight of the land.* As our cities become internal environments the inhabitants become more detached. They are cultural first, natural second. Cultural first, natural second. Though diluted by in-depth urbia and technology, the acts of building and maintenance relate us to nature. Not building allows us to relate in other ways. Oh, give me a home where the buffaloes roam or a tenth storey *box* with a red telephone. The movers are quite different in style to the *accumulators* and lovers of the fixed address. When a Pygmy dies, the tribe leave their huts and build elsewhere. The status of the house among our other life things varies through any Hollywood *boulevard* to the blended thought of Low Carl.

The evolution of a settlement that springs solely from some supportive industry, say fishing, shows house as an industry-associated necessity. Building is fabricated to sustain the industry. We must house the fishermen and the cotton pickers. Food and money in this instance must occur as first priority. We are better off, having eaten, uncomfortable and cold under a jetty than starving in a house. As the settlement develops so do the houses. There is an easier sanity in this sort of settlement evolution than there is in a mushrooming welfare suburb. The deviant *dodo-that-creeps* spawns *houselocusts* - urban sprawl. "Land racketeering in conjunction with railway planning has contributed to Melbourne's urban plan," shouts somebody reflecting in typicality.

The social agendas of settled civilisation are answered very well by the potentials behind street numbers; "But they do not own hospitality any more than me," muses Cheeky Talkabout. "And the country women's association aint got nothin' on Apache women answering their social call together making tipis of sinew, skins and poles."

We build security into our *dwelling-contraption*. Strong walls, social protocols, locked doors. In Europe and the same today amplified in South Africa sturdy roller shutters and small windows often secure the residence. In Australia and New Zealand agape they find large windows with no shutters; an accessible, lighted and relatively open lifestyle.

We make some identity with our own touch. We fabricate for solitude. We provide stimulation with colour, light, saunas, fluid design, expression. Many of us walk newly into an already built house and continue our *domestic doing*. We share our house with family, friends and community. She made the room light up. This is part of our domestic activity. Domestic enjoyment. We share any 'place' by nature, but 'house' is imbued with specific meanings; facility, aesthetics, manners. Expression. The house is an image. It somewhat expresses the personality of family and, more broadly, it substantiates and affects the ethics and concepts of its society.

Tipi décor, amazingly carved woodwork, verandas, and wrought iron - the reason people spend lifestyled time and energy decorating their houses is probably to manifest cherishment, bonding and ownership and for sheer creative delight. Apart from creative sculpture, rock art, and public works building and especially housing are the only possibilities for such external expression or display.

A light in the night; amid squares of lights in the night. A filter for the day; a refuge. Like the platypus burrow with its tight entry designed to squeeze the water from its fur the house rinses off the woes of the work-a-day. Mr Albert Gallopilong, do you hear? Oh! The night fire dome with its twilight circle does the same.

So much time spent relating to house. Your lifestyle and place of work soundly affects your housing need. *Two people holding down three jobs to pay for a house that is, not only, merely a pitstop between jobs, but also, a provision for latch key children.* We inherit this vast Earth, yet most of us spend so much time on and in housing. Time in transit to and from our abode, the variable influence of the time and times spent, and had, in and about, the abode; quiet days, parties, overnight guests, happy occurrences, driving and looking at houses and so on. Outdoor living reduces our time in house as time in house reduces outdoor living. The chances are you spend more than half of your waking life and a third of your work and leisure time in the abode which holds the basin in which you will spit your toothpaste tonight. One's home and its house is one's children's world. Their first experiences will be there. It is for your own sustenance and a setting for your friends. Within its natural confines it may be a temporary dream house, the dream house, or a mess like you maybe.

It can be stimulating. Coming and going from the house, out in the world and home again, home and back out in our world again, from one's own house to another's and home again, to stand a night on the beach with the penguins and then take relative comfort with Gallopilong on the tropical north-west of Australia.

The DOER DOES FOR the DWELLER
EARTH, LOCALE, PEOPLE IN MOTION

Who is doing the housing and for whom is it being done?

Both originally and primarily it is being done for the family, by the breadwinner, dinosaur-slayer or the candlestick maker. Single people, couples, families, groups, disabled, frail, tenants – all those who move in the *ergonomic room*, have their house built or provided by themselves, by builders, tribe, mothers, fathers, friends, landlord or community.

We gather that in ancient times housing generally catered for groups rather than single families; probably for company, economy, security and warmth. About thirty percent of Austrophiles in the 1990s lived in single-family households, one percent in two family, fewer in three family and some in four family households. The other two thirds are in retirement homes, jails, barracks and singles or couples accommodation. Today where we have broken marriage and family values, single dweller households hold a larger and growing portion.

People may tend to think that 'originally' the 'noble savage' rummaged in rocks and bark, snorting a unit together for himself with some *room* for the female, kids and others. That he wasn't capable of the coordination necessary to jointly construct. Original housing is no more likely to be primitive in nature than supreme in nature, given the resources of the time. Nature is perpetually modern and people apply their resources with the available intelligence. Surely Gina for instance would make resourceful use of the sheet of *red and yellow lycra sail cloth* and some nylon line, if we could pass it to her. She'd whip up a clothes-line and twenty nappies. The bloke, Grunter, might have disagreed and using eloquent gender-based domestic politics may do convinced her to use instead two forked sticks and a ridge pole to make it a *'classic'* tent. It seems also likely that other members of the clan might have an interest in the lycra and its applications in *domestic-contraption*. Let's not focus too much on the low browed primitive or the homo superior; but the person in action. The *red and yellow* would pulse their brow somewhat; just like photos of Andromeda did for the groovers of the 1960's and the boggle of the year 2000.

Today the people involved with housing may be quite anonymous in many ways. Grunter, Gina, Cain and Noah built their own – with their friends and clan as applicable. Sometimes it is a routine for the women; culturally making the tipi or bending long sticks and fronds to a dome hut. Then alongside the owner-builder – while he survives - came the tradesman and industry. *Industrial fabricators and dwelling inhabitants never meet.* Social welfare is similar.

The house is not for only the original and subsequent inhabitants only. It is by logic and intent variously a place for meeting and social intercourse. A fixed location. Address. For some a house is also made in order to be near neighbours, for gregariousness or selfish comfort.

A great variety of hats and ritual. The peoplekind race! An immense range of people. The puzzle of life is increasingly more complex when we consider not only the classic man and the gregarious relationships, but also the uniqueness of each person. Some with tents. Some discarding industrial trappings for a lean-to in a magic place. Some *pale* and incubated. Some go wild with colour. Some have no eye to behold beauty. Some are frail. Broke, dynamic, old, creative, small, fat, crippled, starved. All unique and special. Each blade of grass is the path of a star. Each snow flake is unique. How much architecture is in each person in their uniqueness and its worth? How much is in the way they relate to their *domestic-arrangement?* Abide, reside, inhabit, dwell, lodge, stay, live, shack-up, camp, carry, transport. Variations on a theme – like the dwellers. An adolescent may wonder as he leaves ejected from the house of his childhood for a dive that he and his mates will love together for a while. An old women with voids in spaces once filled by children and husband – is she cared for in her new housing needs as she was when a tender baby?

For whom do we build? We are the 'whom'. We all do some sort dwelling thing. Who knows what one's comings and goings may be with regard to housing. Some Jews certainly had a change of mode, by Hitler. The Swiss Family Robinson too, by shipwreck. A molly-coddled penthouse prince may find himself living challenged by the land. Old peoples, orphans, communal livers, unemployed, criminals, 'gypsies'. Quite a range of people are in the housing scenario. But they are not all. Cats, dogs, canaries and bacteria are in the picture. We find mice, possums, spiders and birds in various territories and hides in the structure spaces and incidental shelters of our house - beetles crawling the flecked laminate. There are plenty of microscopic crawling things in your nice fresh pillow. We do not build for them but they are there. The cat assumes we built for it.

For so many, by so many, producing such immense variety on the common theme. From sheltering our tender baby, to provision of special therapeutic amenity for a very tall blind asthmatic dweller, constrained by quanta pragmatics, unable when young to build facility for an intangible old age, one person's dream house is another's bugbear.

All CREATURES as NEIGHBOURS

EARTH, LOCALE: PEOPLE IN MOTION

It rained cats and dogs. This is because houses had the simplest of thatched roofs - thick straw-piled high. The household dogs, cats, mice and bugs slept in it for warmth. When the straw was wet with rain the cats and dogs would slip off.

Cheek to jowl, *box* to *box*, front yard to backyard yard, property to property; some of us meet rarely across wilderness and others frequently across public urban realm or corporate corridors. We contribute to the neighbourhood: our presence architecturally registered even as we may dwell in seclusion. Not just by coming, going, face and song but by design and expression we contribute. By our place - our dwelling property, both land and *contraption* – or perhaps only by our vibes from behind a neutral apartment door.

All of the creatures of the locale are doing their species thing – some leaving little black hard to move fly spots. The people doing their best to respect animal habitat, social distance and character of place. Identity in public and nature. Identity in household protocol and personal distance. Thumbprints, *housemarks* accruing. Indiscretions and discourtesies annoying. Mow the lawn. Paint the place. Invite them for a beer. Leave a biscuit for the wild creature - somewhere where the dog can't woof it. How does a local kookaburra see your abode, the worm under or the nearby tree? They see it quite differently to myself, your neighbour or your cat. We can only imagine, but we do know that they would feel much the same about most people's abodes. Maybe the possums we killed to protect a vegetable garden, the rats we poisoned to shield the pantry or the dead butterfly on the cill had an affection for our human domicile and the bug falling gassed to a nylon carpet. Is our house expression and impact a subtlety to them; certainly more subtle than the Amerophiles' huge domestic nuclear explosion on the Bikini Atoll as viewed by the inhabitants from a 'safe' distance.

As our insectspray tolerant neighbours increase, so does the *crowd of domestic-contraptions*, along with its fence-meshed tapestry of individual properties. With all this life around we variously seek recluse. This is what the cadastral patterns say too. Seclusion. This can be got elsewhere in degrees, but in the house it is more secure, guaranteed and usually more profound. In a country-house seclusion is more abundant, because neighbour proximity is far less a factor. The Japophiles, holding a different attitude, may not blockout suburban noises. Privacy - the exercising of our ability to feel comfortable and congenial about various activities. It is supported by seclusion. We have degrees and types of privacy, false modesty, hermitism, rudeness. How much does a Londoner pay for privacy? Do you value it as much? It takes time, effort, and money to build in privacy with screens, drapes and walls, passages, high fences, hedges and even extra rooms. The degree of privacy varies from eccentrically shy or prudish to rude and intruding. These attitudes show up in individual Western suburban houses. Sometimes an innate desire to be open and neighbourly gives rise to large windows and no fences, but the over-riding cultural trend leaves the windows almost permanently draped and closed, and hedges between neighbours. The front garden becomes an extension of personal territory, a display and a transition from public to private domain. It is nice for the public and it is nice for the private. Where there is no front yard the doorstep becomes the transition, or the front door takes its place. So traditionally special attention has been paid to cultural detailing of the door, step, frame or porch.

The Japophile has no word for privacy. His *room* partitioning makes meagre allowance for it; the rooms serve also as passage. Sliding panels at any side can be opened or removed at any time. Nobody knocks before entering; the panels are paper. There is no guaranteed *room* for privacy; the most private affairs are known to family. Because of such design we may respond with stronger focii on tidiness, and etiquette. We may find fertility for family bonds, cohesive family thinking and unique development of personality. Traditionally the middle and lower class Japophile houses open onto the street. The fronts and sometimes the sides are removed leaving the interior wide open to air, light and passer-by. Westerners generally demand privacy. They make substantive *room* for it. And where some may consider it a low priority, there may be counter constructions by neighbours.

Life in apartment buildings provides a lesser privacy - seclusion here is an accepted compromise. The compromise downside may be balanced by the apartment being conveniently close to a busy socio-commercial realm or unbalanced by swarming mosquitoes. The compromise may be balanced further by various economies and the winds of social movement. Beyond the privacy potentials of the building we may adapt to substantiate privacy. With amplified music, modern lightweight construction, corridors lined with apartment walls and doors, sound transmissions through structure and plumbing, the compromise can be intolerable to some. This is extenuated with the cultural territorial lucidity that we find in Indian corporate apartment corridors; into which 'apartment-holds' spill out domestic life that draws closer to communal encampment than apartment.

The Abophile's *dwelling-arrangement*. Why is it so different to that of the Sinophile and most of the world, we muse? Shaped by the country-earth lifestyle and enhanced by their territorial pragmatic, the Abophile's arrangement suits identity and a flexible scale of community, using ephemeral encampments in territory that accords with practical social planning - suburbs don't exist. The Abophile camp is a forum prioritised to give overriding value to kin and social ties. Architecture is subservient to the room subtleties of daily community. Boundaries and subdomiciles are clearly articulated but fluid for shift. A control psychology exists in individual camps and the broader camp. Subtle self-siting within lore, as distinct from *box*-planned siting. Shuffle around - for sure, there's always *room* for visitors to camp. A household may site its camp within a social distance of kin. Arriving visitors are noted early; walls don't block sound and vision, so child supervision isn't cluttered. Perceptual access is always there along with the familiar subtleties of weather and the life of the land. All fluid. Easily adapted. Almost sounds utopian – but the point is that it is clear that these people suit their *dwelling-arrangements* strongly to their social values. For whom are they building? Even in the face of reported notable occasional male chauvinism, for each other.

/

...

/

URBAN LIFE HAS A VERY STRONG TENDENCY TO DETACH DWELLERS FROM FAMILY, NEIGHBOURS AND CERTAINLY TRIBAL WAYS.

LONELINESS, OVER-BEARING SECLUSION, IS SIGNIFICANT IN CITIES AND OTHER CROWDS OF DWELLINGS. LIKE THE *DEBOXING* OF URBIA, BY THE REINTRODUCTION OF *NATURE'S EARTHY NURTURES*; IT SEEMS WE SHOULD SOMEHOW **REINTRODUCE THE SOCIAL AND COMMUNAL REALITIES THAT ARE LOST TO RIGID WALLS, DRAPES, FENCES AND THE DETACHMENTS OF THE AUTOMOBILIC INTERIOR (IE THE INTERIOR THAT IS HEAVILY INFLUENCED BY STREETS).**

THE WAYS IN WHICH THESE SOCIAL AND COMMUNAL REALITIES DO OCCUR IN AUTOMOBILIC URBIA IS DIFFERENT TO VILLAGE AND CAMP (THE PEDESTRIONIC URBIA). THEY RELATE PROBABLY MORE TO THE WORK-PLACE, TOWN AND CITY THAN TO THE HOUSE ITSELF. AND SO THEY ARE A DIFFERENT SPECIES OF TOGETHERNESS; SOMEWHAT DIVORCED FROM RESIDENTIAL NEIGHBOURHOOD; EXPERIENCING A VARIATION ON THE FAMILIAR GRIPS
OF
THE DOOR KNOB.

CIVILISATION & HOUSE ARE FULLY MUTUAL

Unbaked **bricks**, silicon-sealed glass, trade and togetherness.

Civilisation is in part some result of housing. It is also a resource for housing. Beyond simple beginnings it is the sole catalyst for *the room boom, the house phenomenon*. Houses contribute to the civilising of community. Civilisation took quite a turn as we made our first *domestic-arrangements*. It is a big word - civilisation. Is it of much value? What is it? Do the nomads among us care much for settled civilisation? Nomadism is more Society than Civilisation. There was an article in the fellow passenger's magazine about Freemasonry and nomads, but she couldn't see past her girlfriend's new vogue boulevard disaster. Albert Gallopilong, are you a citizen?

"A jumble of big and little houses," says Dazzler's little daughter, about a city. Plenty of roofed *room* for citizen dwelling and business amenity. Plenty of *accumulated* utility. Plenty of ecological, sociological and psychological concerns - including *dwelling-contraptions*. A city is a manifestation of a civilisation. Some people mistake built environment and technology for civilisation and here is the *room boom*. House and survival things have apriority to modern city technologies. Is house the cradle of civilisation? No. The Earth is. Is house the first people-made step to civilisation? Yes. No. Early houses relative to their time and people were either added to or came simultaneously with survival implements. *Dwelling-arrangement*. Territory. Territorial boundary. Place. Hang about, culture, pizza. Domestic *accumulations*, sheltered and ordered. Man, woman, children and communities growing

civilisation. The house and civilisation are fully mutual but your civilisation may be limited to a lonely house.

Imagine a beautifully housed world; the resultant society/civilisation
(& vice versa).

The HOUSE in CIVILISATION

THE COMPLETE MUTUALITY
OF CIVILISATION & HOUSE

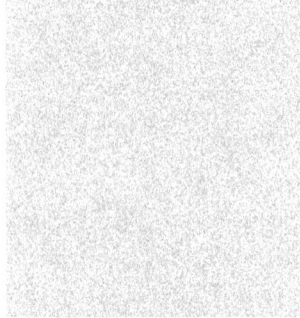

For Eno and Leone Neolithic, their children, friends and colleagues the only manufacture competition to housing fabrication was in survival implements - flints, spears, clothing, ultimately sophisticated traps and maybe a clever bridge or a wheel. Today house building, as an accomplishment, has an extended competition in *mega*-industry's *accumulations* - cars and highways, skyscrapers, fashion, commercial graphics, television, aircraft carriers and astronomical probes. But beyond this, today the *phenomenon of housing*, because of its broad scale manufacture, is melded with most civilised production so manufacture competition is not so clear; clearly however a fighter plane is a far more refined production. Certainly heart of house must be measured by dweller pragmatics – who needs a jet fighter in the carport?

The sense of 'place' underlying house arose from gregarious food gathering and its consumption, along with tarry, security, attraction and dwelling.

Albert's Gallopilong's scant shelter shelters the family as required. "This place aint a house, just some bed *room* offside the alfresco lounge," says a voice with language perfectly harmonic with the lifestyle. His domestic *accumulation* is barely an issue. It and the domestic *layout* cultured by his people are substantially 'outdoors'; they having no 'indoors' until the civilised British bulldog cornered them. The *womb-sanctum* principle does not hold with them; the Earth is their Mother. Perhaps it is because of an ethic of **minimal taking or changing** that their physical domestic order is simply camp based. There is more to their social civilisation than the West can comprehend – ne'er the twain ... Please let us know sometime Albert.

The evolution of the house, as and when accompanied by the temple and barn, is in the taproot of all building including parliament houses. It has enabled development of non-indigenous lifestyle – not necessarily a good thing. **Eastern and Western lifestyles too.** *"There* *are other lifestyles too,*" insists Sitting Bull referring to such as his own. Thinking of *phenomenal* house evolution, he waves a feather over the next couple of paragraphs, the words of White Cloud's grandfather understood in his mind, along with the devastations to his people that were finally drawn by *theodolite*. The lifestyles of the extreme indigenous nomads allow no *room* in their culture for substantial building. Built amenity made by others may in some limited way be useful to them howver.

Domestic activity and need are preliminaries to both civilisation and personal *beingrowing*. As we have noted, development of the house surely was inspired in unison with the pre-house notions or moods of civilisation and personal *beingrowing*; however innocently embryonic those notions were.

Each of the various lifestyles is synonymous with its own civilisation. As the civilisations flourish, some wonderful cultural developments have been made in housing. It is the West, highlighted by the Americans, which has most radically evolved its branch of housing. We see industrial technology warped by economic rationalism and unecologic greed. We see the awesomely inspiring and the sad in context together. The physical impact of especially an Amerophilic house is complex - **components from all over the world**. Full and thorough quantification of its materials and manufacture would be a mind-boggling exercise. Cheekyfella's diplomatic uncle cannot conceal a wry smirk, as his awareness of house grows through these words. Mr Pale thinks it's okay. Evaluation of the worth of the Amerophilic house and its contribution to its civilisation we can manage only with imagination from the stroll in the stratosphere.

Where are the civilised cultures heading in the years of cloning; of cross-cultural commonalities; of racial idiosyncrasies and beliefs? Territory. Human nature. The awakening Building Inspector. The meek and the imperial. The slave and the master. The free. Apocalypse; I'm-a-geddon worried. Battery hens on big macs. In 1945 it was said that a third of all people were destined to premature death, arising from inadequate housing; nearly all those people are now dead. Today we have a billion houses and hundreds of millions of people without one. Give me back the grass hut. Hope and imagination gives me back my creativity; I have an amazing cultural, industrial and environmental resource. We can make fantastic houses. We could provide simple essential houses for everybody. **But as yet we are relatively uncivilised – regardless of everything hi-tech.** The individual Westerners do not share commodity among fellows as much as the Abophile. Our social welfare housing is generally merely politically civilised – and so likely ultimately mercenary. Our wars are more important ... and the territory thefts by theodolite. I'm sorry, some light does shine, but there's too much wrong that is dimming my supreme optimism.

Like *domestic-contraption*, the built portion of civilisation is little more

than an *accumulation*. Individuals, and their individual stuff. In part
amalgamated into public property and law but *n o t   s p i r i t u a l l y
n o r   i n t e l l e c t u a l l y   w h o l i s t i c;* not singly roofed like a
house. Civilisation gives us some territorial reassurance, and some
social welfare; however the priority is the humane reassurance given
to us by our own house.

The house is the handshake between the city and the land
– for the city breaks well away from the land and the well designed
house has at least cosmic symbol, toenail clippings and sewerage.

We note the *handmarks* of *housemarked* people on the conglomerate
that comes from civilisation. And the cities now become the 'cradle of
new domestic activity'; realty, credit systems, global mobility, 'home
owner type', 'urban nomad', immense diversity, eat out, beach house,
commute, insurance, condo, space-age fit-out, home office, vast
rooms, etcetera, etcetera. Etceteras, etceteras.

In this context the house is right there in life impact with the skill of
writing and singing. It is the key in the matrix of our socio-physical
village/city/national conglomerate. Like the individual, in the little
big western world, it is exploited. And often diminished in its ideal
qualities.

Look aside a moment from what you personally consider adequate
  housing. *Inadequate housing is a problem.* From extended time in
  inadequate urban housing, we see negative, deviant, *housemarks.*
  A formal study of the circumstance notes; diminished self
  perception, pessimism, stress, diminished health and satisfaction,
  cynicism about people and organisations, sexual imbalance,
  household management difficulty and child rearing difficulty.
  Arguably the counsel to ease much of this is *attitude.* The society,
  in which the house is set, itself nurtures ailing attitudes.
  Architecture is a measure of people. Buildings partly reveal
  people's subconscious. What is inadequate housing? Think of the
  worst –
and of mere annoyance and of invisible toxins. Think of the
Ecosculpture and mortgage.

The character of the city is made from that of the houses and of the
housed persons *beingrowing* out of househome in the city.

It is politic to nominate housing as a right. But it is only the ideals of
civilised fellowship that make it a right. "An optional right may be a
truer approach," Cheekyfella interjects, noting the blinkered urban
thinking. "There is no such right in the wilderness."

Choked by the *dodo-that-creeps* as also it does in the wilderness,
welfare housing on a global scale is a meagre effort, though in some
instances it shines.

The hallowed 'specific natural locale', the waterhole, the spiritual grotto, the transcendent vista, the incredible natural places, are increasingly rivalled by global civilisation - or rather the sense of civilisation that is delivered by the various communication media, commerce and travellers' tales. *As global civilisation drifts onward there is more stimulus from* **people-created sensory imagery**; *slowly weakening the beautiful uniqueness of each land-based locale*. We meld creative expression and *delights* into both the form and the artifice of our houses; and these respond to the global and local external industro-cultural stimuli. **We intuitively place new nurturing stimuli in our houses to balance those we find out-of-house.** A dweller in the depths of a Big Apple may grasp at the simple natural harmonies; enjoying indoor plants, simplicity of form and natural materials. Even a broad *boulevard* mansion spread widely inward, away from its windows, ceiling shaded, stuffy but beautiful Art Deco lounge, needs potted palms and a spot of moving sunlight. This is a simplistic analogy as the situation is rather boggling when we consider complex environments, people, lives, resources and societies.

Most architectural concept of today was unimaginable in the isolated mini-civilisations of even a century ago. Houses take a lower overall visual priority in our world of pulsing beacons dedicated to commercial, government and cultural architecture - all in all you're just another brick in the wall. However, to the individual homecomer, the front door and its handshake will always hinge things back into the comfortable primeval perspective; but only if the homecomer is *doing* a good job for this circumstance of his own housing. The city in its *accumulation* of our 'from-home' creative developments is an extension of *residential-contraption*, the settler's domestic-arrangement & the spirit of implements. Or - the *residential-contraption* is merely a dormitory pitstop of the city walk*about, wh*ilst **that handshake with the front doorknob** is also the *nourishment* and comfort of our intimate contact with the warm*ing ni   le that* is central to those home amenities synonymous co*incidentally* with precious Mother – a smear of precious milk on the c*hin we cross* the threshold to her comfort, security, familiarity, memories, introspection, future and if we're organised some special stimulation. Can we have left & right door knobs? An organism we know inside and out. Succour.

Mainstream society, in some notional retrogression to Western Medieval times, is putting more public and a little less private into the house. With this I must lock my house in the suburbs whereas in the country I left the door open. And the air and sound waves in town are different from the country house, whether I'm at the frying pan or stepping out to work.

People like Global *Pale* will buy a house image like they do a car. A house style, like the *Classic*, marketed as a trend may well become a trend. Consumer society. Where there is a blend of consumerism and tight regulation there's little left of the innocent building integrity once known in housing. Most Austrophilic houses are of market images and their low cost adaptations.

Societies and communities endeavour to coordinate satisfactory urban aesthetics and qualities in housing – with Regulations. Maddening mediocrity thus increase. Other times we just love it. With industry and vitality the options in housing are staggering - on the face of it. But when one settles down to achieving a specific desire in *domestic-contraption* the limited potentials of the individual become very evident. Money is not a small issue here. But, more so, *attitude* and approach, in the *doing of housing*, are keys.

Where goes the CIVILISATION & HOUSE PARTNERSHIP?

THE COMPLETE MUTUALITY OF CIVILISATION & HOUSE

So what are we up to in housing?! Amid the excellent, in the main, we see inadequate physical outcomes. The bombs of poor integrity fall on people and environment. Is it ecological bombs that rain on Armageddon in a few short years – bombs to reverse ecological breakdown? More likely, it'll be sociological bombs – the bombs of dubious intent.

Wow!? Where do we go - our housing *attitude* being integral with our social fabric and mental health?

Absolute mess or not, the global symptoms do not look good. There is innocence, complacence and domestic 'well-being' for those fortunates who can afford a book. It is obvious that there are the people who do not care at all, those who are not adequately conscious, and those who live sensitively. Our housing situation is exactly that. Definitely it's mostly on the sad end of things, despite the ease of filling magazines with full gloss mouth watering residential photographs. If you are reading from your established dream house, or adequate facility, consider those who are not, along with what possibly could happen to you, your grandchildren or a friend.

It is not my aim here to move everybody to dream *boulevard* optima in housing. That's not possible. Fully implemented *ecopicality* is possible, but the *dodo* weakens it.

We who conflict and have burgeoning law societies shall never be ultimately secure. Socially, economically, environmentally. In any year houses destroyed by catastrophe may well be more than were built - some further stress behind the smokescreen on the *Ecosculpture* scales. In addition to total destruction there is significant disruption. Floods, quakes, fire, shoddy manufacture, rip-offs, war. The problems of housing contribute to wars and trouble. Various industrial materials, even as innocently as cow-dung smoke, have caused us, as *dwelling organisms*, serious and fatal health issues. Catastrophe and inadequacy – typical of human endeavour. Horribly morbid I'm sorry again; we can make absolutely fantastic houses and crowds of houses too.

Given sensible customer economy, if one must *borrow* to build one's house, one's economy and social *attitudes* are in a very poor state. The individual dweller is corralled by the whips of finance and the *theodolites* of town planning. How do we go ahead? First address the causes of the drag. There is no agency to do this. There is no organised agency in our civilisation to find this drag wholistically and properly. Relocate people out of flood plains. Install industry-wholistic energy controls. The *dodo-that-creeps* corrupts effort. First - a blast from some sun to clean everyone.

Nine tenths on Earth live poorly spending an incredible amount of their brief earthly life achieving a much poorer housing facility than is reasonably possible and than is fitting the achievement and potential of the twenty-first century. This can begin to be seen in the money and effort we put to housing, in the frequent monotony and ugliness and suburban sprawl and high-rise flats starved of *nature's nurtures*, in the passing of large numbers of people through crisis centres, in the short lifespan of modern houses, through the scientific understanding of engineers, economists, psychologists, and architects; and through the experience of our builders, social workers, and politicians.

Our compromises in building have been poorly based. We have chaotically come together in housing sprawl. *Waste and error are rampant.* The fabric of housing and other building is very substantial and semipermanent. It has momentum. **Renovation is our key to improvement.** In the world we share, we continue to use, maintain, alter and add housing to the existing fabric. As we slowly become accustomed to the future-shock of the multitude of industrial developments we grasp values to suit. Our compromise values are reviewed. To date we have not compromised well in blending industrial resource with tasteful and healthy domestic life.

The house will *evolve*, lead by an earth-water-air-creature-person-society balance – in accord with our values and compromises. *Domestic-contraption* compromises will be based on a *fully integral* domestic-city life, whether this life be township with remote area links or a short interior walk to a public laundry. By *'fully integral'* I mean - from a city based coordination system of industro-economic logic, balanced in the sustainability of satisfactorily minimised environmental disruption; each house unit evaluated for approval. The *megamonster* is rinsed away. How much longer? Bye bye grass hut.

Fifty years ago in Australia it was easier to own a house than it was to be half a century later, albeit a different house. This pattern may well occur for some time yet; given the rabid consumption of world banking credit. Also, the sky is the limit, subject of course to conquer, dinosaurs, ice age, ecology and plague.

Whilst the suburbs and villages remain in renovation; gradually we begin to build, in the city, a *continuous interior*. From the front door of the dwelling apartment we go by enclosed walk, car and subway to work and shopping in a huge complex interior and home again, six paces down the hall, to more less-than-natural air conditioning and indoor plants. We begin to yearn to see the sea and the wildlife – for the ceilings to take flight and the walls to open to *nature's earthy nurtures*. **We begin to suffer too from tribal, family and even friend detachments.** On the other hand the **remnant nomads** may be essentially very close group entities, moving in close association with each other and with no worries apart from the 'no camping nor poaching' signs that may become common everywhere, except at locations where they are replaced with 'please pay at reception'.

Whereas once the city was an adjunct to a person's free house, it becomes more and more the case that the house is limited to the regulated city.

We see that which is happening today in regard to housing is fantastically vast, yet it is something that in another two thousand years Mummy Nature could absorb back to her nurture as compost, given, either, the absence or a thorough awakening of her peoplekind.

On the fringe some may manage beautifully in the economic deserts of the countryside. By and large it may well be only those with helipads.

Join all the common hearts, all the *ergonomic room*, of all houses – a big common heart in some Godcity.
Imagine a happily housed world. Imagine the resultant society.

YOUR ACTION
THE COMPLETE MUTUALITY
OF CIVILISATION & HOUSE

Our monetary systems are modified to meet excessive and mistaken demands in our housing amid problems caused by iniquity in other areas of human activity. Housing is used in political manoeuvring, and to increase land values for the greedy or the well meant selfish capitalist. Are you involved in these areas, or any of the other of peoples' activities that shape housing; writing, toxic paint manufacture, bulldozing? Oh you're supposedly innocent. Millions upon millions of people are caught up in a mad whirl of keeping or just finding housing with little time or quashed desire to use what they have. This goes on day after day while others nonchalantly enjoy and abundantly make good use of luxury – and the stars of the story strive in *ecopicality*.

So much of the quality of houses is potent in civilisation. Your vote, your domestic manifestations, must safeguard the utopian *ecopian* politic against the existing politico-social adversity. Seal out the *dodo-that-creeps*. And aim for rich earthy and industrially facilitated houses for all.

These comments are not based on the politic of anarchic pig-headed capitalism, but on community spirited togetherness and joint endeavour with a focus on individual capital freedom and democratic claim.

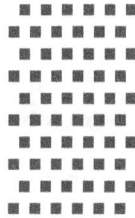

■ ■ ■ ■ ■
■ ■ ■ ■ ■
■ ■ ■ ■ ■
■ ■ ■ ■ ■
■ ■ ■ ■ ■
■ ■ ■ ■ ■
■ ■ ■ ■ ■
■ ■ ■ ■ ■
■ ■ ■ ■ ■
■ ■ ■ ■ ■

It happens with materials and tools, to make a bench for
tooth brushes propped in a lemonade glass.

And how much of your physical manipulations, money (which is the same),
thoughts and imaginings expended so far have gone into yours?

RICH EARTHY BRICK & SHEER WALLS OF GLASS

In the full breadth of our globo-social context, a steel
bolt-mechanism turns tight under a clear-hearted builder, to
fix a fresh orange-pink Oregon pine bearer an inch from your
lichen flecked masonry – instant carport. Fantastic materials
with unique qualities give the familiar, and the rare,
fundamentals of structure and form to our houses. Sealants
and finishes to give *mother of pearl finesse* to internal amenity
and external purposes. *Playdough-of-the-Earth.* The joy of
building for some. Simply the enjoyment of the built for
others. A beautiful sensual relationship with the Earth
through the house and the encampment. *Nature's earthy
nurtures.* An appreciation of the crafts. From the ancient
igneous production of Tasmanian granite to the modern firing
of cool clear glass and colours that would send Eno Neolithic
to neuronic orgasm, we have the stuff for creative housing like
never before. Do our nomads care; does it compare with the
earth mattress and magnificent land clear of three-
dimensional graffiti and 'civilised' industrial commerce?

Machinery aside building is a kind of 'tilling of the Earth';
sweat of the brow; a bracing integrity, taught by the different
characters of materials in extraction and fashioning? The hot
fired glow behind the cold steel of your door handle. The whir
of the sewing machine follows as you draw a lace curtain. The

196

study and research of the chemist drying in the durable film of rich yellow gloss on the back door. Its molecules humming with atomic energy and bio orders, the *threshold* wood is in the act of holding back the thresh.

Bone structured flesh, fingerprints and hob-nailed boots, toeprints in domestic action, in touch with materials that are truly far more than mere *playdough*. Feel, patina, mark. Warmth, wear, scent, clang. Thump, grain, colour, texture, shape. Weathering, static, chip, chink, hard, synthetic, natural, structure, *mother of pearl*. The long crosscut saw, a man each side, sends wood crumbing from its cut; fresh sap in the bush, a blue thumbnail, healthy *armpit*, sweaty singlets and a cup of cold tea; a long, long way from Manhattan - today. And a long way from the hunter-gatherer.

Zen and the art of materials with countenance clicks in with Pirsig's book 'Zen & the Art of Motorcycle Maintenance'; everything clicks in with natural principle. Nature's physics and *nurtures*. The soul of material integrity. The heart of architecture cradles the crumbs on the table. Rich earthy brick and straight sheets of glass calling out for space, corners and shapes; garnished with a fragrant breeze from the rose garden and the eucalypts in neighbour Dazzler's grotto, and some *synthetic aesthetic* as part of the *inhabitants' touches* and the designer's way, harmonious being and whim. No industrial dwelling machine or little *box* on any hillside can do without it.

Nature's

EARTHY

NURTURES

JOIN

The Inhabitants'

SYNTHETIC

AESTHETIC

RICH EARTHY BRICK & SHEER WALLS OF GLASS

The coming into existence of a house brings a significant change to the air and amenity of the space and ground about it. Acoustics, visuals, biological comfort, scents, the taste of piped water, the light from contrivances. Peoples' breath on cold window-panes, a joy of interior and of the bus in winter, hazes the value of the untouched nature - finger draws an eyehole to see what once was there. It was natural place such as which the indigenous have only lightly built out; and since then was pasture, wild and crops.

We must compensate for our loss, to wall, floor and ceiling of nourishing natural amenity - *nature's earthy nurtures*. We compensate by adding and permitting the *earthy substitutions* and ventilations of the *nurtures*. In so *doing* we return some semblance of the indigenous enjoyments to our rooms – a waft of Sitting Bull's feather over our décor, a constellation visible through a skylight and the enjoyment of simple axe-split weathered boards and stone. And to it **we must add the much loved *synthetic aesthetic*** of peoplekind and dwellers – internally and usually externally too.

"What's with this pathetic *synthetic aesthetic*," *pales* the bus driver, himself an unwitting master of the art. "Only famous artists know about that sort of thing." Dusty corners; these are where *synthetic aesthetic* doesn't land. Move into a second-hand house of an unfavoured idiom, or a cave of no idiom, but hang your hat on your talismans, your *attitudes*, your flair and your renovations. These when manifest are your *synthetic aesthetic*. *Synthetic aesthetic* – the myriad of design taste modes of people, as distinct from the wholistic mode evident in nature. It is always a little sad to see the landscape gradually blocked out as a wood frame is clad, soon to carry our groovy *synthetic aesthetic*. Suddenly the intimate place in the land becomes an intimate interior.

In spite of what our walls block out, locale itself has much to do with the presence of *nature's earthy nurtures* in our house - land energies, resources, atmosphere, outlook, sounds. Any manipulation to optimise these *nurtures* would notionally parallel the Feng Shui arts. There are many aspects of nature, such as gravity, that cannot be blocked out and many that can be coaxed indoors, such as the sun's warmth.

Frank Wright renovated convention to reintroduce *nature's earthy nurtures* to a naive generation.

One might channel roofwater to make a little waterfall into a hallway pond. On the other hand, the famous Wright house, 'Falling Water', strikes a high note with *nature's nurtures* by the placement of a stair going down to the stream, not primarily as a jetty nor for swimming, but to physically and aesthetically connect house and river. Apartment towers popularly use balconies in a similar way to connect with external space and vista. It was an open mind that selected that *nurturing* house site. There are many ways to bring in the *nurtures*. Colour, pictures, views, internal-external connections, view scoops such as bay windows, accessible land at hand or vision, sounds, plants, scents, air, materials, toenails, glass, landscape, roof form. The indoor climate and aesthetic must be ventilated with outdoor airs. Outdoor materials inside. "Air to every corner," said Florence Nightingale. Limited *room* for domestic *armpit* air though.

The New Jerusalem, a huge arcological *ecopian* cube with giant pearls as gates – no street number nor brass knocker but a slot for a particular ethereal card. They say it will glow from within with the light of God – putting *nature's earthy nurtures* into a different perspective. It's not here though. At least not today.

Dust-free air, freshly ionised and with a measure of moisture content enhances tranquillity, whether by Dymaxion or natural ventilation. Needs that appear to be metaphysical are sometimes answered by physical presences. Calm energies from stone may be masked by static electricity from synthetics and electro-magnetic fields. Some stone though may continuously give off mild radiation or a little radon gas. The magnetic effect of metal framing, nails and screws in house construction may add a little pizazz for one and discomfort for another. Like the dowser one may magnetically sense these metal items all around, behind wood and plaster linings. The synthetic cabin of a modern car and the leather and wood of a vintage model; enough said. Wood 'breathes', absorbing moisture at times and giving it off at others; sealing it with clear plastic will steal the value of this moisture buffer so the air may at times cause a little discomfort. Air is a more prolific in-house nature need than is say wood, silver or soil; but these latter things are needed for spiritual comfort and some indescribable, subtle contentments.

The clang of steel pots and echoes from walls, the loss of the bush's rustles and clouds bumping together, the stillness of earth-covered houses and a heavy truck rumbling by. The body hears, not only through its ears. Sound is usually barely considered in house design. It's a *playdough* of sorts.

The body feels the thermal atmosphere in many ways. From surface contact, air temperature and radiant from surfaces or heat sources, sun to an enjoyable zephyr over your bare brown indigenous back. Humidity and the heaviness of cool air. Warmer upper areas in the enclosed stillness. Thermal comfort. As the body feels the cold when walking near cool block walls, so it feels the static electricity in materials. Microwave comfort. If you have breast cancer the electro-magnetic field from your electric blanket will cancel the effect of your medicine -switch it off when in bed.

The subtle sensitivities of our bodies can be catered to by the materials and atmosphere of our built interior; sometimes in ways more comprehensive than in nature. A body in the blazing sun is better sensitised with shade. A week in the snow is better when sensitised with a house full of diverse materials. You may find its the electric field of the refrigerator motor behind the wall behind your pillow that breaks your sleep.

Some say that too much plastic stifles the psyche – others know it. Material-to-person, person-to-material and of course person-to-person communications are frustrated when an inert film of plastic is

used. But all materials must change when we adapt them to houses.
Materials of the interior are of the exterior yet they are different.
They may be chemically transformed by industry or coating. They
may be cut and relocated, showing as surface that which once was
below the surface. Grain and granule; part of a tooled flat face that
is learning the touches and patinas of a new environment. An adzed
and oiled wood beam may be 'natural' but is alien to the exterior -
Mother Nature's *surface* is bark, lichened, mossed, eroded, different
after each day.

We note potentials and nature present in our houses. Some of them
we can only grapple as feelings, atmosphere, gender things and vibes;
things that can be overlooked for lack of orthodox credibility. Bio-
energies - lovely light-blue orgone can be *accumulated*, adequate for
therapy they say, through a copper, steel-wool and wood enclosure.
There is mystical cellular wisdom and history in the structure of
woods, bamboos and straws. Molecular and crystalline wisdoms in
igneous rock and metals. The magical qualities of sunshine in the
house; whether through glass, canvas or void opening. The
translucent buffalo hide, natural materials, the land at hand ... the
lanolin in the wool of the first Great Southern Land lamb held curiously
in Talkabout's great grandfather's endemically dialected hand.

Potted plants, talismans, flowers and new window vents. Often
introduced only by after-thought. Careful design time thought may
bring worthy effect. It is similar with all materials. In the city, a
beautiful mass of stone-wall may substitute a natural window view.
Mrs *Pale* sees these things as foreign to the indoors, but she is not
properly sane. Baskets of fruits bring a similar spirit. Like the
inhabitants themselves these natural additions, especially when well
placed, complement the synthetic of our own fallible touch. There is
a complement in the occasional beetle, praying mantis, eucalypt
fragrance or even a menacing wasp that may enter the domestic
scene, which to them is pretty natural. Mother Nature is hand-in-
hand with artistry in aesthetic venture; artistry is not totally
indispensable. Aesthetics is not all visual; listening to the rain on
the roof, the overhang of the tree, feeling its moisture, the path to a
little llama's lounge. As a spiritual light, the basket of fruit may
outshine a Picasso painting.

We may let colours be introduced purely by the nature of the various
materials. The Japophile and Sinophile were prone this way;
simplicity, integrity of construction materials. Others elsewhere,
often used preservatives and surface sealants, like the old
whitewash, to colour rather than preserve materials. Fabrics, rock or
lace, whether dyed or not, bring in colour. Many today enjoy a *red
and yellow sail cloth*, but in early housing you would find paint
mostly used for preservation and sealing rather than its colour. Gold
and other metals, stone, plaster, wood etc were complemented with
pigment and so mosaic murals appeared for the rich. In the very
earlies of housing evolution however, the main colours are those

inherent in mud, skins, reeds and sticks. Ochre pigments and white burnished lime plaster came into use at the latest in Eno's time. Often floors were pale pink, cream, or white, or sometimes red matching the walls that may have red dado to a metre high, with white or pictures over. The Sinophiles, thousands of years ago used a limited range of pigments in building. Today in a different economy we may still create murals of coloured clays and use the inherent colour of materials, but we also have the amazing alluring colour resource coming from our chemical mastery in paint and plastics factories. The Sinophiles' new China is reflecting western city resources and amenity; will their traditional ways weather the rage, I doubt it in general with global electronic networks and trade arcing to a common sky. Shockingly rapid conversion, urbane but challenging valley neighbours to the lure and foisting of beautiful city flats.

We add our *armpitted* urban nurtures to *nature's nurtures*. There's an urban room around the nomad. I won't close the door – for fear of shutting out the extended open space and the scent of the street tree. The lanolin in Dazzler's wool blends nicely and there's a pizza *box* on the floor. All vital in the greater *playdough* design-conglomerate that is; they were all there, waiting in balanced utility for the *inhabitants' touches*. All three;

1. Nature's earthy nurtures,

2. The substance of dweller idiosyncrasy (the very *armpit* of *synthetic aesthetic*) and

3. Local urbanics (town soul, fabric, stuff, boundaries).

All three lie around the inner city ground-floor apartment, draped over the built-in sandstone-slab book shelves, fluoro-green steel-pipe stair rail and your own reading *room* chair, climbing slightly damp up the wall and floating dust, light-dancing, in the straight lines across the air. Put these modified *playdoughs* together in accord with your own selection and filtration; your *synthetic aesthetic*. Add a hank o' hair and a piece o' bone – and what y'got is a comfy home. Citizens gradually internalise. *Nature's earthy nurtures* get filtered out by walls and pavements. Place becomes cultural first, natural second – yet we thrive on nature. The ecological chickens come home to roost in the offices of the sprawl. Knock, knock ... we know you're home, mother of the world's most totally new city. Fill the *room*. Lift away the stifle and breathe your ancient breath, to greet the hyper-industrial objects newly born into peoplekind's home-made *room*. There's some roam in the room. It's safe to close the door.

The flickering fluorescent or the powerful settler television can do more than damage or weary your eyes. Artificial illuminants, from coaxed flame and electricity, are used for aesthetic enhancement and vision as a supplement to sunshine and incoming streetlight. Some of it has fairly natural solar qualities; kerosene, paraffin candles, illuminating gas and the early carbon filament electric light bulbs. Some of it is less than wholesome; mercury and sodium vapour, neon and fluorescent. Yet for the purposes of seeing, whatever could be economically produced was acceptable. Where our contrived artificial light does not have some equivalence to sunlight there may be some *adversity*. Incomplete or unbalanced light can have ill effects. Neither mouse nor human would thrive if exposed solely to mercury or sodium vapour light. For biological health lighting requires a balance of spectral energy; like daylight in quality, if not in degree or intensity, with some ultra violet radiation. Daylight varies; a breeze moves some foliage in front of the mauve wall that reflects tinted light onto your face. Using architecture we can do magic with light and dark, often by proud accident.

The *playdough of the Earth* is many 'materials'; rock, light, lace. Use them to bring both *nature's earthy nurtures* and people's *synthetic aesthetic*. Use them also to renovate or modify an over-*boxed* residence. At times we love the ceiling to fly away - even from a grass hut, merely a most tolerable *box*; though perhaps a little short on contemporary utility, view window and cleaning convenience.

ROCK & LACE
as NACRE

RICH EARTHY BRICK & SHEER
WALLS OF GLASS

*H*eavy, *hard rock*. Fluffy cotton balls. Polyurethane foam. The variety and potentials of house materials is an incredible wealth. The *playdough* put together. The *nacre* that houses the oyster. Across the world and in your locale, now – onward, the lush saga goes. Rough hewn or sawn and polished stone. Grass thatch, or woven to rattan. Seed to cotton, to lace curtains. *Lamb across the sea to wool carpet*. Bamboo cladding. Steel beams. Iron wrought by machine or hand. From our *playdough* we produce fabric - ready for assembly and refinement on site. Fabric to create the fabric that is the built *nacre* of the house. In our delight we must acknowledge the future ecological truth – further, the *ecopical* truth. In our *delight*, materials support *nature's nurtures* in our houses; bringing aspects of *commodity* and *delight*. For security, as the 'three little pigs' learned, materials support *firmness*. Materials for structure - fixings, frame, membrane, mass, bond. For amenity - screening, facility, comfort, aesthetics. Thermal comfort - heat sink, reflectance, conductivity.

As builders we either; find a material to
suit, adapt the material we find or adapt to
the material we find.

Glass for workaday windows demands flat sheet rectangles. We're looking for - malleability, spreadability, waterproof, non-conductivity, shear strength or some other quality or mix. Increasingly toward *ecopicality* we choose materials for environmental sustainability, various othe ities, and hugely for cost economy; *buildability, availability* and *aesthetics*. And for comfort and cultural tradition. And, as we wake, for ecology. These qualities and variably other considerations in the overall design conglomerate when altruistically valued, weighed and balanced, having been tuned with compromise give us the *ecopical* outcome.

Traditionally we have chosen primarily for *structure* and for built *form*. They relate strongly - a *structural* technique to suit a prerequisite *form* or vice versa. A flat roof is not going to work with stone; we need beams or curved or trussed steel. Stone may crack in span, and is not likely to be long enough. Weight is very significant too. It relates to manpower, machine power, on site and in transport. And it is here where very substantial evolutionary developments have been made through the strengths, economies and potentials of steel engineering – from hugely abundant iron ore - in house design – shapes, long spans, fine lines, huge cantilevers, fast construction and few adverse concerns. We must evaluate the impact of the noteable amount of heat necessary in its production.

Material fabric. Add some corners, space and shapes and it's the shell, the *nacre*, of a house – the fabric.

The properties and qualities of the earth's stuff are hugely diverse. As Frank(y) Wright expressed too; they have been disintegrated by temperatures, ground by glaciers, boiled as magma, eroded by wind and sea, sculpted by tireless forces, nourished by the daylight and rains of many historic dates, cut and ground by tools; perpetual change, the brick and plaster of the wall will be different after the next ice age. This diversity of materials is extended by people with tools and industry. It is initially astounding to observe a huge granite mass and imagine how to deliver some of it to a house site converted into beautifully smooth or flat glossy surfaces, sharply arrised and squared into manageable sizes. Wonders have been done with stone without the aid of power tools. Like the silicon chip in the door-lock, it boggles one until one knows how. By showing unevenness in light & shade the reliably straight sunray is the measure of trueness of the work in stone as well as the fall of the lace drapery, something for the draftsman's apprentice to skirt. Hard stone and soft stone - we have learned its tricks, compromises, disciplines and its worthy stability. Today it is heavy and costly for housing, but more viable as wall and floor tiles or slabs. It is still used a little as traditional masonry. Certainly there are plenty of old stone houses. And old stone buildings to recycle. Many types of

stone are beautiful enduring building materials, useable to many
effects. Including some novel effects; Eno Neolithic as evidenced in
the Orkneys made stone built-ins and furniture. In Puglia, Italy even
recently, stone is laid into peaks. Stone to roof as well as wall. A
stone church spire refines this principle. The staggering lace-like
finesse of stone construction in Gothic cathedrals and the proud
weighty Classical refinement of Greek temples highlight the
potentials of stone; much of which is beyond workaday housing. The
lace-like *finesse* of carved limestone wall screens colloquial to India
have a residential potential; thin slabs of probably limestone,
beautifully carved and reasonably light and modular for installation.

Wood is beautifully fragrant crumbing from a bench-mounted
circular saw. Wooden wedges swelled with water will split stone face
from a quarry.

Glass is highly significant in the development of housing and
especially the needed new solar-energised wave. It increases solar
light and heat gains – thus reducing the environmental pressures
from heating. It opens walls to scenery while blocking wind and to
the contrary forms a main component of the mirror. There is down-
to-earth pleasure in the creative use of our *playdough.* Harmonious
composition with materials is part of architectural design; weighing
in all things, oh God, the poor architect - *patina, weathering,
machining, crafting, repair, aging, surface, cost, strength, porosity,
acoustical impact, static, toxicity, extraction ecology and on and on.*
It's all just surface and texture to most. What's behind that *surface?*
What can we read in it; are there chisel marks, flecks of mica, a
fossil, a knot? Is it totally homogeneous, a furnaced metal?

THE OYSTER MAKES THE *MOTHER OF PEARL*, THE INNER FACE OF *NACRE.*
MOTHER OF PEARL IS NOT THE CAVE *SURFACE* BUT THAT WHICH WE *DO* WITH OR
APPLY TO THE CAVE SURFACE.

The raw material may need paint, machine polishing, or carving.
Making the interior fully comfortable – burnishing, cherishing home.
Softening and draping, clarifying and smoothing, relieving visual
monotonies and taking up creative opportunities or placing artefacts.
Cushioning, cleanings, colouring, hangings, rugs and lacquers. The
exterior of our *nacre* (be it or not merely the gnarled old exterior of
the of the original shining layers of interior) we make robust to the
elements and aggressors – and being people we culture it with urban
aesthetic. Rough cut stone, hand split hardwood slabs.
Whitewashed weatherboards. Heat bonded plastic on sheet metal.
Rendered plastic foam.

THE GROUND IS A READY-MADE STRUCTURAL, WEATHER-RESISTANT FABRIC.
The underside of an on-ground concrete slab is exterior *nacre.* Or
the topside of a concrete roof slab also, where the house is
underground. *Lithotectural* houses, as they may be called, can be

partly or completely earth-covered or in-ground; sometimes with natural or man-made earth berms. Roof-lights and court-yards light them well - a view window through an embankment or a lookout room on top. In all other ways this style of *dwelling-contraption* has the same *mother of pearl* as any above-ground house. More costly in structure, more economic in exterior maintenance, land use, insulation, burglar proofing and fireproofing.

Dominance of any material tends to characterise the house. Local abundance of particular *playdoughs*, local industrial product or tooling stimulates the growth of colloquial architectural features – in both region and period in history. The blend of materials too can be interesting. *Materials, locale, people in motion.* Language and writing varies so much, just using sound and letters. Houses do too. Interestingly, a house with brick walls, despite a steel or tile roof and plaster lined interior is called a brick house. Some house materials suit the common roofing structures - pitched, flat, skillion or butterfly. These materials are concrete, log, stone, mud brick, tamped earth, timber frame and log pole. Some house materials suit construction with integrated roof and walls - *unhatched chickens know about this integration plus with floor integrated as well.* These materials in association with uncommon roof structure are polyurethane foam, ferro-cement, reinforced concrete shell, stressed or inflated membrane, geodesic frame, 'A' frames, stone dome, ice blocks, flexible tree limbs and grass - making organic forms.

Marco Polo travelled with a huge tent of stitched lion, ermine and sable skins. It was capable of holding thousands of troops they say. Membrane stretched over framework. We call this 'stressed-skin' structure - the wings of a glider, a simple tent or and air supported tent. Ballooned membrane may be used as a formwork for sprayed concrete or foam. Pneumatic structure, like car tyres, is pressurised air in tubed-membrane framing. Houses of glued and painted cardboard layers formed for strength as polyhedra have been used, mid twentieth century, in long-term temporary special purpose dwellings and are on offer as a basis for a low cost house today.

Concrete is a relatively recent breakthrough. Footings, the correct term for that which is often called foundations, have been of stone, rammed earth and plain ground. Even when one of these primitive methods would sometimes suffice today, we are usually obliged to contribute to the countless tons of concrete being poured into footings around the world. Concrete is sometimes pumped into containing spaces to base prefabricated houses. *The source of concrete, its weight, consumption of precious water and the sheer immense quantity of its use make it a target for environmental value analysis and other use logistic considerations.* It is a marvellous material though, made from a base of wood ash if my memory serves me and of course sand and gravel. It has a multitude of established uses in floors, walls, decks, landscape, driveways and steel reinforced structure.

Plaster allows a precision in mouldings and corners that eliminates timber cover strips and opens scope for curved detailing. It's a substantial bonus to the *mother of pearl* palette of materials; sealing away spidery cracks, smoothing and adapting.

Earth, stone, slate, flagstone, marble and granite are useful for floors. Floors are for toes, lying down and washing machines. The tatami floor mat is unique to the Japanese house; six by three feet and two inches thick, of rushes woven over a wooden frame, additional mats sewn on top; a continuous yielding flooring, through half the house - other parts of their house have wooden floors.

Walls contain elbow *room*, are for minds to climb or count flowers on and for the daily eye to see. Machined timbers, logs, canvas, polyurethane foam panels on wood stud framing rendered over with acrylic or oil based slurry of absolutely any colour with an integrated stabilising fibreglass fabric. Walls may be partly or wholly glass or of limestone, bluestone, sandstone, any stone, tooled or natural, chunks or sliced, any earth, can be left as is, rendered or clad over. Concrete poured in-situ, or precast as building blocks, tilt up slabs or as an aerated block or panel system.

Some magician says wood is the material of life. It is thus to the woodworms too and a supermarket to the wood-pecker. Love the wood like the craftsman does and the carpenter, black cockatoo and bushwalker. Hear the wind rustling the leaves through the annals of its grain rings. Follow a young knot out into last year's sunshine where it grew; possibly pushing through some microns of lead based or acrylic paint bearing somebody's *synthetic aesthetic* thumbprint. Today economy and ecology has forced out nearly all of the most skilled wood workers and most beautiful woods. Beautiful carving and turning is seldom seen new where industry rules handcraft. Many timber species – and the forest systems they support - are threatened with extinction. Wood can be used in modern space frames and geodesics. It can be polished or rough cut, green or seasoned, as cheap packing or feature work and like sportsman keep breaking records so farmed wood will be developed further. It can also be used as plastic when treated to chemical transition. Wallpapers once always came as paper from the tree that falls to the ground.

Heat is for comfort and cooking. It is both architectural amenity & tool. Like the saw, chisel and loom it is used to process materials; to melt sand into glass, bake clay bricks and roof and floor tiles, as an option to dry timber and for metal; not quiet the igneous magma but a process that is natural though managed by people. Large and small kilns, fires, black smithery and welding. Piston chambers and warm delivery truck tyres. The architecture of fire is another storey.

Some materials we take for granted, <u>overlooking them as</u>

environment, but they are part of domestic fabric; fire, light, the stabilising ground and – as in igloos and clay brick - water. They have always been around. As we say, a spot of sunlight moving across the floor should be valued as design. Sunlight is hygienic and delightful; build it in. Patterns thrown from sunlight or 'artificial' light shining through lattices, translucent textures, and weavings; and mood setting coloured lights, variable at the flick of a switch. Fire is a master comforter, warmer, lighter and a general delight; the delivery truck would be lost without the small sparks in its motor. Water is handy for making mortar and industrial manufacture.

Metals, far more than ever before, can be efficiently cast, amalgamated, moulded, rolled, carved and treated for use in latches, hinges, and nails, screws, wires, plumbing, roofing, window and door frames, beams, concrete formwork, concrete reinforcing, decorative sheeting, light fittings, stoves, and so on.

Roofing materials are usually best when lightweight but structural integration can vary this. They must be selected and processed to suit also the wind, rain and sun; not to forget manual delivery into position as required. Tiles can be concrete, fibre cement sheet or pressed zinc-alum. Concrete slabs can be used, or a shell concrete dome tapering to perhaps an inch thick at its top yet spanning up to a marvellous twenty metres. Cement packed into multiple layers of chicken wire, can be freely shaped as roofing and walls and boats as well - ferro-cement.

Vinyls, synthetics, acrylics, polyurethanes, polystyrenes and fibreglass have been used both horribly kitsch and clever as imitation natural materials, like plastic grainy wood beams and table tops, weatherboards; or waterproof under floor membrane, a substitute for metal as fittings, paint, sealant, glue, bench tops, soft furnishings and many colourful aesthetic uses.

For colour and astounding finishes we generally sell our souls to toxins - however there are paints without this problem. In some precious older houses the beautiful blackwoods, teaks and pines carved with caring craftsman skill, in the times when their wages were adequately affordable, are blandly covered with gloss paints. Paint for its own sake. It would seem people were taken by an early 'future shock'; like the sharp edge of today's industrial manifestations swamping the gentle organic heart of home. A heritage story; in a recent today we spent time stripping off the very same paints - to paint it again with clear plastic.

One plastic differs from another. Some emit dangerous gases, especially if they catch fire. All are breathless to touch. Most are toxic non-biodegradable and non-ecological in production. Some people will argue the pain of non-ecological production is balanced by their lightweight and therefore low transport energy consumption, and their permanence. In light of this, subject to regulation, if you wish you can have a freely formed house of chicken wire and sprayed polyurethane foam; incredibly light and easy to shave into any shape. Or a urethane panel cladding. The lightweight makes fixing quick and easy. The acrylic render poisons on its war through manufacture and application. Plastics arise from laboratory mutated cellulose, oils & various but what's the problem ... It must lay in the mutations, the afterbirth and the non-biodegradablity.

Plastic, earth, water, fire. **F e n g   S h u i   w i t h   p l a s t i c s**. *With electromagnetic fields. Does it balance? Cross your fingers and say, 'In some ways it balances but o n t h e w h o l e w e d o n o t l i k e t o d o i t'.*

The INHABITANTS' TOUCH

RICH EARTHY BRICK & SHEER WALLS OF GLASS

"*F*eel the climate Bobby," shouts *Pale*? Alas it's the weather feeling *pale* from melting polar ice. Feel the rich earthy brick and walls of glass *Pale*? Alas there's a wall feeling *Pale's* touch - burred joins, oil marks and torn edges. Dear *Global's* bricks are images on worn photographic wallpaper. He is about to remove them in favour of a pink pastel plastic paint, for dear Maggie, complemented with a print of Colonel Sanders. A fully culture-warped *synthetic aesthetic.* This is the uninhibited *inhabitant's touch* on the *playdoughs* of his house.

We would not know materials as we do without our *touch* in their extraction, study, tooling, <u>use</u>, daily proximities and incidental experience. **In housing they give us *limits* and sometimes *nature's nurtures*.** The limits may create warming incubation, imprisonment, subtle coercion or harmony. The **limits** may be stressed with crowding, rowdy activity, holed plaster or loose hinges. Seven paces to the vacuum cleaner, living skin oils the wooden knob, smudges on the chrome, dirt walks in, elbows bend to many household contacts, bodies warm it and moisturise it, windows open, chair across the floor. Polishing the basin is an act of renovation. *Inhabitants' touches* wear, modify, innovate and renovate – glaze *mother of pearl* over the *nacre's* tough rudiment. Active habitation; echoes from voices and pots bounce off the glass muffled by the curtains, worn out floors, comfort, broken windows, twelve stone children, bums on seats leaned against the wall, graffiti, dweller art, décor, ancient tapestries, *mother of pearl* and design. Accidental, intuitive and conscious house *doings.* Visualising, planning, enhancing, modifying and developing the place of abode. Busy little oysters, go, go, go. Little chickens cracking out of the egg. Bodily *touch* weighs into the physicality of things; hardened clay, woven fabric, dirt resistant benches, gravel paving crunch, stair post. Concrete gnome, mammon marks, grubby human edge, *lowly human touch.* *Mother of pearl* is layered with loving *inhabitants touches.* And their *synthetic aesthetic.* Ah and the Gallopilongs; **no building to *touch, touch* the Earth** - their abode, their ancient mother. Bobby Dazzler, known to find *touch* with the earth as well as his house, painted his door high gloss yellow, to meet their mood for Spring. "It was brown last week. It works. It really does," she says, the gorgeous arbiter of physical beauty. "What colour would you paint my legs, Cloud; for my walk into the mountains," **quips Cheeky** ... " ...'*my legs are my front door'*..."

Rearranging furniture, fixing a leak on the roof - the house feels your *touch.* The materials and structure are in both serious and whimsical function – threshold holds. They culture us somewhat to suit their **limits**. W e   c a r r y   o u r s e l v e s   o n e   w a y   i n   a   h o u s e   w i t h   r i c e p a p e r   w a l l s   a n d   a n o t h e r   w a y   i n   s o l i d   b r i c k . Boots off, don't throw the cushion, bounce the ball off the wall. Let the dog out.

> The whole architectural consideration is about health and wellbeing. About the rich earthy inhabitants with clear eyes and hearts.

HARMONIOUS BEING & WHIM

RICH EARTHY BRICK & SHEER WALLS OF GLASS

A little more than an *inhabitant touching*; a living being creating all manner of comfort. I seem to be a verb; manufacturing *mother of pearl* starting from the outside. The inside of the nacre is integral with the outside. The outside may come first because the inside needs it – but the inside rates as first in our motivations to house. The **founding layer of *mother of pearl*** depending on choice may be; the *foil* from our first resistance immediately at the frontier of weather and urban imposition. Or it might be the Harmoninnies' motion picture *wallpaper-of-locale* (trees, sky, wildlife, rock) – the deft legworking art of managing the weather by movement and minimal fabrication. A mutual first resistance may be the *foiling* of the threatening hard earth for sleeping.

210

The inner face of the material of resistance is the mother of pearl. The outer gnarls with the weather and graffiti; the inner smooths with the inhabitant's touch – pull some grass over the hard earth. Locale, facilities, materials, aesthetics, hygiene, order. Engineering, art. Mandatory necessity, comfort, cultural expression and whimsy.

Art is made impure by the *dodo-that-creeps*. Gender-bending disdained; the purity of a man's house is in the purity of his art.
     The purity of a woman's art is in the purity of her home.
Now, the Greeks did not have a word for art, yet they were 'great'. Art like house and civilisation is an *accumulation* of a number of doings and manners of doing; in various media and commercial circumstance. The **media of house *playdough*** allow a diversity of artistic *doings* and *touchings*.

In this sense consider the *doing of housing* in accord with wholistic intuition, knowledge and love. Not surgery but craft with no short cuts. Full of generosity of spirit quickened by the demands of expedience. *Doing* for both need and whim – excreting some dwellers' *mother of pearl*, laden with *synthetic aesthetic, nature's nurtures* and succinct expression. One might venture to say that all art supports the purpose of the house of the artist and sometimes the houses of others; but let us not venture to that which may vaporise.

The city develops some of its various amenity to make an extension of the house and also a communal house. We are all variably artistic, at least leaving the *marks* of our nature in what we do; an engineered house does not, consciously, express culture nor individual *touch*, though such expression is unavoidable due to the nature of people.
     A door is nothing other than wood to go in the access opening; it has
     no need of expression. This is the correct engineering attitude. *The*
     architect assesses the urbanity value of using the doorway in order to
          express cultural celebrations or whims (or to clarify the way to go).
And so sometimes doors are happily quiet and other times they are large or grandly decorated. Art, when not corrupt, enhances urbane amenity; individual song in cultural context encouraging greater well-being. A totally engineered house, a machine for living, Dymaxion or otherwise, like the facility of a recently discarded campsite discovered on walkabout, must feel the effects of the *inhabitant's touch* before it is complete. Some of the *inhabitant's touch* is often pre-empted or occurs during design. The culture of the architect understands the culture of his clients and their direct requests - kosher culture. Sinophile people might have a traditional red front door for happiness - nothing at all to do with the seasons or where Cheeky's legs are going. Door is facility; the culture it may express is amenity. Pulling together the available materials in the best way to produce good art and engineering is what we are doing in architecture.

Engineering is a prerequisite to art, in building. And the reverse, as happens in the fickles of peopledom, the artist will specify to the engineer. *A good architect cultures engineering elegance, using art so as to humanise the work as it meets the laws of physics* - sculptural, expressions, pattern. Full integration is the harmony to which we aspire. 1. The traditional Sinophile has put structure secondary to artful *layout.* 2. Finely engineered for its time and even now; the Dymaxion dwelling-machine puts culturally artful *layout* secondary to structure. A mental marriage of the two illustrates this wholistic housing harmony.

Why tack on ornament? What does ornament do? Ask a woman in the home. Ornament does nothing to a house but be there. It does a lot to home; to individual culture and community culture. Icons of expression; meanings, visual talismans. The whims of the dweller are not all *armpit* psychology. Art, and spiritual and emotional triggers, like façade detail and mantelpiece mementos are desirable in housing to the extent that we would have it as a facility about our abode even if walls or roof were not required. Except: if we're on the move and must depart the attachment.

Can you imagine life without walls? Without visual art? Is art a substitute for something left in Eden or lost from the wanderers' landscape? The meanings of things is a factor. An old apple-crate as a cupboard may equal fine mahogany joinery; where did it come from, where has it been, what has made its patina; "We're making it on a shoestring" - emotional embodiments. Honest resourcefulness will often achieve artistic effects that can belittle expensive magnificence and award winning architecture.

The artistic quality of the house may be enhanced by naming it or flooding it with music; the legible atmosphere; the infinity of interior and expression of external presentation. The elaborate door or feature wall is not always necessary. It may not be missed when absent, yet may be appreciated when present. Conversely a house may scream for some feature, being the lesser without it, or be ruined by excessive features, ornament devices or apparent facilities. Your daily thing, your special ways. Lingering on crafting the house, even by spending your wages on an artisan, brings various qualities as rewards for the caring and even casual doing - cockle warming enhancement.

An aspect of ill health has taken many like the *Pales*, as they have become tied up in their house - basic earth perspectives lost. Stuffiness, eccentricity of decor, lagging energy occur, as they become *housebound*, attuned to an 'ailing symbol' of house, the surface of house, forgetting the ground under; tons of rock and who knows what, through to the other side, and out into the stars and the breezes that waft through. This suffocation can happen in the country as it can in the suburbs. This stuffiness must be cleared as a priority in any housing *doings – natures physical nurtures.*

As paper walls make you walk more gently, so the cultural harmonies and sense of individuality imbued by our own whimsies make us walk in a tune - song-lines of sorts. Even so we have an option to follow our own drummer, no matter what the house says.

Conscious culture creation, unlike *nature's nurtures*, is not critical to house, except in that culture for the settler is a sustenance that must be got or expressed to some extent from somewhere. And the house is an obvious source. To some character and poetry is sufficient;

the house can simply occur any old wa^y.

INDUSTRIAL
MANUFACTURE
RICH EARTHY BRICK & SHEER
WALLS OF GLASS

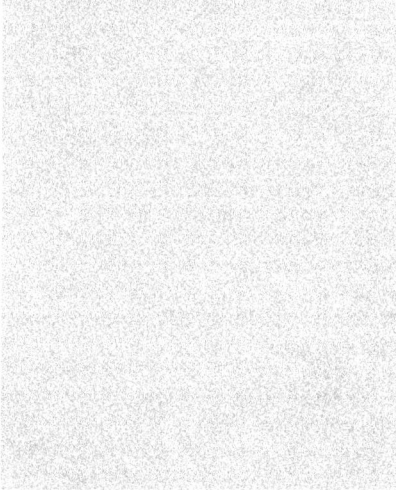

In most of the world still, houses are built with a minimum of machinery, electrical energy and processed materials. The Luddites should be pleased - decreasingly however. Mud, woven grass, rectangular cross weave and straw in Africa; reeds, nut leaf, bamboo in the South Pacific; stone, mortar and whitewash in Greece. No plywood, sliding glass doors, sealant cartridges nor stone-cutting saws.

The buildings blend with their surroundings because they are products of those same surroundings.

Metal sheet, plantation timber, plastic foam, fibre and particle boards, and concrete panels are the most common basic components of contemporary industrial 'housing systems'. Buy and assemble a house kit as instructed. The house component industry was noted in 1970s Sweden - stair flights, refuse chutes, kitchen fittings, walls, floors and complete rooms as factory stock. Reinforced brick slabs, prestressed concrete, and reconstituted wood have long been commonly used there. We can transport built houses - as far as we want. Modular housing systems, notably more popular with the Swedophile, account for perhaps half of single-family Amerophilic and Francophilic dwellings. So-called mobile houses set permanently in caravan parks are also very popular – a third of single-family Amerophilic dwellings are ostensibly mobile. They are very large caravan size, economical and can be used to dodge planning regulations to enable small, cheap houses – usually kept permanently in parks or private sites.

Industry modifies organic materials in ways impossible to the hand and simple tools. We persevere toward development; of window plastics that frost over to block out or reflect sunlight when the sun is too hot and of concrete with enhanced and variable thermal capacities. Sometimes the modifications are simply mechanical - a wire cut granite slab; a machine-sawn roofing shingle. Sometimes the modifications are chemical - plastics and preservatives, galvanising of steel, baking and bonding finishes to metal. Sometimes they are conglomerate and clever; layers of paper in resin capped with colour - plastic laminate. Sometimes the modifications assorted bits & pieces - gang-nails, corrugated roofing, plastic pipe, light globes, wall panels, pre-cut housing kits, fake fibreglass timbers, electronic circuit sets for all manner of screens, sensors and coordinations.

Plaster was a key innovation in *mother of pearl* and in functional *finesse*. It became an industrial and ecological issue very quickly after its exciting discovery. (Don't know the date sorry). Lots of fuel is required to burn lime to make plaster. Lime fuel, inevitably local trees, plus building, local trees again, plus goat feeding, caused deforestation and hence the collapse of some early towns. Industry and economy go hand in hand. And ecology is with industry and sociology too. *Machinemark*, chemical process, huge scale, mass produced repetitions. Things happen more quickly and economically. Specialised production. Wonderful potentials. **No soulful *handmarks* or friendship with a craftsman; the factory is too distant for that.** Industry creates new relationships in building. There are dangers there for the architect and the dweller. No *handmarks*, time warping processes, credit economy. We are losing touch with individual scales. There he is; person with grass hut. Around him we can plainly see the source of her house. Another person, Global Pole, an electronic plastic house. The source and impact of his house materials is not plain for us to see.

Developing industry is in fact the beginnings of 'virtual reality'. And it is more prone than pre-electronic industry to amplify the instances of *lowly human touch* whilst also working magic in our modern world.

We have yet to adequately adjust the amazing strides of industry to match our cultural needs and urbanity. The languidly lined vernacular buildings on Thera; white hand-formed houses clustered on the side of a volcano, where curves and straight lines are handmade perfection. When it was partly destroyed by earthquake, the lines and surfaces in the redevelopment were made industry straight geometry. Thus, by losing *handmark*, the key uniqueness of each dwelling modified its cultural companionship. Thereby much of the vernacular charm was removed from the corners, spaces and shapes. Some of the locals therefore deserted their new houses.

The *machinemark* and industrial systems are crisp and guaranteed.

The potentials of organic materials are expanded. If selected and well managed in design, industry and the associated well civilised economy, the industrial ingredients open an ever expanding world of housing development opportunity; developments in size, structure, speed, colour, form, creativity, durability – lifestyle, utility, *delight*.

< >

The enclosure of space
makes a type of *room;*
corners, new forms and shapes.
Shaping the inside and out.
The near and far.

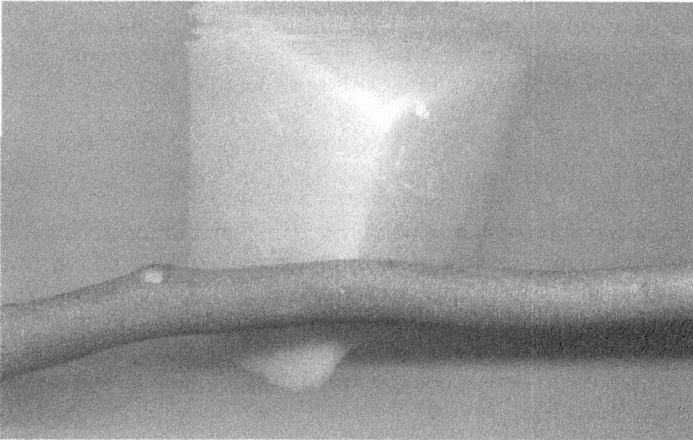

CORNERS, SPACE
& SHAPES

Corners, **space and shapes**. Elbow *room*, reach. Stride,
lay, meet. Nook, cranny, hall, yard. Capacity, scope, *layout*.
Depth of cupboard, height of sill. *Ergonomic room*; bus aisle
accesses an emergency stop button, grandfather's coffin and
his grandchild's cradle. All this shaped not only in the laws of
materials and buildability. Knobs, rails, seats, stair-risers
and treads. Door sizes, ceiling and pergola heights.
Ergonomic room - it is tested by our designs, perversions,
gambles, industry, genius. The *room*, to access, to move and
to be still in our houses and camps. *Ergonomic room* has as
many potential forms as there are snowflake designs; more
actually.

R o o m : in a place, to fulfil domestic needs - the basis for house and
camp.

Playdough materials, style, *layout*, domestic culture and
precise location are variables that enhance this basis and
affect the physical form and any compromise of the *room*.
Space may be sculpted to facilitate both legible and easy
access. It may be orientated largely outward as in
Gallopilong's communal domestics or enclosed, but with a
'view', as in *Pale*'s sense of domestic place.

The *playdough* at hand is traditionally our first limit in construction.
The form of our *room* may be basic or dream refined. Cuboid, eggoid,
broad, tight. High, low, corner, space and shape. The fundamentals
of the form of our *room* as I said arise from the *playdough* more so
than vice versa. That is to say form is shaped by building materials
more so than the materials being selected to suit required form – a
matter of practicality. However, to qualify that, the required *room*,
enhanced for movement, appeal, utility and storage is always the first
house former.

Room accommodates: the resident, the *accumulated*

possessions and access, the house shell (with its redundant spaces), outbuildings and the landscape. Not all of the space in the house is *room*. The *ergonomic heart* will leave dust in redundant corners and hard wear and patina on traffic spots – corners however are part of the shell form and may even arise in some form in the garden. Other quantities in household need *room* too; smoke, water, things, electricity, light, sound, air, driveway and patio. Some *room* needs no urbane amenity. The interior and exterior shapes become very much part of the daily life of the dwellers and passers by. These shapes

were unseen on the land before houses. In your room cast your eye to the wall top, where the ceiling is. Very often; three lines meeting at right angles. Two walls and a ceiling. This *three-planed-corner* is one of peoplekind's most significant creations. It happens at the floor too, but there it's usually lost to shadows and furniture – not lost to the handy square fit of the cabinet though. Its creation is owned more by physics and the nature of *playdough* than by us.

We're looking at and using dome, *box*, gable, rectangle, planes, vent, conduit, flue, pergola. These unify in ways that are cohesive, fragmented, cluttered, harmonic, functional, ergonomic.

LOOKING LATERALLY
CORNERS, SPACE & SHAPES

Shapes about the house; windows, floor, walls, ceiling, fireplace, cupboards, little room, large, floorboard, mat, vestibule, antechamber, foyer, corridor, inglenook, reading nook, computer nook, boudoir, courtyard, door, sill; and our corporate products in streets, side fences, parapets, back fences.

An incidental interesting dichotomy we see in the architect's shape relationships; the predetermined natural land form, stamped by the townplanners grid, sometimes blends bipolar with the forms of the house, as the house strives supposedly to relate with it all. Both the natural and urban forms are married by the *private synthetics* of the house, the id in public dress leaning hog-like into the ground and against a boundary in one site and flying eagle to the horizon in another. The Harmoninnies scratch their heads.

The traditional Abophile, it has been commonly held, at least in certain sense of colonial scientific assumption, has no racial memory of permanent *domestic-contraption* - since the Ark perchance. The square-rigger that delivered the Anglophile was a 'great white bird'; "Not far short of a 'ufo'!!!" exclaims Abophile Talkabout. Certainly

218

some traditional Aborigine Peoples dwell occasionally with rudimentary *boxes* of sticks and bark, fully *nature's earthy nurtures* – complete with webs, but only if left too long. But what was this new sharply arrised, gabled *box;* the first sealed, light-coloured interior with its eight crisp *three-planed-corners* at floor and ceiling. This *box* was far from *ticky tacky*, for it was awash with novelty and sitting in rich context. And imagine that there is still a few totally uninitiated Harmoninni people in company with Uncle Gallopilong, yet to have first time experience of a modern suburb and a sharp block of flats sitting on red Australian earth. In the *box* are squares, prisms, right angles, door, window rectangles and a cupboard drawer holding a match-*box*. A match-*box* - something fallen to Earth. *Elsewhere an appropriately proportioned pyramid-shaped room gives a surprising energy which is a little more physical than psychological.*

So many people, for so many hours of so many days for so many years, are subject to the quiet bombardment of so many *three-planed-corners*. The corners seem to counterplace the circular belt of sky that blends with the horizon below it and the dome of the heavens above. That belt is there, however. Maybe it's shrouded by depleted over-head forest leaves and life, distant it mooches warmly present, bombarding orgone glow, behind the flat white ceiling, walls and that skewed corrugated roof of unknowing. It's quite significant: so increasingly many people, for so very many hours of so many days for so many years, are subject to the quiet bombardment of so many *three-planed-corners*. The roombooming corners rather counterplace the powerfully sweeping belt of sky that blends with the horizon below and the awesome dome of the fabled heavens above. That belt is there. Depending on where you are it may be shrouded by over-head forest leaves and life, distant it mooches warmly present, bombarding orgone glow, behind the shade of the flat white ceiling, walls and that skewed corrugated roof of unknowing. ("... the tight *little boxes* were cracking like egg shells and surprised lizards were too slow for the hawks," notes the Building Inspector in the *psyche of flying ceilings* back in our chapter 'Doing of Housing')

The interior with the *three-planed-corners* moulds our attention habits; into forms that differ to those habits made from embrace of the dome of the horizon. Have academic architectural psychologists measured that one? Of course not. The nomads have. 'Closing the door may have a touch of adversity,' notes Little White Cloud. We need the solid tactile mooch of a polished tree limb flow through the windows of the eight cornered white box interior.

Ergonomic room flows from activity to activity, facility to utility, merging and melding into a composite whole that we call 'living at home'. People do not move and bend in accord with fixed right angles; though they can train themselves to do so, and in fact are usually compromised in that direction. Dazzler has found that, providing he isn't carrying a bowl of soup to the television couch, he can make a fluid either-hand turn at speed by executing an exhilarating, snappy swivel, born from the ball of his leading foot. We very often happily face the containment of *boxes*, so as to have, ready and reserved, the *room* to perform many domestic things. Albert Gallopilong's fluid ephemerality is not an answer for the furniture and seclusion-disciplined needs of Bobby's urban planning office.

Spatial forms required for **mind reasons**
need *room* in the very same way
as does furniture.

"Get out of our *room*, get out of our face," say Albert, smiling hatless woolly of hair, and Bobby, a corrugated slouch hat roofed across his university brow …, his feet stirring the sandy floor of stone broken by a million frosts, a few small kilometres below the stratosphere, chatting peaceably in an open air country nook, in a song-line corridor, *nature's earthy nurtures* bucketing through, *galloping* too, undisciplined by the Feng Shui and the magazine kosher. They're speaking, to a couple of cloud ceilinged larrikin kids impinging the sanctity of their space, crowding their spontaneous *room* and the purpose for which they need the *room*. Never-the-less, accommodating curiosity, Bobby takes a bucket of the sand to demonstrate the art of concrete to a curious progeny of Cheekyfella Talkabout.

Room has form. It is the space necessary as contained by the pragmatic shapes of building or landscape. In this the required obstruction-free zone is the *room* we need plus usually some redundant. *Room* may be created-protected by physical fabric, maybe earthy brick and Whitefella's concrete. *Room* is enhanced and permitted by physical fabric. The fabric may be all primary natural or it may include contrived fabrication. The contrived fabrication we may call a wardrobe, a room, shack, house, *contraption*. Add some *mother-of-pearl* acoustic panels for *room* to enjoy music. For *room* to swing a cat we need, ergonomically, only a circular space, but we may build a square room for it – dusty or otherwise utilised corners arise.

Draw a line between us. It is bound to be straight, unless it wiggles with a stream. Boundaries are limits; lines between. Concise interface; a meaning of square. Where limits meet. Draw a line; beginnings of the polygon on the way to the square. A *grid* is the best way to quantify uncropped crops - for an ancient Egyptophile and a modern Amerophile. Floor tiles are usually orthogonal, but they could be any arrangement of polygon.

There is something to be said for the right angle (& its *box*).

It seems the *quicksilver* needs it. For us rectangles as a rule are easier than beehives. Post and lintel, taught string, spear, basket-weave and loom. We need a horizontal bench, the pragmatic squaring of joinery and construction, the adzed rectangularity of the first tooled beam. Sit the rock on the horizontal face and shape the end to meet the other – cut stone, bricks. "Is it square apprentice?" "Yes boss, we now have concise interface sir." "Good on you kid; things don't fit well if they ain't true, square, ay?" "Yes boss." "We do 'ave *room* for curves at times though apprentice." "Sure boss. Depends on the manner of erection boss." "Yeah! A *box* ain't a *box* if it's a dome." And so the site boundaries are similar, but more strongly interfaced with irregularity due to the *quicksilver* of mounds, valleys and neighbour opinion.

Before *shape* however, we have the pragmatic of the <u>horizontal and vertical planes</u>; children of gravity - essence of *box*. They are the parents of the *three-planed-corner*, the unfathomable prime-former of building. Gravity along with the dimensional requirements of our bodies and psyches, and ergonomics, are the first aspects of our quadrangular prisms; our *boxes* with quadrangular yards. Material and weather affect shape too - ice dome and pointy snow loaded roof.

A science fiction homo superior chap, match-*box* in pocket, fell to earth in a time-space craft that swayed and warped in the cosmic winds, but held firmness to the strong currents of air. This mobile house was in essence a culturally dressed rectangular prism, like a large unwheeled Gypsy wagon and not a lot like the Tardis. It was a marriage of cubic geometry with silvered flowing chaos; maybe a beautiful technology to come that adds encouragement to settlement as we know it today.

> The rectangle, perhaps, is mandatory for our earthly balance. However, we do not seem to like having it stare us in the face too much. We very often mould the edges, soften the corners, use curving visual overrides, or simply break the enclosure by flowing together bits of rectangle. We marry rectangles with organics. Rectangles with *nature*. Give me freedom. Don't fence me in. Yet, make me house.

Rectangles, right angles and straight lines though are not altogether artificial. Broken stone may be in the form of approximate rectilinear prisms that are similar to house *boxes* viewed from a distance. The rays of the sun and candle-cast *shadows* show straight lines and edges. The curved surface of the water is reasonably flat and a tree trunk or cliff face may be perpendicular. Some of this object imagery is external and some may vaguely relate to internal rectangular imagery, but;

NOWHERE IN NATURE IS THE THREE-PLANED-CORNER AS SEEN WHERE BOTH FLOOR AND CEILING MEET WALL MEETING WALL. INDEED, THE CAVERNOUS SHAPES WE WOULD KNOW, BUT THE GEOMETRIES OF INTERIORS WE WOULD NEVER KNOW, IF WE DID NOT BUILD.

The whole story of interior and exterior unfolds. We note some of it.

Even domestic facility as a camp has interior. The *heart* of the interior is the dwellers space. The fabric of the interior is simply domestic facility; fire, campstool, conceptual boundary, or maybe walls and roof. The amenity of this interior may include simply warmth, or seating, or it may include windless air and shade. The exterior is the reverse side of the fabric that creates the interior, even the reverse side of a conceptual boundary. *Surely without built interior the world would never have been thought of as open air, nor external nor outside;* except in the sense of outside a realm or a copse of trees. A cave is in, one would go out of it, but this 'out' doesn't seem to fit the outdoors scenario. We have become *pale* – unless we were originally simply soft enough for Eden.

Panels that open and close - doors and the like. If there were no houses you would never see mother with sunny window-pane patterns warming her blouse – nor father. Captivated aside a moment from a *boxed*-in workaday, as to the where's and whys of the house, by a sensation mysterious to him, in fact a deep engulfing *nomurbic* vortex in the swirl and rhythm, he snapped back to routine and *wakely* places a shirt in the washing machine, framed by the doorway to the laundry. Open the door, close it. Space, light, interest, movement. There one moment, the next changed at the motion of a hand; a sound as the jamb is struck; the wood is in the hole. The bead curtain has flopped back to straight. A door is a door, a window an air vent, a straight line a part of the aesthetic profile, inside and out. The lounge lizard isn't moved.

A circular driveway is sometimes a barbecue place, some *room* to walk and tend in a garden grasping the returning hug of a house.

GARDEN & YARD
CORNERS, SPACE & SHAPES

*N*ot all houses have them, and some houses have only the native land, yet as part of nature's vegetated surrounds, the garden offers rich potential to bind house and land – *earthy nurtures. And the house offers rich potential to enhance life in the garden;* as distinct from life in the land - that is, notwithstanding the potential *traps of interior.*
By utilizing the land around for living we can make do with less by way of building.
There's some eco wisdom there; one step towards an *ecopian* urbanity - *nomurbics.* The nomadic land-living ethos embracing settled interior-valuing ethos – at that *nomurbic crossroads.*

The garden is a spatial wrap, containing interior. Interior is a wrapped space in the garden. Patio merges inside and out. This is true even without a nearby doorway. The house exterior, in association with the floor of the yard, offers to the garden some interior aspect. Veranda, pergola, inset patio or an adjacent out-building enhances this psychology. In addition *a house is a 'thing' in the garden,* albeit more commanding than a concrete gnome, pergola, garage, footbridge or vegie patch. Sometimes the garden is simply part of the house *layout.* Like limbs and roots from the stem of a tree, paths moving out about from and to our residential place add living beauty to its nurtures and garden. Similarly there may be similar movement from a special garden place, a bunkhouse or a neighbour.

Being composed of natural components, *playdough,* that have not been adapted for building; the garden is in physical contrast to the house. It is of natural and living forms, partly or wholly designed in *layout. The contrast is a powerful thing.* In simple we might put white *box* with polished limb; immediate aesthetic energy. Garden is a mediating space that brings together the contrasts of technical and organic, and of peoples' and nature's scales – reflecting the *cosmic symbol,* and usually negating the need to express it by other means. As we work and create in them they reflect our attitude toward nature, life, and the universe. And, like house-culture, garden-culture may develop. The twain should be one.

The value of domestic garden is very often omitted in cities. We are wise to consider seriously our gardens in association with our houses, with the natural land that rolls under and unites even the most intruding suburbs, and even in complementing and harmonising with the gardens of our neighbours. It may be forgotten, that the original natural contour of the island or continent that supports the *theodolite*-surveyed limits of the garden are ever present. The rock outcrop in the backyard may be part of the outcrop that was cut to make foundations for a distant *dwelling-contraption,* which also appears as a low cliff at the local recreation field and furthermore creates the desert nook in which hatless Albert speaks with Bobby.

Consider the garden as you consider other aspects of your planning. No need to conform to nature - simply respect it. For the Sinophile and Japophile especially, the garden and house are homogeneous; for in a sense we start with encampment in the native garden. The Japanese have a tokonoma; 'indoors', a garden acknowledgement, a small room, nook, inset, element in the house, maybe three square metres, about 15 square cubits, or a few tatami mats. This tokonoma is like the small garden at the front of some city dwellings.

Perhaps the little garden
tea-house is the reverse of
the tokonoma.

Align a tree, a window, an indoor plant and a favourite chair. The space around a house can be used to enhance or construct the meeting of house, nature and urban context. In most modern western residential areas the outdoor spaces are the last, and at times a remnant, consideration. Having said that; they are often energetically redeemed by lively *Housefandango*.

Outdoor spaces can be used for security, vandal-proofing, *room* for social contact, psychological shelter and so on. Spaces can be loose or tight, path-like or wide open and definite or vague. They can support the domestic *shape-up* between the road, shed, car, yard or garden jungle. They can be visually and aromatically integrated with interior amenity, wafting eucalyptus fragrance into the Dazzler's kitchen. They can often minimise need for expenditure on *nature's nurtures* materials and design for the interior. A picture window to a birdbath offers more than wallpaper; subject of course to warmth, privacy and other factors.

A *box* in a
garden isn't so
boxy.

Gardens are also an interface between interior and the wilderness land that brewed the *hud – hud*, the basic hide-shelter. Nature's vegetated surrounds. The track through may grow over and a new one be trodden. They grow and change. Some end up covered in the ubiquitous lawn. Lawn has a story of its own. And it is not all good.

Garden and yard being part of the dwelling amenity are considered in parallel with the items in **A CHECKLIST FOR HOUSING**.

LAYOUT & SHAPE-UP
CORNERS, SPACE & SHAPES

When we have our domestic location *established,* bearing in mind the land orientations and any existing building , and we know the amenity and utility that we require we can begin the bones of house design. We now *lay out* site and floor plan - with *shape* in mind. This may have already occurred to form your house a century ... any time ... before you moved in.

The building(s) & garden or camp is set out by plan but the need is for space, or more so ... *room* - not simply ground area. Overhead limits such as a limb, regulation or preferred ceiling may be there. It's the upward third dimension, that we build onto the two dimensional plan; call it the '*shape-up*'. It's more in your face and at hand than around your feet – both internally and externally. The *shape-up* may retain the large oak blocking the water view and simply set a circular limit for built interior. The *shape-up* here is a dome in a garden with a tree; in air and cosmos of course. Sometimes simple, sometimes complex.

224

The land orientations relating to *layout* and *shape-up* may include such as sun orientation, neighbour courtesy or the incorporation, rather than the removal, of a rock outcrop at the front door.

The building structure also has much to do with shape.

Houses once were partly dispersed across the site or garden. Walk unsheltered to the toilet. Laundry in the shed .... "Hello, it's Cheeky here! ... We are all over the country too Monte. And we don't put our front door in a built core, smack bang in the best part of the garden, b'cause our front door just keeps on walkin'." "Anybody try t'bang his knocker betta watch out," Bobby plays, tongue in cheek. Cheeky was not impressed. And it's not true. Abophiles do more than walk, and they don't sham the land with their encampment ; that's what he's saying. Their camps have a sheltered area, for night and day, sleep, storage and cooking out of the rain. With this are activity areas; lounge, workshop, kitchen & probably more at times; and a refuse area. In circumstance there may be domicile over a wider area; an individual camp may be relocated within its wider domicile. They need little by way of *shape-up*; the ground may equate to bench and to seating and they'd be looking to use a limb rather than remove it . So what you're doing Cheeky is taking the opportunity to share your love for flexible indigenuity at a time when we're talking about building zephyr-stifling walls – well thanks, but unlike me your physique and lifestyle were not forged from centuries of forebears in chilly Scotland ... and don't ask me why they were silly enough to stay there rather than move to sunny Australia.

The stimulation of building and relating to the land may generate an urge to create additional *layout room*. To bring the land back into our *box*, we may make *room* for patio, deck, pergola, polished tree limb, garden interface or tea room in the garden. These along with garages, sheds and simple garden places are often forgotten during layout time. People are prone not to think of them as house, as fundamental 'hud' priorities and so they come to them as afterthoughts; so that the *layout* flow from bed to land is disjointed, not optimum and the *dwelling contraption* has a blunt edge confronting its land and out-places. Glass in the evolution of the *contraption* has very significant implications in this aspect of *layout* and *shape-up*. Glass allows the outside's visible values in. Whilst doing so it encourages the blunt footprint. It reduces the inclination to create open verandas which soften the visual profile of the house – we just sit by a window with our knitting.

The diverse collection of *room* amenities that we feel we require in a house in part can be merged or overlapped with one another into a common space or room; multi-purpose *room*. The overall household *room* contains lots of smaller *room* provisions – bathroom cabinet, *room* for bedside lamp. There are many *room* entities. The basic *room* amenity required, most often, is founded in partitions, screening, separations and 'nice' finishes. Separations may be for odours, light, individual seclusions, aesthetics and shelters. Walls create the separation but often walls are more for towel rails, mirrors, shelves, posters, nearby colour, texture, the backs of benches, wardrobes and hooks than for screening. Little White Cloud, is set in a mind-frame suiting her boudoir - soft mauves, exotic laces, polished blackwood and scented mirror. At the boudoir doorway transition she eases into the habitual buffalo land stroll and through another doorway, feeling a mind-frame transition as she perceives her daughter's room - strong yellow and green with a full window wall onto the garden, a fairy princess poster and some muddied blue jeans tangled with her chiffon dress amid her *room* amenity – it is some ephemeral *mother of pearl* layered in and contributing to the *shape-up* of the *room* amenity. Note the general psychology of changing rooms, or in this case moving from room to room – cheeks flush or bladder stirs in response.

'Rooms' are challenged by 'open-planning'. Warmth is an amenity. Warm cosiness encourages traditional heatable draughtless rooms – the enclosure psyche encourages them also. Traditional rooms are also justifiable for security, dust control, sound insulation, tidiness - many reasons. *Traditional rooms though are only a part of the spatial amenity palette.* Spatial amenity (*room* amenity) is three dimensional and often adaptable. Moveable, flexible and partial partitions. Double doors, awnings, furniture arrangements, ceiling form, special lighting, materials and colour. Internal windows and 'open plan', as *Pale* calls it, come into the picture as well.

Ducts, space, bulk storage, equipment space, food storage, passages, stairway ... are *room* entities too. We need *room* for these but we don't necessarily call them rooms – let's call them *room-entities*. Rooms are *room-entities* too. *Room* is for people or their things to be in. Rooms are nearly full of *room* – and space and shape and designed amenity and a-priori reality. I say "nearly" because of the useless corners, if you only need to swing a cat.

Whether resolved by traditional rooms or other means, some of the activities that generate a *room-entity*, which needs urbane amenity, are - sleeping, bathing, dressing, reading, making things, entertaining, cooking, meditating, washing clothes, playing with children, love in the garden, sitting in revelry, entering the house, leaving the house, changing from activity to activity, transition from eating to chatting, parking the car. The activity of sleeping - to make a point - encompasses associated activities, each with their own *room-entity*; maybe eating, bathing, dressing, undressing, reading, copulating, talking, etc. 'Open planning' facilitates wholistic integration of *room-entities* with fewer *three-planed corners*.

The traditional Japophiles have a culture of economy and refinement of planning and design that contrasts open planning & also the rampant *boxing* of the seemingly crass culture associated with the production of the Western *box* with the *shape-up* of its *three-planed-corners*. They conserve space. Space is a key amenity of *room*. They kneel on a mat rather than absorb space with furniture. Keep the bed quilt in a cupboard and roll it out in the living space for sleep. No space is solely dedicated to passages. There are special compromises and values for each culture and application. Sleeping in a niche on a yacht is one compromise, or another, sleeping on a big permanently located feather mattress with ten others as a Medieval Anglophile.

Planning is ruled by mentality: the *layout* of the traditional Japophile house is in three areas. A raised tatami area for living rooms; a raised floor-board area for verandas, corridors, lavatory, and usually the kitchen; and a comparatively small lower part with an unboarded floor for the hall, bathroom and part of the kitchen. Note that fixed walls are kept to a minimum. The use of sliding or even removable doors and partitions enables the house possibly to be transformed into a single room, opening onto the garden. The corridor or passage, necessary in larger houses, is hardly possible in small houses; they may use the veranda as a passage - and make thoroughfare through rooms.

The complexities of *layout* planning options across the world is vastly simplified by an understanding of the principles and their application to your own culture, locale and pocket. If you require focus on any particular style of *layout* you must research.

No *layout* is complete without the third dimension: the complete household *layout* couches the total homogeneous *room-entity*, that is, the space taken by every possible move of every dweller, visitor and item in the house. And each *room-entity* has its own ideal spatial refinements to do with movement and psyche. As we locate windows and wall masses to suit interior as well as exterior; so it is with *layout* and *shape-up*. And so we *shape-up* with attention to ergonomic detail, interior aesthetic and external appearance, as we can afford it - structural implications in mind. And also in mind the diversities of the human organism – size, agility, vision, hearing, strength, frailty, numbers and grocery bags. Different human, different movement. And so *shape-up* may warrant some modification to *layout*.

If possible it is good to create an interior long-distance sightline. This can be done with open-planning, a hall or aligned doorways. Link this view line through a window or external door with that garden feature and distant locale feature, a mountain peak – to good effect in orientation and *nature's nurtures* and *cosmic symbol*. Maybe it goes for miles and miles – certainly further than the surface of the mirror where you might be with your toothbrush. Or the inside of Maggies blinds.

The overall *shape* - and detail moulding of the *shape* - of any *room-entity* can be receptive to an activity. And also expressive. Inviting reach and channelling walk; to the entrance, to the toilet, upstairs, beckoning doorway, ease of access, coaxing balustrade. Access to light switch, exit, handle. *Familiar skinned hand turns the chromed doorknob, room enough to avoid marking its knuckles on the lacquered arrised timber jamb.* Receptive. In addition to these aspects of physically based inducement, shape is useful in creating psychological amenity such as spatial symmetry contrasting with ad hoc. We create tranquil space for bedrooms. Maybe a *deboxed* noble tranquil *space* for a lounge using say a domed inset in a rectangular ceiling. Or an egg-shaped room in an otherwise ramshackle farmhouse. We create flowing *space* using lines in the floor to move us with the North Wind or just along to the front door together with an inviting alcove inset. On his way to the car, the Building Inspector passes the filigree shadows casting skewed lines across the portico's boarded deck.

More than a track worn through grass, sometimes paths are intricately ornate and coloured. *Shape* can be similarly creative. They serve a purpose and stimulate while doing so. Our front path means a lot to us. It is a transition; we probably go through typical mind-frames each time we walk it from the public realm to our private seclusion. Walking down that passage can become a notable experience, given design and maybe a notion of translucent buffalo hide overhead. Design to create beauty and flow, with enough power to convert a settler television daze to a bush television daze – or some *ecopical* in-between. A staircase may simply be *boxed* up and down, or curved swooping flight. And the cost for such design, apart from loadings put on by cautious builders, who may find it difficult to do something unconventional, is not necessarily more. The entry to the house is not just a door and maybe a multi-purpose air lock. It is an opportunity to be polite to visitors, to shape an experience, and to meet public and friends. Like Mick Jagger or was it his wife or both, had two front doors; one for your wife and one for you. Maybe two bedroom doors. A gender aspect to your house. Here goes the PorticoFandango. Even just a door or window can be a design focus. Wow, the DoorFandango Now! Fantastic things doors, important doors, locks, detailed doors, artistic doors, frequently and rarely used doors, doorways, internal, external, the quality of approach, the expression to the user, psychology, hand on the handle, the refinement of the hinge. A knock and it opens. A bolt and it's barred. Or its only for keeping the warm in; so we can use the fabrication for cultural and whimsical expression. Doors can be double, sliding, swing, roll up, curtains, folding, carved, painted, metal, wood, heavy or light. Doors are part of a partition, an option to screen or not. Doorways conversely are holes in the partition, passageway, access through; ergonomic provision. Different shapes, rectangular, arched, wedge, key hole, or circular. Some ancient people, now, have low doorways; about the height of a dweller's lower chest - they stoop, bow, to pass through; in a sense, passing under the wall. "What a different feeling that gives to a room," the Inspector notes. The same people have their front doors in the roof. In some cases this was a safety measure; pull up the ladder, the garden path, from the ground outside to be safe from intruders.

Doorways, windows, arched openings, pergolas, roofs, furniture. Shape potentials abound. Maybe the threshold is knee-height above the floor.

228

Symmetry is a power. It's a *shape* and *layout* thing that binds the viewer to the viewed. A very significant psyche thing. It creates more than focus – breadth, space in front and behind. It can be a *deboxing* device. It can also accentuate *box.* Vertical symmetry is different from horizontal and one wonders if angular symmetry, or curved air refractions, is symmetry at all. Symmetry is often challenged by building practicality and economy. Often most pleasing are the aesthetics based on simple building technique, the grass hut, the gable cottage. Bobby's new gable barge would have been asymmetrical if he had widened one side to make a porch. Instead, in discussion with a friend, he made more complex construction to secure a symmetry. It was a bare necessity in a very tight budget. Symmetry provides.

With *layout* and *shape-up* the house can help us see where we are in the cosmos, in the domestic scene and in the community – a *cosmic and social symbol.*

We in the West tend to snare ourselves with low flow *boxes.*

PSYCHE
CORNERS, SPACE & SHAPES

Let's lean harder to the lateral *understandings.* **Beyond even the office bound house jealous whims of the magazine glossed passenger. The awakening Building Inspector obliquely notes, "... *psyche* saturates this writing". The psychological impact of shape and space is as powerful and delicate as that of colour and light. When shape, space & light come** together **- and throw in a little** *synthetic aesthetic***, pattern, sound, fragrance and graphic artifice - we have potent architectural potential.**

We may impulsively square-up a barely skew window or picture on a wall; why? Can Gallopilong relate to this? It's there as he squares up to spear a fish in accord with its refracted light. He doesn't mind if his entrance lintel leans; his need for order is absorbed in his spear thrust. **The order in his house is not in geometry but the finesse of frugality. They are real needs:**
the needs for some order, symmetry, closure, completion of an act or a system - *finesse.* They are cognitive, aesthetic or neurotic - 'needs' never-the-less. The camp abode becomes ordered. Order is the result of economy, sustainability - we sustain what we like. Order has an aspect that ensures its parts are harmonious with its whole. Cost and construction-time are aspects of the whole. What we like is a balanced whole; a balance that complements our own. Hierarchy too is an order matter; the entry door is dressed best. Gallopilong's encampment has minimal impact on his whole; his doorless entrance may lean a lintel.

Don't take space for granted; the possum has no awareness of it - a farmer once told me. Between it and its walls is nothing. People generally are emotionally more comfortable in limited spaces. Generally we prefer the natural enclosures to wide-open spaces, even for special purposes. As an occasional happening only, we desire wide open space; mountains, deserts or at sea. A psychologist said that; **typically no doubt never having met any Harmoninni.**

Roofs can be most economical flat or skillion. Many seem to prefer pointy ones. We wonder. Their pitches may vary beyond structural dictate, relating visually to the sky, landscape and viewer. I prefer the mid range pitch in most circumstances; it seems to join the sky and the ground without making me feel dominated by the house. That farmer also said, "The steeper the pitch the more birds sit on the ridge and crap, and that's not good for your tank water." "Didn't think of that," said a frilly necked architect. "Nor me," said the builder's draftsperson. "Nor me!" echoes the fabled draftsman's apprentice, "but I have noted that the vertex of a 45 degree gable is a right angle" – as, and quite aside, his eyes fell to the window by the smoking red clay chimney, causing his delighted reflection on the physiology of lace and cotton folds enhanced by the flesh warmth of the evening sun glowing against the moist mortar in its slightly up-cast horizon plunge, throwing all manner of domestic bliss about a cranium. In the old days, he afterwards thought passion limpen to matter-of-fact, roofs were often flimsy straw arrangements. Cats and dogs usually wouldn't but bugs and other droppings could fall through onto one's clean bed. A sheet awning supported on four posts could be set up for the sleeper's protection. This little act, of *doing one's housing*, evolved into the intimate little four poster canopy bed, which is popular even under long run corrugated iron and sealed plaster ceiling and cornice. It began for protection and remained popular for its own interior *room* appeal. A *room-entity*, a little room in a room; useless except for mosquito net, the psyche of **delight** and sometimes, with curtains, some extra warmth.

"All building distils into *firmness, commodity* and *delight*. But **an oasis, of any form, gives delight**," the little pig tells the llama.

My Reader please note in readiness; 'familiarity' breeds all three - 'contempt', comfort and simple acceptance. Now; ingenuity of design allows the disciplining of 'familiarity', to avoid the 'contempt' and allow the 'comfort'.

In concert the llama verbally imagines, "Ingenuity gives *delight*; and beauty gives joy." Hmm, yes, it thinks, "Land context aside, to be *delightful* the form of a house in all its intricacy must convey cleverness; whether it be wit or sheer handiness. Otherwise it is simply okay and not particularly *delightful*; except in its innocent simplicity during simple use."

"Well," snorted the pig in the matter-of-fact face of the llama, "knock me over with a feather. And I thought I was telling you something!!"

My small 'r' readers may agree in part. I love us small r people, we're my type.

Utility like amenity also cause psyche responses. Moods arise in association with the user utilising. Bump your head on a jarred door. Skin your knuckles, again, turning the knob. Not delightful. Such moods relate to nomadic minds too. And also design and construction create motivation and excitement. There is much complexity in the *psyche* and our housing is *rippling* far and wide in there in the *psyche* of *room* as the hot chimney falls back to a mound of wet clay and the cotton curtains to freshly plucked cotton balls in the flushed afterglow of the reconfirmed knowledge that there's not much between the house and the camp when it comes to the very fundamentals of domestic *armpit* bliss relaxed by curtains drawn by the draftsman's passionate apprentice.

In the aesthetic of your house and oft it is but subliminal is the hand of the builder, his thoughts as he ate his lunch, his sweat and blued thumbnail as he raised the stud frame and his slapping brush as he mothered the pearl.

Room for a spear. Put it in the *hud*. *Room* for some space; the mind needs space, but the head is all gray matter. Make *room* for space; no use space for room.

ECONOMY & BUILDABILITY
CORNERS, SPACE & SHAPES

It is interesting how the *ripples* roll. Shape impacts psyche. Structure impacts shape. Structure impacts psyche. Economy and buildability impact space and shape. The chosen manner of construction will stimulate some built forms and prevent others. We have spoken a little about the rectangular (orthogonal) logistic based on fundamental pragmatics in building. It is easy to see the simple shape logistics of indigenous dwelling, except perhaps where economy of time is waived to produce shapes of religious significance. We do not try to build a gable roof of ice on an igloo; we do not try to build multiple flowing curves in a low cost timber cottage. Sometimes we stress our construction limits to achieve specific spatial effects – like our Sinophile. Sometimes we let the natural integrity of structure carry the day for the beauty we need and simply make best use of the space it allows – function adapting to form.

Rooms and the *accumulation* of *room-entities* (like nooks, passage and ducts) are brought together to fit the dwellers in accord with structural conditions. Our traditional Sinophile was preoccupied with stretching his spatial achievements for the sake of amenity. Structure was a relative after-thought. So at times the buildings were frail whilst being beautifully spatially integrated and orientated. At the turn to this century they would still test the engineers with Feng Shui demands in their skyscrapers. Conversely others may confine their *room-amenity* to the form limitations of some pre-established structure. Accordingly people enjoy the economy and ease of construction of geodesic domes, despite their limits. Similarly people tolerate and adapt to *ticky tacky boxes*. Economy, buildability despite wholistic inadequacy.

The Sinophiles would (& will) experiment extensively with space – as an enhancement and creator of *room*. For them, foremost, before beautiful structural proportion, is their own position, in the centre - rooms and gardens around them and the city too. With respect and wonder Albert Gallopilong says, "Our Mother Earth is our centre (the Abophile centre)'. The Sinophiles' highly integrated *room* elements were not separable like those of the Greeks and the modern sham *boxes*. Each component space was integrally dependant on the others. The *box* culture's concern is not beauty nor is it the dwellers position per se, but practical minima as industrial market-commodity; albeit by slowly awaking unsatisfactory standards and values. Their eyes seem shut and bolted against the economies of nature and flowing ergonomics. *A major aspect of beauty though is practicality; the Western box has an appeal to the Third World; the modern Sinophile will use it with real style.*

We all, like our Sinophile, can manifest design flair by bending seeming structural axioms to create motif or aesthetics. Passionate ingenuity puts a seat where a column was demanding to go. Structure, though does come with strength into the play of the impact of construction on shape and space. The truss shapes the roof. It is likewise with materials, pipes, wires, landform etcetera. These things may impact, either, only detail shapes and space or the overall form, depending on design priorities. Our potential to build easy lightweight domes is derived from geodesic structure. Not flair, just ingenuity and mathematical discovery.
   An aside to the point just made; partitioning, acoustic and waterproofing difficulties in geodesic domes are balanced by beautiful arcing window configurations and structural economy; combined with their beauty on the land, this makes them enticing. Domes can be joined in multiplicity. There are formulae for various shapes; ellipse, half round, five eighths, egg shaped. They can be of myriads of small geodesic triangles or fewer large triangles. The triangles are a size module for the dome.

Japan's tatami floor-mat is used as a domestic *layout* sizing module. The brick and available lengths of wood affect the detail sizing of houses, window widths and proportions, roof spans and *room* widths. 'The Modular' is a seemingly wonderful system of measurement that enables, in a building under its principles, the harmonious interfacing of all sizing and quadrangles. *Deboxing* may use harmonic quadrangles. Look up 'the Modular' and read about it. It is a magic ideal of proportion developed by architect Le Corbusier ('the Builder') more than half a century back. The shame is that industry is by no means coordinated enough to make use of it. This beautifully harmonious form, pattern and shape ideal is not pragmatic in common building cultures. It also says a lot about the pertinence of orthogonal buildings and interiors, that is the 'rectangles' – horribly unnervingly close to *boxes*.

A *shape* item, the eave, is there to protect the walls from weather and interior from sun. Very often we do not need eaves all around the house, because of durable materials or directional weather and shade circumstance. The pragmatics of building however often gives eaves all around. It can be easier to build that way. As the bonus dusty corners, which arise from building pragmatically around the needed floor area, shape our *room-entities*, so we may have bonus eave - if we want any eave at all. It is said, probably therefore, that traditional cottage houses 'look better' that way – common sense.

Building always has its say; and so once did drawing boards. Tee squares and set squares enhanced the entrenchment of orthogonality, straight lines and right angles; but by choice, also fit the natural harmonic that gives us post, lintel and brick, with dome and other venture as rarer constructions. It is not as simple to draw a dome on a drawing board but it can be done, like motorcycle maintenance in Zen.

Sometimes we limit our building potential to facilitate unskilled construction to meet an economy favoured by an owner-builder.

BOX
& FLOW
CORNERS,
SPACE
& SHAPES

*G*et *some hearty quicksilver flow* into the pragmatic *box*. *Debox* in *layout, shape-up* and renovation. I live in a 1970s second hand ad hoc *box* myself, but it is now bountiful with *nature's earthy nurtures* and I open the way to *ecopian* qualities by using the reality programming vision of my aims for future developments.

One of the world's most acknowledged architects intentionally set out to destroy the *box* in building; "Architecture is creative only while we are true to Earth ... the *box* is science taking the place of art," said Amerophile, Frank Wright. We note that 'The Modular' is science - a little bit fudged some suggest. He seems to say that science is led by art in the quest for trueness to Earth. Perhaps he is saying the *box* stifles by shutting out *nature's earthy nurtures*, by being limited in design to inadequate considerations. **The squared *box* crops up in natural construction of course just like the grass humpy dome.** But the square most strongly rings the harmonies in the marriage of dweller psyche and common pragmatics – I'm sorry I don't know why I said that. Whilst *boxy* inside some forms of in-ground house may be moundy outside, having no visible exterior walls or roof. Some may love their *box*, but really when it is too *boxy* it is a horribly demeaning place of abode. The egg is shaped for birth delivery and chick comfort. The over-*boxed box*, the *ecopically* poor *box*, is shaped for economical construction - shape streamlining for environment and urbanity are barely addressed. House must not be merely a container. *Debox* the container. No severely distraught Harmoninni would suicide in unbearable anguish in a cell that didn't stifle the songs of the land. If *Pale* could find the molten looking-glass he would be poulticed against the *box*.

Rectilinear configurations are an amenity of house valued for their mental impact. This is because their rectilinearity relates to both manufacture – ie not from natural occurrence - and the intended domestic function. Rectilinear thought is a maker of domestic amenity - and other building - which is exclusive in nature. This exclusivity creates the fixed aspect of house in physical and ethereal space ... we may say ... or at least an ethereal aspect in physical space.

Box harmonics are part of people's *synthetic aesthetic*. We fuse box and flow – water cubed in a glass fish tank is a terrific happening, even better from the domestic viewpoint of the goldfish. A *box* caravan camped at the seaside. A *box*-roomed, orthogonally planned, house, with garden and light spilling in from all sides – in contrast to the over-*boxing* of a black, lead-lined cell. The over-*boxed box* syndrome can be solved by *nature's earthy nurtures* – through materials, curves, artistry, colours, music, planting, beautiful doorways and windows; and through having Albert Gallopilong and Sitting Bull for tea. Leave the door open for them during their stay. The dweller's touch, and also the builder's touch, relate to *nature's earthy nurtures*. This is so by virtue of their own innate nature. Hence organic aesthetics and ergonomic lines, and visibility of the builder's construction too, help to resolve *box* syndrome. The act and credibilities of construction relate to ergonomics; relate to people in action as they take discernible proportion in space and *contraption*. Ergonomic lines are part of the 'streamline' aesthetic; call it *ergothetics* - no obstructions nor snags, just welcoming shapes and leg room. *Room* to move and perceive comfortably, by nature, is not *boxy*. *The mind, when relating, via perception or understanding, to the act of building, is less boxed.* The act of construction is visible in the likes of battened wall panels and exposed beams. A shallow dome space formed in a flat square ceiling, though not easy to build, may be mental ergonomic amenity, carried by the form and space; *ergonomic room* for the mind to stretch – certainly it *deboxes*.

I think perhaps Le Corbusier's Modular, with its system of harmonious rectilinear proportions, enables a near fully orthogonal house to be not a *box*, but a beautiful piece of *synthetic aesthetic*, that is highly linked with nature's flow. Occasionally we see them,

234

whether by Modular design or by intuitive parallel, sitting delightfully in the landscape – maybe with their minor *boxed* imperfection, tweaked to *deboxed* perfection, with a gentle, doubly curved, archway and some fine detail, linking to the pattern of the leaves, to balance the broad perceptive links to wide open planet.

New Jerusalem, being a giant cube, is a curved ball in this *deboxing* theory - as one might expect.

Deboxing is a designed linking of *synthetic aesthetic* and nature.

There is a house that rises maybe four storeys, but with maybe seven split-levels. Inside are a central pole and spiral stair with seven landings. Off each landing a spoon-like floor pod - providing scope for a *room-entity*. No walls, just a number of spoons in a large tipi-like space. Though the furniture may have been *boxed*, it is more venerating than a series of *boxes* inside a *box*. Bobby is realising what we have missed. A landscape of tipis, too, is more pleasant than a landscape of *ticky tacky boxes*. The ball and chain of ailing orthodoxy is one problem here. A comfort somewhere between this tipi-like *contraption* and the *tacky box* is probably a better orthodox. This of course is subject to concurrent implementation of bulk ecological issue resolution; arcology, *ecopicality* and population control. We can do it by *ecopical Housefandango*. Carlos Santana gently melts *deboxing* and *nature's earthy nurtures* into chamber music – best of course with huge speakers, in homely chamber and a view to a sunrise. 'Can we get a speaker wire run to the mob's camp Monte?" calls Cheeky.

It costs more. It costs more!! It costs more!!! But it's cheaper for the progeny. Much cheaper!!!!

The wilderness doesn't need *deboxing*. Some *synthetic aesthetic* perhaps may help it - unless it's heritage listed. Some cities need *deboxing* - Central Park helps - more than others; the multistorey welfare housings need it desperately. A rumbling train is in part a synthetic substitute for some absent natural sustenance as it rhythmically hoots at the skyed arc of the horizon, steaming through the crowds of *boxed* contraptions crammed with *three-planed-corners*.

Why be mean by limiting ourself to 3D *box* pragmatics. There are four dimensions. The *time-cost-effect* evaluation scope of the dweller is the critical fourth – the design zone of getting the best we can when we need it for the money we have. When this simple fourth dimension is over-limited, by lack <u>or</u> meanness, then maximum *box* is the only way to go. A saving grace; the fourth dimension may then, at least partially, be achieved through arrangement of furniture, choices of décor , links to the land and future enhancements. Even small details of *deboxing* design can be tedious and expensive – as often a convention has not been developed that makes details of construction become routinely economical. *Being beyond dire necessity and orthodoxy (common practicality), sometimes product of design that stretches the fourth dimension is questioned as to its buildability and economy.* In this situation it is necessary to fully utilise, with shrewd priorities, the scope available to the fourth dimension.

We may *debox*, in renovation and new house; beginning at key areas, say the lounge, and keep laundries *boxed* to conserve our fourth dimension scope for the high point priorities ... which, sometimes, may be an even dispersal of *deboxing* throughout the house and a high-point feature at a lounge-kitchen transition or the like – might be a kitsch little arch as the *Pales* aim high.

'Practicality', in a sense in which we sometimes use it, is actually only that which can be done within our self-imposed limits. We can adapt to our *boxes* constructed with our self imposed limits. Self imposed – restrained by lack of independence, venture, courage, faith, generosity, imagination – by lack of *ecopicality*. Most houses today are orthogonal with flat or sloped roofs. Curves are beautiful but not always practical. Some of us need them, some of us do not. Some subconsciously love to use arches in *box* houses. They simply like them without knowing why. It gives them a break from the rectilinear slavery they inflict on themselves. Arches, though kitsch in some uses, are a device that can relieve tension and assist with nurtures in a house. As we say, house fabric is not just floor, walls and ceiling. It is planes, lines, curves, shapes, and can be related to sculpture.

Indigenous techniques cannot create the stereotypical problem *box*. If they could, the *box* would not be anywhere near so bad; ie without a suburban pattern around it. A '*box*' is a *machinemark*ed rectilinear house with rectilinear rooms, around a passageway, and nothing else. Windows and doors appear to be cut into the fabric. Millions of people live in *boxes*. They are the cheapest and most publicly acceptable houses available to the growing small proportion of 'Earthlings' who make dwelling arrangements with the Western ethos. They fill by far the largest tracts of suburbia. They are even *boxier* in apartment blocks. The best standard of *box* may be in Australia & New Zealand. Their general standard of finish design can be quite reasonable by the measure of our industro-cultural limitations. People do like them and resist most changes that designer's attempt. Either they are mere *shadows* of people or our famous architect is missing something. The people who live in them can either make them *boxier* or, with spirit and décor, open them to nature. Some are so tied to staid orthodoxy that any planning or structural adventure is bravery. It is not an easy problem for designers of low cost houses either, because of convention-economy. Safe and secure, it seems to some. Convention is like a seat belt, but often it holds you in a *box* - a seatbelt restraining a spear.

Eno and Leone were Lindenthalers, where Germany now is. Hairy as they may have been, they had time to kill and they had no fibreboard factories. This allowed freedom for room-space configuration. They sculpted earth floors and wicker-worked shapes for reclining, comfort and movement. Shapes speak many languages. Pyramids are a shape of unique capacity. Domes, tipis, broken integrated rectangles and occasional curved walls are tremendous - in their places.

It is the work-a-day socio-economic condition that limits awareness and hope, bringing psyche adaptations and compromise that makes many people happy with their *box*. House is not everything. A good lover, peace, food, flowing *box*, the blessing of window glass and beautiful weather are enough on which to hang your hat and survive happily. This little paragraph is not an answer though, if only in that the weather *is wilting*. Not to mention that we should not accustom ourselves to even second best.

Within the industry and sociology we can, little by little, introduce *nurtures* to join the practicalities and beauties of *box* logic - squeezing out the stifle. A beautiful organic entry, along with a breezy *mother of pearl*, may be adequate to resuscitate an entirely *boxed* small house. Applying other design rules to this basic orthodox can produce beautiful results. Structural timbers can be left visible and the garden design can be set integrated with the house form and close views. The Japophile as part of their roof structure may use a natural log not necessarily straight, possibly bow shaped, as a main tension member in their milled timber gable roofs. Such a technique can be used and left exposed in Western orthodox housing to introduce the gentle beauty of natural form; *nature's earthy nurtures* introduced by stealth of design, in the face of adversity. Don't stay too long in a *box*. Flow into the *box*, as does God into New Jerusalem; fill it with pheromonic; fill it with the vibes of a remote beach; marry it with the land of the site and then start on the roads and city. Consolidate the lot. Go Bobby go.

The person invents to discover and use. To enjoy.

I discovered the telephone, which I use. I prefer my personal relationships to be based without the phone.

I installed one, to make appointments; which I use. I prefer the **unanticipated knock** on the door to the **regimented forewarning** of an appointed visit. But both are better than the former alone – if the latter is managed well. If the latter is managed well.

I prefer a relationship with **village and land**, which is **unencumbered** with the facility of walls; yet I have a relationship with walls. But both are better than the former alone - if the latter is managed well.

If the latter is managed - is managed well. *Only* if it is managed well.

I discovered the silicon dna ....

SURFACES, BITS
& RESPONSE TO USER

Why **do I *do* it?** This chapter focus brings us full circle on
our discussion of motivation for housing. Beyond love of a
place; domestic facility, utility and comfort are where we
begin; not the first stone nor the alluring front door. And
again we sharpen our appreciations here by relating the
settler and the nomad alternatives.

Earthy brick, sheets of glass and industrial components are
shaped-up to produce the *nacre* to create *room*. The blending
of orientation, material and method produces an overall
amenity; a style, a tastefulness, an atmosphere - *room*. A fit-
for-purpose zone, serviced by the mechanics of fundamental
utility - *room*. The *surface* of things too; this is of common
significance to amenity and utility – *mother of pearl*, easy to
clean, nice feel, looks good, reads tastefully, will not scratch,
will not chip the cups, soft, polishes well. Polishing the
bookshelf is architectural *fandango*; momentary completion of
the unfinished. It should be acknowledged in the draftsman's
pencil along with the dirt from dig. Utility helps us to control
and tune our interior amenity; draw the curtain, latch the
door, dim the lights. The responsiveness of the household to
the inhabitants' whims is a primary aspect of house quality -
convenience. The easy action of the curtain rail, simple
microwave electronic latching, easily adjustable kerosene
lamp, practical ventilation, no jamming door or faulty power
switch – kinetic *finesse*. A log-seat handy to the camp fire.
The *services*
grid attached to the fibre optic cable from the gable. The
satellite dish attached to the moving star in the sky

ITEM, ACTION, USER

Building on the ancient cooking and warming fire and jugs of water, we seek to fully service our homes. Plumbing. Water in. Sewerage and sullage out. White Cloud, while feeling the warm wet cleanse, looked the brass

shower-rose in its spirit. Seeing through the pipes to the big indigo clouds and the provision of a waterfall, she wondered as watery well about the conveyance by outward flush of her leftovers from yesterdays food. How very significant sewerage is to the settler. And should this be managed some other way; compost toilet, balanced eating, a spade in the bushes, septic tank, dunny cart?

Washing tub, water heater, sink, chopping bench, scullery, furniture, warming arrangement. Utility items; part of the housing *accumulation*. Our housing itself generates further utility; doors for control of heat, security, spatial amenity and privacy; vents, shutters, letterbox. We have control of artificial and solar light. Our utility items result from; indoor climate control, ablutionary needs, storage arrangements, food preparation, cleaning, relaxing, etc. Open and shut, squeaky hinge, grime in the crack, glare in the eye. Dead possum in the water tank, broken chain on the drawbridge. A wasp in a nomad's wine gourd, an easy rolling disability stair-lift. As the years go by we consolidate life-assisting utility as nomad or as settler. Making our domestic complex in the manner in which we wish it to promote us, in the way we want it to take us. Coat hangers; bring a significant space-saving & tidiness evolution to the house. Electricity; a big word in utility and house evolution. Some say that it is what has broken the back of settlement sustainability and our natural rhythms. Gallopilong still sleeps in the desert cold. That aside, we *do* it well - make our domestic complex that is. We maintain it. It *responds* to its limits to the call of its master. To the strenuous demands of the family and the party animals - the lounge-*room* is sometimes a gymnasium.

We dream of house. Dream of a new pool. Laud the perfect laundry with the WashLaundango. Sit on a splintered chair. Life is lead by dream and ruled by reality. Sometimes circumstance puts beyond our practical scope the wish to fix the leaky tap. The unfinished garden and fading wood-fire complement our need for work.

The utilities vary from house to house. They have weight, volume and cost ; *quanta*. Often they rely on the shelters of house for both their birth and ongoing effectiveness; being useless when wet, sun burnt, blown or stolen. They are a highly significant portion of housing *effort* and *impact*.

Do we wonder why on earth it is that we need utility? Can the dolphin put her fins in his head. Oh no. Utilities; we don't wonder about them a lot. Our hands know the reason and our feet; that is enough. They inform the designer. The designer makes do with what he has. Ingenuity stretches the mind and the man is extended. The woman dims the light. The lamp is well oiled and the sturdy old pumping machine doesn't miss a beat. *Doing* it; *doing your housing, Housefandango!* A wonderful activity if unstressed, The complex wonder that answers so much. An empty house and one in use. While **the *movement/utility* interface is a constant vital presence** in the house, the house's visual appearance *pales* away with familiarity - except for only Sundays, new visitors, a backdrop and resale time.

Surfaces; we are really coming home to house. A squat lounge tabletop ready for an artefact. A hand height standup bench. An elbow height sitdown tabletop. That pressure on the bottom of your foot is the floor. And the soft knee high bench under your hamstrings is a seat. The children's fingermarks will clean easily off the gloss door surface. And you know you are lucky if you can drag furniture without scuffing the floor ; a different utility to dirt floor. Glaze the rough with *mother of pearl*. Let the dwelling organism slide through the silky curtains and the mental *ergonomic room* all around, glazing surfaces, colours, temperatures, resilience and textures. No elephant pats; everybody's happy. Plenty of warm cooking glaze. Time brings on an extension; a *sink*ronised women's place. The kitchen sink; only joking. Give some gusto to one of the most mundane activities. That activity is punctuation in the story of your daily life, a riff in your daily music. Give it more space, set the sink with soul in a soulful setting. The Dogon people know. Do not let the electric dishwasher steal the whole story; nor let the frozen meal for microwave cooking finally rob the house of its ancient heart's primary beat. Mother charming children in the kitchen, flour on her cheek, potato peelings by a warm glow, fingers in the custard bowl – fresh cooked carcass by the camp fire. **The heart of architecture!** Yes *Pale*, come on now, you must at least mourn. The city supers and eateries sell immense variety, but from a relatively hollow kitchen.

Stove, mechanisms, equipment, furniture; a mere hovel with one state-of-the-art ergonomically adjustable swivel armchair is no longer such a hovel. A hovel with one fully ergonomic Albert Gallopilong is never a hovel. *Is the utility more closely a part of the dweller or of the house?* Regardless of your answer to that interesting question, Albert never having trodden a floor nor ever likely to be near a town, if coming upon a hovel with an ergonomic chair would use it, his own new wonder aside, in the same way that nephew Cheekybugga used the *Classic* sedan.

Utility can make a lot of noise in the *housing contraptions* of the mechanised times; refrigerator, cake mixer, sink grinder, vacuum cleaner, stereo in another room, fan, telephone. Always a click at each of the great multitude of switches we flick. In association with simple bangs on the easy slip and grip of the chill wooden floor, voices, pot on the sink, sliding chair there is scope for a maddening cacophony. Selected materials, form and the utilities themselves can soften the noise. People often forget in design and in purchase of goods; *accumulation* making itself known, as nerves fray. This noise extends beyond our small Western World, which today, in this way, is being joined by the East and the giant corporation market places.

BITS

SURFACE,
BITS &
RESPONSE

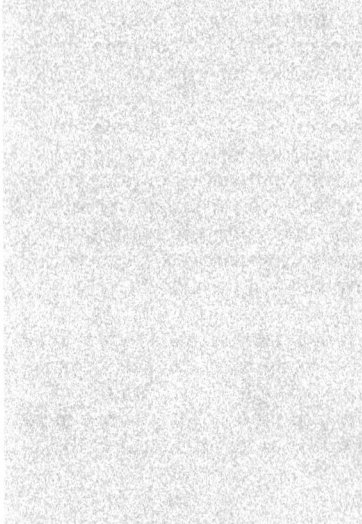

With the house are the *miscellanea of* cover strips, window sills, mortar joints, cracks in the slab and cupboard shelves. Let's not be tedious. Plaster, laminates and sealants have reduced them.

Especially in this age of industrial manufacture, we should learn more about the art of uniting all the bits and pieces of our house into a tidy visual and tactile *pearled* harmony. Factory standard sizes and shapes tend to run parallel with *box* syndrome. They're economically practical but can grind a bit hard under the mind's comforts. Le Corbusier's 'Modular' system of sizing was trying to harmonise all these quadrangles to a sort of musical rhythm.

The mix of separately manufactured bits in the house is a little similar to the separately designed big bits that front each street address; so we understand this pattern of things and tend to tolerate or enjoy it through our *understanding*.

It was bad luck to stand on a Chinese threshold and maybe it still is - a little *bit* of miscellaneous information *accumulating* in some adhoc order.

SMOOTH LATCHES & AUTOMATION
SURFACE, BITS & RESPONSE

To warm, Eno and Leone Neolithic build appropriately to bring in their animals, to partly supplement the warmth of the fire and to care for their animals and their productivity. Fire becomes ecologically and environmentally unsustainable with the modern severity of population. Electricity is smooth but part of the ancient essence of fire is replaced by the switch click; and some corporation's turbine powered by something.

We cannot expect an enchanted house that responds to the rubbing of a magic ring; but we may be well on the way. Door closer, electronic sensors, flushing mechanism, spa jets; the refinement of operation and ingenuity of design and manufacture very largely limits such items to industrial product; rather than *handmarked* product. The indigenous man, autonomous man, cannot have them without gift or money. "No! Thanks anyway Global," responds Cheeky, ever-faithful to Uncle Albert, "I'll stick with the automatic ancient essence. It has its hardships too, but I like it. It's not that I'm silly, oh no, I know what I like." Low Carl knows he likes his fine little spirit stove and snow-zone sleeping bag too; but the automatic ancient as well. "Well maybe I actually could latch onto the ease of the *finesse* of some smooth automation. Just keep the country on top," **says** Talkabout, by 'country', meaning land, biodiversities and landscape.

ADAPTABILITY & MOOD
SURFACE, BITS & RESPONSE

Albert's mood is based on his lifestyle, as is anybody's. It's to do with weather, seasons, happenings and time. Our interface with utility shapes our daily movements. As we have noted, it can affect our mood; especially if the required *response* does not avail. Effective *surfaces.* Our *acts* with our house.

Giving hygiene. Reducing maintenance. Making us move. Saving our time. Smooth operation. Lower the awning. A romantic *Housefandango*. In the mood. Dim the light. Sharpen the carving knife. Under the roof of a hard days work. The sounds and actions amid the *Pale* family at home are very different to those amid the Gallopilongs. Lighting, colour and texture effects *room-amenity* whether the room is interior or whether it is in Gallopilong country; the interior effect is largely to our own tuning, the exterior awesome but without air conditioning. Utility of campfire creates a room of light – a mood in it and one out of it.

The full amenity of the house then is a blend of functioning utility, *nature's nurtures*, air conditioning, space and visual aesthetics. "I can beat you with all that Low," chides the cheeky one; "... and they're all superior design coordinated by the ancient authority, perpetually modern nature, not like your plastic mismatch." We know that design which celebrates the utility functions is not likely to produce a totally *boxed* house, because there is nothing *boxy* about any action nor function and because the celebration of movement in a house relates to peoples' love for arms, legs, crutches and wheelchairs. It's all agreeable focus. Create an entrance experience to and through the doorway. Celebrate the sink. Make the items shake the hand of the master; and contour to his bottom. Where is the *box*? It's lost outside with the dusty corners - the intimate inner responds nicely.

An air vent, especially if adjustable and visually enhanced, contributes to the dweller's mood of anticipated ongoing amenity. A door bolt promotes a safety feeling allowing tranquillity. Provision of visibly encouraged direction for access and handling sets a mood of ease and uncluttered thought. **Utility access is part of the whole ergonomic flow of the house**, both as function and aesthetic. There once was a tendency to build the furniture to suit the style of the house; a wholistic aesthetic. The pragmatics of the domestic *accumulation* and industry, updating included, however, mean that the leading aesthetic of each item is either a commercial trademark or an earmark of sentimentality or practical economy. Indeed there is a serious danger of house simplicity being over-ridden with the visual clutter of utility items - the city creeping into our privacy. Even into our genome. Indeed, slum dwellers with hi-tech utility, like nomadic people stuck halfway between indigenuity and city are freak societies.

"Well maybe I actually could latch onto the ease of the *finesse* of some smooth automation. **Just keep the country on top**."

keep the country on top

keep the country on top

keep the country on top

keep the country on top

keep the country on top

keep the country on top

keep the country on top

keep the country on top

keep the country on top

keep the country on top

keep the country on top

keep the country on top

keep the country on top

keep the country on top

keep the country on top

keep the country on top

keep the country on top

keep the country on top

MAKING, BUILDING, DESIGNING

ere in the studio-workshop and on site, feet in grass about to be covered with foundation rubble, we may see some solidification of the multitude of gossamic allusions made on our butterfly accompanied journey to establishing domestic site and *contraption*. Earthy brick, clear sheets of glass and lace laid-up into ordered utility, space, corners and shapes through the making-building-designing of *domestic-contraption* on land and usually among other people. The interfusion of design with the act of fabrication is a fact. If we're in touch with the *Housefandango*; we think, evaluate and envisage as our hands go to making. Or as the hands of others go to making for us – and, if we accept an existing-building scenario, we simply unify with the process of its origin in our understanding, thus making its future. Filigree on the veranda roof, style, vogue, avant-garde, vernacular, pragmatics. And as we design, in mind or on computer, we program a potential reality for construction.

In the case of utilisation of existing building; construction may simply be addition, **adaptation**, renovation. In fact, architecturally speaking, existing land is fundamentally the same as existing building; hence <u>any construction is</u> **adaptation** *of existing dwelling facility*. As we construct we detail and sometimes modify the design. Whatever; we make an ordered arrangement of our domestic *accumulation* and *room* requirements in accord with our taste, caution and inhibition – and all the *armpit* magic and profundities of the foregoing chatter. Here in the drawing room we also understand more about the built heritage (land is heritage too) – what to keep and what to lose.

The way in which we go about making houses and developing

domestic open space affects our lifestyle. It also affects the design and the physical outcome of the domicile. Design itself has vast impacts. People in the actions of resourcing and visualising, communicating and fabricating; people as a tribe, individual, friends, community, society and as customers and providers. Some animals *make*; insects, birds, trapdoor spiders. Angels; we wonder. Many of we Western-types simply buy the package, or something similar. For Cheekyfella, it's like scratching himself, or spearing a lizard; set some rocks, grab some limbs. Pounce on the chance of a secondhand camp and he's streets ahead.

Many people and communities in the many locales, varying in culture, skills and resource, produce the many different houses and renovations. Thatch, mud, aluminium, plastic. Adze, power saw. Bushman, carver, carpenter, block layer. Lifting. Stringlines and microchipped satellitic *theodolites*. Biceps, bruises and lunch breaks. Bushman, nomad, owner, architect. *Handmark* custom. Machined en mass. Lifestyle, soul. Daily work, expedience, money. A particular domestic circumstance is cradling yours now. Another circumstance may eventuate too. And another.

Abundance of time, timber and space. But that was yesterday. Whilst some are not fazed. Many are profoundly moved by the process of designing and building their own house or that of a friend or client. Or renovating; in effect pouncing on the advantages of adapting a secondhand camp to a brand new day. Or establishing regulation. "Yet, for the industrially civilised, this design and building *Housefandango* ought to turn to corporate war tactics," agrees Bobby supported by White Cloud and a passing Gypsy in earshot of Global. Building for your own, having it built for you or moving into an already built *contraption*; regardless, your world, health and dwelling enjoyment are best served with a feeling for the building of your dwelling – not to forget the preparation and modification of your site. Oh! And the land under the road that leads to it – and the land under the industrial building that is also behind the *Ecosculpture* smokescreen.

CONSTRUCTION, BUILDING, MAKING

MAKING, BUILDING, DESIGNING

They may be erected by ladies, beavers, spontaneous passion, ornery contractor, plan or handy machinery - made by intuitive indigenous reflex or greed for money.

248

The constructed designed house *contraptions* come about in many ways. Tradesman and administrators or indigenous woman alone. Tools, cranes, trucks. Materials; simple-natural, prepared-natural, factory made, on-site or in-factory. Program and coordination. Weather, foundation, neighbour. Building seems to suit settlers; the love of it may have encouraged the origins of housing. Or the routine has simply become second nature.

Playdough, methods, skills and tools set a scene for construction. Design is disciplined within this. Design ideally should suit the predilections and certainly the potentials of the builder – in which case, design follows a predetermined style of construction.

We must measure. Rules, tapes, levels. Cubits, spans, feet, metres. Verticals, right angles, *grids*. Calculations. Scale. Measure is used to tailor building to function. It will transfer requirement from full scale concept through the scaled down design drawing process, through specification drawing and on through to building set-out, resourcing, pre-cutting and fabrication; and then on to establishing the Council rates bill and the size of the heat pump.

Design does not necessarily imply the builder working from drawings. Where the builder may be the architect, or working closely with him, it is quite reasonable in some circumstance to proceed with building and design simultaneously. Of course the townplanner and building inspector may each skew an eyebrow at the thought. Sitting Bull's in usual routine as his camp comes together. Construction is a factor of design. Design is a factor of building. 'Architect' is Greek for 'chief builder'. Every construction has a chief builder. Even the simple ice dome. "Pass me the comic!" calls an Aussie builder on site referring tongue-in-cheek to the architect's plans. The manner in which the architect refers to the builder's Progress Payment Claim can be equally satirical. When all boils down architect and builder are one.

The builder cuts and stacks blocks of ice in such a way as to make a *nacre* that is logical to the local material. Or lays Persian mats from trade direct to the ground, with no concept of a carpeted reinforced concrete slab. By another method, machine cuts and assembly lines produce items for anonymous cash. These items are then installed by a detached process far away in another land. This is industrially civilised logic; an excellent logic if we can resist the temptation to sell our soul. We must buy a little scope in our construction for the lifestyle magic of the building process. The value of the joy of building is immense in our settler well-being. This will improve the product. We cannot buy this scope, we do not have the wealth, so we review the priorities and put the 'pragmatic' assembly-line item close to the balancing enhancement of *nurturing* countryside. Oh, catch 22. We cannot often do this either, so can we mix prefabrication and mud, or ice? We have ingenuity. But the indigenous call it wit. Here 'building' is thoroughly 'design'. And ideally building with partial 'prefabrications,' i.e. dazzlingly modern building 'products', can become thoroughly 'vernacular'; matching the ceremony of building celebrated by some indigenous peoples. But this is not the case in reality. The women of some tribes make artful basketry humpies with driftwood and green branches. They simply select and order 'products'.

A forest dweller from Borneo, briefly away from the home of his leafy forest skin, observing a Western *box* being built, is gobsmacked by the stress and complexity of the whole thing. What are the handy items at which the Westerner grasps to make its house? Certainly not mud and fronds; land purchase, mortgage, lawyer, regulation, plans, estimates, tender, contracts, progress payments, inspections, insurances, deadlines; deadlines, extra costs, nine to five. Where is the simple soul and joy of cottage construction? Even feature wood carving is too expensive. "Pity the Westerner," frowns Low, but the villager is extremely impressed with the product; subject to a little intricate homely *deboxing*, wood carving and streamlining. Will handmade houses phase out like the grass hut or simply become the prerogative of mainly the wealthy? Such stress and complexity is born of the industrial commerce and society necessary to produce the impressive product.

In the face of market commodity psyches, allowing callous-free hands for life; Western individuals perhaps should exercise some general diversity of skills, rather than speciality alone. Get a little dirt on your hands. The industrial method over-rules. And, sadly for impassioned spirits and healthy community, regulation is trending to reduce the potential for owner-building, only to secure a social standard and resolve a taxation loophole. The ordinary person is often intimidated into giving up trying to do it for himself, making him a slave to experts that likely he can ill-afford – for novice owner builders are usually in the humble end of the market where surely there is social justification for some constructive freedom. So, though one may be able to build for oneself, it is often in that industrial attitude. One really should be reasonably prepared by oneself to remove a wall, build an awning, pull up the carpet and old boards and install an earth floor; build newly even though one is already in a house. It is your environment, work it. Make it. *Do* it. Don't necessarily just settle for your own specialty. You may be an ice-cream vendor or barrister, but you are a bit of a builder too. Like the house itself the process of getting it or building it must suit your circumstance. If you can't see yourself with a hammer, too frail perhaps, select the carpet and have help to put the floor under it and the roof over - you, yours, here.

Beyond the owner-builder potentials with its place for some experts working with the owner-builder; there is scope for houses made completely by experts – houses waiting completed for dwellers to enter and adapt to their own needs, if they have not been fully tailored for the dweller by an architect.

250

There is not enough *room* in this workshop to guide you through all the details of building the many varieties of houses. Nor can I hope to give you your own localised inventory of *playdough*, manufactured materials, services, special conditions and personal idiosyncrasies. You are best to find the right Inuit to teach you of igloo building, or to take a course in basic bricklaying if you intend building in brick; and of course the same applies to the arts and skills of specific design. The right expert may be exactly what you need. That expert almost certainly needs you. And you need your house; the way you need it. It's your *domestic arrangement* and your responsibility.

The further you go from the local orthodoxy in your building the more building problems or adventures you are likely to face, and the less expertise is readily available. You may look to cheapness, greater individual building convenience, beauty and other advantages. Such advantages inherent in your uncommon technique may easily outweigh the difficulties. For many reasons, especially 'minimum cost' and well worn tracks, most people and apparent bargains will tend to sway you to the orthodox manner; whether or not you are engaging expert advice and tradesmen. *The convenience of convention reclines in the jungle of innovation.* There to be utilised, modified or discarded at will. Discarded for a lack of need, or inspiration, to make new innovation. New innovation must sometimes precariously face the many traps that the jungle conceals.

Part of construction are the fiddly trims, installations and the owner's *mother of pearl* décor. And cleaning, tidying, maintenance and renovation are part of construction in some minds. And if you are moving with a domestic lifestyle masterplan anything you *do* toward your next abode location is part of a building process; part of the your Housefandango - producing the continuum of your housing tunnel. This includes design, collecting materials or raising money.

And don't forget; the joy of building is best in its relation to the dwellers and their friends. We must fight so that industrialisation doesn't drown this joy along with the arts and crafts of ornate timber work – this real, healthy, irreplaceable, immense joy. Almost a woodpecker, if not a thylacine or dinosaur – in the West.

The MEANING & POTENTIALS of DESIGN

MAKING. BUILDING. DESIGNING

Design is not God – the devoted student gasps, hand on heart. Nor is it *Magazine* – the devoted Maggie gasps, hand on heart. Life in a cave has amenity and influence, even though the only design may be the choice to go there. Life in a *houselocust* is similar. *Gravitymark, handmark. Toolmark, machinemark. Mindmark, housemark.* These, in house manufacture, say as much if not more than design. Not alone but a known champion and so a good token, Australian architect Glenn Murcutt will very likely agree. But where does he go with culture sculpture. Ecological response is urgent, sure. Delightful functional response is fantastic but there's certainly *room* for arty socio-cultural creativity – especially in the depths of the existing sprawls. I guess he goes there too – in his own way, and when the few opportunities, made very rare by the *megamonster*, may arise. Ayn Rand in 'The Fountainhead' tells of *megamonster* sociology and architecture.

New residential design is applicable to more than a bare untouched site or totally blank slate. There is always existing cadastre stamped by our corporate multigenerational architecture through townplanning, which is not commonly accepted as architecture but of course it is. We, 'modern' architect or Zulu villager, must roll passionately with the punches thrusting from the inherited unfolding urban realm produced by our own kind. There are always existing conditions and vernaculars; which we adapt, renovate, modify, extend, alter or demolish; whether it's virgin landscape conducive to houses or camp, an existing building; or any landscape, be it the landscape of mental mediocrity or a conventional old apartment. Rather than making new dwelling facility, we are always making additions, renovating or remodelling. Renovate convention, remodel the landscape, renovate mediocrity. *Make house additions to the land.* Renovate the industry – feed some discipline to the *megamonster*. Hurry.

Ecology, culture, economy etcetera come together as we build.

Vernacular building, and taste, is based on native locale; usually the product of generations of 'inexpert' lay development. It has a beauty like that of local people and language. The *accumulated* built bits that make up the *housing-contraption* fall innocently into a delightful visual unity, under the integrity of simplicity in taste and technique. The formulae for vernacular design and construction aren't known - how do words come, or a smile? Why use this type of door? Simple - tradition modified by today's new resource or people. A vernacular is an agreeable local orthodoxy rooted in urbane tradition. It can be fascist, but it usually relates to humility and idyllic community. It has more to do with the building of culture than the building of conventions. Familiarity and tradition underpin convention; as much as does the comfort of using the known, the tried and tested.

In its vernacular simplicity, design is the intuitive action of bringing in appropriate materials and putting them to suit requirement and whim; whatever works works and the way it looks is the way it looks; a basis on which we can be creative in design, to make it work better and modify the looks to suit the required amenity.

For the grass hut builder, the words 'design' and 'build' are probably a single word – maybe *'thinkbuildthinkbuild'* or *'buildthinkbuild'*. There'd be a significant amount of recall in the think. In large societies though, the hard-hatted builder will lampoon the truffle-fronted comic-making architect who in turn will bemoan this brawn based pragmatician. Design is the outstretched dream fusing with the rigorous facts, the oft obstinate cultural orthodox, the industrial melee, the time of day. Both the most aesthetic and the most practical position of the toothbrush holder are issues. And the myriads of even minor hang-ups the builder may face.

Convention is handy where it can be relied on to make easy assessment of existing structure for modifications. It is handy as a common language, skills and industry for efficiency and economy. It is handy for easy design. But it is linked to regulatory standards and the limits of bureaucratic change. And to lazy minds. Within the decrees of nature and society, our housing is what we make it, and have already made it. We often are quite happy with our lot until we see something we like better. Any brief lesson on design may improve your own innate knack for it. You. The Architect. Vernacular. Classical. Abstract. Aesthetic. Orthodoxy. Any old way will do; no design. Plans and specifications - a pencil helps, but it is *room*, utility and address we seek, not pretty drawings. Drawings are simply a means. And so is a house.

Design, for housing, involves all of the foregoing and the upcoming chapter rooms in this book. Design applies to renovation, conversion, addition, toothbrush holder, town planning and ecology. It should be performed with an enriching spirit; receptively, boldly and delicately. No less for rudimentary practicality than for complex cultural specialty. And never never perfect or all-considered.

Seldom today is design the work of only one person. Planning and health authorities, public taste and industrial pre-conditions prevail. But in addition every dweller relates directly to his *dwelling-arrangement* through personal design. The choice to walk into a particular dwelling and make the bed emanates from design thought, as does the engagement of an architect.

One's egocentric delusions and off-key hopes and creativity are sobered by pragmatics and the momentum of the Western orthodoxy. Idiosyncrasy may appear off-key in the face of a cultural orthodoxy. Rooster feathers don't grow in duck flesh. A society tests our idiosyncrasies. Sometimes they may be a new style emerging. A new style. Or even a single item; sprouting through the hard clays of habit, convention, tradition and momentum. The sprout must be well watered with determination, effort and possibly money. The clay may be laden with public taste. If so, it may take stealth through the planning laws to achieve any particular appearance or scale outcome; another test of individual with society.

Design must not be fettered by habit, a shadow of convention, but very very often it is wise to roll with it; accepting habit and routine as part of the designer's palette. It might be routine to put a little *box* on a hillside allotment but one's own peculiar circumstance may provide one with opportunity and motivation to fight for something startling. It could be anything. A friend of Low Carl obtained a redundant river ferry, a beautiful old thing, very cheap, to place artistically on his site. Some props, plumbing, an entrance stair and strategic planting; eventually the local council is proud of it and a neighbour does something similar with a group of railway carriages.

`°□°◀■Δ°◻

Beauty and the *bits*. Like *boxes* to suburb and city, so industrial *bits* to the *dwelling-contraption*. Much of a house may be prefabricated components – *bits*. Window frames, cupboards, shower units, air conditioning, roof trusses. Prefabrication can form just part of a house. For example an earthy-looking stone house may have a fibreglass plumbing-cum-ablutions core, a bath-room, toilet, laundry, sauna, and kitchen segment, all in one delivered by truck. The plethora of *bits* sets a challenge to sensual and economic harmony. Is it cheaper – or, better still, more *ecopical* - to use a steel or wooden beam? The satellite dish looks misfitted. The treasured old dining table clashes with the retro flecked laminate benches.

Like the submerged part of the iceberg the orthodox and the prefabricated can be a part of, or a base under, some sensitive architecture, leaving a beautiful vision for the eye – or a beautiful flow for movement. So, the orthodoxy becomes just another valuable basis for building, like the properties of available materials.

Houses should outlast their original inhabitants. So there is a strong case for universality, for rudimentary pragmatics, in design character. Even for resale. Make use of orthodoxy, conservatism, vernacular, conventions, universality and societal taste; but do not deny the id, the roosters plumage, one's unique requirement and individuality. Be cautious as to resale and cost, should you go too far in eccentricity. Where is the id in the Gallopilong family camp? It's in the design on, and ownership of, the spear. Where is the id in the Murcutt-style living place, which is a rudimentary *delight* as a pragmatic architectonic response to the land, sitting alone in the bush? It may be in the construction, if it's owner built. Or in the colours or the obstinate Art Deco stair rail installed in a later renovation. A cute spouse is all you need really. But that would sprout id all over – and maybe that's okay.

Sometimes it is clever to imitate, to build convention. No need to reinvent. Use the discarded camp just as it is. Best design is not necessarily obvious. It may look just like that which is next door. There is a lot of good logic to the *box* neighbourhoods – Dazzler might not agree. The point here is to carry on one's palette all the conventions, colloquialisms, regulations, trendy styles and routine.

But load the palette also with the colours of White Cloud, Dali, the swallow, maybe Zen wisdom. And include one's master programmer; that is - informed idiosyncrasy and cosmic economy. Use nothing of some if you like. A broad sense of design will indicate even the country in which one should live; or the lands which one should nomadically inhabit. Lifetime masterplan, omniscience, established houses, the beautiful design of an architect may not suit as well as an old shack at the base of a cliff by the sea. Unless, some say, the Lord built the house they who built it labour in vain. Remember? *The domestic design solutions that we need now, even more urgently than home quality, are those for town planning and ecology.* Remember the *Ecosculpture* ... deeply - thinking *ecopically.*

Ecopicality in design is far more important than powder-puff vogue appearances or even avant garde visual-cum-spatial delights. Weigh up the ecological issues alongside the sociological and the personal. Give whatever consideration is available to these aspects. It's only where we strive for the cutting edge, the absolute best possible up-to-the-minute design, that it may become complex or require new science and product innovation. The assessment as to whether the design is up to a reasonable standard can really be answered only by professional calculation. And, even then, neither readily nor indisputably supremely accurately.

The quality of design could be measured, maybe crudely, by giving an ideal value weighting to each design aspect. Then, after the compromise wash-up resulting in the finished design, estimate a score for each aspect based on the weighting. The sum of the ideal weighting on all the aspects is the goal - a reasonably perfect house and site for the dweller. We say perfect, rather than optimum – lest we settle for the best possible in poor circumstances. The score will usually be a fraction of the ideal weighting. Some aspects may be down, some up. Using maths we can come up with a total score. Call it the *Design Quality Quotient.* For example an aspect of design consideration is the *'impact on immediate local endemic flora and fauna'* factor. Best score would be, weighted at 10 say, for no undesirable impact at all. An improvement, perhaps by removal of weeds and soil contamination, may bring a score of, say, 12 out of 10. Another factor is the *'satisfaction of dweller with external aesthetic appeal'* factor. This is less important; weight it at 6. The prospective dweller isn't all that happy but has conceded; the score may be 2 out of 6. Now, there are quite a few factors to consider, maybe 10, or even 500 if we go into deep detail. We can simplify by taking the more general, not so deep, view. For example, the *'endemic ecology'* factor can be considered in the same basket as the *'global ecology'* factor etc; giving a more general *quality quotient.*

A version of this *quality quotient* idea was, originally I'd say, conveyed in the 1970's for non-residential building by a firm called CRS architects in a book (ebook too), *'Architecture by team'*, WWCaudill. A very successful and expansive firm, they found it a handy means of gauging their design success and of improving their designs – achieving design excellence. As yet I haven't followed through with a complete itemisation and weighting of design factors specifically for residential design. Never-the-less the Reader hopefully can see that such a *Quotient* is there to be found, regardless and notwithstanding counter philosophy. There exist a score cards in some countries for industry assessment of energy efficiency in house design.

Canvas framed up by the engineer. Palette loaded by Dazzler. But which brush do we use first? What colour? Priorities, beginning. Design is quite an animal. It happens all at once. And also at the end of some ordered process. Values and attitudes impact priorities; taste, orthodoxy, affluent excess, unnecessary amateur effort (where an expert may have been best), great or even moderate debt, complacency, apathy, zeal. The universal biological necessities aside, people hold different priorities in their housing needs. Monetary allocation may, for one, go to an exuberant front door, and for another, instead, to subsidise a tennis court. And though making the cost of the house extra, another may omit the lounge dado, make his own wooden door latches for cheap, reduce his lounge space, saving enough expense to justify a central courtyard. Or an electric wheelchair for an old spinster. To another, image is everything; spend a fortune on the façade or a high-society allotment.

Floor *layout* may be secondary to many things, style, shape of allotment, neighbours view; but all things in mind it is usually the floor plan that is first developed by sketch. There are the many things ahead of it in mind though, and in the colloquial way – a vague finished concept perhaps.

Design, like the *Quality Quotient*, can be scant or thorough. Recognition and use of valuable unintended outcomes is often a feature of design; originally the attic was only a practical structural necessity, not intended as storage space. Some left-over space by the stair now works well for a fish-pond and fountain, saving a lot on material costs for *nature's nurtures*. "Oh, this is what it is like when built, I thought it would be different; I see a spot by the warmth of a sun-soaked stone wall around the corner where we can set the patio table." Some design is incidental or accidental. Thorough design considers the ephemerality of people's inclinations, whilst weighing and juggling all. The time factor in design is complex. Is there time to persevere? The perseverance just 'may', as distinct from 'will', save construction time and also improve the job.

"If only I had been more considerate in planning," thinks a thwarted dweller. At design time you can save money, hone special details or change your mind completely. It's not too late during building either. Maybe it's worth knocking down a newly built wall, having realised a more appropriate plan. A built design may have been warped, pushed, moulded, compromised, and recompromised by its architect, client, site, climate, the laws it is built under, the amount of money available and by the customs traditions and history of its location.

The other side of compromise, needs and problems is inspiration and opportunity. Design is not purely problem based. *Limitations* may be opportunities, or inspirations; "They have always been the best friend of architecture," said a great architect. He was Wright – to be frank.

Dream the requirement then invent the technology. Make what you can of existing technology. Build the space, the *room*, not the structure. The place, not the fabric. The comfort, not the chair. The beauty not the eye; somewhere the *blueberry pie*. The facility and amenity. Not the bench and the paint. Please the senses or at least do not offend them. Like a baby walking, or me learning to type, you should eventually find your way, for your own unique home enhancement. And you may be already flinging full *Housefandango*, or satisfactory *Housefandango*. If not ... walk baby walk. Yes there is a proper way. It is the way that suits the dweller in action. There are a vast number of proposed *domestic-contraptions* for which professional design, standards, regulation and copying are somewhat impractical.

But what of the Classical discipline. Indeed professional territory – proportion, entasis, even the Modular; but these are only incidental. Two and half millennia ago, Sinophile, Loatse correctly noted that the essence of building consists not in walls, floor and roof but in the space within; the space to be lived in, the *room* provided. Duh! The humble dweller is the measure. Any designed amenity to create *room* of some specific quality may as an option be Classical. Keep Classical in perspective. The commendable Classical style was substantially developed by just two architects more than a century ago. Squared and true geometry, domes, clean lines, palatial dwellings designed to stress the importance of the dweller and the individual generally, to assist and not to intrude; a lovely vision of universal human dignity - not only local. And built forever. But it does have to suit one's taste. It can be sullied too. There came heavy Classical representations, where the buildings intruded, fancy stonework and facades stood like doors slammed in front of the dwellers and visitors. It is quite reasonable to utilise Classical proportions to make *room* for disciplined thought, and some balanced focussed mental comfort, but one may think best in a *room* of mixed idioms. It is not the building we want, but the service it gives. But the building as a by-product must respect our majestic world. And we must note that the disciplined geometry of Classical design must somewhere meet the aesthetic of 'wilderness', of the indigenous and of the builder limited in resource. That also applies to the limitations of industrial modules and proportions. "The Classical's makin' too much 'f a big deal 'f interior ... shoulderin' away the country. It's okay 'f it's a bit gentler at the edges where it meets the land. It kinda makes me think it's for dwellers who feel insecure, ...,"sings a dark figure, as he chisels a series of wide circles - across two and three treads and risers at a time - over the white marble entrance steps, always agrin. But still the earth happily supports the sound and balanced structure. And the turtle from inside, a fob watch in his vest, skips gaily over the steps into its firmly fenced Classical garden which is devoid of uncultured plant and not a creaturely neighbour near.

One needs only to look about to see the *incredible diversity of design in housing.* Rules are flouted here and there, sometimes ad hoc becomes beautiful, styles mix and much can be observed.

Some people value the building fabric, the *nacre*, firstly or solely – taking it as the source of the *room* – it generates *room* by its action and form, as noted at **A DISSECTION OF THE OBJECT**. On another hand, some dwellers value the space or *room* firstly or solely – taking the *nacre* as merely necessary hardware. In a third stance the *nacre* and form of a house can be used in design to interface the two attitudes – *room* blended with fabric. The *nacre* then, rather than being sole focus, is a sort of additional company, a helper, to the dweller in her room and her neighbourhood. Perhaps I fail to communicate here, never mind. The house belongs in kinship to the terrain and cosmic space on one hand, and to its people on the other. Rich earthy timbers, clean sheets of plaster and people in motion – some reaching for a beer to clear a plaster dusted throat.

Taste in our dwelling designs - conceptions of beauty and
   expression, relative to society. We need beauty. It has meaning.
   It is legible as a social document - interpretable. Taste is beauty
   that is interpretable by community and dweller together. Some
   beauty is purely personal or family-based; professional architects
   may not manage this. Taste relates to locale and epoch; to
   accepted sets of aesthetic values - vogue. As part of objective
   design, taste strives for our timeless universal values. Taste is
   tested in our response to décor, surface, essence and substance.
   The prominence of taste in societal values gives a clear notion of
   practicality to this aesthetic, this emotional relationship between
   people and the world. Avant garde, vogue, timeless, ordinary,
   different. "Monte I love you for saying that!!" I hate to say it Little
   White Cloud, but, it's just professional knowledge. I rather liked
   it too. Unfortunately, taste is not as securely urbane as it was.
   Machinery, electricity and money have been allowed to devalue
   taste as a societal binding force, where it is provided by both
   architecture and fashion. People stuck between the *megamonster*
   and the divine logician. Science and invention often dominate
   creative faculty.
Creativity should be first and science the servant. Socio-cultural matters should lead engineering. Conform the engineering to the social. "Design in these conditions is too difficult, building too easy," said our world's greatest architect. "That'd be right," smirks Cheekyfella. Slowly, through the future shock, we find new aesthetic

integrities, solutions to suit the storm of industrial forms, materials and processes and the greedy pace. Design evolves with society and technology but sometimes evolve is too good a word - warps, leaving warts.

We have talked about taste in another context and we have seen 'order' through the dwelling-organism's idiosyncratic glass onion.
Order is in part integrated with taste. The Modular, the golden rectangle, Classical proportions, mixed idioms. Order has a facet in physical function as well. Order in the *dwelling-contraption*, including its site and locale, is physical and spiritual coherence. All items are made a harmonious whole. Established order in nature and society must be met or modified. Cyclones are an order. Tidiness is an order. Order is a utility too. It makes things easier.

A place for everything and every thing in its place; aesthetic and functional order. The relationship of colours, textures, materials, and surface treatments; the relationship between buildings, blocks, streets, and landscape; rainbow harmonies, the Modular, beauty, *room* to flow, physical and sensual music, music, music, music. Order, rock and roll, brick on mortar, Classical, jazz, taste, music. Builder's program, order, commercial radio or thumbs-up with the weather. The nature of the entire constructive conductor's performance. Out of that nature comes whatever character one can give to the building as a creative artist; or as a carpenter. Some chaos too, if you like ginger in your chocolate cake.

Ah yes! It can be very complex ensuring that you have considered everything, that they will fit well together, to come up to the standard of your superb house. A domestic considerations list and the formula for the whole constructive performance is a few pages ahead for you to adapt to your situation. The right specialist or experienced assistance will possibly improve your hopes. Without professional design a home-made house may cause problems and look ugly, yet usually it will reflect the better qualities of its locale, designer or builder; its inadequacies healed by quaintness, local affection, stories of construction, identity. Proper design comes through the door of refinement and discipline stemming from the vernacular truth – vernacular, local *growingbeing* to your very own site. The use of industrial resources and global information to construct in an intimate locale can ideally lead to a professional, less innocent, vernacular, but the pace of industry and global anonymity tend to quash this.

On site. Need being the mother of invention; resourcefulness produces qualities and features of construction that are not existent in less intimate academic design. For example, a strong, naturally curved piece of wood found on site would not be included, with its cost and aesthetic advantages, perhaps as a visible internal roof brace, if the construction had been planned and organised from an alien city centred design office; instead a factory stock item would be specified. If we broaden the 'on site' concept and forage far and wide for our materials taking in say an old bay window from an auction, a beautiful piece of sandstone found in an old quarry near a favourite camp, a bargain buy of seconds in milled timber and perhaps a tremendously expensive stained glass roof light, the design approach becomes more specific, intimate, unique and more distant from the usual 'design then buy' manner. A ferry boat or a *box*. A local 'classic' or an avant garde architectonic masterpiece.

The *vernacular* builder proceeds and rounds the rough edges, makes the odd change as he abides. In vernacularism is an ultimate simple beauty that is polished by colloquial inheritance. Unlike its cousins, *orthodoxy* and *convention*, it takes optimum advantage of spontaneous development and generally proceeds with innocent integrity. A Classical designer may attempt to rubbish vernacular architecture, or at least to neutralise it – a Minimalist I know most certainly will. Vernacular is never ugly - as such people are beautiful. Is Classical in fact a refined vernacular? No, it denies the ephemeral compromises that will suit the tastes and circumstance of the immediate locale. But also, yes; when it's not stuffy, or when it is in its native land and developing with the day.

Now hear this. *Experienced imagination can three-way marry the Classical, the local vernacular and the avant-garde trend.* And commercial imaginations can evolve all sorts of pastiche and pretentious surface imagery to mask a cheap *nurtureless box* - the *Classic* and even more *pale*.

We can't make a silk purse from a sow's ear. We must tailor design to suit the inevitable builder, the resources, colloquial context and much more. And above all, to suit detailed environmental integrity.

All that, for you, is a little toward profound understanding of simple truth. Invention, creativity and resourcefulness can produce the novel, the ingenious, the cultural harmony, the natural harmony, a good contribution to the locality, a house that is 'different' to tell a story like a snowflake, a solid cavernous house, or a light hearted occasion. We come up with all sorts of ideas, stemming from simplicity and honesty; including dwelling places in megastructures.

So take a site, maybe one with a building on it, and begin your new domicile, being autonomous in selection and placement of material and skill resources - a visit to the Building Surveyor at the Town Hall. Three tins of purple paint, the local tradesman in overalls and nail pouch, and you be the architect if you want. You are the main one who must live with what you do, so you can do it, if you can keep the Town Hall happy. When all is said and done the Town Hall is helping your interests and your neighbours.

Town Hall won't be fussed if you want to match your spoons and all other paraphernalia with your construction detail and the overall house form. Design has gone this far. Pugin is one architect who did this on a wealthy scale. Frank Wright, in his time of its own style of gender balance, I have read, made his wife's clothes in coordination with his house. If you don't like the house in which you must live, push it into the dusty corners and dwell in your creative consciousness. *Mother of pearl* renovation will eventuate.

It can be done. But do you want to? And does it suit you in your circumstance?

WHO CAN DESIGN?

MAKING, BUILDING, DESIGNING

Yes, you can do it, but not necessarily alone. *You are the designed foundation of any consultant's designs for you anyway.* Forgive me if you happen to be an architect or a Patagonian builder, as you know you can design. And townplanners, urban architects and urban planners continue to wake from the colonial two dimensional landscape, onward through the fine substance of local landform to ensure that lounge meets lounge. Lounge to lounge. Like people at a party, a conference, as quiet neighbours and as energetic company.

A New York architect going to tiny Patagonia, in far south South America, will experience his lack of expertise in the Patagonian vernacular for dwelling design. He would have to acquire local knowledge and reflexes in order to build to economy a house to suit the simple local culture and resource. The architect, in seeking, would work with a local builder and that would leave the New Yorker initially redundant. The builder would do it all, but after some extended observation the architect may begin evolving the vernacular. Locale means a lot in dwelling design; though, economy aside, globalisation allows culturally sublime dwellings by foreign enterprise in local colloquial settings - the design must be sharply disciplined though. If the architect was in fact a layman, she would do well to ride with the local style, taste, regulation, orthodox, norm; making her idiosyncratic affectations only where she felt confident or where she could see past the builder's shaking head.

This is the way people will usually design; base it on that which they have seen. That which is kosher. The layperson is limited when it comes to extending or over-riding the familiar, the orthodox or the trend. And Bobby knows only too well that there are too many *pale* houses trending in our larger societies. He notes though that the *Pale* principle works well in small communities but that many could do with alien aid.

Everybody can design, within their limitations. Who can design adequately? The person who seeks the best available skill and knowledge and applies it. The *Pale* failings are most often the failings of regulation and commerce. These will taint the designer and the designed, like impurity in water and weeds in endemic ecology. To purify against the taint is often to add expense; good investment, smaller house or something. However, render to Caesar that which is Caesar's. Though make positive developments to Caesar's rule - to regulation and the industrial culture *megamonster*. He is a big big boy in design. Vote with your dwelling.

Design is preparation for an intervention in a common world. There is most often more than one person to directly use the house. There is cultural gusto, suggestion and inspiration. Therefore most often there is more than one person involved in design. It is a rule of thumb that one person coordinate all the inputs as part of an over-riding creative-cum-engineering process. The ruling figure is the dweller but the dweller's reign may be relatively miniscule. Town planners. The children. Architect, draftsman's apprentice, designer, builder. Housing Department. Prefabricator. Many belong to the *Pale* family or are slave to some *dodos*. Many are awake, adept and courageous. The first government houses in Australia were wattle and daubed mud. The government is people. They all design.

Often small houses are designed by builders, built without knowledge of architectural philosophies and at times with keen implementation of superficial architectural fashions. They may mimic expensive design in cheaper materials.

By adopting convention for its own sake, like others, you get the benefit of years of learning in that particular style, you will have little trouble with builders, councils, and material, and the price will be very predictable. However you will fall short of the optimum, you will in most cases add to the unsustainable *pale* sprawl and monotony; and the house's dwellers will benefit, and be fulfilled and stimulated to a lesser degree. The lay reader may see the author's bias here.

There are many books on design, covering many different angles. Without natural talent or experience, one may gain only a working knowledge that will give a better liaison with some selected designer, or that will give at least some improvement on one's own previous design potential. People have produced manuals on the specifics of most circumstances that any doer of housing will face.

ARCHITECTS CAN

MAKING, BUILDING, DESIGNING

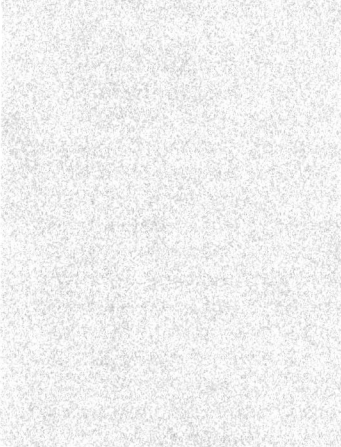

Naturally, an architect is very likely to open doors in design and implementation for residential developments, which enhance the potentials beyond your own horizons and existing *three-planed-corners*. And conversely it is true that your presence in the designs may in ways enhance it beyond the architect's horizons, in that you are the dweller with lively idiosyncrasies and nous; with personal attentions and attitudes. A wise architect may simply confirm that you should role with your local vernacular. No architect is an island. Tune up with your architect who may or may not tend to prefer that you take some of his own design attentions; those attentions cultured by his professional growth, and/or those which should remain out of your picture. Your personal attention may rightly be absorbed by a weatherboard cottage full of bookshelves and other *accumulation*; whilst an architectonically avant-garde, slick, well proportioned, steel and glass, cantilevered delight won't hold you but for a moment of obtuse admiration. In this instance your personal attention is held by your *accumulation*, its accessibility and companionships. The architecture that contains it for you, rather than be a focal addition to your *accumulation*, may be incidental, over-bearing or even distraction – "Architect, please make it quiet and let my *accumulation* dance fantastic." "Certainly madam. At your service madam" ... thinking, "There'll be no award in this one." In fact there was.

Architects seek the motivation behind the client's design requests and reinvent the client's visions. People may love to think something is their *own* design. If their own design is built, they may never realise that an architect's design may have been better, whilst just as much their own. The same goes for architects who fancy their own designs. Their client's or colleague's designs may be best and in acknowledging this they will own them too. It's a tough work-a-day call at times. In today's cultural climate of commercial packaging psychologies, it may behove an architect to provide highest priority to a certain 'look' or 'appeal' ... and in fact the client may demand that the packaging take a higher profile in the budget than the goods. The goods being *ecopicalities* and practical amenities. The 'look' may make a popular trend whilst leaving behind the function that formed it - hollow, pastiche, sweet painted lady, perhaps an ultra Classic.

The devoted architect today - for less than 1% of the world - more than ever, must sharpen his pencil like a spear, to defend the ethics of the day, whilst cajoling the enemy for bread and butter. The *megamonster* battles are often lost. Yes it can be a battle to break a bit of convention, and architects may prefer to treat every project as a new innovation, up-to-date with technology, current affairs, current conventions, current fantasies and the avant-garde. In the late 1930's as conventions were reviewed; an Austrophile student-architects' ball made comment in song on community attitude to architectural newness and change of the time, as enshrined by their now eminent Robin Boyd: - "There's a bright vermilion door, with chromium plated handle. We create a little scandal, when we build a modern home. There's a cantilever sun porch, with green and yellow awning, where we sun-bathe in the morning, when we build a modern home. There's some concrete and some steel-work, but most of all the walls are glass. But the painter does the real work and the rest keep off the grass. We'll have rubber on the floor and sound absorbent ceiling. There's contemporary, feeling in our very modern home." The architects' torch lighting the frontier and the change-over to Modernism. Bear in mind though that Architecture as a university discipline has developed only over the last couple of centuries – a bit like the saxophone.

Behind the frontier, it's business as usual. If it's a *dwelling-contraption* you want, an architect can do it. A client makes up his own mind as to whether the architect can deliver in accord with his own cultural circumstance. It's part of his *fandango*. Architects are susceptible to a version of dodo cultural cliché and frozen thinking, as are their clients. The pressures of the tunnel-vision effect, of years in some niche in the 'noblest profession', may make it difficult for the architect to appreciate good spontaneous or 'untrained' design. They may be afflicted with the goading of what is deemed unprofessional by their colleagues whilst endeavouring to break this orthodoxy for the clients economic or design benefit. The word 'professional' is frequently heard highbrow. It means, simply; expert, thorough, fully informed, efficient and complete; and of course kosher. It doesn't mean indisputably perfect; but an architect who acknowledges his fallibility and responds to any challenge is pretty good – even in the face of one who may be better, albeit only better in the area of the challenge. The notion of a *quality quotient* style of assessment of architects, as distinct from assessment of buildings, is interesting but impractical, so we go with our intuition and hope. Circumstances surrounding the client and the client's requirements may necessitate an unorthodox approach within the professional process. The approach may be similar to that used by the farmer who successfully uses rocks rather than nails to hold down his barn roof.

Architects manage design and administer construction contracts for built *contraptions* other than houses as well and are involved in public urban matters also. Generally they must earn a living. They are not necessarily a luxury. Their design may save you money. Yet also, they may at times see the necessity to persuade you to spend more. Within design cost-effectiveness, assessing the real cost of the architect may become difficult. A lower budget means possible savings become less and the architect may find more work than his normal fee justifies. Often time-consuming complexities in house design are not covered by money available from the client, especially when compared to income from other larger or simpler projects. That's why Bobby Dazzler's grandfather calls the profession 'noble'.

Less than five percent of houses in the West are designed by architects. Building firms are responsible for a greater fraction of houses today, and along with builder-design, owner-design, direct copy, 'architectural' designers, 'building' designers and draftspersons they make up the remaining ninety-five percent. The difference between an architect and a building designer? An architect has an objective wholistic basis to design and the building designer will be basing his design on merely trends and conventions set by the architects and regulations; or some lesser avenue. If he does more, he's becoming an architect. There are special practitioners who may in circumstance and talent outshine the best architects whilst having no right to call themselves an architect. Frank Wright, in fact a revolutionary in architectural design and once a shining light for many aspiring architects, was 'qualified' only as a civil engineer. The reverse applies too. Some achieve architect status and for various reasons and, possibly only in various circumstances, fall short.

The architecture curriculum is very broad; sociology, engineering, aesthetics, building technique, contract management, materials, industry, salesmanship, drawing and on it goes, and so some are more expert in some areas than others. As we have noted architects are not a divine masterplanner and they may resist doing things the ordinary, conventional, way. Often, tendering and contract administration is not requested by the client as part of the architect's services; though to request it may be valuable in safeguarding design through construction. A draftsperson is sometimes a better option, in that he may work totally within convention. The architect can coordinate the draftsperson. In such a case it may or may not be worth avoiding the architect.

Architects are not all the same. Philosophies vary. Maybe the broad demands of the job suggest to some of them that we ought to be arrogant. Some treat clients like children. Others encourage them to take a strong hand in design. Both attitudes can produce satisfying buildings. On the other hand, the dweller should make her best choice. The architects who have spent their entire expertise accrual in multi-storey buildings and may flounder - not founder - if moved straight onto the business end of house design.

An educated eye may observe, in their products, that a swag of local architects have attended the same school. Their work is cultured by

the school and locale. This is potentially a birth of some vernacular.
It may be stuffy. It may be refreshing. Like artists they will all
exercise their own natural ability and talent, giving various legitimate
accents and character to their work. Some may be less experienced
but not necessarily less competent for a particular job. But they may
at any time need to be advised as to some knowledge held only by
their client. The architect's client is a microcosm, like his local
community, whether in the Bronx, Patagonia or outside Sydney.

Trends begun by architects are adapted, mistreated, misunderstood,
developed, degenerated and copied. The influence of the architect
upon the seas of housing is but mild against the influence of the
vernaculars and the *locusts* of the modern consumer orthodox.

Is the architect;

ζ An **EPHEMERAL NOMAD**, so as to be *nature's earthy
nurtures* landscape-designing the interior, and

Ω A **SOCIAL BEING**, so as to be tweaking the synthetic
address and the regulations, and

$\daleth$ A **PERENNIAL SETTLER,** so as to facilitate hallowed
halling and fruitful continuum?

Are civilised and social coordinations just like the winds, sands and gravities
that shape, weather and shake?

COMMUNAL
COORDINATIONS
& MARKET

MAKING, BUILDING, DESIGNING

Tradition, adaptation, mediocrity,
industrial limitations, marketability,
mortgage conditions, regulation, by-
law.

These are all societal contribution to
and societal impact upon design.

Within permitted discretions it is mandatory in design to accept
regulation and established planning. Along with regulation and
planning, it is optional to accept economic and cultural conventions
or trends. Building regulations limit what can be done in design and
sometimes enforce a house that is more than needed – if not a mere
dog *box* relative to healthy lifestyle. But the accurate supervision of
hygienics, land-use and security by authoritative process is
invaluable. "Or should we say, *would be invaluable* if it set to
reducing excess such as the traps of our huger interiors!" comes a
passionate *nomurbic* voice. ***"What use is stringent energy
regulation, without the curbing of gargantuan playdough and
landscape consumers embodying huge energy per dweller***

capita in huge houselocusts." The applause of the *stratospheric strollers* rings long and loud for Low Carl's call.

The only thing plainly tangible about regulation is printed text. The meanings have unclear roots. As well, I have read some terrible English in formal planning documents. Are the public authorities and their lobbyists *doing* it correctly? Too much. Not enough. Red tape. Bias. Yes and no and also the *megamonster* kicks in and Bobby's task in Arcosanti is clear.

Environmental regulations are becoming more stringent, with respect to energy, building materials and planning. Change is happening too quickly. Politics is often expedient. Bureaucrats can pretend. Community opinion is usually diverse and pointed to selfish ulteriors. Democracy can mean apparent rule by a mistaken majority. With passion, the underground strives to save environments and species' and people's habitational amenity - its integrity proven by lack of pay. A large proportion of the underground too is mistaken in essence. Whence comes the blast from the sun, to rinse clean everyone. Or are we all bound for last earthly days looking for the one fish in simmering soupy oceans. Low Carl straightens his torn collar and heads for the city library internet. His email is to you. "If you haven't already done so, put it down now. This is serious. We can't leave it all to Bobby! Don't invest in a 'hot brick' dwelling. Put it down. Convert it. Change the orthodox. One vote and you are not guilty." *We are all participants in public authority and cultural development.* Let us help Global *Pale* to detox his bus and *debox* his residential property. Ingenuity may find the antigravity hover-car. The harmonious dwelling circumstance. The pure *playdough.* The dream bubble is burst by some pins from both regulation and orthodoxy. It is not easily answered. Call for the blast from the sun.

It is not all bad. In regulation the sinking ship has order on board also. As in the following analogy, there has been a vernacular in some locale somewhere that incorporates an
> adversarial aspect to house development. An annoying neighbour is narked by a new wall in front of his view. So, to regain, he builds out past the wall. The wall is extended. It happens again. He vanishes. His fleshless bones are found a year later in the neighbour's drinking-water tank. He suicided, so as to have the last nark. *Truly – I think.*

Sometimes people are so stupid they need to be handcuffed and led by law. We cannot easily complain about government design dictate and demand affectations on our habitation amenity.

Planning and habitability standards. Who wants to make them? Certainly not people who live in paradise, or artists. Or people who spend forty hours a week in an office plus additional in transit and at lunch; brave souls maybe needing a better working environment - but that is another story again. Are bureaucracy and office life part of the problem – probably it is, along with political folly?

The following is symptomatic of Low's dilemma. Social consequences
from design. These examples are decades old but they make a point
that relates to contemporary circumstance.   The Brazilian
Government built apartment
    blocks for the inhabitants of a shantytown and then destroyed
    their shacks. Later the tenants moved back and rebuilt. And;
    a once modern residential facility was built by the Hungophiles,
    Hungarians, for families from a dilapidated city precinct. Many
    sold their new apartments to middle class families from the old
    district and moved back to their old but familiar slum. And
    another; in Jamaica it is said that riots were partly prompted
    by resistance to public housing that was to replace their
familiar slums. The causes of these reactions are complex and
demand investigation. The situation though is partly encouraged by
technically adequate public housing that is socially inadequate. The
people have not been involved in their own dwelling decisions - the
short arm of bureaucracy. In Europe, the large Pruitte-Igoe building
was demolished at high cost whilst still serviceable after twenty years
costly vandalism and dilapidation, caused by the unhappy
occupants. Designed for anonymous users and in a purist language,
it was at variance with the sensibilities of the inhabitants. Where
housing is a public service, there is a particular meaning in the
fabric. It's a public service in communist countries. In others it is a
consumer good. In others it is vernacular and in some cases it is art.
Each case produces different social reactions.

Another instance. Low engaged a switched-on architect to design his
mother a granny flat, a dwelling unit auxiliary to his brother's house.
The design was inspiring by his mother's requirements and compact
and there was plenty of open space on the property. The regulations
required it to be ten square metres smaller. So, away goes a
significant quantity of happiness. Frustrating. "Forced into a dog
box," winces Low. But; are civilised and social coordinations just like
the winds, sands and gravities that shape, weather and shake?

The so-called 'Australian Dream', home ownership for all, is
frustrated by regulation. Certainly it is modified by regulation.

Building '*standards*' and methods of regulation restrict our potential
to make new building for new social functions. Even old ideas of
dwelling amenity are encouraged by a bureaucratic mediocrity. The
limitation is not as major as it was a decade or less ago. In recent
years most systems face further review. *Standards* seek to prevent
the bad. As well, they limit innovation, economy and naive building.
They create socio-economic barriers and distort household budgets.
Incentives rather than more restrictive standards may be the means
of achieving better, cheaper and fairer housing. Rigid controls on
design and siting of houses constrict the creativity of our convention-
breaking, residential planners and architects. *Standards* give us
inefficiency, social segregation, restricted happiness and mundane

uniformity. In urban planning we are faced with the paradox that higher *standards* often produce poorer cities. Minimum *requirements* presented by many local councils are beyond those that would be chosen freely in the market place. Habitability *standards* supposedly guarantee pleasant and safe interiors. Such *standards* affect no-one but the occupants and should be regarded as matters for the dwellers rather than society. However, mediocrity is a secure politic.

A house that contravenes many regulations may still provide excellent housing amenity and locale subtlety. Low Carl's friend's old ferry boat and Cheeky's camp are examples.

Australian cities have developed at relatively low densities. There is nothing intrinsically wrong with low-density living and the evidence is that most people variously choose it, or would like to. The potential range of low-density dwelling types is broad - from single dwellings on large lots, through small lots with more public-open-space, through town houses and cluster housing, to flats set in private parks. The range can create stimulating variety in architecture and people. Regulation, it seems for the sake of its own simplicity, may for example, rule out of certain areas all but probably the first in the range. Military-like uniformity occurs - soldiers in rank more than hippies in San Francisco. It is the nature of the paperwork. Street-front setbacks demands are not flexible so that the occasional street edge house can break monotony. By area-planning affluent people are encouraged to low income housing districts, but never vice versa.

Greater flexibility is sought and is being attempted in part through performance-based *standards* rather than quantitatively based. To cut to the quick; *simple courtesy cum creative community protocol, armpit psychologies, should form the basis for land laws relating neighbours and passers-by;* `a la Abophile camp. The housing facts in any country reflect the general consensus attitude of the people. While their unwieldy bureaucratic paperwork is not an easy tool to use, it has more impact than the bulldozers.

It is not easy to make regulation. They are inherently complicated, like most legal documents, in order that they are not misunderstood or taken advantage of; again a reflection of consensus attitude. There is wordy defence against the criminal greed and inadequate values of the *megamonster*. In the same documents is simple, and ideally creative, assistance for the innocent and unskilled. The law, by the *accumulated* nature of its makers, must be an ass. The users are baffled and often need to consult experts to interpret the regulations. And even the interpretations can be challenged and very often demolished. It occasionally becomes obvious that something fundamental is wrong with the miracle of peoplekind.

A rule of thumb; stand your ground, persevere with what you see as fair, but if you detect a losing battle accept the regulation demands and *do your housing* accordingly. Just as you accept the demands of a hurricane. Resistance at times is futile.

Perhaps production of simple generic guidelines, backed up by separate publication of the intricate and legal matrix, could help. Nevertheless the regulation makers face a difficult task. Arcosanti is just too far beyond the fragmented steps and personalities of public authorities. *Ecopical* arcological cities are substantially fundable from cost savings from roads, services and transport, but regulation is not leaning that way.

If the generations of public authorities were wholistic in outlook and made some courageous decisions, just maybe the physique and aura of human habitation would be burgeoning pure on the Earth and countryside like the mighty Amazon, before the rat of its pollution, and the magnificent ancient forests, before the *dodos*. Where are you in this consensus culture; in the market place in the temple, on your way with the true grit, or are you a part-time television cow with a permanent drip-line, giving life to the consolidating *megamonster*.

Mighty mankind. Spaceship to Mars. Ha!

An operating manual for *dwelling-contraption* Earth is what we need, before a restaurant at the end of the universe.
The options are many. On which branch currently am I?

WAY TO GO

Pling **it all off for a minute,** all your domestic

attachments –your hud, mortgage work, empty petrol tank.
The egg room too. Atrophied professional mind too. Make a
clear organised perusal of your array of residential options.
Dreams and practical options. Half options and balanced
compromises. Radical change, long shot chance. New
country, an indoor toilet. A penthouse or a pair of jeans and a
plastic gourd. Or settle for a new cloth over the dining table.
Come to think of it, everything is sweet, let's go to bed. But
the lovely Little White Cloud in the moonlight would not let
Bobby sleep. She was feeding his new inspirations. He was
sick of the bus rides and she knew it. "Global's bus is part of
your own domestic locale Robert. Let's build an office, you
can work from home." "No, I like the people in town. I would
rather move across the bay, a better view and catch the train
to work." Comes midnight she is still kneading his concerns,
but ..., "Robby darling, daring, Dazzler take me to live in
Arizona." There was something missing in her own domicile
as well. She'd miss the neighbours, the cute house and the
big old gum tree that was cracking the bitumen out by the
letterbox, and the whole charisma of the hillside suburb, but
Arizona tickled her genes. It was ancestral memory and she
also just knew that Bobby would thrive at Arcosanti right
there in Arizona. A master plan was coming together, as,
when Bobby said maybe, pheromones went crazy.

*We need not review our options if we are happy where we are.
But by reviewing them along with the thoughts in this book we
may discover an inspiration to be active in some owner, client or
public domiciliary revamp. As your life-span continues where
and with what you will, the wallpaper of your community,
culture, family, friends, individual aspiration, destiny and
functionality dwells with it and maybe some old compromise
falls away. Throw away some crutch or catch some wave. Or
stay - but watch those house psychologies in relation to your
wellbeing.*

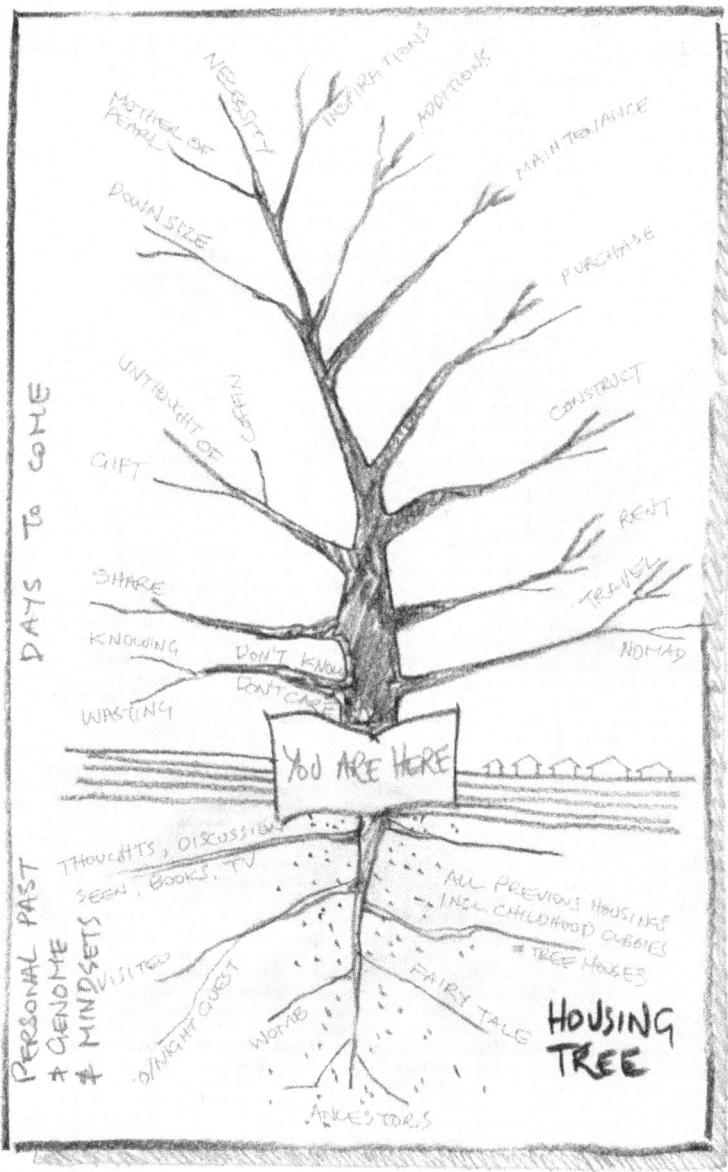

DAYS TO COME

NECESSITY
MOTHER OF PEARL
INSPIRATIONS
ADDITIONS
MAINTENANCE
DOWN SIZE
PURCHASE
UNTHOUGHT OF
CLEAN
CONSTRUCT
GIFT
RENT
TRAVEL
SHARE
NOMAD
KNOWING
DON'T KNOW
DON'T CARE
WASTING

YOU ARE HERE

THOUGHTS, DISCUSSION
SEEN, BOOKS, TV
ALL PREVIOUS HOUSINGS
INCL CHILDHOOD CUBBIES
TREE HOUSES

PERSONAL PAST
+ GENOME
+ MINDSETS

UNVISITED
0/NIGHT QUEST
WOMB
FAIRY TALE

HOUSING TREE

ANCESTORS

Take out a wall, a regulatory clause or let go with Low Carl as a guide. *Do your dwelling* in ether vapour, as well as dense molecules. Walk through some ley-line corridor to Arizona and make some new *room* for the same purposes of the same old dwelling-organisms, you, with your few *accumulating* talismans. Walk a line with Providence.

From a drawing room at Arcosanti, Bobby and the Cloud could best beat out messages to the settlement authorities back in Australia and across the world as to the array of options in detailed settlement planning and the doored cataracted windowed walls of bureaucracy.

Options for hut and palace dwellers. And policy makers. Stepping seemingly backwards; Ritz room to snow-zone bag under a Hong Kong bridge, Director of Housing to postman; somehow we manage?

BUILD
A NEW ONE
WAY TO GO

A fresh new, up-to-date, personalised design. No sign of weathering or previous *armpitted* tenancy. Let's build a new house! A new house has a very appealing commodity. Certainly.

"But - why the penchant to build newly?" Low asks the couple with a Government house builder's grant, or 'home' builder's, as the oilers say. "Well, we have total control over what the house will be, in that we know what we want"; delusion in most instances and you may miss out on a well established garden maybe with an ancient English Oak. Waiting for you; with an old house just begging to bend to your avant garde renovation. "There is no need to put up with the taste and odour of previous dwellers"; not always significant, clean existing renovatable house options are numerous. "The romance of seeing it grow"; relative. "We can start small and add on as we can afford it"; to a limited extent. "We can build where we like"; vacant allotments are fewer than existing houses, overall. "We know the best locale for our lifestyle, there are no houses available there, we have extra money and we want to create a state-of-the-art cultural contribution"; more than enough reasoning, probably - we cannot be certain in light of ecological circumstance (there are some very delicate ecological situations and some straws do break the camel's back). "We want the therapy of growing a picnic place into a garden with interior"; a regular bushwalk may suffice.

Existing houses provide a wealth of commodity in both significant and humble heritage, renovation potential and established gardens. Usually they are available quickly, more cheaply and with no further environmental concerns. They do not have that newly built commodity that has a special worth to many. However, in balance, to build newly, at times, is plainly a poorer option. Often people who take the poor option don't clearly register the mistake - life goes on.

Of course building anew may be an option. It can be very exciting. For some it is merely a task – or that which you can do yourself - and it will teach a lot to many. But wait; rather than build it on a brand new allotment of land, you may find a creative opportunity to do something unique in an old warehouse - nine metres floor to rafter.

Owner building. Owner coordinated building. Architect coordinated building. Builder coordinated building. Small and large contracting businesses. Contracts, payments, quality control, programs, rights, liabilities. Coordination, expertise, reliability, unforeseeable problems, opportune adaptations. Research the subject thoroughly if you are not clear in detail as to how it will all happen. We are not referring to mud huts here, the monetary and lifestyle quanta are significant and the physical outcomes must be safe; sleep easy in a severe windstorm. There are some inspiring books.

GLOBAL ARRAY, LOCAL ARRAY, DESIRE

WAY TO GO

The first issue here is the selection of option(s) in accord with informed desire. The array of options need not necessarily be fully examined. Any shirt off the rack may be acceptable, or one may hunt endlessly; Gallopilong has never had the experience. The arrays fall into broad categories - broader than individual dwellings of particular size, amenity and location. The nature of their potential occupation for example; by squatting, rent, ownership, mortgage, loan, share, board, overnight lodge, pre-arranged, impromptu. By environmental consideration; off the services grid, on the services grid, ethically available. By disability access, by garden and so on. The process of sober analysis and selection is the academic method. Providence may favour the seeker; recognition of the provision and acceptance of Providence may save a lot of work and provide valuable amenity and opportunity of which one had not thought.

As we note, the options begin with remaining where one is and range through many extremes, types and variations. To name a few; a mobile house in a permanent caravan park, mobile caravan, houseboat, tent, travel in one's own way, short term change, owner build, shared house, cooperatively owned flats, join with an Arcosanti, a unit in a cluster house, any new or second-hand house.

The choice comes as we consider other aspects of livelihood; health, locale, climate, domestic work, finance, ethics, romance, site configuration, nebulous family - all lifestyle matters. These sorts of things may prompt change in both housing facility and amenity. Keep them in mind for **CHECKLIST** time.

Several hundred thousand people globally live in houseboats. In some cultures the tradition is centuries old - Lake Titicaca and the Huang Ho River and the Chinese junks for example. Bobby's neighbour on the bus is stunned at the thought. "How could they?" And the driver's wife *pales*. But maybe the quaint glamour is lost to those quaint boat residents who themselves may swoon at the *pale* suburbs – lured by another culture's blood-and-boned greener grass.

It is all in the *doing of our housing*; the action of domestic development, maintenance, refurbishment, renovation, modification. Out of wholistic, energetic domestic development comes the string of options that we have taken up or will take up throughout our lives. And we know how important it is to apply ourselves to optimum housing for both ourselves and our world; even if the domestic activity is simply cleaning the kitchen, or removing toxicity from the household smog.

STAYING WHERE YOU ARE

WAY TO GO

New air in the current house. New paint. New site for the current career movement. New building. New ruck sack. They are all results of *doing our housing*. This *Housefandango* ♪ ♫. It's what you're *doing* as you read and as you move your chair.

By remaining where we are, we may still have options in renovation or modification. Trimming off deadwood, additions, sentimental creativity, working through life transition and keeping up with the times. There is often work to be done in updating and pursuing the daily dwelling frontier; tuning and refining. *Doing our housing.* Revamping as needs alter; a growing and changing *domestic-contraption*, master planning the house. Just masterplanning the current house, because, in this case, choice is against the relocation options. Remaining where you are, in the face of apparent duress, can sometimes be a good compromise. A family lived several years in Findhorn, Scotland, cramped in a caravan before they eventually saw how it had consolidated them as a family. The cost and effort of relocation may be better used in revamping, or in the bank. This shows the quanta impact of psyche.

Review the house *layout*. For example; an area may initially be used as combined living/family/study/studio *room*. As needs change, it may be given over to dining and new arrangements made for the other uses. When the children leave, their sleeping area becomes a studio and later a separate apartment for when they return to visit with the grandchildren. Changes like this are simple. More subtle changes to do with décor, *deboxing*, technological updates, improvements in natural lighting, solar gain and so on take some informed analytical envisioning. In this regard; cleaning, an aspect of maintenance, may justify serious renovation. Maintenance will generally be for hygiene, safety, security, comfort, facility, longevity and *grid* services. For any reason; extend outwards, upwards or downwards or buy a prefabricated out-building or railway carriage. Redundant space may be appropriately redeveloped as a garage, workshop, boarder's *room*, self contained flat, rentable store or offered to the local women's guild for monthly luncheons. Redevelopment may involve modified integration with the garden, veranda patio etc.

A SNOW-ZONE SLEEPING BAG

WAY TO GO

*B*oth *itinerant city life and resourceful living off the land - indigenous life - may leave one without a house.* It'd be a compromise in a cause-based lifestyle. Housing is a lower priority. Low Carl knows this, "No time for the house, not any more; none left to devote to life's love and safety boat; there's too much else of urgent demand; fragile world, a fundamental which comes before house and your lover's hand."

Ultimately though there is no alternative. We need at least a minimum domestic facility; and once accustomed to warmth and cushions we need more than the Gallopilong minimum.

For the cost of a house you may fund say six years in motels or buy a few thousand acres and wander it with a tipi.

You want MORE

WAY TO GO

*M*ore. More may bring you to a level of satisfying sufficiency, or put you over the brink to gluttony, waste or over-burden. It may be that a fascination with *more* is what turned some to, eventually intense, settlement; from nomadism or light indigenuity. The domestic *accumulations* and the nature of the consumer *megamonster* warn us that a whim for more may be a problem. Luxury is that which is beyond reasonable or orthodox necessity. Perhaps it is necessity itself at times. We look to options because we want more of something; a more compact house, more refinement, more simplicity, more *room*. More or less. Wanting is more the issue here. Wanting can sour a perfect reality. Should we cease to want, in housing? Should there be an end to the a-priori hierarchy of needs and wants? Rationality makes the answer variously obvious.

We all have a limited understanding and imagination in all things, including where and how we might optimally live. It is said that a very wealthy and well housed rock-star, unwell from his life, had to rediscover himself in a humble hamlet somewhere. The value of simple fundamentals devoid of automation and synthetic, *machinemark* and bright colour, sumptuousness and elaborate interior in an intense urbia had to be reintroduced to his life. An obliged abode for a sheik in a mud hut is similar, a suburban soul to a country camp similar again. This is updating to meet our current psychologies and functional requirements. *Looking for optima rather than more.*

Looking for optima rather than more – looking to **ecopicality**.

We must work together responsibly to achieve optima; at least work with whom we trust and as far as we trust them. Whilst proceeding with caution we stop to seek where doubt exists. There are optima within the limits of current orthodoxy and there is the developing frontier of optimum orthodoxy. We are a far cry from the latter.

A house is a house, but a beautiful house is a beautiful house. It is more of a house - we thrive on beauty. Beauty though is relative to practical reality, circumstance, emotion, ownership, 'seeing' and romance. Beauty is not necessarily expensive Taj Mahal style design and it is often adequate in a vase of flowers among ordinary appearances, a visual moment to carry one through the plain hallway. A house with abundant beauty is a tremendous success. One with minimal beauty is probably a sign of a dweller needing creative company to assist the action on the daily housing frontier. Or maybe the window's holographic wallpaper effect provides all the beauty required and therefore the person is encouraged away from the inward-looking *trap of interior. Nature's organic nurture* is outward looking. Indigenousness is outward looking. Urban interior risks excessive inward looking. One's outward garden might be a distant fishing lake and the yard at home merely the space between the house and the fence.

Refinement in housing will arise from disciplined planning. It will also arise from construction technique. There is something beautiful about the farmer holding down roofing iron with field-stones. This is refined, some may say professional. The farmer did a refined job within his constraints. Practical, efficient and complete; in accord with time and resource priorities. Beautiful, in its vernacular way. Kosher. It is only more refined to nail the roofing iron if in some different, probably more orthodox, scenario. We grow accustomed to housing refinements that may be beyond our means. Frozen thinking, cultural orthodoxy, regulation, professional habits, keeping up with the *Pales*. Frozen thinking in building as well as design.

Doing with less is an environmental necessity. Making the most of the fait-accomplis in already built extravagant housing options, such as in any Hollywood *boulevard*, is the best we can do with them.

The Japophile and Sinophile live in very small houses. A large lounge in Australia may suffice as space for a two bed flat in Tokyo.

To move house in order to gain housing amenity is tricky; certain aspects of your old house you take for granted and certain bugbears with the proposed new one you will not notice until you have dwelled there. Gain in functional value is assessable. The whole real estate situation is tricky. However, it can be excellent to have moved house, to have stepped into a superb update.

Building for more amenity is often tricky also. Visualising and describing what you want is only the first step. Building it is another. And it may not be as you imagined. Nor as you intended.

EMPOWERMENT
TO DO IT RIGHT
WAY TO GO

Resourcefulness. The professional is already informed but dwell on the perspective of the layperson. The lay dweller; seek and you will find. If you are not sure where to live, or in what, search for some loose beginnings. Ask around. Be wary at the market. Do not be overly prescriptive or rigid. A place I once found, for what we thought was a short spell, was too big - we thought. Knock us over with a feather; we had four children there. Later we were obliged to move to a place that we said was too small. Now we happily live closely here.

Bub may want a lolly but he really needs a carrot. A bumblebee buys a unit in an ant's nest. He thought he knew. It was a hard thing because the ant laws would not allow his bee adaptation proposals. The bee was convinced by a magazine picture that of the many possible solutions to his needs the ant salesman was right. Watch out for the proverbial rut but keep yourself free. The market is generally limited, like the orthodoxy; no cosmic orientations and genome sensitive concerns.

If you liked the idea of living in an igloo, you may spend a lot of money on refrigerating equipment, or move to the icy north. Depending on how strongly you felt about the igloo, you may adapt your *doings* appropriately. It is said that Jesus once said that there is a cure for every ailment, maybe a mountain breeze. Maybe an igloo or a hamlet cottage would cure your lethargy, the simple act of changing your shirt to suit the mood of an hour, or rolling up the sleeves to get down to clearing a drain. Or smoothing plaster on an egg-curved wall in a weathered weatherboard house with ancient tapestries in a grotto; a world of its own that you found, through perseverance, very cheap, but beautifully sited even though behind the city dump.

Doing it right. There is a message in the *Zen of motorcycle maintenance* and many other philosophies that link environmental intervention and personal *beingrowing*. Unlike the mechanical truths of motorcycles, Lancastr bombers and structural physics; the aspects of décor, conservation, taste, tidiness and aesthetics can be affected by 'seeing'. 'Seeing' is *doing*. 'See' the broken-down bathroom drawer in the perspectives of your efforts, passions, responsibilities and potentials, unbiased by the predilection of social norm or the expectation of a visitor. You may 'see' a perfect justification for this drawer-of-some-character in your house that serves you well. Bugger off with the snappy interior designer's upturned nose – Cheeky might say. You only wish the designer could 'see' the beauty of that drawer as you see it – a sow's ear working perfectly. When the time is right you will see that the drawer should now be straight. In the meantime let it lean a lintel. The daily dwelling frontier and the *doing of housing* eventually becomes an exciting *Housefandango* ♪. "Bobby darling Dazzler, my dream house - it's a complete romance needing a handbook with a *checklist*."

A *checklist* can enhance the dance. It will help you to understand where you are and where you might go. There is something prepared in the following chapter. Let's have a look at that, now that we have some more background for it.

Please own it in your own language, spill tea and beer on it and take to it with a fat pencil or fine edge as you please.

And always remember that like the quanta of your house, the eco-quanta of your public realm is sensitive to your *doings* whether they be politically pointed or residentially.

Better check that we're on the ball.

A CHECKLIST FOR HOUSING

This **list supports** *ecopical doi* in;

For your SITE & LOCALE.

It's for both; DWELLERS & the HOUSING WORKFORCE - and is
generally useless for nomads.

You may need further information; no *list* is an island.
Make your own *list* based on this, for your own circumstance.
You may well discover some unlisted items.

PLANNERS & DESIGNERS using this checklist may need
organised enquiry of client, future tenants or ratepayers.

BUILDING & PLANNING REGULATORS may find implied research
to be complex and urgent. A multidisciplined summit will
always be an advantage to REGIONAL & NATIONAL PLANNING.

Domestic location and fabrication are subject to the following
and so the *list* is to be read within your specific circumstances
regarding;

Abstinence, adaptation, lack, time of sojourn, city and local
resource,
Inhabitant numbers, mobility, alertness, health,
Type and quantity of goods, chattels, perishables.

The chapters and sections of this book allude to the needs,
impulses, lures, fears, dangers, frustrations and options that
we face in

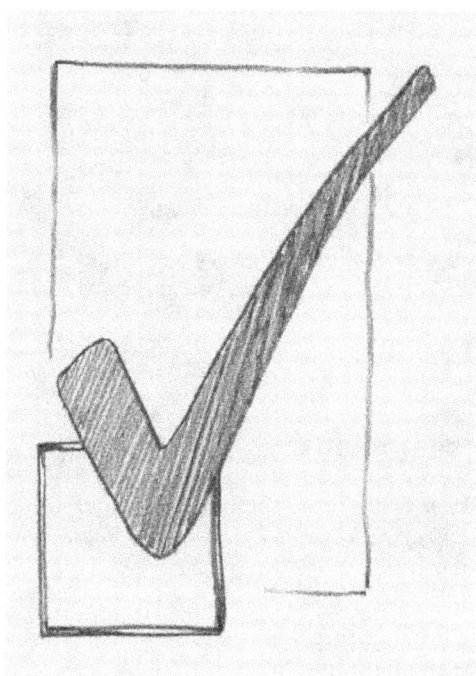

arranging our domestic place and achieving *contraption* to suit. This list is a framework relating to all of this allusion. It is for your reference to help compose or modify your mental stance and note down your particular requirements in planning, renovating, relocating and/or constructing.

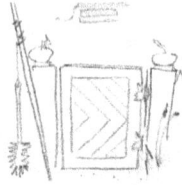

Do your mother of pearl.

Do your housing.

Do it for whomsoever you please.
There are **five** categories.
Ω

1. The GENERAL NEEDS

Ʊhese general needs are those common to ordinary people. Today nomads are not so ordinary.

There are four sub-sections here;

1.1 PHYSICAL WELLBEING
1.2 SUSTENANCE and ABLUTIONS
1.3 AMENITY, COMFORT and CONGENIALITY
1.4 *LAYOUT* and *SHAPE-UP*

1.1 PHYSICAL WELLBEING
Provide for, avoid or shelter from;

Air borne elements – climate, winds (all directions, seasons and types), rain, hail, snow, lightening, heat, cold, dust (internal and external), sun heat, glare (sun and peoplemade), ultra-violet light, unhealthy gases and fumes, smoke, bad odours, nuclear fallout, quality interior air, fragrant air, allergy air.

Ground elements – fire (urban, on-site and bush), ground stability (avalanche, landslip, subsidence, clay movement and cracking) volcano, tsunami, earthquake, flood, radioactivity, radon, cliffs and balconies, water hazards, excessive shade and damp (permanent and seasonal), falling branches and trees.

People and animals - undesirable neighbours, marauders, predators, attack, kidnapping, snakes, spiders, insects, animals, pests, fungus, aggressive bacteria, plague.

Industrial devices - traffic hazards, sound and vibration from machinery and air and ground traffic, bombing, dangerous micro-waves and factory emissions.

1.2 **SUSTENANCE AND ABLUTIONS**
Provide for;

Nature's earthy nurtures.
Clear orientation of dweller in the land and cosmos (including *cosmic symbol*).
Contact with open air, sunlight, directional breezes and the land.
Access for coming home and going out.
Preparation of food, eating, sleeping, resting, washing, toileting, dressing, grooming, laundry.
Interaction for couples, family, social, pets.
Solitude, unique dweller activity, ambient and task lighting (for night and day activity).
Satisfactory air, light spectrum, humidity, temperature.
Preferred fragrances and any other bio-interactive commodities and materials.
Food storage and/or production and preparation, quantified and specified - secure from vermin and spoiling for appropriate timeframe.

1.3 **AMENITY, COMFORT AND CONGENIALITY**
Provision of;

Architectural amenity (including economy), beauty and expressive design, optimising and enhancing *nature's earthy nurtures*.
Synthetic aesthetic.
Appropriate *room-amenity* (aesthetic and ergonomic) for each dwelling activity. Turn cartwheels across the floor.
Scope for cleanliness, tidiness, order, soft furnishings.
Spa, sauna, orgone energy, art, aesthetic and cultural manifestations, personae and spiritual support.
Physical, emotional and intellectual comfort for all.
Ventilation and cooling, glare control, warming, ultra violet control for fabric and people, ephemeral controls.
Whimsical potentials, novel creative opportunities arising from and value-adding the job at hand.

Flexibilities.

1.4 *LAYOUT* and *SHAPE-UP*
Consider;

Size, with *Ecosculpture* in mind.
Floor(s), 'room' amenity screens (corners, space, shapes, front porch, walls, windows, ceiling forms, dividing elements, box, flow, etc), *ergonomic room* (access, easy motion and mental ergonomics for all dwellers).
Placement for all goods and chattels, personal trappings – domestic *accumulation.*
Grid connections where required – electricity, gas, lights etc
Facility and site inter-relationships (eg. road to path to *room* to *room* to patio to sun to tree to views, cater for or contain infants, disabled and all inhabitants, review orthodoxy limitations against potentials).
Dweller and social and architectural expression.
Scope for the miniscule activities and multiple use potentials (reading on the front step, useful corners and niches, places discovered after construction, particular windows and so on may be tuned to suit convenience and opportunity, handy locations for pickup and put down of hats, mail, shopping, cups, etc).
Maintenance, cleaning and future additions and alterations.

2. THE UNIQUE NEEDS OF EACH DWELLER
Provide for;

Affordability – affordability and optima.

Personal trappings – *ecopical* decisions, safe, convenient and organised storage for all trappings considering the future; cars, clothing, laundry, crockery, cutlery, cooking utensils, appliances, tools, hobby, entertaining and professional trappings, recreation equipment and toys.

Special and routine activity - house cleaning and maintenance accessibility and minimisation, potential spatial and furniture rearrangements, fun and games, dance, tea and garden parties, banquets, lounge parties, hobbies, eccentricities, exercising, barbeques, meetings, work at home, coming and going, strolls:- all in day and night, winter and summer, weather change, holiday and work-a-day conditions.

Emotional and spiritual stimulation (the way you want to feel and be) -
Based on *Delight* - cosiness, quaintness, uniqueness, sense of freedom, aesthetics, cleverness, feeling, response
Based on fragrance, sight, sound, nature - all through sunlight,

colour, surfaces, textures, materials, desirable insects and pets, earthy and floral scents, garden, sea/landscape view, breezes;
Based on artefact and _room_ – memorabilia, artworks, religious keys, the dwelling itself as a sight and feeling, photo gallery, artwork space, contemplation space, colour, shapes, materials, design, seclusion, Dreamtime potential.
Based on participation – _do your own housing_ with your family, friends and community.

Special identity substantiation, in addition to that gained externally – personae; taste and order; privacy possibly by personal space; family role maybe by dining order, fathers chair, children's art wall etc; personal creativity manifestation by decor, taste, garden etc; social relationships by presentation of dwelling, activity etc.

Personal life-path and location - land-mark; ancestry by heir looms, photographs etc; renewal by up-dating, fashion, constant house development, diary facility or memo board, consolidation of facilities, growth of garden, development sophistication and refinement of the dwelling.

3. SOCIAL & CULTURAL ASPECTS
Provide for the countryman, citizen, fellow, neighbour, family and individual aspects of dweller activities, accumulations and location. Review of and allowance for;

The privacies -
shyness, coyness, discretions, secrecy, neighbourly differences.

Citizen and national considerations -
the global tale, ecopicalities, architectural styles, heritage, political security, consider the indigenous lifestyles and environmental aesthetics.

Government and law - property, financial, legal, building and planning pitfalls and advantages. And _ecopical_ development thereof.

Individual and group ergonomics;
Social distance -
room for comfortable movement and activity, privacy, seclusion, separation of groups,
Social interaction -
things external to council regulations, neighbours view and their environment generally; neighbourly links; encouraged family life, guest provision, visitor provision, and socialising in house and out.

4. LOCALE, SITE & EXISTING BUILT WORK

Choosing or adjusting to location. People living closely together have different housing requirements from people living alone in nature.

Include locale aesthetic - views, birds whistling, soil, rocks, trees, flowers, busy city outlook etc.

Environment for work, neighbour, community, social & cultural - consider also crèche, church, sporting facilities, neighbourhood house, entertainment, recreation, health services, shopping, community spirit & expression, *room* for you, and your contribution.

Travel - wheelchair, automobiles, public transport, taxi cars, walking and running distance, travel abroad.

Safeguard ecology and resources - household pollution, sewerage, grey water, smoke, microwaves, noise, energy efficiency, conserve rare timbers and the *playdough of the Earth* generally.

Health - allergies, asthma climate/air, radon, energy points, water near, earth-water-fire balances, ley lines, various phenomena.

Public Design – assess the implications on location of regulation and public taste.

Advantages of the site – assess the value of pre-existent built facility and the amenity pre-existent in the site or on it - handy historic sandstone wall, animal thoroughfare and habitat.

5. DESIGN & CONSTRUCTION

Maximum consideration of up-to-date developments in dweller circumstance, and social and industrial contribution to housing -

Generally - lighting, plumbing, electronics, telephone, solar technology and change in number, condition and feeling of dwellers.

Protection of the building itself - the elements, vandalism, internal fire, corrosion, salt air and industrial electrolysis and oxidation.

Good and wise planning and design - to bring all needs into whole and complete satisfaction in the optimum architectural manner.

Reasonable buildability.

Safe building - re sharp edges, glass, trips, house fire, fumes from toxic materials whether burning or not, constant air (people have suffocated by their fire using all the oxygen from an air tight *room*).

Optimum responsible use of natural and laid-on energy - sun, wind, hydro/thermal/nuclear electricity, wood, coal, oil, hot springs, man-styled fuels, all combined with insulation and draught proofing.

288

Design, including making *room* for, for current and future installation of all energy, liquid and air reticulations.

***Ecopical* selection of materials and builders** – in particular consider the required appearance and utility qualities of all surfaces (*mother of pearl*). Think like a turned on *building inspector*.

Wise personal economic-cum-life impact.

Future potentials – developments in the 'unfinished' house; additions and reductions, other uses, getting furniture, changing needs, flexibilities._

╪

You may need professional help.

▶   *Let's do it.*

OUR DOING
OF HOUSING

*D*oing your own housing. *Doing*
another's housing. *Housefandango*; doing, using, responding
to and living relative to housing. Domestic activity - creative
building, making, designing, habitation, hospitality, cleaning,
renovating, resourcing, checklist ticking and enhancing. This
chapter is about the actions that have caused you to be
housed as you are – choices, attitudes, attentions,
predilections and freedoms. And the actions and reactions
that occur as a result of your abode - enjoyment, hard work
and chores. It touches on the *doing* of nomadic domestics and
those *doings* that culminate in the industrial frontier – your
connection to *nomurbics* and *ecopicality*. **It also relates
strongly to those who *do* housing for others - welfare
programmers, architects, regulators, commercial
developers and domestic item producers.** With the
foregoing chapters it goes a distance to empower you with
respect to your own domestic immediacy and your political
and social potency. It is more a corridor through the book
than a room. Lining the corridor you may recall :– 'We know
why', the checklist, the dignity of dweller *quicksilver*
abstractions and your *synthetic aesthetic*, calling your own
shots, simple *ecopical* action and use of *playdough*, your
accumulations, the *ergonomic matrix*, preening it of *grid*
infections, a person in motion, *cosmic symbol*, your place in
your continuum, the sociology of the doorknocker,
compromise, attitude, *deboxing*, the *trap of interior*, the
architects' perspectives, the *domestic-contraption* is a key.

Dreaming is *doing*. Using is *doing*. The *happening organism*
is *doing*. We have talked a little about original, primitive and
evolutionary *doings* and what Albert Gallopilong and dolphins
don't. The happening settled person today generally spends

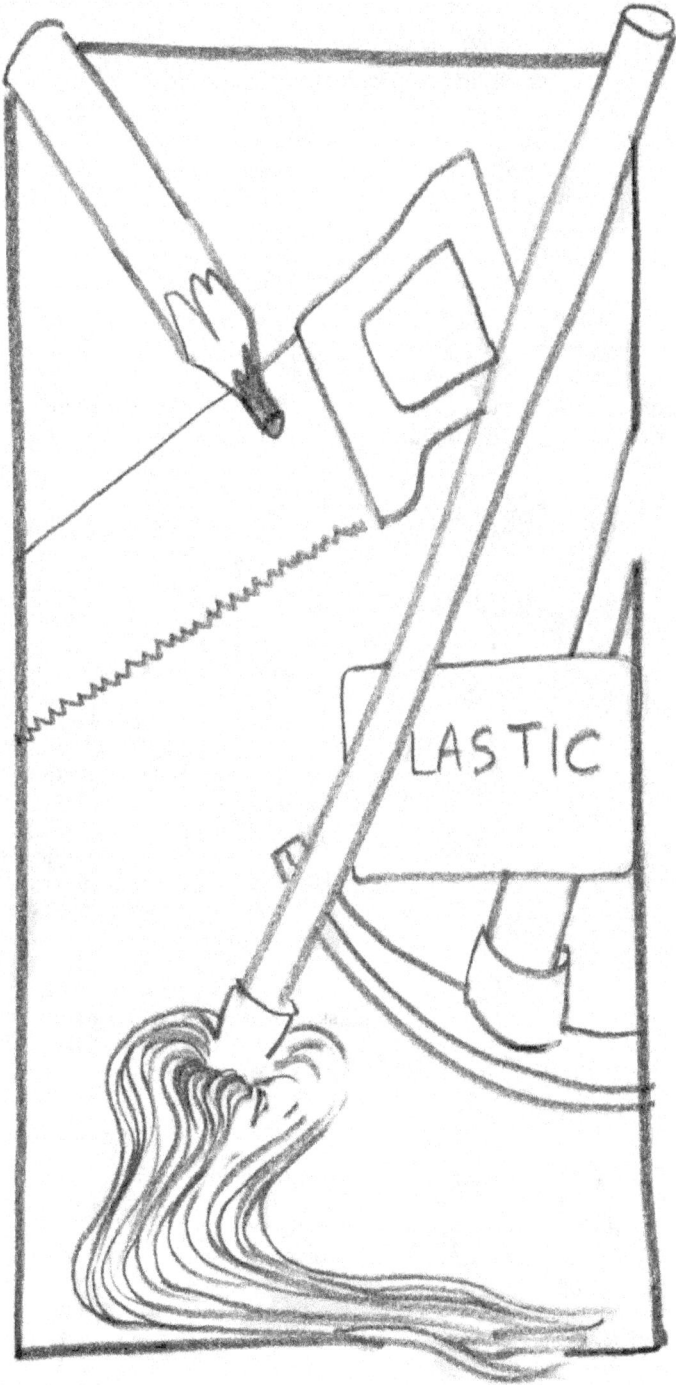

much of its time *doing* something associated with housing. Very significant quanta. You are *doing* some now as you read. It's something we do - housing. It's the Housefandango. It is usually very big in our lives. As big as that which it makes and hones. And that which we afford or borrow. "Jesus is preparing a place," comes a surprising comment from *Pale*. "In the heavenly city we may be nomadic in our prepared abode," suggests Cheekybugga.

We do other things too - recreation, investigate the world, socialise, help each other, eat, collect stamps and create. The nomadic person
 spends more time *not doing* housing things than does the settled person; and far more than the rat racer.

TUMBLEWEEDS ROLL, ROOTS ANCHOR
OUR DOING OF HOUSING

The mood to build or not to. The mood to 'wander', the mood not to. The desire to move on for food, joy or whatever weighs against the desire to settle for different food. This *nub* of common ground, discussed earlier herein under **A MAKER OF FOOTPRINTS & RIPPLES** is a critical point in belief, psychological inclinations, intuition and discipline. Cheeky, Gallopilong and *Pale* dispute endlessly the best way to dwell. The most extreme nomad case may never, ever, even conceive of permanent settlement; being motivated by a satisfaction with a lifestyle of which he would never conceive as transience. He may never make a choice not to settle to the extent of substantial building. Should the serious world see Gallopilong's dwelling style simply as contemporary preference – rather than a primitive stalemate?

The urbanite out camping on holiday is closer, than he was at home, to the *nub* of *nomurbic* domestic arrangement. Wanting not to go home; does he settle and build or does he follow a nomadic way? Why won't he build? And what is the difference?

Which of our doings make the difference, at the *nomurbic crossroads*, where we may turn toward nomad or settler? Is it *accumulating*, preparing to cook, *making* seclusion? One doing is that of permitting substantial barriers, screening, between inhabitant and neighbours,

292

and indeed inhabitant and nature. Allowing the loss of openness, immediate social contact with the encampment, early observation of visitors and the loss of wind on one's back. The loss of convenient and spatially encouraged local forum. Another; the acceptance of some environmental intervention, say, ploughing, building, permanent change and indifference to barriers formed by interior. An *attitude*. Whatever, it is it's in the roots of our cultural acclimatisations. It is safe to note that, within all reasonability, there is some middle ground where people may build without disruption of another's reasonable domestic option, be the option extreme nomadism or ecopical settlement, or indeed, Nature's own environment. There is some middle ground, where the hunter-gatherer is content to accept contained horticulture by the settler and hyper-industry is hyper-ecodisciplined. Where natural selection is supplemented by contraception. *Ecopia*, as yet a figment township at the *nomurbic nub*, the *crossroads* - a modicum of building which is extremely sensitive to ecological extrapolations and respectful and encouraging of extreme nomadism. Extremely disciplined. Spirited by the flighty *nub* butterfly. It is protocoled by universal nomad-cum-settler domestics - *nomurbics*. A physical reality arranged about the *nomurbic nub*. Its Australian symbol can be Albert Gallopilong shepherding a descendant British lamb with a handcrafted spear. Its global symbol can be a *theodolite* shared in indigenous and industrial hands.

The house and its one alternative, which is the people capable of living without the house, have in common essential *domestic-arrangement*. Nomadic domestic activity varies from people to people, person to person. Hi-tech gear, adapted resources, Gypsy tradition, Gallopilong's skill. Low Carl sees the potential of wholistically good city-life knowing it to be non-existent as he wanders the globe. He is still an urban nomad; today with a little methylated-spirits cooker and a shower stolen from a corporate stairwell. A distant friend rubs sticks and steps freely into a billabong. Traditional wiles and newly learnt resourcefulness. Domestic survival, food included. Domestic survival can certainly be tough for the settled soul too. Poverty can make it so. The way in which we manage is unique to each, nomad and settler, even within the breadth of tradition, when tradition is effective.

When fuelled by eccentricity or ritual, even matters of domestic *finesse* may put us in a lather as much as do matters of basic survival, cultural protocol and *layout*. If Global had not changed the colour of the front door Mrs *Pale* would have divorced him - *finesse*! It was luminous violet, yes luminous violet - settler Global after all does have a soul, albeit gasping smothered in that plastic pastiche. The oyster surely would not live but for the *mother of pearl* it generates - *finesse*. Our oyster is our persona. Our *mother of pearl*, our personal comforts.

Three key fundamentals of housing are;

» 𝔉inesse – mother-of-pearl, refined function, synthetic aesthetic

€ ℭultural Protocol – privacy, courtesy, taste, vernacular

¤ 𝔏ayout – siting, environmental orientations, efficiency

These, at times, seem to be of equal importance. Perhaps because of that *nub*. Lying in that *nub* within the acids of our psyches is the origin of our mode; tumble or root. The *nub* flutterby flitters or lands. The mood or need. To build or be mobile. Or to stay but be very light. The choice. Finesse the desire prompts the action which makes the noun. Something we do by tradition, habit or reflex. A fundamental sense of doing or happening that takes us either to the billabong in the bush or the sauna in the city's interior heart. The country locale or the synthetic locale; and those between.

Consider the most everywhere nomad, unaware of building (as distinct from making), absolute minimal intervention in Mother Earth's harmonies. What is he doing - great grandfather of Gallopilong? He is not being 'a transient' – "Just a transient," sniggers dear Mrs *Pale* in arrogant ignorance, supported by much industry.

The most devoted penthouse-owner boggles at the indigenous nomadic everywhere-man and cannot imagine exchanging his well-rooted street-alligator address for a pair of legs with muscles wiser than a satellite navigation *box*. What is he doing this jetting homo superior? He is not being 'a settler' - there is some smiling cheek from Mr Gallopilong who is fascinated by the new apparent star, a satellite, crossing his beloved red-earthed sky.

In their foundational context; Little White Cloud found that Robert is her journey and Robert now finds White Cloud to be all the *room* he needs. Together in this way their cleaving grew an ethereally founded nature and *playdough* force-field, blasting with *hyper nurtures*. The nurtures forged the childhood memories of home for their children in *ecopical* domestic *nomurbic* dynamics; a masterplanned corridor blending changing landscape and diverse temporal abodes with a hallowed supremely functional, renovated, intimately internal base-camp, which would raise Dali's eye. The current aspect of this domestic continuum is shrouded to the public in an ordinary largish once-*pale box*, a *delight* for Global, on the delightful country fringe of 'secure' suburban mediocrity. There was no *room* for an architectural award only because there was no explaining the architecture. **All the dwellers there, it is obvious, are** architectonically **nurtured.**

This *nub*, in the foundation of our *dwelling doings*. The two ways may blend. There are the lessons of the tried and the decisions for today. Dwell upon them; transcendental and matter-of-fact. One of the ways that should be a winner is losing oppressed to the one that is wide-open to the *dodo-that-creeps*. The nomad, just like the wildlife, is dozed-in and *theodolite*-surveyed into a tiny remnant corner, while the dwelling settler increases epidemic potential. Another meaning of 'dwell' is 'astray'. The big, big mess has got to change, change, change. It is all in what we do, do, do, do. *Do*. . .

NOMAD MINIMA
BOULEVARD BOLD
OUR DOING OF HOUSING

*D*oing it. Placing slabs of bark against a limb frame or refurbishing the open fireplace are *doings*. Purchasing a title deed and installing a stove are *doings*. The quanta, values and meanings whisper through the *nomurbic nub*. The whispered messages are distorted by the powers of money and sometimes are even not understood because the culture of the dweller is foreign to locale. And money has warped where people forget, relative to their capacity at the oft ominous point of purchase, that the quanta of a house, site or locale is rather a lot greater than that of a new shirt or hat off the rack – a renewed affection for the old shirt and a repair to the walking shoes makes a ninety degree phase shift an exhilarating option.

Doing our domestic activity. We may negotiate our way to some new locale. We may *accumulate* our way to fixed abode. Abode, a *doing*; the act of waiting, a stay before proceeding. Abide; conform, make do with, live with. We reside. We stay, but only awhile, we are on the move. We depart when we die.

As the *accumulation* increases so does the domestic action and so the settler culture grows, dream house and bitumen. Nomadism grows in the time that is not spent on housing, dream time, and in the nature of the simplest of *domestic-arrangements* - natural bounty and hard work.

How we manage the *doings* is unique to us all, while in part it is common like the attires of tradition, culture, place and language. With the newness of the day it is wise to be ever ready to take stock and renovate or even transform your mind's inherited architecture and lifestyle. This is what sent Bobby's ceiling away and awakened him to the non- repetitive heart-beat of Little White Cloud. Their reconditioned love easily counterbalanced the loss of Bobby's job. He had ignited a small ecological bomb in his corporate property-development workplace. At the time he still walked the checked vinyl floor, but it was now, clearly, converted *playdough* with a twist of

dieing culture – and eventually magical *residential continuum* in a
renovated *pale* box *(ecopically* supreme – **for a settler that is)**.

If you are not already so armed, arm yourself Reader with
Gallopilong's legs, Bobby's candour and Low's conviction.
Somewhere there is value in *Pale* too. Review and renovate or
refurbish your mind as appropriate and open the louvres to the new
day with either changed or sustained actions in your housing. Seek
direction from the local or global resource, quickened with the
transcendental. Think about simple domestic facility on one hand
and your own personalised masterplan on the other. Any culture fits
this process. Different resources, personalities and climates blended
with time produce the different buildings and lifestyles. Similarly
people produce their own swagger.

As we note, across the world there is some difficulty with housing.
This is a main motive for this book. The process is very often
frustrated. Even the wealthy by and large are in a personally
unsatisfactory house – even if they're assumed architectural delights.

If you are locked into some dream-house mode, take a serious look at
your limitations. Our limitations are the fences and walls of your
true domestic space. They are what fit you and today's world
together. Respect them. Work inside them, with their *room* amenity,
to achieve what you can; maybe its very humble, *nomad minima*. A
very wealthy man must consider that his money may be an
obstacle concealing the mud hut, which can turn his heart to
health. There was something irritating about his bold *boulevard*
mansion. He was puzzled. The obstacle can be moved. The
limitations cannot. A limitation for him may be discovered by his
doctor. "Limitations may also be ethical – as distinct from
physical," points out Low, always earnest on this issue. Hope,
attitude and knowing the meaning of success; what you get by
due process is probably just what you need. Greed is not due. It
is not a limit but an obstacle.

Within the limitations we make actions. Economy of action adds to
opportunity and worth. The feeling of beautiful action; graceful and
aesthetic.

We resolve and understand our needs; fresh water, four bedrooms, a
house that represents some son of a god lying on his side, a timeframe. Our needs. We resource; obtain information, expertise, skill,
site, fabric. In either an *ecopian* town or the *megamonster*'s
orthodoxy, we usually need to call on others, perhaps designers,
tradesmen, gardeners, estate agents, advisors, neighbours, window
cleaners, money lenders, and so on. Cheeky notes of most of these
people, "They's doin' time ... house-time ... f'ra living."

Location is a resource – sometimes worth more than the luxury
lounge. We may relocate, and certainly we create when we do so, to a

new town, a design, a strategy, a building, an opportunity, a lease. Civilised cooperation is a sensible thing; compromise and mutuality are basic to working together. We exercise faith courage, perseverance and trust as we house, as we do in all endeavour. We recognise and reject, resist or resolve obstacles and frustrations. We dream. We take a Sunday drive looking at houses and locales. Our actions bring reward.

While we are busy making house plans, life for Albert and Low is happening, with its own ups and downs. Also things happen in spontaneous creative house *doing* that would not happen by design and life plan. An obstacle or faint domestic opportunity seen through the eyes of a dweller at home in daily motion will be invisible to the planning eye. Gradual evolution of *room-amenity* as the dweller dwells. A 700 square meter lot at a bitumen road. A front landing a little awkward and unfriendly to an expanding family. The step widened, a shrub moved, a vision of a transition place. Eventually a new significant residential attribute is developed; a much lauded two metre diameter sandstone landing, radiating like a sun to the paths of the world and drawing in the energies of the same, throwing radiant streaks of sandstone across the still-functional driveway to reject the assumed impost of the car – an inspiration at every passing and place to sip tea. *Similarly things happen for nomads but in what the settler sees as minima.*

§

There is sometimes a domestic circumstance of which one dreams. Dreaming is automatic *doing*. One's voluntary psyche has got everything to do with achieving the reality. By way of *attitude* you may make the most of the sense of order, form and adequacy of your domestic things as they exist. Appreciate the wealth that is around - molecular energy, the air between us, the abundant, music … . By this appreciation and by a psyche response to one's extant house, in time, one achieves a state that is optimum for one. One's spirits affect one's perception. Many soak up *boulevard* house innocent of its *unecopian* birth

Maturity settles, whilst youth underpins the fulfilling wisdom. With all this still we drift toward the orthodox mode and on through the other side we drift innocently to the elegant veneer of the costly *boulevard bold.*

And so we go on *doing*; within our capacity to perform, different approaches, romantic enthusiasm, utilitarian gusto, any old how. *Doing our housing* constantly, unconsciously, zestfully, partially, olympically or another way that suits. Having some *done* for you, *doing* it for others.

The having of creative ideas is hopeless unless the idea is appreciated and fed to the future of your action through a broader activity that you know how to enjoy – work. Or perhaps you are a bit different in your motivational manner.

In a sense one's overall life is one's *domestic arrangement*, house for the settler. Nomad bold, big broad world. *Boulevard* minima shape our life.

MAKE
BUILD
CLEAN
REPAIR
OUR DOING OF HOUSING

*M*aking is simple building. Grass hut. Stud wall. Maintenance and cleaning are the ongoing *finesse* of building to perfect the *mother of pearl* amenity, making and renewing hygiene, refinement and functionality. The priority order of built ergonomic *layout* is the same sweep of order principle as *ephemeral household tidiness*. These things differ in permanence and physical quanta; otherwise they are a single domestic activity.

The only single traditional word that comes to mind for this activity is housing (houzing); the verb, housing. Designing is part of housing too. So housing work begins at the review of psyche and attitude, and carries through cleaning the teeth, removing belly button fluff at the *nomurbic nub*, designing, building, cleaning, updating and maintaining. The same objective is served by each item. That objective is simply for people to personally grow, become and interact in being with the *accumulations* and ergonomic whole of the house in locale. This is
the backbeat of the domestic *Housefandango*, the *Campfandango*, a short dance underpinning any Corroboree, a long dance in industrial reality, a beautiful circadian party in *ecopian* balance.

Our housing action is a quality imbued in the house, even if purchase is the action. Like the imbued memory that makes the hallowed halls, our establishing actions exist consciously in our own appreciation of our own house. The father gorilla builds a new nest every night for his wife and family. Maybe an action for hygiene, or maybe a token. Making camp, patching the tent, re-establishing the fireplace. Domestic acts, build, dwell, abide, reside, inhabit, boil, fry, roast, acts in privacy, withdraw to seclusion, batten down the hatches, home-making, hospitality. Many things we do in our time in house. Building consumes time as a fundamental, and often seemingly repetitive, domestic action.

The completion of building usually results in some degree of celebration, a response to elation and high spirits *rippling* from housing as well as simple achievement. At this time the traditional

Indonesian may ceremonially eat yellow rice. Under the roof of a good days work we relax and talk for a time to let our hands be free again. White Cloud at the coffee table relates the story of the Swiss Family Robinson house built in the trees on a lonely tropical island; a heart rending account of the intimate joys that ought to be associated with the building of a family home, and of the possibility of a house supporting and promoting our physical and mental health. The house, though in fiction, is an example of simple, honest and natural design. In building the house, many things were learned, not only of planning and construction but also of the builders' place in nature and family, of scale and measure, of time and possibility and of many other things sustaining to good life. Such building activity could well be one teacher of the Way. And another case of noteworthiness is that of the construction of community, domestic and other facilities at Findhorn, Scotland. Incredible as it may seem to some, and of dubious spirit as it may seem to others, the construction went ahead regardless of availability of resources following faith in guidance from nature spirits. "They aren't Jesus," she again insists. Building went ahead day-to-day and the *attitude*, materials, expertise and approvals needed always manifested when required. There's no indication they may be Allah.

The making of mud bricks and tamped earth walls is in itself an experience and when combined with spontaneous design, and sometimes vernacular technique, this manner of building strikes a chord all of its own. "I'm awed by their imagination ... and what their hands have done. Look at my clean fingernails. I wish for mud." emotes a passer-by who was once lost to a *pale box*. Somewhere else someperson is wishing for steel structure, glass and curved corrugated claddings.

The many emotions and potential complexities must always be cautioned with a check, as far as possible, of the whole implication of building. Otherwise other parts of your life may suffer due to attention lost to excessive housing. Often it takes longer and costs more than what one expects. This is often the excuse in the smaller microcosms of the same domestic activity, maintenance and cleaning.

The DREAM,
the COMPROMISE

OUR DOING OF HOUSING

Now, of course, some things some people are not ready and able to do. Money, time, ability or inclination may be lacking. In some instances this creates new limits. Bones limit the flexibility of your body; limits are not always a problem. It may be an advantage to find oneself landless and poor, limited, unable to fund a house.

We do *dream* and despite their fragmented, sometimes fluffy, nature dreams are critical to our physical designs and *beingrowing*. Sleeping-dreams may be linked to day-dreams. It's day-dreams that commonly bear dream-house visions. Whilst they oblige us to notice the short-falls of our current circumstance, they spur us on to optimise our potentials. Tune your psyche, grok the facts, acknowledge the humble truth of faulty inheritance. Adjust, to *compromise*. You will be burden free; dancing the *Housefandango* by impulse. A practical dream. A house with walls of cloud, hot and cold running servants; the dream may be a variable and will probably be quite unlike the reality that you eventually marry and learn to use. Other houses that you admire are only a part of the fabric grasped by the creating chemistry that generates your dream. Do not let your visions of ivory houses, moats, automatic kitchens, or Hawaiian hammocks sour your present circumstance. Your present is truth.

We must act out perfect individual solutions, and the magical romantic truths, that are possible in this miracle existence. This is where one *doing* one's own housing is exponentially more potent than the hiring of the most honoured architect or real estate agent. They are merely steps on the way.

The owner-dweller is in an odd situation with respect to his capacity to have an ultimately significant impact on her own house. On one hand we see avant-garde and eccentricity in houses – shots called by owners. On the other we see the prime formers in nature and economy and industry calling the bigger shots.

Gallopilong's dream is to do away with cold desert nights - from the outdoors of course. Reality is an obvious *compromise* and so Gallopilong has not dreamed this since he was a teenybopper. *Compromise* - agreement in the face of constraining pragmatics. Who knows if in fact these are our just deserts? In the case of housing, *compromise* can be a loose concept or appear as adaptability, changing circumstance, lack of omniscience in design, flexibility of use, unexpected or unimagined gains. Compromise seems to lie between success and failure; but success relies on compromise. "Chasing illusion can get quite confusion because heaven can turn into hell," Cheeky hears Jimmy Buffet.

Always when dreaming, lacking omniscience, we relate to only part of reality. When dreaming of delicately gardened courtyard, one may be even forgetting the children or the practicalities of maintenance. Dreams are like that, a little undisciplined - minima, budget, get real. Dream bubble bursts but we acknowledge the children as being sustained by the proper dream, so we simply realise our mistake as we blow another bubble. Some mistakes we don't notice. We build them and then adapt - a little compromised but we understand; foibled reality justifying the ego of our most intimate *Housefandango* moves - the secretion that is *mother of pearl*.

It is easy to dream up excess. Or for the dreams to shadow one's current house. This is where the process of *doing one's housing* becomes a *key*. *Attitude*; one's understanding of one's own unique and general requirements and ones ability to realise the requirements, grows with that *doing*. Also one's understanding of the current facts of one's housing grows. The growth eventually melds dream and pragmatics.

The achievement of the dream-house eventually becomes less poignantly demanded and people settle for what they have and then act on whim. A mild realty in hand is worth two in a dream. Always it can be much better until you are guilty of nit picking your idea of residential *finesse*.

Compromise is an ally of the dream. Some of the allies of *compromise* are human adaptability, *armpit* psychology, omniscience, expedience, practical optima, reality, and ecology.

An optimum dream obviously must be in harmony with the times. There was no point in dreaming of a waterbed in the days when straw was the mattress. Yet there is nothing wrong with dreaming of servants attending your abode in the future to take care of your housework.

Dream your locale too, as part of the whole *domestic-arrangement*. If your place is lacking and pop posters are not as good as Picassos, hang your focus on the beauty of the big world. Some sound and maintained contemplation can flood the place with *nature's earthy nurtures*. A star is as close its light; you can touch it. A molecule of air is really something. Learning to love it. Basically it is a sickening, destructive mess that rules, with the genuine, intelligently thought out, sensitive abodes taking a beautiful, fragrant, tiny minority. On the other hand it depends how one looks at it. Error is innocent, people are adaptable, greed is misdemeanour, and thoughtless design is simple intuitive design. Assume the appropriate spirit your glasses haze over to rose colour and the sickening destructive mess becomes the minority and a place of lessons for those who need them. It depends very much on your own attitude to working with it. Be clear on that. It depends on your own attitude to working with it.
Dream your helpers too.

No dream; just housing in a simple matter-of-fact manner. The dream is matter-of-fact and the awareness of the dream, the creative vision, fosters the practical move and simultaneously brings a reality to your life according to how well you *do your housing*; rational dream, romance. All good things will be added unto you.

UPDATING the daily FRONTIER

OUR DOING OF HOUSING

Some of your many housing actions are in your daily frontier, the current edge of your house developments, on edge for a full-wall paper-thin plasma screen, tumbleweed thinking, scraping paint, cleaning behind the refrigerator, adapting a garage cupboard to hold the lawnmower, anything. Once established in a house or once *Housefandango* proficient; sour-grapes compromise and all, you can sweep the floor on automatic pilot while your spiritual adventure works with your developing dream. And if you are adept enough you can manage the tin-tacks work whilst your dream is fulfilling. Renovation, next abode, imagination. Attitude is the father of invention. The ethers fuse your wishes to produce the facility and amenity that best suits your character.

If you are living properly, *doing your domestic facility* correctly, you will be optimising your housing. If there are a few things missing, compromising limitations, handle it right and enjoy it. Necessity is the mother of invention. Go to square one in *doing your housing.* Or maybe compromise with status quo and go surfing instead – or go give Gallopilong a hand with his parallel lifestyle chores. He may be five miles from camp gutting a kangaroo.

The place you have now may be any of perfect, adequate or hopeless. Whatever - it exerts on you its power and you bring power on it. It may mean dweller action is prompted in renovation, decoration, moving on, addition, a celebration, a spring clean, a talk to the landlord, some regulations lobbying, gardening, vacation, attitude shift, lateral thought or going out for the evening. If you find yourself in a dirty dive sometime, a symptom, do not just woe, do your *dwelling activity.* It will teach you while you shape it. A hopeless ramshackle flat in a bad part of town. Keep your shirt on. You may deserve it. It will undoubtedly, though depending on your spirit, get you moving in search of improvement which will be appreciated when found. Why should you accept a squalid flat in the first place? Any reason will do. Accept the challenge. Be ingenious, make it great, talk to the landlord; make the effort called for, refuse to go there, whatever. Roll with the compromise appreciating where you are on the track to paradise. Open your eyes to paradise. It may come as a new short term flat-mate in Low Carl. Low might suggest, "This flat would be ideal for sobering the sheik of petulance." Who knows where the daily housing frontier may take one. Bobby, many years ago, spent a few winter weeks with his lady under a sheet of roofing iron propped up on sticks, icicles and all, while he built the preliminaries of his first hut. It was good for their spirit and story telling. Not that Cheeky was interested.

A smooth and stimulating ride is available. Consult your local guru, church, friends, mother, father. Search your soul, pray, but face it square on accepting your racial circumstance, social situation, mysterious needs, known needs. Keep moving. One man's junk is another's gold. Your basic lot may be a wealth to your spirit. Get it on, rock on, tally ho, tarry not. Be active in meeting nature and society through the intimate truths, potentials, challenges and tonics of the housing you will need through your life and now. Your maximum wise effort is the basis for optimum housing. Housing to meet the reality compromise where work quickens the spirit.

We have our housing roots, our housing now and various future options. Your past housing experience will be consciously and unconsciously considered in your future doings. The need for life-long housing security encourages many of us to cling to what we have; afraid or shy to move. Change abode on reasonable impulse. Always be ready to use those wandering legs as they were designed, and move on. Always! When your heart is anchored, and your roots are spread you will know it, and nothing will move you. Until then always keep the moving options open. Ease of moving house is one of the new marvels in industrial life today, a further dimension available in housing, possibly a way of quickly changing your circumstance.

Are you *doing* it well in your house now? Are you using your facility fully, keeping it in order, giving it daily life, and discovering its flexibilities of use. If your tastes or your needs have changed, subject to whim, soup up your house and move on as you feel. You are not a cultural mistake if you originate fashion and style yourself. It is your business. Stand by your dignity as any person of integrity and *armpits*.

The close familiarity of the house can lead one astray; a vision of greener grass, a better place for the family to grow. Frustratingly limited one feels that it should be an immediate update.
Unachievable one tends to think. Daylight dawns through the strato-stimulus clouds of compromise. One sees that the new house sought is in fact the house that one is already in, as a new light falls over its therapy and facility. If one had not been limited by compromise one would have gone straight to realising the expensive unnecessary dream – the new house. One was desperate to own what one thought one needed, yet it would have changed the balances in one's life.

One of the morals, there, is to keep housing in the light of all your other necessities. A single-issue vote is a waste.

Visual, aural, tactile and fragrant comforts and stimulus form the basiis of domestic *surface* treatment. They change with the days, by the *mother of pearl* and updating processes. Tuning the house to the time of day, current living fantasies, moods, visitors, happenings and doings; colour, stereo, aroma therapy, the new Picasso, remake the stair rail with a perfect piece of drift-wood from a beach stroll, mount some photographs, a new computer terminal, a door-flap for the cat. *Doing mother of pearl.* Some empty space, item, feeling or facet of your house will always be knocking on your doors of conscious or unconscious creativity and solutions. Overcoming bugbears, make an easier flow. Improvement is a fundamental value of house. How does it make you feel? Good, at least, if not exuberant.

The intimate knowledge from habitation combined with leisure activity may create spontaneous hobby-type house developments, unique creativities not possible by any form of planning; some rare pieces of wood from the shed, some time to sand them to best grain, glue, a couple of cramps and a piano hinge and you have almost by casual accident created a unique cupboard door in a highly prominent location and who would have thought you could have done it and that it would have such impact.

Unfinished. It is a kind of pleasing amenity at times, raw, fresh, something happening, something to do, a rough edge to highlight the smooth. This idea in a Japanese garden hinges on renewal and development, flux and change, the constant developing activity of the gardener, rather than simply additions, subtraction, and maintenance. Working her frontier White Cloud explains, "That which I have, though I like it, is not what I would have if I could, but because it is something that is getting me there it is kind of okay; it is highly important to have a place you like; even furnishing goes a long way, I think because it is closer."

Life goes on to later frontiers and new considerations. When should the ageing organise low maintenance, easy access, safe housing. At the right time - before the inevitable slip in the shower breaks the hip.

If the Earth shifts on its axis relocate the front door to face the rising sun, update, inhabit.

INHABITANT ROLES

OUR DOING OF HOUSING

*M*asculine roles, feminine roles, children's roles, hosting, chores roster, owner responsibilities, custodian, lordship, authority, hostess and working together in the *Housefandango*. Functionality, activity, taste and expression coming from all inhabitants. All dwellers have a role to play in the full development of the house and in particular the daily frontiers and *mother of pearl*. The husband might latch the door, the wife polish the bed-head; having entered by one of two bedroom doors, one for he and one for she.

Houses can be organised with sub-domiciles, the hall being like the public realm accessing private rooms, and the lounge a community hall. Domestic politics, sanity, parents' realm, children's realm, personal solitudes, personal *room*. They can be organised in family harmony or group agreement with intermingled expressions and senses of order.

The inhabitants may be comfortable in allowing a designer's taste to rule their order, but this should be rule in some ways only. The *Housefandango* requires the participation of the inhabitants, for the glow of the house and of the inhabitants. Taste involves many things, the manner in which the colour hues, tones and tints come together in your house, whether glossy, matt, or textured, of natural or synthetic pigments, lighting, forms, patterns, shapes and more.

The dweller needs to be involved. We have seen repercussions in welfare housing. Almost all the problems with welfare housing can be traced to the fact that the user does not play a proper role. Disorientation. The ape, even a *shadow*, within a zoo-house away from his native habitat makes his nest, regardless of an uncongenial environment, making the most he can of his materials, even just a circle. He sits in it - home. The culture of housing becomes part of the tapestry of life including the deeply rooted moods and motivations.

Our cities, regions and countries are our communal house. Our globe is our ocean liner, spaceship Earth.

USING this DOMESTIC FACILITY

OUR DOING OF HOUSING

Although we make houses to use, we tend to think of ourselves as living in them; 'living' in the sense of 'being' where we belong. People who belong on the road notice this clearly because they contrast with the loungeroom lizards. The essential use of the house, i.e. both facility and *room* to do things, allows the loungeroom lizard ethos to develop, which is a use that is more of a non-use. When we rise in the morning we tend to be in habitation, inhabiting, just being there, because it is cosy and handy. This though is the amenity that gives *room* for us to make our daily bearings, like Bobby as he splashes cooking oil on his work shirt. We are in fact using this *room*. And we are cosy only temporarily as eventually we must ... something.

This does relate to the use we may make of the very natural world, but then the house is blended with this world; Gallopilong, through Talkabout's heart, with a freshly gutted lizard nods as he wanders through the egg shaped lounge to make use of a refrigerator. We use *room* and facility to both enjoy and continue. There are spaces in the bush formed by natural landscape that a walker may identify as providing *room-amenity* for contemplation, lunch, sleep or some manual work. Bush – ie wilderness and rampant nature - is there in house, even as Mrs *Pale* hermetically seals out that which she can – *a house filters*. Old Gallopilong is through the kitchen and out the back door in fluid motion enjoying the *ergonomic room* flow of his visit while thanking the absent custodian for his sharing; he continues as part of *nature's earthy nurtures* on his way out the back track through the bush, the lounge-*room* lizard still quivering at the thought of his spear and afraid to touch the berries the nomad had left on the unlacquered kauri-wood dining table. The Building Inspector finds himself united with Bobby in the psyche of flying ceilings. He has not used the house for other than exploration. He heads back out the front track into a small mobile interior and back towards the Council offices. He notices people using the laundromat, the community hall and cafes and sees the ceiling of each joined with the ceiling of every house, and notes that the old Blackfella he saw seemed to utilise some interior whilst rejecting other; the tight *little boxes* were cracking like egg shells and surprised lizards were too slow for the hawks. People had been using the *boxes* to hide away from disciplined activities and neighbourly truths.

Both profoundly, almost-eternal and simple automatic daily *doings* are the long and the short of the myriad of uses, of the *accumulations* of *domestic-contraption*. We use them for the purposes for which we made them - and more. We take actions that traditional nomads have never experienced. Opening a window, turning a knob, pulling the chair out from the table, checking the letterbox or putting a saucepan into a cupboard. On the other hand some of these actions may have parallels in principle to nomadic manner. Answering the door is like responding to a request to broach your personal space to share a fire. Hospitality happens in all lifestyles. A native basket is a utility from which the user seeks response just like the plastic refrigerator drawer. Where there are hands there are things put to use and where there are minds there is spatial amenity making *room* for various mind modes.

Again we see the limitations of planning and the want for adaptation and spontaneous invention, this time in the utilisation of things intended for specific use only. We do mix the uses of our facilities;

sitting on the stairs, cooking on the fire, coming through the bathroom window or, if you live in a draughty house in cold winters, camping out by the fire in the loungeroom. The kitchen is popular at parties; a down-home feel and provision of seating on chairs, benches and table, and leanings everywhere, and a heart for children too, with mother cooking. It is good to make coffee tables to double as seats and stools.

Many actions and uses of household inspire *Housefandango*, while others remain dreary because we do not understand where their beads fit in the great 'glass bead game'. Sleeping, toileting, washing, passing along a passage way, dressing, reading, stamp collecting, entering the house, entertaining, changing from activity to activity, cooking, meditating, leaving the house, washing clothes, playing with children, tuning to the day, and sitting in revelry are a few. Roll over on the bearskin rug in front of the fire, grab the remote and tune the lights and stereo - "Now you know what houses are for," smiles Cheeky. "Be cautious warns," Low. "Your house may well have potential beyond which you are currently using it and it may well have potential to draw the wealth from your spirit."

And in all this we must adapt to the work of the Director of Housing and the makers of the Building Act, as we do to a cave or a suffocating cup of tea in Maggie *Pale*'s very own lounge.

Okay! Let the dog out for real this time.

Whilst he's lifting his eyelid, finding an excuse to stay inside ....

SKIP THE
Housefandango

Afterglowing **cinders** and smoke spilled under the
colonial mantelpiece curtaining up to the sooted ceiling. Some
twigs and a spud in the coals. *Anyone for a cup of tea and a
blanket now!?* Compact disc transmutes bed-time music,
...walks with personality, talks with ecopicality ..., as the dog
quietly holds his curl. Our hands have created. Brawn and
brain. *No sugar, only milk? .... Here ygo!! Howsat?* We
express artistically with our houses. Domiciled on a hill by an
airport, a resident conceived; it might be fun to build my
house to look like a crashed plane, for the interest of the
people flying overhead. A tall skinny bloke with a nose of note
thought of ferro-cement to form his house to look like it was
dripping off the cliff edge. Merely thoughts. A wacky
Anglophile in a traditional row house thought and did. He set,
poking through his roofing tiles, a large fibreglass shark,
looking like it crashed from the air. As it is when orthodoxy is
breached, there were complaints - neighbours, council issues.

A Building Inspector, somehow turned cartwheelingly
romantic, groping with newly found views as to cosmic versus
street *grid*, was looking to arrange a window or skylight so
that the sun falls on his dining table, at dining time, on his
wife's birthday, and another so that they faced a full moon
while eating on their wedding anniversary. They laughed at
their mistakes. Oppressed by the rectangular *layout* of their
immediate locale, they found that a simple gateway through
their fence to a friendly neighbour had a significant
psychology of allowing *nature's land nurtures*, back into their
property, *deboxing* the rectangular fence corral gridded across
the hill face.

Beauty and the bits, the *three-planed-corner*, the smell of the
cooker and the new sun rising over the mountain through the
large glass window that once was not. The fantastic and

308

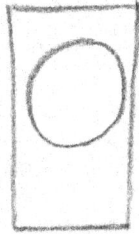

tremendous experiences and inspirations we gain from our own housing and even simply looking at those of others pale into insignificance when we realise the part these *dwelling-contraptions* have already played in our personal and social development. This paling though is not without the focused glow - the onward development of our personal
housing dream and those others to which we can relate. The future always seems to be more infinite than the past. The housing dream so often equates in intensity with the dream of our *beingrowing*. Rock, lace and time melded with wood, water and space fused by feelings, family, people, love, action and dreams; ingredients of the house phenomenon, parts of earth parts of the spirit. Sweat, tools, muscle and money make footways, seats and food places using choices, selections and preference made by pragmatics, desire and fantasy.

There are many things we learn and do that simply would not be but for houses. And the nomadic people remaining to sharpen that knowledge are every day fewer and more diluted by settler culture. There is not an answer here - just an enhanced void for our own answers to grow to light as the fire embers dull still warm.

The good Albert Gallopilong eventually traded his vast wealth of *nature's earthy nurtures* for the infinite wealth of the light of God that filled the entire residence of New Jerusalem.

As time rolled on Bobby Dazzler established *Debox* Renovations. It was a subsidiary of Residential Evolutions. Another subsidiary was Desnag Innovations. It provided a legal and research service regarding the frustration of innovators wishing to over-ride conventions that are tangled in standards-based regulations. Bobby's interests expanded into a rigorous challenge to bureaucratic negligence and political shamming ... his organisation House Peace was able to free many wage enslaved devotees of *Ecopia*.

Hopefully you have been stripped naked for a romp in rigorous land, to bivouac against your societal *dodos*, and allowed to redress with some new wisdom and awakening here at hand. The motivation for this book has been to highlight and facilitate the magnificent options available through houses and the frustrations of achieving the delights, without ruffling the world. To promote an approach to responsible creative housing. To acknowledge that whereas we know why we build houses we cannot deny that there may have been another way for the world, while for some the way is right now an innocent reality. An innocent and energetic vote ... whilst these voters were feeling kinda seasick, the crowd called out for more. Its clamour came from the dream we are about to enter.

TREMENDOUS RESULTS from dancing turtles & penguins in this PORTICO TO THE AFTERLIFE

SKIP THE HOUSEFANDANGO

Imagine. The house. A living machine, alive that is, albeit body without soul - the primitive beginnings of living crafts of freedom. A Jonathon Livingston house. A two-saucer garage house as converted from a laser-built restaurant at an end of the universe. Seems better than the dank cave at another end. A *ticky tacky box* couched in tar and cement at another. A silk lined coffin overcoat at another. The great uniting ceiling – *galloping* full flight. A mansion full of rooms, framed up by words at another end. The word was not Architect. The glow of deep interior. The step that steps via the mind into deep emotion and personality. The heart of the *dwelling-arrangement* is deep within the dweller where we unite at sea. This is what matters, is it; the Dream Time. In God's house are many mansions. This mere portico to some eternity, we may currently enjoy. Like penguins crowded on the dolphins' shore or turtles plying the aqua blue, our happening human organisms do their thing. Like the unique beings we can be, we create, all three, beside, in and separate from nature. *Do your housing* with love, but absolutely first and without being overly materialistic, look after your soul along with the souls of your people; the key to this lock is also a frame of mind. I mean make sure the house takes second place to the use for which you designed it. Live fruitfully. *Doing our housing*, the *Housefandango* only as people break bread and remove the cork, and followed by celebration.

Like the acts of drifting, siting and planning; kitchen is a state-of-art that we are, as is ablution, lounging, rising, copulating and daily dancing. Aesthetics is a performance. To build is to physically fulfil an understanding of an increased freedom to be. Maintenance, gardening and housework are simply building. We come and go regardless to the house or campsite. To house though we must pave and floor. Reeds and newly manufactured plaster perhaps. Build. The grass will return to the old campsite as an ephemeral floor. The transient makes do. To bless building or camp is to be unified with building or camp. Potato baked in the lounge fire. It may be that the house will go. Pack up camp. Earthquake perhaps.

Years ago a hippy said that the buildings on one dimension of Venus are a low density hemisphere of translucent cellular material stronger than our plastics. It is into this vibration that an event in the making will project our Earth. Appropriate dome structures here will survive this change into the fourth dimension. The dense and ninety degree structures, most houses, will fail the hippy sayeth.

While that sort of thing is going on, as it is, or may, or may not be, right now, bureaucrats become more active in housing and environmentally friendly laws may yet become very strict and less token. Many fault lines we guess will still be zoned residential. We must consciously and even massively revamp despite some built heritage and establishment. Inner city office space is freed by the impact of the microchip. We look to convert the vacant space to housing.

Obviously enough it is your moves afoot now that create the future fact. The *dodo-that-creeps* lies in ambush at the step that we must take to save another erg increment toward global disaster. Like the pioneers who would travel deep into the country, meeting new frontiers, which have become old frontiers, so will any spot in the future soon become old. There will always be home and four walls. The rooms will always be humming harder at some times than at others. There are trends, which in the short term are quite predictable.

Today very few people head out into deep country and hack a house out of the remnant bush. One could frame up on an iceberg, lake, mountain top, valley or the roof of a skyscraper. People at Lake Titicaca live on floating islands of reeds. They constantly renew as the reeds sink. Simply bring on soil for gardens. Huts and canoes are of reeds. In the Far East many are born and raised on ships and floats, seldom setting foot on land. In early times there were floating islands of bamboo with sometimes two hundred families with stock, orange trees, vegetables and flowers on the Huang Ho. They drifted downstream and were towed back to drift again. A far cry from the common suburban block of both today and say the less populated early Rome. They drifted along with an empire. We flock to the cities. They can make us crazy. We can change their presence.

Our houses are becoming more sophisticated and quicker to build. Increasing variations and industrialisation. Yesterdays modern bakelite switches are outmoded today. Let us hope today's nuclear power will be outmoded tomorrow. Like social distance and sunlight, natural materials will always be. Earth for bricks, trees for wood, sand for glass. But their use, like cotton in clothing, will be reduced by planning, technique and synthetics. The globe may hold together. Probably with additional expense to individual comfort.

Art trends in houses will change due to industrial componentry. The old furniture you see was once a current artistic expression. Now it's old hat and maybe absurd, or even enduring. There will be increased reliance on trappings for natural items, art and craft to bring urbanity to industrial houses; to bring *handmark*, nurtures and *synthetic aesthetic.* Utensils, furniture, hangings, graphic pattern, television, recorded music. There will, though, always be a variety, and variance within the varieties. And peoples' characters and individualities will always rebound and expound from housing. Poetry will always live, and ingenuity, romance and adventure will always be available through housing – "I'm sad to interject your optimisms, but that can be an impossibly tough call for some," interjects Cheeky's Aunt with an extreme circumstance in mind; the vital *nurtures* of the songs of the land smothered out of the environment of a friend by *nomurbically* ignorant *dodo*-infected settlers.

It is hard to imagine life without the sarcastic face of common commercialism, selling housing packages, planning obsolescence, and producing disposable houses; even some so-called architects designing with magazine photos more in mind than living outcomes. We are mostly blinkered and *bound* into life as we know it.

Moon houses will not cater to heavy gravity, winds or rain, but will need additional shielding from the sun and so on; the influence of environment. The influence of people. To repeat a beat; the house that in plan is a spiral of stone, which tapers upwards twelve metres is an inspiration. Stairs run up the spiral and off them are, not *boxed* rooms, but suspended spoon-like pods. Imagine an the oversized tipi with a twist in it and pod trays suspended at various heights and spacings inside. The pods are designed for privacy, but are open to the tipi-like interior. *Room* without *box.* One pod for sleeping, one for lounging and so on. The kitchen and indoor pond, garden, fireplace and patio are on the ground floor. The house is approached by a small suspension bridge across a river. This is the 1950's. There is a beach house that looks like a large boulder and another designed with not one straight line inside. All flow, an endless house. Clever and different. Day in day out.

Yesterday and simple organics: It is said that it was kosher for Gina and Grunter at Catal Huyuk and elsewhere to build platforms, a half metre off the floor, plastered and covered with matting as a base for cushioning and bedding; under lie deceased relatives, right there in the lounge. They did it their way, even with brown eyes. Interesting ideas. Architectural tricks and delights. The feats of ingenuity by the 'primitives' can leave us for dead as handymen. In traditional New Guinea special houses may be shaped like sacred animals, a wild boar, an alligator with six metre skyward jaws wide open.

As Global *Pale* is blind to the *finesse* of eco-sensitive beauty, many are blind to the cultural essence of simple indigenous dwelling.

An African dwelling may appear to be quite rudimentary, unpretentious or even artless. We may note the owner's freedom to build, untroubled by modern bureaucracy. However complexities may go into the planning. In Mali the Dogon people have a house that represents their Son-of-God in his human form lying on his side, procreating. Lightly speaking it has a central *room*, the *room* of the belly, around which are the kitchen, three storerooms a stable and a big room with an entrance flanked by four conical towers. The towers are limbs. The kitchen is the holy placenta; no plastic laminate or black and white checks. The stable its earthly counterpart. Hearth stones are the eyes in his head. The arms are the two lines of store-*rooms*, two jars of water placed at the entrance to the central *room* are breasts. The genital is the entry that leads by a narrow passage to the workroom with jars of water and grinding stones. Corn liquid extracted on these is carried as semen to the shrine of the ancestors left of the entry and poured on. I'm not sure of the gender implications here but I know that the account I have found in some old notes gives a fair idea of the depth of meaning to which the house was built. Is there a soul in a nylon carpeted rented flat? Not so much as under a Manhattan bridge with Low Carl or in the frugal amenity of a Tufa apartment.

In Turkey, are thousands of Tufa cones, or lava peaks. Many of them eroded in a peculiar way so as to appear a surrealistic moonscape. The cones have been hollowed out, up to six levels and ornately carved and decorated to house thousands of people. Ancient earth houses and modern earth houses. Imagine a refined house superb interior and very fine Classical stonework, with ornate trim, windows and stairs, pushed into a low cliff, with shrubbery hanging down over it. There is one in Europe somewhere and it is not a *box* blot on the local terrain. At Coober Pedy, Australia, the underground is a solution to both the heat and the remoteness of materials. Spacious skylighted houses are tunnelled out using opal-mining equipment. If you upset your neighbour he might kick in sand from up top.

Nobody kicked sand at a particular Yaqui Indian sorcerer, though. His ways it seems have power. He resurfaced the earth floor of his student's on-ground bedroom, moved his bed to an angle to meet angular fluid lines that he had newly set into the floor. The lines worked with the powers of the Earth to bring the student and the North Wind together – *nature's earthy nurtures*. It was done to help his development in sorcery. A kind of mouth gaping shamanic Feng Shui. If you read the series of books by Carlos Castaneda this little architectural gesture will mean more to you. We shape our buildings and our buildings shape us. *Corners, space and shapes*. "Align your bed as you feel it best to sleep well," suggests White Cloud placing a last fragrant log to pick up the paling cinders.

There is a circular house, around the upper trunk of a tall tree, connected by a bridge to a nearby land rise. Today with flexible materials we can do marvellous things with tree housing, even extending over more than one tree. They can rock and sway in the breeze. A very therapeutic household can be had. An elliptical timber geodesic dome. Like a flying saucer on a stem. An immense amount of custom cutting in the panelling of triangular modules.

Earth, locale, people in cities. A glass house is built in a large city as a work of art. Completely transparent, bath-*room* and all. Temporary home to a gorgeous oyster living privately in full view of the public. Surely she was inventing *mother of pearl* in her sleep in an endeavour for private comfort.

Like a tattooed man somebody painted pictures all over their house.

Electronically tuned houses may have sensor controlled light changing as one moves about. Voice activation if you like. Automatic internal climate control and plant watering. Sunlight and temperature sensitive louvers, curtain motors, glass tinting. 3D audio-visuals and teleportation finally does away with the driveway and streets. Except as styled for a scenic stroll. Lots more of course. Electronic intrusions, telephone salesmen, spies, viruses, junk mail. Appliances evolution. Electronic locking. Bio-electronics. Living houses. But is it as alive as the house of God. The 13 metres high, 27 metres x18 metres house for the Ark of the Covenant which King Solomon built for Jehovah was of stone, gold, cedar, fir and olive wood. By today's standards the house cost hundreds of millions of dollars. It was detailed in unison to the dress of the priests and built silently, without the sound of even voice, nor tool. Plain without and rich within; of kingly appearance. Sometimes it is called the House of God. Many a lesser house has been named. The romance of life shows up in those names and in the feelings of the heart as we recall congenial Sunday afternoons in a favourite room, as we walk from one part of the house to another, as we celebrate with a 'house-warming' party or a new encampment gathering. We can compare a house with chemistry; various manifestations and reactions. A synthesis of a whole lot of explained, unexplained but understood, and subconscious people activity, emotion, desire and fulfilment.

Your abode now may not be your dream house yet it may suit you all the way in the truth of your current reality. The things that it teaches you, the way that it trains you and the activity that it encourages when faced square on will help you achieve. A dream house is only as good as that which the dwellers can comprehend, harmonise with and achieve; that is it is only as good as a state of mind. Abophiles in Western houses, as a rule do not comprehend them and are unable to harmonise. They are not an Abophilic dream house. Dreams are ultimately individual. By picking up that dream thread in your abode now, and working on it, your dream will improve, become clearer and more practical and grow about you in the nebulous reality of your daily life, until your home roots strike too deeply for transplanting and your ideas become fixed and perfected. At such a time you may think back and be glad that that naive dream you dreamt, when you were young, turned out quite differently in the end.

A complete house, one that is working in every detail, greatly assists in the sophistication and broadening of our home. Much of the

settlers' civilised life is absolutely dependant on the shelter, facility,
activity and home as provided by the *domestic-contraptions*. Some
houses we care to pass through as temporary dwellings. We may
swap our ultimate dream house for another on inspiration. The
whole house process and fact from birth to death gives a rhythm to
our lives. Do not let your housing needs be thorns, and do not be a
slave to desire. The very aspects, that you consider inadequate, of
the abode you are in are the seeds of improvement. Simply apply
your comprehensive effort. Understand. Break out your hammer
and saw, or spend your wage to foster those seeds. Suddenly
inadequacies are sprouting directions and dream fulfilments.
Working on your house may entail multi-generational political battles
to challenge regulations or perhaps the right smile might encourage
your wife to bring in the flowers. Simple or complex, the basic truth
gives to home far more than comes from any misconceived luxury or
expensive fashionable trend. So, cardboard *box* in the middle of a
road or the good ship Britannica, when you have your dream house
you are free to *dance* with your *dancing* friends. Like a diesel
mechanic or a ballet dancer. Free to move with housing *delight* and
to move out if you like. It is immensely important for the Earth,
other people and yourself that we house ourselves properly. Please
encourage others to be *doing* it too. Edify your visitors perhaps.

♪♪♪
◎

A traditional *dwelling-contraption*,
high on a Japanese hill.
They set the zig and zag of the paths so that, in approaching uphill,
visitors are treated to exciting glimpses of the house. But no glimpse
of what must be an increasingly breathtaking panorama below. On
reaching the dwelling, they thirst for a spectacle from the living room
window. But … no glimpse. All available windows treated lovely
views of the garden and other parts of the house. The visitors are
puzzled. Certainly frustrated. Frustration is no aim of the builder.
Toward proceeding with the tea ceremony they comment. No
panorama, you're nuts; a missed opportunity!? In the tradition they
bow, kneeling to wash for tea.
Bowed, and having washed, introspective, they lift their face.

Eyes opening, still bowed and face glistening with purifying water
droplets;

the small low window, whilst allowing the trapezoidal patch of
sunlight to bathe the contents of the basin, reveals -

T   h   e   P   a   n   o   r   a   m   a   .

The only glimpse.

Tremendous.

M e a s u r e   t w i c e,   c u t   o n c e.
T o   g e t   i t   r i g h t.

♥

Would anyperson like to make a book about the great Australo-Kiwi lounge *room;* the bloke, the sheila, the kids and the family, as it was before settler ship's captain, James Cook, was delivered by an awesome great white bird, a great white *square* rigger? Singing it in the sixties but echoing the noughties, looking past the teens. Or maybe a Namibian lounge, or a Korean, a Greenlander, Mexican, any loungeroom, its practical and romantic heart throbs.

Dear Kiwi Maggie *Pale*, again with a dip, lift, drip and slap, flops the mop into the already clean coved vinyl toe-space at her pink glossed kitchen breakfast bench, not a breadcrumb in sight; in some *'Home Beautiful'* concert with Queen Elizabeth.

HOW'S YOUR HOUSE NOW
... this very domestic second, whether between pulses or on pulse
...NOW?!

The infinity of *room*.

ROOM

In land, neighbourhood, garden. Interior and kitchen
drawer.
A time lapsed infra-red tracking
of organisms moving through domestic ergonomic *room*.
Hot spots and cool.
Flows and edges.
Housefandango.
Just a step to the right.
Never ending.
Flinging on.
Guilt free dancing.
There at your unnamed *ecopian* township.
Even as the township may be a newly conceived view
of you and yours
here and now.

∞

We Skipped the Housefandango,
Turned cartwheels on the floor
We so lost some shades of
... Pale

♪ ♫ • ∎

I don't need this house no more
Won't have time to fix the windows
Won't have time to lock the door
I'm so busy spinnin' wings
Soon be leav'n this cacoon
When I pass away might I join
The space that's hold'n
our living *room*

....
....
...

.

Okay Rover! Out to the kennel boy.

R O O M for a book on your shelf?

R   O

Where will I find it, how can I make?
Whatever you don't do there will always be the truth of your future
domestic contraptions; the next one is right there if not in form at
least in place awaiting materials that may currently be in the earth...

Come on boy!! Out now ...

... O U T !! ... c'm'on fella ...
time for bed ...

GLOSSARY;

THE DAZZLERS' DICTIONARY

NOTE
DD: indicates that the word or its specific meaning is listed in the Dazzlers' Dictionary and nowhere else at this time.
EW: indicates standard English word and described according to the Dazzlers definition.

Abophile:DD; Aborigine; member of the aboriginal race, known as the Aborigines, of the continent that now supports Australia; *Blackfella*; Harmoninni(DD); similar Austrophile, Amerophile etc.

aboriginal:EW; original people; origin of *Aboriginal*, pertaining to the native people of the Australian continent.

accumulation:EW,DD; everything we collect and take with us when we move house plus everything that we gather around to make our house- including walls and roof.

beingrowing:DD; ephemeral development and unfolding of personal or cultural being.

Albert Gallopilong:DD; fictional Aborigine (Harmoninni(DD) who has never seen anything of Western culture. Friend and mentor of Cheekybugga.

Albert:EW,DD; Albert Gallopilong.

alfresco:EW; outdoor domestic lifestyle.

amenity:EW; valued quality of place; useful persona, spiritual, mental experience; as distinct from facility.

Amerophile:DD; member of the American race.

a-priori:EW; a priori; progression of developments/needs based on pre-establishment of earlier development/resolved-needs.

Arcology:EW; city design including on integrated architecture and ecology; term by Paola Soleri; similar *ecopicology*(DD).

Arcosanti:EW; centre for arcology (non-fiction), Arizona; built on Little White Cloud's native territory (fiction).

armpit protocol:DD; personal domestic protocol.

armpit psyche:DD; psychology, mindset, mental outlook, attitude unique to universal domestic place or specific domestic place at most private.

armpit psychology:DD; the down-home domestic truths and fallibilities of people's thoughts, character and bodies; psychology, mindset, mental outlook, attitude unique to universal domestic place or specific domestic place.

armpitted:DD; affected by *armpit psyche or psychology*(DD).

Arthur C Clark:EW; well known futurist author.

Austrophile:DD; member of the Australian Western race as typified by those Westerners who first settled the land that is now commonly known as Australia..

Bauhaus:EW;a university of arts and architecture in Germany, famous for its contribution in 1930-50 (approx).

beatniks:EW; counter culture people of the 1950's in America, England, Australia.

beingrowing:DD; actualising, uniquely unfolding influenced by place.

Big Apple:EW;DD; a big city like New York.

biocity:DD; completely autonomous city, with self sustaining food and power generation.

biohouse:DD; completely autonomous house, with own self sustaining food and power generation.

Bioshelter:EW; completely autonomous house environment developed maybe 1980s, with own self sustaining food and power generation; *biohouse*.

billabong:EW; type of waterhole/lake left when a bend of a meandering Australian river is cut off.

Blackfella:EW; colloquialism for Aborigine; Abophile; member of the aboriginal (Aboriginal) race of the continent that now supports Australia; Harmoninni (DD).

blueprint:EW; architects plans – in the mid 20th century plans were white lines on blue paper due to printing process.

Bobby Dazzler:DD; Dazzler, Robert, Bobby; fictional Sydney urban architect who is moved to solve housing issues; married to Little White Cloud.

Bobby:DD; Bobby Dazzler, Dazzler, Robert, Bobby; fictional Sydney urban architect who is moved to solve housing issues; married to Little White Cloud.

boogies:EW; creepy crawlies, aggressive beasts or people.

boulevard bold:DD; Western housing at its richest, as typified in any Hollywood boulevard; *ritz boulevard*(DD); as distinct from nomad minima.

box:DD; typical western houses, low cost or large; "*little boxes* made of ticky tacky" (song from 1960s); houses devoid of *nature's-physical-nurtures*(DD) or satisfactory *ergonomic room*.

Buckminster Fuller:EW; inventor-designer of the Dymaxion House; well known thinker-designer.

Bush television: EW; campfire.

cadastre:EW; plan showing land allotment boundaries; cadastral – stemming from cadastre; DD; sometimes creating cantankerous site shapes on awkward landform from which to found a house that honours the cosmos. The shapes of the cadastre are from sentiment sometimes unsympathetic with that of the designer.

Campfandango:DD; the indigenous nomads' celebration and performance of activity for *domestic-arrangement*(DD); a dance of doing domestic activity; version of *Housefandango*(DD) and *Localefandango*(DD).

Catch 22:EW; in the best made plans there's always an unsuspected catch; as per well known book of same name.

Carlos Santana:EW; contemporary musician-guitarist:*ecopical*(DD) musician.

Cheekybugga Talkabout:DD; Cheekyfella, Cheeky; fictional Australian Aborigine (Harmoninni(DD)) who relates cross-culturally with those of Western culture, through visits to Sydney and the like; friend and devotee of Albert Gallopilong.

Cheekyfella Talkabout:DD; Cheekybugga Cheeky; fictional Australian Aborigine (Harmoninni(DD)) who relates cross-culturally with those of Western culture, through visits to Sydney and the like; friend and devotee of Albert Gallopilong.

continuum:EW:DD; wholistic ongoing event; life-story; of a domestic property or locale or nomad territory or tradition.

contraption:DD; house; *domestic-contraption*(DD), built *dwelling-arrangement*(DD), *residential-contraption*(DD); *housing-contraption*(DD).

Corroboree:EW; traditional Aboriginal ceremony including dance and fire.

cosmic symbol:DD; *dwelling-arrangement*(DD) as a symbol of a dwellers place in the cosmos; a device to acknowledge the same.

couch potato:EW; colloquial Australian for lazy indoor dweller; similar *loungeroom lizard*. *crowds of domestic contraptions*:DD; suburb.

crowds of domestic contraptions:DD; suburbs.

cubby:EW; small play house usually built by children.

Daleks:EW; fictional space creatures housed in mobile life-support apparatus; as in Dr Who, TV series.

Dali:EW; late surrealist painter of note, who, incidentally, had sculptural eggs as part of his house *synthetic aesthetic*.

David Attenborough:EW; revered pioneering producer of magnificent TV nature study shows (ironically ecological horror is complemented by TV nature shows – TV & eco-horror are both products of housing)

David Gulpilil:EW; a person of the Australian Aboriginal People who is well known for his film roles and his cross-cultural liaisons; a dignitary greatly respected by the author; in the bush hunting roo for the family one day, sporting a dinner suit and a broad grin in the city the next..

David Suzuki:EW; famous ecological scientist.

Dazzler:DD; Bobby Dazzler, Dazzler, Robert, Bobby; fictional urban architect from Sydney who is moved to solve housing issues; married to Little White Cloud.

debox:DD; verb; avoid/resolve over-*boxed* housing (see *box*); optimise the practical applications of orthogonal construction simultaneously with dweller and community *synthetic aesthetics, ergothetics* (DD), *nature's earthy nurtures*, locale landscape and ecology; supports *ecopicality; deboxing*(DD), *deboxed*(DD), similar *degrid*(DD).

degrid:DD; verb; similar *debox*(DD) but applies to urban realm, streets, parks, open space, compensating for losses by walls on society and dwellers' contact with land.

different strokes:EW; the harmonious, non-conflicting, differences among people; a colloquialism.

dodo:EW:DD; thoughts that creep into minds and corrupt wholesome housing; person/bureaucracy afflicted by the *dodo*; urban deviance caused by ignorance, apathy, greed and desperation; feeds the *megamonster*(DD); responsible for *pale* people(DD), *boulevard*(DD) excess and deceptive opulence; destroys *ecopicality*(DD).

Dogons:EW; a People of Africa.

doing of housing:EW,DD; also do, doing; any action by a dweller that immediately or eventually, supports, implements or updates the dweller's housing; *Housefandango*(DD): *Localefandango*(DD).

doing:DD:EW; also *do*; when in italics it is the *doing of housing*; any action by a dweller that immediately or eventually, supports, implements

or updates the dweller's housing;
Housefandango, Localefandango(DD)

domestic-contraption:EW:**DD**; house; any on-site fabrication which contributes to dwelling or domestic arrangement; *housing-contraption*; *residential-contraption*; *dwelling-contraption*; *contraption*.

Dreamtime:EW;**DD**; Australian Aboriginal cultural exploration and understanding of life, the universe and everything – please refer other sources for formal definition.

dwelling-arrangement: EW;**DD**; any physical arrangements made to support dwelling in a place for domestic activity.

dwelling-contraption:**DD**; house; any on-site fabrication which contributes to dwelling or domestic arrangement; *housing-contraption*; *residential-contraption*; *domestic contraption*; *contraption*.

dwelling-arrangement:EW;**DD**; any arrangements made to support dwelling in a place of domestic activity.

dwelling organisms:DD; dwellers.

Dr Who:EW; What! You don't know who Dr Who is!!; TV series of 1960s, featuring Daleks and the Tardis.

Dymaxion:EW; a housing system developed by Buckminster Fuller in the 1940s.

Ecopia:**DD**; *Nomurbia*(DD), an ecopian Utopia; socio-ecologically perfect urbia; *ecopical*(DD), *ecopicality*(DD), *ecopology*(DD).

Ecopiala:**DD**; fantastic *ecopian* city, loved by nomads and urban stick-in-the-muds alike, frequented by nomads, introduces settlers to nomadism.

ecopicality:**DD**; a wholistic quality of any environmental interventions (incl. house making); aspects of this quality are harmonies in: ecologies, economy, community, dweller compatibilities, *nature's nurtures*, dweller personality, urban design, *synthetic aesthetic*(DD); an urgent modern way of dancing the *Housefandango*(DD), of *doing our housing*. *ecopical*(DD), *ecopology*(DD); if a house has *ecopicality* it's a winner, so we sing to the tune of the old L Price song "she's got personality ... "she's got *ecopicality*, walks with *ecopicality*, talks with *ecopicality*..."; term developed during the writing of this book.

ecopian:**DD**; according to *ecopicality*(DD).

ecopical:**DD**; pertaining to *ecopicality*(DD).

ecopology:**DD**; as yet undeveloped science-art of socio-ecologically perfect urbia incl. housing, in association with *nomurbics*(DD).

Ecosculpture:**DD**; impressionistic illustration of house quanta and its sourcing, its impact on environment, relative to the dweller.

eco-status:EW;**DD**; degree of ecological harmony (of house).

Eno Neolithic:**DD**; Neanderthal person of the Neolithic era living at Litherland, once in the vicinity of Germany; husband of Leone.

Eno:**DD**; Eno Neolithic.

ergonomic heart:**DD**; The *ergonomic heart* is the fusion interface of dwellers and the *accumulation*(DD); relates to ergonomic room.

ergonomic room:EW:**DD**; basis of the *access matrix*(DD)that unifies the *accumulation*(DD); the space and *psychospace*(DD) necessary for any movement required for functional & ethereal living; detail & generality of *room* necessary to access & live in a house & its place; a *unifying matrix* that brings physical & metaphysical singularity to our domestic accumulations; a heart of the house; 'Ergonomic' is not the perfect word as pertains to work; 'domestonomic' could be coined but no; also applies to this room in private outdoor & public realm, incl. barbecues, city square, streets, public buildings; see also *room*.

ergothetics:**DD**; art of shaping the house fabric to fit its *ergonomic room* with minimum obstructions or snags & instead welcoming shapes, leg *room*, accessibilities, *room* to move comfortably, provide for people in action scaled in space, with a visual aesthetic; streamlined design; a rather beautiful word invention, term developed during writing this book.

facility:EW; useful physical apparatus or arrangement; as distinct from amenity (environmental support useful for persona, spiritual, mental, bodily experience).

Fall:EW; the event caused by the original sin that we suffer for now; per Moses' writing.

Fandango:EW;**DD**; Housefandango. Campfandango, Localefandango.

Feng Shui:EW; ancient Chinese art of architectural and land design relative to the land, cosmos, spirits and the place of the dweller.

Fern Hollow:EW;**DD**; fairytale paradise village by a river.

filigree:EW; decorative architectural fabrication not so popular today; jig-sawn or assembled woodwork, wrought or cast ironwork, or other.

finesse:EW;**DD**; simply fine finish, assembly, operation or technique; *mother of pearl*(DD).

footprints:EW:**DD**; existing impact of house.

Francophile:EW;**DD**; member of the French race.

Frank Lloyd Wright:EW; early-mid 20th century American civil engineer, produced revolutionary architecture.
Frank Wright:EW; Frank Lloyd Wright, renown architect.
genome:EW(DD); any person's genetic map or the impact o f that which it maps, dna, intuition, instinct, nous, talent, predilection, genetic persuasions.
glass bead game:EW; book by Herman Hesse involves a game about the complex aspects of life.
Global *Pale*:DD; suburban entrepreneur, bus driver, developer, *box* dweller, husband of Maggie; inspires '*pale*' life; Global, *Pale*.
gourd:EW; small hollowed pumpkin or the like, a portable receptacle for the nomad's most precious goods; may also be used for drink (taking care not to drink a wasp).
gravitymark:DD; the affect of gravity on the form of building, physical balance in structure, loaded beams, rain flow needs flashing, horizontality, vector shapes in props and struts, etc; relates to *machinemark*(DD), *handmark*(DD), mindmark(DD), *housemark*(DD), peoplemark(DD), toolmark(DD).
Great Southern Land:EW; early name for Australia.
grid:EW:DD; city supported services available to dwellings by cable, conduit, microwave, delivery or in fact by a short trip; also *hypertech hypernet grid*(DD).also street grid.
Grunter Palaeolithic:DD; Grunter; person living in the stone age; husband of Gina.
Gina Palaeolithic:DD; Gina: person living in the stone age; wife of Grunter.
handmark:EW:DD; the affect of the building or decorating hand on the house; thumb mark in a brick, swirls in render, hand sawn wood, brush marks, hammer marks, inaccuracies etc; relates to *machinemark*, gravity mark, mindmark(DD), *housemark*(DD), peoplemark(DD), toolmark(DD). Harmoninni:DD; an imagined People of Australian Aboriginal race.
Henri Thoreau:EW; writer-philosopher.
Henry Ford:EW; developer of the car and production line; creator of T Model Ford car.
hippies:EW; people primarily of the 1960s and 1970s inspired by psychedelic drugs toward social change, flower power.
Hobbits:EW; earthy foresty little fellows who live in organic earth-mound houses with complimentary round doors etc; as per Tolkein's story.
Hollywood *boulevard*:EW:DD; exampled as a socio-cultural pinnacle of Western housing development; relates to *boulevard bold*.
homo superior:DD; ultra modern person; adopted from contemporary musician David

Bowie lyric associated with the man who fell to Earth in a shimmering orthogonal craft.
housebound:EW::DD; lost & blinkered in the house, not waking to the great outdoors when leaving home.
Housefandango:DD; the *doing of housing*; living relative to, celebration and performing of *domestic-arrangement*(DD); dance of doing domestic activity including construction, polishing furniture, writing cheques, design thought, etc; relates to *Campfandango*(DD) and *Localefandango*(DD)
Houselocusts:DD; key components of the destructive suburban sprawl; *box*(DD) houses; *megamonster*(DD) spawn; plague as the *machinemark*ed(DD) *grid* of *boxed domestic-contraptions*(DD)
housemark:DD; the affect of housing on dweller; relates to *machinemark*(DD), gravity mark(DD), handmark(DD), peoplemark(DD), mindmark(DD), toolmark(DD).
housing-contraption:DD; house; any on-site fabrication which contributes to dwelling or domestic arrangement; *residential-contraption*(DD); *domestic-contraption*(DD); *dwelling-contraption*(DD); *contraption*(DD).
hud:EW; hide; probable root of the word house; simple place to secure vital possessions, spears, skins and kindred or to sleep safely, perhaps, or to hide, have personal sanctity, privacy, security for the hunted.
humpy:EW; small organically constructed interior, usually indigenously placed but could be of industrial materials under a city bridge.
hypertech hypernet grid:DD; *grid*; urban *services grid*, enhanced by the continuum of development of the internet
id:EW; the individuality of people, their idiosyncrasies and unique initiative.
inglenook:EW; curtained-off nook about a fireplace, to optimise warmth.
Inuit:EW; native People of Alaska; often known affectionately as Eskimos (and sometimes derogatively); Inuophile(DD)..
Inuophile:DD; member of the Inuit race.
jerry:EW; receptacle for urination and defecation, often of porcelain, usually for convenient in-house night use where there is no in-house plumbed toilet, to be emptied in the morning.
Jimmy Buffet:EW; contemporary country-rock-folk musician-singer.
Jonothan Livingston Seagul: EW; character in book by Richard Bach; bird breaks away from flock orthodoxy, strives and reaches great heights.
Kyoto protocol:EW; international endeavour to overcome ecological deterioration.

layout:EW;DD; floor plan of house and property; similar in principle to urban public realm *layout*.

Leone Neolithic:DD; Neanderthal person of the Neolithic era living Litherland, where Germany is now; wife of Eno.

Little White Cloud:DD; White Cloud; Cloud; wife of Bobby Dazzler, mother of his daughter: American Indian by decent

Localefandango:DD; doing of the locale aspect of housing; a dance of doing and celebrating local activity as an enhancement to dweller life and communal dwelling; similar *Housefandango*(DD), *Campfandango*(DD).

Lockwood:EW; well known trading name of contemporary lock manufacturer.

lounge lizard:EW; loungeroom lizard; colloquial Australian for lazy indoor dweller; couch potato.

loungeroom lizard:EW; lounge lizard; colloquial Australian for lazy indoor dweller; couch potato.

Low Carl:DD; urban nomad from New York who has cast aside successful urban residential and married life to pursue a cause to resolve vital ecological issues.

Luddites:EW; culture based on avoidance of mechanisation.

lycra:EW;modern fabric.

machinemark:DD; the affect of machinery on house, such as power tools, factory processes; relates to gravitymark(DD), *handmark*(DD), mindmark(DD), *housemark*(DD), toolmark(DD).

Maggie Pale:DD; Maggie; wife of Global.

Mega:DD; *megamonster*(DD); *megathing*(DD).

megamonster:DD; *mega*(DD); *megathing*(DD); the commonly acknowledged unecologic giant multinational current pragmatic of industrial society which harms the nomads, ecology and wholistic residential life; counter *ecopicality*(DD); spawns *houselocusts*(DD).

megathing:DD; *megamonster*, *mega*.

mindmark:DD; the affect on a house of thought and feeling from designers, builders, dwellers; relates to *machinemark*, gravity mark, *handmark*, *housemark*(DD), toolmark(DD).

molten looking glass: see sky's molten looking glass.

mob:EW; social group, family, gathering, tribe of Aborigines.

Modular:EW; system of architectural measure and proportion based on mathematically complementary rectangular pattern developed as a life work by early-mid 20th century architect, le Corbusier, allowing variation in size and proportion of rectangles whilst retaining overall integration.

mother of pearl:EW:DD; term here used for lack of an established architectural term; inner face of nacre; interior honed for soulful *beingrowing*; some result of the ongoing *emotional kiss* from person to place, not the first fabrication except that some understand it to include the full thickness with exterior of shell as begun from the interior to block urban / fauna / weather adversities; inhabitants like the oyster produce; an intimate organismic comfort, honing the raw basics, rough edges, irritations, finishing, changing, decorating and colouring to personal delight and to coordinate with similar considerations in pre-construction design; includes wall hangings, colour, polish, *ergothetics*(DD), comforts, bacteria resistance, *finesse*, decor etc; outer face of nacre (roofing, weatherboards, footings) is a foundation for & cause of *mother of pearl*. Refer **HOUSE EMBRYO**

Murcutt:EW; Glen Murcutt - leading Australian architect; producer of beautifully pragmatic responses to the land and the dweller.

nacre:EW:DD; the constructed shell of the house through to the inner; the fabric; adapted from nacre, oyster shell; see *mother-of-pearl*.

nature's earthy nurtures: EW:DD; the product of optimum retention and introduction of natural amenity in the house and urban realm; natural materials, forms, fragrances, nourishments, sounds, sights, textures etc.

noble savage:EW; the image of the primitive indigenous person given to desperate self survival as being nobly destined to become as good as we think we are and as we think we may become.

nomad minima:DD; minimal domestic baggage or *contraption* as by indigenous and urban nomads; as distinct from *boulevard bold*.

Nomurbia:DD; underpins *Ecopia*; nomurbic urbia; nomadic urbia.

nomurbic crossroads:DD; geographication of the *nub*(DD) of thought as to the inclination to settle or to roam; the nub butterflies fly here.

nomurbic:DD; alludes to *dwelling arrangement* and urbia based on a ground of convergent mutual acknowledgement among the nomadic and the urban; term developed during the writing of this book.

nomurbics:DD; an as yet undeveloped science based on *nomurbic*(DD) and *ecopical*(DD) principles.

nomurbic crossroad town: DD; indigenous nomad-friendly town in the country with minimised hitech essence emanating from the *nub* of thought as to the predilection to settle or to roam; alludes to dwelling arrangement and urbia based on a ground of convergent mutual acknowledgement among the nomadic and the urban; *nomurbic crossroads*(DD) with some settlement; manifestation of *nub*(DD).

nub:EW:**DD**; the *nub* of thought behind peoples inclination to either roam or settle & so become nomad or settler; the *nub butterflies* are the thoughts at the nub; see *nomurbic*.

orthogonal:EW; relating to or composed of right angles and straight lines and planes; post & lintel, quadrangular floors, vertical walls.

Orwell's 1984:EW; worldly urban existence as imagined decades before 1984 by author George Orwell, illustrating an extreme of interior syndrome.

Pale:**DD**; Global *Pale*, Maggie *Pale*

pale:EW,**DD**, adjective pertaining to syndrome and environmental product resultant from lifestyle and attitude similar to that of Global and Maggie *Pale*(DD), see *trap-of-interior*

Palaeolithic:EW:**DD**; Grunter and Gina Palaeolithic.

Paolo Soleri:EW; courageous contemporary urban architect determined to counter the perpetuation of urbia that is destructive to the Earth; promoter of arcology; builder of Arcosanti (refer www).

Patagonia:EW; City at the tip of South America.

peoplekind:**DD**; cousin to Mankind.

peoplemark:**DD**; the affect on the house of people in community and the social continuum; relates to *gravitymark*(DD), *machinemark*(DD), *handmark*(DD), *mindmark*(DD), *housemark*(DD).

playdough:EW:**DD**; *playdough of the Earth*(DD); materials taken from the earth for building, including fabricated and synthesized materials.

Pugin:EW; an architect.

punk rockers:EW; members of a socio-cultural movement.

quality quotient:EW:**DD**; design quality quotient; a measure of design quality; based on a sum of scores given for each aspect of design.

quicksilver:**DD**; the abstract of people, *synthetic aesthetic*; as distinct from orthogonality and nature; the hard to grasp essence of what we like.

residential-contraption: EW:**DD**; house; any on-site fabrication which contributes to dwelling or *domestic-arrangement*(DD); *housing-contraption*(DD); *dwelling-contraption*(DD); *contraption*(DD).

ripples:EW:**DD**; the ongoing impact of house on environment, people and society, by visual, industrial, waste, cultural conditioning, maintenance necessity, mortgage, isolation etc.

ritz boulevards:EW:**DD**; like any Hollywood *boulevard*(DD).

Robert:**DD**; Bobby Dazzler, Dazzler, Bobby; an urban architect from Sydney who is moved to solve housing issues; married to Little White Cloud.

Rococo:EW; a flamboyant architectural and design style pre 20th century.

Robinson Crusoe:EW; character from a story book who was obliged to make a life alone on an uninhabited island and eventually had a helper.

roo:EW; kangaroo.

room-entity:EW:**DD**; any *room* enhanced or otherwise to serve a particular purpose, regardless of size of space involved and regardless of any need for walls; exampled by niche, nook, *room*, hall, inglenook, cupboard, garage, tokonoma, pergola, matchbox.

room:EW; 1) traditional component of house interior, as in bedroom; 2) space, scope to occur, space to receive; the amenity, including space, needed to undertake an activity; may not include walls – bed-*room* is *room* for bed and the activity of using bed.

room-amenity:EW:**DD**; the amenity, including space, needed to undertake an activity or to suit purpose; may not include walls – bed-*room* is *room* for bed and the activity of using bed.

salamander:EW; small water-land creature according to the theory of evolution linking the movement of people's ancestry from primeval sea to land.

services grid:EW:**DD**; see *grid*.

shadow: **DD**; person or ape depleted by possibly many generations of housing and urban constraint.

seven league boots:EW:**DD**; there's a fairy tale where a lad has boots that allow him to step seven leagues at a pace.

shape-up:**DD**; the third dimension of house construction or design arising from the floor plan and below the floor.

silo:**DD**; any isolated university/high school faculty or subject, government portfolio/department or policy that doesn't relate with its cohorts of other disciplines.

Silicon Valley:EW; a bustling electronic industrial urb.

Sitting Bull:EW; renown native American, chief of a People.

sky's molten looking glass: EW; Biblical phrase relating to timely personal interpretations of Godly communication carried by cloud waters vision.

Smogton:**DD**; grotty, over-crowded urbia, low in country soul; third-rate urbia resulting from land scarcity.

soma:**DD**; tasty distraction that lulls one into carefree oblivion; word borrowed from some science fiction classic, maybe Orwell or the author of Time Machine; also has another, irrelevant, meaning.

Song-lines:EW; Australian Aboriginal cultural relationship with Dreaming, each other and the land (refer formal definition elsewhere).

Spaceship Earth:EW: planet earth as a limited entity; term from Buckminster Fuller.

stargate:EW; hi-tech programmable gateway allowing one step passage to anywhere; Arthur C. Clark term.

Suburbophile:DD; member of any suburban lifestyle.

Steve Irwin:EW; recently passed away, cherished centre of dynamic TV wildlife communication (ironically ecological horror is complemented by TV nature shows – TV & eco-horror are both products of housing)

stratospheric stroll:DD; viewing life at home from a mind movement out to the stratosphere looking back.

Swiss Family Robinson:EW; fictional family ship-wrecked on a tropical island, built magnificent tree-house; similar well known Robinson Crusoe story.

synthetic aesthetic:EW:DD; the *quicksilver* of personal abstraction: the myriad of design modes of people, as distinct from the wholistic mode evident in nature; housing developments emanating from the id.

T Model:EW; first market successful automobile, from Henry Ford.

Taj Mahal: EW; an icon of beauty in architecture in India; a right royal building.

Tardis:EW; Dr Who's transport, a mid 20th century styled London phone booth with a vast space-warped interior; time machine.

televisory device:EW,DD, television set.

theodolite:EW; telescopic instrument used to mark out urban set-outs and boundaries.

theodolitic:DD; as by *theodolite*.

three-planed-corner:DD; three lines meeting at right angles, same as two walls and a ceiling meeting; *one of peoplekind's most significant creations*; the corners seem to counterplace the circular belt of sky that blends with the horizon below it and the dome of the heavens above.

thylacine EW; unique Australian marsupial believed made extinct by dodo *theodolite* syndrome; known as Tasmanian Tiger.

ticky tacky:EW; relating to *box* houses; term from popular song by Malvina Reynolds, sung by Pete Seeger 1962, assumed to allude to manufactured materials, *pale* lifestyle and credit.

Tierra del Fuego:EW; at the southern tip of South American continent.

tiki:EW; part of Maori culture, fearsome carved figure to frighten of all things bad.

Tolkein:EW; well known author of Lord of the Rings and the Hobbit.

toolmark:EW:DD; the affect of tools on the house; chisel mark in wood, straight cuts, brush marks, hammer marks, inaccuracies etc; increases house potential yet relates closely to *handmark*(DD); relates to *machinemark*(DD), *gravitymark*(DD), *mindmark*(DD), *housemark*(DD), *peoplemark*(DD).

trap of interior:DD; the lure of interior that snares the dweller, makes him *pale* (DD), promotes larger interiors.

tv:EW;television.

unifying matrix:EW; see ergonomic matrix.

wallpaper-of-locale:DD; the amenity of locale that surrounds and benefits the house, incl. shops, beach, roads, buses, hospital, beauty, conflict etc.

wakely:DD; a bit of word play relating to the inspiration of another author and the awakening moments that we sometimes ignore; for that author, gday Mark.

Whitefella:EW; anglophile or any fair skinned person, Aboriginal colloquialism.

wooden overcoat:EW; colloquialism, wooden coffin.

yuppies:EW; young up and coming professionals; people on their way to some *ritz boulevard*(DD).

Z factor:DD; the unknown as to the consciousness and lifestyle of Adam and Eve of the Bible.

Z mode:DD; the circumstance of those of the Z factor(DD).

zincalum:EW;contemporary sheet metal used for roof & other cladding,usually with a bonded colour finish.

Out ! !   !

with thanks
Monty Luthenmann

www.ingramcontent.com/pod-product-compliance
Lightning Source LLC
Chambersburg PA
CBHW062156270326
41930CB00009B/1556